T0211861

Lecture Notes in Computer Science 12207

More information about this series at http://www.springer.com/series/7409

Qin Gao · Jia Zhou (Eds.)

Human Aspects of IT for the Aged Population

Technologies, Design and User Experience

6th International Conference, ITAP 2020
Held as Part of the 22nd HCI International Conference, HCII 2020
Copenhagen, Denmark, July 19–24, 2020
Proceedings, Part I

 Springer

Editors
Qin Gao
Tsinghua University
Beijing, China

Jia Zhou
Chongqing University
Chongqing, China

ISSN 0302-9743   ISSN 1611-3349   (electronic)
Lecture Notes in Computer Science
ISBN 978-3-030-50251-5   ISBN 978-3-030-50252-2   (eBook)
https://doi.org/10.1007/978-3-030-50252-2

LNCS Sublibrary: SL3 – Information Systems and Applications, incl. Internet/Web, and HCI

This Springer imprint is published by the registered company Springer Nature Switzerland AG
The registered company address is: Gewerbestrasse 11, 6330 Cham, Switzerland

Foreword

The 22nd International Conference on Human-Computer Interaction, HCI International 2020 (HCII 2020), was planned to be held at the AC Bella Sky Hotel and Bella Center, Copenhagen, Denmark, during July 19–24, 2020. Due to the COVID-19 coronavirus pandemic and the resolution of the Danish government not to allow events larger than 500 people to be hosted until September 1, 2020, HCII 2020 had to be held virtually. It incorporated the 21 thematic areas and affiliated conferences listed on the following page.

A total of 6,326 individuals from academia, research institutes, industry, and governmental agencies from 97 countries submitted contributions, and 1,439 papers and 238 posters were included in the conference proceedings. These contributions address the latest research and development efforts and highlight the human aspects of design and use of computing systems. The contributions thoroughly cover the entire field of human-computer interaction, addressing major advances in knowledge and effective use of computers in a variety of application areas. The volumes constituting the full set of the conference proceedings are listed in the following pages.

The HCI International (HCII) conference also offers the option of "late-breaking work" which applies both for papers and posters and the corresponding volume(s) of the proceedings will be published just after the conference. Full papers will be included in the "HCII 2020 - Late Breaking Papers" volume of the proceedings to be published in the Springer LNCS series, while poster extended abstracts will be included as short papers in the "HCII 2020 - Late Breaking Posters" volume to be published in the Springer CCIS series.

I would like to thank the program board chairs and the members of the program boards of all thematic areas and affiliated conferences for their contribution to the highest scientific quality and the overall success of the HCI International 2020 conference.

This conference would not have been possible without the continuous and unwavering support and advice of the founder, Conference General Chair Emeritus and Conference Scientific Advisor Prof. Gavriel Salvendy. For his outstanding efforts, I would like to express my appreciation to the communications chair and editor of HCI International News, Dr. Abbas Moallem.

July 2020   Constantine Stephanidis

HCI International 2020 Thematic Areas and Affiliated Conferences

Thematic areas:

- HCI 2020: Human-Computer Interaction
- HIMI 2020: Human Interface and the Management of Information

Affiliated conferences:

- EPCE: 17th International Conference on Engineering Psychology and Cognitive Ergonomics
- UAHCI: 14th International Conference on Universal Access in Human-Computer Interaction
- VAMR: 12th International Conference on Virtual, Augmented and Mixed Reality
- CCD: 12th International Conference on Cross-Cultural Design
- SCSM: 12th International Conference on Social Computing and Social Media
- AC: 14th International Conference on Augmented Cognition
- DHM: 11th International Conference on Digital Human Modeling and Applications in Health, Safety, Ergonomics and Risk Management
- DUXU: 9th International Conference on Design, User Experience and Usability
- DAPI: 8th International Conference on Distributed, Ambient and Pervasive Interactions
- HCIBGO: 7th International Conference on HCI in Business, Government and Organizations
- LCT: 7th International Conference on Learning and Collaboration Technologies
- ITAP: 6th International Conference on Human Aspects of IT for the Aged Population
- HCI-CPT: Second International Conference on HCI for Cybersecurity, Privacy and Trust
- HCI-Games: Second International Conference on HCI in Games
- MobiTAS: Second International Conference on HCI in Mobility, Transport and Automotive Systems
- AIS: Second International Conference on Adaptive Instructional Systems
- C&C: 8th International Conference on Culture and Computing
- MOBILE: First International Conference on Design, Operation and Evaluation of Mobile Communications
- AI-HCI: First International Conference on Artificial Intelligence in HCI

Conference Proceedings Volumes Full List

1. LNCS 12181, Human-Computer Interaction: Design and User Experience (Part I), edited by Masaaki Kurosu
2. LNCS 12182, Human-Computer Interaction: Multimodal and Natural Interaction (Part II), edited by Masaaki Kurosu
3. LNCS 12183, Human-Computer Interaction: Human Values and Quality of Life (Part III), edited by Masaaki Kurosu
4. LNCS 12184, Human Interface and the Management of Information: Designing Information (Part I), edited by Sakae Yamamoto and Hirohiko Mori
5. LNCS 12185, Human Interface and the Management of Information: Interacting with Information (Part II), edited by Sakae Yamamoto and Hirohiko Mori
6. LNAI 12186, Engineering Psychology and Cognitive Ergonomics: Mental Workload, Human Physiology, and Human Energy (Part I), edited by Don Harris and Wen-Chin Li
7. LNAI 12187, Engineering Psychology and Cognitive Ergonomics: Cognition and Design (Part II), edited by Don Harris and Wen-Chin Li
8. LNCS 12188, Universal Access in Human-Computer Interaction: Design Approaches and Supporting Technologies (Part I), edited by Margherita Antona and Constantine Stephanidis
9. LNCS 12189, Universal Access in Human-Computer Interaction: Applications and Practice (Part II), edited by Margherita Antona and Constantine Stephanidis
10. LNCS 12190, Virtual, Augmented and Mixed Reality: Design and Interaction (Part I), edited by Jessie Y. C. Chen and Gino Fragomeni
11. LNCS 12191, Virtual, Augmented and Mixed Reality: Industrial and Everyday Life Applications (Part II), edited by Jessie Y. C. Chen and Gino Fragomeni
12. LNCS 12192, Cross-Cultural Design: User Experience of Products, Services, and Intelligent Environments (Part I), edited by P. L. Patrick Rau
13. LNCS 12193, Cross-Cultural Design: Applications in Health, Learning, Communication, and Creativity (Part II), edited by P. L. Patrick Rau
14. LNCS 12194, Social Computing and Social Media: Design, Ethics, User Behavior, and Social Network Analysis (Part I), edited by Gabriele Meiselwitz
15. LNCS 12195, Social Computing and Social Media: Participation, User Experience, Consumer Experience, and Applications of Social Computing (Part II), edited by Gabriele Meiselwitz
16. LNAI 12196, Augmented Cognition: Theoretical and Technological Approaches (Part I), edited by Dylan D. Schmorrow and Cali M. Fidopiastis
17. LNAI 12197, Augmented Cognition: Human Cognition and Behaviour (Part II), edited by Dylan D. Schmorrow and Cali M. Fidopiastis

38. CCIS 1224, HCI International 2020 Posters - Part I, edited by Constantine Stephanidis and Margherita Antona
39. CCIS 1225, HCI International 2020 Posters - Part II, edited by Constantine Stephanidis and Margherita Antona
40. CCIS 1226, HCI International 2020 Posters - Part III, edited by Constantine Stephanidis and Margherita Antona

http://2020.hci.international/proceedings

6th International Conference on Human Aspects of IT for the Aged Population (ITAP 2020)

Program Board Chairs: **Qin Gao, Tsinghua University, China, and Jia Zhou, Chongqing University, China**

- Inês Amaral, Portugal
- Ning An, China
- Venkatesh Balasubramanian, India
- Alex Chaparro, USA
- Honglin Chen, China
- Jessie Chin, USA
- José Coelho, Portugal
- Francesca Comunello, Italy
- Hua Dong, UK
- Katharine Hunter-Zaworski, USA
- Hirokazu Kato, Japan
- Jiunn-Woei Lian, Taiwan
- Chi-Hung Lo, Taiwan
- Eugène Loos, The Netherlands
- Brandon Pitts, USA
- Jing Qiu, China
- Peter Rasche, Germany
- Marie Sjölinder, Sweden
- Wang-Chin Tsai, Taiwan
- Ana Isabel Veloso, Portugal
- Konstantinos Votis, Greece
- Yuxiang (Chris) Zhao, China
- Junhong Zhou, USA
- Martina Ziefle, Germany

The full list with the Program Board Chairs and the members of the Program Boards of all thematic areas and affiliated conferences is available online at:

http://www.hci.international/board-members-2020.php

HCI International 2021

The 23rd International Conference on Human-Computer Interaction, HCI International 2021 (HCII 2021), will be held jointly with the affiliated conferences in Washington DC, USA, at the Washington Hilton Hotel, July 24–29, 2021. It will cover a broad spectrum of themes related to Human-Computer Interaction (HCI), including theoretical issues, methods, tools, processes, and case studies in HCI design, as well as novel interaction techniques, interfaces, and applications. The proceedings will be published by Springer. More information will be available on the conference website: http://2021.hci.international/.

General Chair
Prof. Constantine Stephanidis
University of Crete and ICS-FORTH
Heraklion, Crete, Greece
Email: general_chair@hcii2021.org

http://2021.hci.international/

Contents – Part I

User Experience and Aging

Aging and Mobile and Wearable Devices

Contents – Part II

Well-Being, Persuasion, Health Education and Cognitive Support

Aging in Place

Cultural and Entertainment Experiences for Older Adults

Contents – Part III

Aging and Social Media

Technology Acceptance and Societal Impact

Involving Older Adults in HCI Methodology

Older Adults' Participation in VIAS' Mobile App Design

Cristina Azevedo Gomes$^{(\boxtimes)}$ ⓘ, Sónia Ferreira ⓘ, and Bárbara Sousa ⓘ

Polytechnic Institute of Viseu, Viseu, Portugal
{mcagomes,sonia.ferreira,barbarasousa}@esev.ipv.pt

Abstract. The literature is consensual when it tells us that the choice of the inter-generational approach brings significant advantages, both for the youngest, the oldest and even for the technological products under development. Given this reality, this article describes some of the intergenerational workshops developed within the ViseuInterAgeStories Project (VIAS), although with a special focus on the participation of the elderly. VIAS promotes collaboration between children and the elderly in the creation of georeferenced stories in a mobile application while touring places of culture, heritage and a natural interest in the city of Viseu. To do so, they can publish local images, texts or audios or access stories already shared by other users, creating a city identity network. The project followed a Participatory Design approach, involving children and older adults during inter-generational dynamics and practices and to co-design the app. The results reveal the appreciation of the city's history by the seniors and the importance of thematic categorization in the organization of the mobile application. Thus the App integrates georeferenced historical information. Even assuming difficulties in using the technology, participants built meaningful ideas of what they wanted and could get from it. Intergenerational experience and the co-design process have revealed positive implications for self-esteem and satisfaction among older people.

Keywords: Older adults · Mobile app · Participatory Design

1 Introduction

The known contribution of the economic, social and health evolution, as well as the marked tendencies of the aging population [1, 2], contextualize the challenges that increased longevity entails and justify the emergence of programs and studies aimed at the promotion of active aging.

Focused on individual development, the concept of active aging was adopted by the World Health Organization in the late 1990s and privileges the continued social, economic, cultural, spiritual and civic participation of older adults within the community, as opposed to the mere ability to be physically active or to participate vigorously in the labor market [3].

In this sense, active aging appears not only as a challenge, but as an opportunity for society as a whole. It demands accountability and the participation of all, fighting against

Q. Gao and J. Zhou (Eds.): HCII 2020, LNCS 12207, pp. 3–17, 2020.
https://doi.org/10.1007/978-3-030-50252-2_1

exclusion and discrimination and, according to Carrilho and Craveiro [4], in promoting solidarity between generations. Society has a responsibility to design different, safe and accessible social spaces, as well as to ensure and promote civic participation of the elderly. This promotion of social solidarity, voluntary life, and civic action is the collective's responsibility as well as the individual's duty and right. In turn, social support networks and the existence of meaningful relationships involve affective and solidary investment and come as decisive capital throughout life and aging [5].

The increase in life expectancy will lead to greater opportunities for social interaction between generations. This opens the way for the innovative creation of services and products that respond to the new needs, by integrating the elderly population within society and valuing their life experiences. Intergenerational practices emerge as beneficial experiences, not only for the elderly, but also for children and young people, manifested in the transmission of knowledge and greater social cohesion [6].

ViseuInterAgeStories (VIAS) Project, presented in this paper, is an example of an initiative whose goal is to promote intergenerational practices, in order "to develop a greater sense of belonging to a certain community and to support healthier and more inclusive lifestyles" [7: 2]. Although we have used intergenerational workshops, this paper focuses, specifically, on the results of older adults' participation.

2 Technology and Intergenerational Initiatives

With this context in mind, increasing relevance is being given to intergenerational programs mediated by technology, as demographic trends go hand in hand with the rapid introduction of technologies in the most diverse sectors of our society.

One example of practices, involving older and younger participants, is the "Engaging Generations Program" [8], developed at a New England public university and inspired by the documentary "Cyber-Seniors". This documentary highlighted a program developed in Canada, where high school students taught seniors how to use technology, and used a number of interesting moments, such as seniors chatting via video calls or making new friends online. Younger participants underlined how the program helped break stereotypes, not only about older people, but also about their ability to learn to use technology.

In the "Engaging Generations Program", students worked closely with the elderly in order to teach them how to use technology. In return, students got to acquire some teaching skills. The analysis of the program showed that, in fact, there was an improvement in the attitude of students towards aging and an increasing interest by the elderly on technology. Results showed that the most effective intergenerational practices included "multiple meetings with the same pair as means to deepen friendships, in-person training for student leaders, student responsibility for scheduling, tailoring sessions for each participant, student documentation of meetings, and active involvement by community partners" [8: 1].

"Nobits - Nostalgia Bits" is a particularly interesting initiative as it bears conceptual similarities with the VIAS project. Nobits has developed and evaluated an online memory platform, by establishing a meeting place for different generations where users of different ages share and (re)create personal narratives and memories [9]. Given all the characteristics and peculiarities of the different audiences, the usability of the portal has been a major concern since the beginning of its conceptualization.

The portal's assessment was divided into two phases and involved 220 participants: 44 older adults and 176 children. In the first phase, the usability of the site was evaluated in a sample of older adults' participants. In the second phase, the effectiveness of online reminiscence was tested against a control condition in which the elderly shared their memories with children without the support of technology. The main dependent measures included self-esteem, loneliness and pleasure/involvement with activities (flow).

During the phases in which reminiscence and usability effectiveness were evaluated, usability showed positive results. However, the use of the platform did not significantly improve the effects of intergenerational reminiscence.

Another example is the "Grandparents and Grandchildren Keep in Touch" (GRANKIT), a European project co-funded by the EU Lifelong Learning Program under Grundtvig Multilateral initiatives, which seeks to bridge the gap between older people and the use of technology, by using intergenerational practices [10]. GRANKIT's main goal is to promote active citizenship, regardless of age, and to explore the relationship of first and third generation reuniting seniors (grandparents) with their grandchildren through basic Information and Communication Technologies' (ICT) education courses. This project involved participants from four countries: Cyprus, Germany, Greece and Romania.

As a result, older participants acquired basic ICT skills - accessing the electronic world for information, communication and lifelong learning opportunities - and found more opportunities to spend time profitably with their children and grandchildren. In turn, younger participants the opportunity to take on the teacher's role and transfer their ICT knowledge to their grandparents while simultaneously getting to know them better.

Mix@Age [11] is a European Project conducted in Austria, Belgium, Germany, Scotland and Slovenia. The intergenerational workshops were developed in arts institutions, museums and community settings and combined arts and new media such as iPod movies, audio guides for a museum, art blogs, Tagtool performances, digital music and photography. Regardless of educational background, the main goal was to explore the potential of older people and to share their experiences and social skills, as well as to recognize and learn about young people's skills and perceptions.

Although these activities focused mainly on art and on the development and use of creativity, participants have collaterally developed digital skills by using day-to-day technology, such as mobile phones and tablets, as an artistic tool.

We can see some successful intergenerational programs using technology as process-facilitating tools, but it is important to develop further studies that reflect on the roles of technology in promoting daily intergenerational moments in older people's lives.

2.1 Participatory Design and Active Citizen Participation

Technological development towards ubiquitous and transparent devices increasingly immersed in our daily lives poses Human Computer Interaction (HCI) some important challenges, widely recognized and discussed in the literature [12, 13]. Boundaries between technology, human and the environment are rapidly reshaping and, in this complex and diverse context, HCI needs to explore new design methods.

Understanding users and user-centered designs has been the main goal since the beginning of HCI. However, the panoply of interaction design approaches calls upon different end-user roles, from simple testers or informants to full and engaged partners in the process design [14–16]. Nowadays, the complex interaction design context clearly calls for the active participation of end users throughout the design process. Contemporary HCI must acknowledge that technology is now embedded and used in our daily lives, and, in this context, design activities in the laboratory and in controlled situations are moving into the wild, valuing in-situ development and engagement in significant contexts with the end-users, seeking to understand new technology interventions in everyday living [17].

Participatory Design approaches explicitly engage end-users in the design process, and should be centered on mutual learning, fostering interaction practices for users and developers to explore possible and useful technological solutions. Mutual learning is supported by embedding the design process in participants' practices, allowing them to explore and experience how emerging designs can affect their lives, which gives them the conditions to construct their own meanings about technology [18].

Participatory Designs value democratic practices as well as the idea of equal partnership between designers and users [19]. More recently, several authors have argued about the need for rethinking how we conduct Participatory Design in order to fulfill democratic issues. They advocate more attention to the values involved in Participatory Design projects [20]. Focusing on participants' values could be the key to support them through the discovery of meaningful alternatives while they explicitly feel, their influence over the design process, leading to products shaped to fulfill their visions and values [8]. Several methods and techniques, such as workshops, design games, or paper mockups, can help the participants see how emerging designs affect their lives, while making the development of better digital products more noticeable.

When it comes to older adults there is a widespread tendency to underestimate their abilities. This trend widens when dealing with technology. Undoubtedly older adults experience more accessibility challenges in using technologies than younger people, in consequence of their aging process, health constraints and digital exclusion [21]. It is also true that technology is of great help to the elderly population with increasingly sophisticated assistive, adaptive and rehabilitative devices.

However, the focus on health issues, whether physical or cognitive decline, leads to an extremely reductive approach to technology and elderly relationships. Older adults are a highly diverse demographic, and in HCI field one must consider not only their assistive needs, but also the characteristics of their life stage, including the generational perspectives about their social context and the experiences lived while facing technologies, seizing what they can give back to society and their communities.

Societal challenges related to health, demographic change and wellbeing encourage real Participatory Design approaches with older adults. For older adults to find value in digital technologies they need to be designed in ways that support the full diversity of their life experiences, bodies, and skill sets [22]. In this way, active participation and the centrality of mutual learning are unavoidable ingredients for the design process.

3 Aims

VIAS' main goal is to develop a mobile application that allows both children and the elderly to create stories about the city of Viseu while walking and interacting with historical, cultural, and natural places. Through this process, we intend to add multimedia layers of georeferenced stories developing a greater sense of belonging to a certain community and supporting healthier and more inclusive lifestyles for children and older adults.

In this paper, we present and discuss the importance of elderly participation in the design process and their real contribution to the app development. We also present and discuss the possible impacts that this participation may have on the elderly, namely in the appropriation on the use of technologies and in the value and importance of their role in the process, affecting their self-esteem and fulfillment.

4 Methodology

VIAS | ViseuInterAgeStories project follows a Participatory Design approach. For over a year we have invited a group of children and older adults to participate in exploratory workshops destined to develop and co-design a collaborative intergenerational app that helps to create stories about significant locals of their city (Viseu). Through these activities, urban spaces become "places", while participants' reminiscences, meanings and re (meanings) are deposited in multimedia formats across the urban space.

We ran a total of six intergenerational workshops, counting with the participation of children, older adults, facilitators and designers. Elder participants were recruited in the Senior University of Viseu, which means they are active older adults, and children through professional connections, namely family of workers from the IPV and word-of-mouth.

The workshops took place in a significant context, some of them touring around the Viseu city and others within a specific area. We valued intragenerational dialogues, while participants explored a set of technological devices, such as mobile phones and tablets, combined with bags filled with a wide variety of art craft materials used to represent their ideas.

In the workshops, we mobilized several methods to collect data: participant observation; a questionnaire about the use of digital devices in participants' daily routines and about their digital skills; an open-ended questionnaire about what participants learned and taught to the other generation during the activity; focus-group.

4.1 Previous Workshops. Participants and Procedure

To contextualize the process, we give a short overview of the workshops developed for over half a year. For the purposes of this paper, we will focus our analysis on the last three activities, exploring the perspective of the older participants. Table 1 summarizes, for each workshop, the participants, the main goals and a short description of the activities.

Even though, it was difficult to count on the availability of all older adults and children to spend one morning attending each workshop, it was still possible to create dynamics of mutual recognition and collaboration amongst participants.

Table 1. Short description preliminary workshops: Participants (Children-C and Older Adults-OA); Aims and procedures.

W	Participants			Aims and procedures
	n	Gender	Age	
W1	13 C 10 OA	♂4 | ♀9 ♂9 | ♀1	[6–13] | M = 9,7 [60–78] | M = 67,8	To explore children's and older adults' perception of interactions and learning outcomes in an intergenerational activity. To explore how they use ICT to narrate stories about their favorite places in the city In a school library, each intergenerational group could use tablets, laptops, paper and pencils and printed photos to tell their stories
W2	6 C 8 OA	♂2 | ♀4 ♂6 | ♀2	[6–13] | M = 9,0 [63–78] | M = 71,0	To explore intergenerational dynamics in the creation of collaborative stories about significant cultural heritage elements of their city. To explore how children and older adults use an app and mobile phones to create multimedia stories. While touring in the historical city center, intergenerational pairs created and posted multimedia (text, image, sound) stories, using mobile phones
W3	6 C 8 OA	♂2 | ♀4 ♂8 | ♀0	[9–13] | M = 10,2 [63–80] | M = 71,6	To explore the same goals as workshop 4 in a different context, the city park, with significant natural heritage elements

The first three workshops contributed to explore intergenerational dynamics, having the children and older adults' stories and reminiscences about the city's heritage sites. These workshops were also very helpful in exploring how technology is mobilized and used in intergenerational contexts. They also helped to situate participants within the scope of the project and its overall goals. The procedures and results of these workshops are described elsewhere [23, 24].

4.2 Designing Paper Mockups. Participants and Procedure

In Workshops 4 and 5 children and older adults have developed paper mockups, proposing the app design. This was the only activity where they didn't work in intergenerational interaction. We adopted this approach, having the differences between each generation in mind, in what concerns drawing and writing practices. In this way, both children and older adults would be more comfortable and confident expressing their ideas to their peers. Table 2 presents a summary of the participants and aims and procedures of this activity.

Table 2. Short description of the mockup design workshop: Participants (Children-C and Older Adults-OA); Aims and procedures.

W	Participants			Aims and procedures
	n	Gender	Age	
W4 W5	6 C 5 OA	♂2 I ♀4 ♂4 I ♀1	[9–14] I M = 11,3 [73–80] I M = 73	Co-design with participants the apps' features and requirements In separate moments, children (W4) and older adults (W5) explained and designed the app functionalities, in paper mockups

Participants were questioned about the use of technological devices in their daily routines. All participants tend to use their mobile phones to make phone calls, most of them also use this device to take and view photos (5) and receive and send emails (4). The computer is mostly used to search for specific information (5), to receive and send emails (4), to watch videos (4), to use maps (4) and to search for common information, such as restaurants, cinemas or pharmacies (4). Only one of the six participants said he felt able to use technology for everything he needed, while others said they felt more or less capable. Regarding what they would like to learn to do with technology, two participants mentioned making videos and other uses for the computer.

The design activity with the older adults lasted 2 h. We started with a short "ice breaker" activity, about the quality of life in Viseu city. Then, older adults were invited to explore the collaborative stories created by them and the children in the previous Workshops. In order to project and foster participant's engagement, we edited place marks with the stories on Google Earth.

We organized the participants in groups and challenged them to design the app. Three of the male participants decided to work individually and the other three participants drew the mockup in a group. They used a bag of stuff with art crafts, city images and maps, and models of the screen mobile phone to create their proposals. Each group presented and discussed their work with the other participants and with the research team. In the end, they answered two questionnaires. The first about technologies in their daily routines and the second about what each older adult learned in the activity, how much they enjoyed it, and if they were satisfied with his/her proposals. Figure 1 presents some moments of this session.

4.3 Evaluating the Prototype. Participants and Procedure

The main goal of Workshop 6 was the evaluation of the prototype, developed according to the results obtained in previous workshops. Table 3 provides an overview of this activity.

Fig. 1. Designing paper mockups.

Table 3. Short description of the evaluation workshop: Participants (Children-C and Older Adults-OA); Aims and procedures.

W	Participants			Aims and procedures
	n	Gender	Age	
W6	10 C 6 OA	♂3 | ♀7 ♂5 | ♀1	[6–13] | M = 10,1 [68–74] | M = 73,5	To test and evaluate a prototype with participants Intergenerational groups were challenged to wander freely in the historic center and use the (app) prototype to create and post stories about their Christmas memories associated with locals

Considering the use of ICTs, the characterization of the participants reveals that all older adults use their mobile phones to receive and send emails as well as to make calls and most to take (5) and view photographs (5). Everyone uses their computer to receive and send emails, use social networks, watch videos, and view photos. Most also use their computers to use maps (5), search for common information such as restaurants, movie theaters or pharmacies (5) and to listen to music (4). Asked if they felt able to use the technologies to do everything they needed, four of the participants answered, "more or less capable", one answered feeling "capable" and the other "not capable". They shared that they would like to learn how to install and play games, use social networks, make video edits, solve phone technical issues, and improve their computer usage.

The workshop lasted 2 h. It was held shortly after Christmas and began with an "ice-breaker" where children and seniors shared what they enjoyed most about Christmas. Next, children and older adults briefly explored the prototype, organized in intergenerational groups, before walking in the city, using the prototype to post memories and stories about Christmas time in places of the historical center of the city. In the end children and older adults answered the questionnaire about technologies in their daily routines and a questionnaire about the app usability issues. They also pointed out what they have learned and taught in this activity, and how much they enjoyed it. Figure 2 represents some of the moments of workshop 6.

Fig. 2. Evaluating the app during the workshop 6.

4.4 Focus Group. Participants and Procedure

Given the profile of older participants, we felt the need to understand better how they assess the app, by mobilizing another form of data collection, which would allow for deeper insight than the questionnaire survey. So we ran a focus group in another session with the older participants. The focus group lasted for about one hour and a half. Table 4 presents a summary of this session.

Table 4. Short description of the Focus Group to evaluate the process: Participants (Older Adults-OA); Aims and procedures.

W	Participants			Aims and procedures
	n	Gender	Age	
FG	8 OA	♂7 l ♀1	[68–79] l M = 73,0	To test and evaluate the prototype with older adults One session only with older adults

In a focus group approach, we gave the opportunity to the older adults to express and discuss their feelings about the project by organizing the debate around the following topics: In what ways older adults perceived their role in the whole project, and if they recognized their contributions in the app. If they thought, they could use the app in a different context.

5 Results

5.1 App Layout Proposals and Experience Evaluation of Workshop 5

As described in topic Sect. 4.2, participants presented four proposals for the app (see Fig. 3). All chose to value and integrate the stories of the places in Viseu. In the first proposal the user would choose between the past or the present; in the second and third the application would present suggestions of nearest places and; in the latter, the places would appear organized by areas such as nature, sport, tourism, etc.

The next step in the first proposal would be the emergence of more local information accompanied by images. After a minute, the user was asked if he would like to tell his story about the place, with a yes/no button answer option. Choosing "yes" would open the options "audio", "photo" or "video", and before publishing you would be asked if you would like to review it. This option may reveal that this participant already has some digital skills, suggesting usability concerns.

Fig. 3. Older adults' proposals

For the next two proposals, users would choose to interact with the app by choosing to be able to hear local stories, take photos, or choose other places nearby.

In suggestion four, after choosing the area, the map with the geolocation of places of interest would appear, which, according to the choice, would present a gallery of images, description of the place, stories already shared by other users and link to similar themes.

Thus, one of the suggestions that result from these proposals is the idea of the app presenting information about the reference places of the city of Viseu. With this in view, it was decided to integrate a new option in the app, that would give access to the history of Viseu, sites within a perimeter close to the georeferenced position of the user and not just the stories deposited by the VIAS community.

On the other hand, the structuring of the information in categories was contemplated, since to upload a story the author must add one or more tags that allow to triggering filters to search stories and information. A rigid information categorization framework was not integrated, as the app was not designed as a tourism app. Figure 4 presents the results of the prototypical interface developed after the five workshops described.

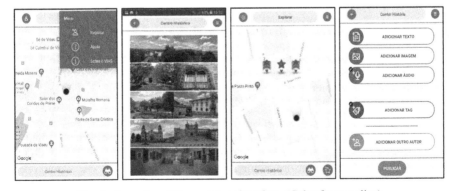

Fig. 4. Examples of the prototype interface. (Color figure online)

When the user loads the app he can see his actual position (the red point on the first screenshot). Clicking in the binoculars icon, you'll be given access to a second mosaic screenshot where each image gives access to textual information about the cultural or natural heritage near that specific local. When a user logs in, he can see nearby stories added by other users, (stars in the map of the third screenshot). He can also add a georeferenced story about the place, by clicking in the star at the bottom of the screen. He can add text, image, audio and tags to create a story (fourth screenshot). If he adds another author to the same story and if the second author is from a different generation, that story will be represented with a golden star, valuing intergenerational collaboration.

After performing the task, the participants answered a questionnaire directly related to the activity. Regarding the question about what they have learned, the seniors said that they gained more knowledge about the city of Viseu, about the use of technology and about the development of applications, as well as the improvement of group work skills and relationship with colleagues.

When asked if they were satisfied with the app project, everyone answered "yes", arguing it was a great experience to learn and develop brain fitness, as well as to start feeling self-utility. One of the participants shared he thought that the project would have a bright future.

5.2   App Usability Evaluation

The usability evaluation of the app, performed in workshop 6, revealed ambiguous results, suggesting that there is room for improvement in this area (see Fig. 5).

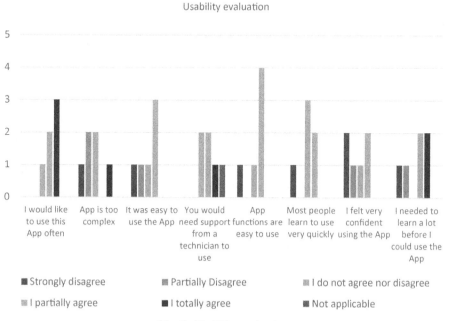

Fig. 5. Usability evaluation

When asked if they would like to use the application frequently, three of the six participants answered that they totally agree, two partially agreed and only one that neither agrees nor disagreed.

Regarding the app's complexity perception by the users, the answers are not unanimous and reveal some need to review usability issues. Two of the participants reported partially disagreeing, two neither agreeing or disagreeing, one strongly disagreeing and the other strongly agreeing.

In addition, when asked if it was easy to use, three participants revealed that they partially agreed, one that he totally disagreed, one that he partially disagreed, and the other participant neither agreed nor disagreed. Regarding whether they would need the support of a coach, two of the seniors said they don't agree or disagree, two partially agreed, one fully agreed, and the last participant replied that it did not apply. Four of the seniors reported they partially agreed that the app's features were easy to use, one said that he strongly disagreed, and one that neither agreed nor disagreed.

When asked if they thought other users would have it easy to learn how to use the app, four participants reported partially agreeing, one totally disagreeing and the other neither agreeing nor disagreeing. On trusting the application, two seniors strongly disagreed feeling it was trustworthy, two partially agreed, one partially disagreed and one neither agreed or not. The last question was whether they needed to learn a lot before they could use APP, two seniors said "yes", completely agreeing, two partially agreed, one partially disagreed and only one totally disagreed.

After the session, all participants were asked about what they thought of the intergenerational moment. Regarding what they thought the younger ones had taught them during the activity, the older participants stressed the ease with which they used their mobile phone, the friendliness, respect, responsibility and joy of young people, the importance of being creative and one of the seniors even said that "in interacting with these young people, we feel a bit like them."

When asked about what they thought the younger generation learned from them, the seniors said that the young people were able to learn about the city of Viseu that existed in other times and to hear stories about places that no longer existed today. In addition, it was said that the youngsters learned the importance of family respect, and that, older people also knew how to live and understand them.

Regarding what they liked most about the activity, the opinions are unanimous in emphasizing the contact with young people, remembering the places and being able to tell the stories placed in the city.

The seniors left as suggestions the possibilities of extending the activity to more people, allowing more time to do it and creating a mobile application that covers more areas in Viseu.

5.3 Focus Group Results

When asked about the main difficulties while using the app, participants stated their general lack of ability to use technologies and not this particular app, "as it would always indicate where to click". "I have had the phone for a few years, but I'm still not sure what an application is", "I personally felt little interest, I saw no use for my life".

They recognize the role of the youngest in exploring the app. "Without the support of the youngest, it would be difficult to do the job".

About what did they like the most about the app and what did they dislike the most about the app, the seniors did not express sound opinions, but left as a suggestion for improving the creation of a support tutorial. "In the future we should have an explanatory session before going to the field", "the existence of an explanation (tutorial), or an explanatory video to support the use of the app". These tutorials would help people using the app, as they feel that, from one usage to another, "you forget about features and operations".

When asked if they think that it is possible for other kids and adults to use the app, they asked objective questions about the features of the app envisioning its exploration. "Will the app only work in the Viseu center? It will be interesting to have some places outside this area that may also be important". "We must wait until we have the app on our mobile phone, is it possible to use it with our grandchildren? But we will need a tutorial". Questions as "how is intergenerationality reflected in the app functionalities?", "how will the app be disseminated", "the person who posts can delete that content", "the contents are supervised?", unveils the appropriation that older adults make of the app.

Finally, when asked how they perceived their role in the Project, they stated that, although at an early stage they only did it as a favor, they enjoyed it and wished they were able to follow up. "At first, I participated just to do the favor, but then I liked it and wanted to continue. We learned a lot". They also stressed the interaction with the younger ones, referring to the moments of learning and how they felt valued by them. "I enjoyed interacting with the younger ones, I felt valued".

6   Conclusions

VIAS | ViseuInterAgeStories aims to develop an app that fosters collaboration between youngsters and the elderly by creating and sharing stories about the cultural and natural heritage of their city, (re)creating some of the places' appropriations and meanings, while adding a multimedia layer to the living city. The project mobilized a Participatory Design approach, working with children and older adults as a path to explore intergenerational dynamics and practices, as well as to co-design the app.

In this paper we have presented and discussed the results of the design and of the evaluation workshops, emphasizing the meaning of contributions by older participants.

We have followed the idea of embedding the design process with the participants' practices, by exploring in-situ the way how children and older adults interact to create collaborative multimedia stories, while touring in the urban space as they use mobile phones. For over a year, exploratory workshops guided the context and the conditions for the participants to develop paper mockups, with significant contributions, and to evaluate a prototype of the app.

Results show how older adults value the history of the city. Faced with this fact, we decided to integrate georeferenced historical information into the app. Another issue pointed out by older adults was the importance of categorizations. In fact, one can say elderly users have important and significant opinions about what should be the app's requisites. Although they assume the difficulties faced while confronting technology, they have been constructing their own meanings as much as possible, and they want to do it by using technology.

The intergenerational experience as well as the co-design process both showed implications for older adults' self-esteem and fulfillment, and gave value to their role as productive and important members of the community.

Acknowledgments. The VIAS Project – ViseuInterAgeStories (CENTRO-01-0145-FEDER-023485) was funded by FEDER (PORTUGAL2020). The Polytechnic Institute of Castelo Branco, the Municipality of Viseu and the 2PLAY+ company are co-sponsors. We would like to thank the students of the Senior University of Viseu and the children for their partnership.

References

1. European Union Ageing Europe: Looking at the lives of older people in the EU. Eurostat Report (2019)
2. PorData: Indicadores de envelhecimento (2019). https://www.pordata.pt/DB/Portugal/Amb iente+de+Consulta/Tabela. Accessed 21 Dec 2019
3. WHO World Health Organization. Active Ageing - A Policy Framework. In: Second United Nations World Assembly on Ageing, Madrid (2002)
4. Carrilho, M.J., Craveiro, M.L.: A Situação Demográfica Recente em Portugal. Revista Estudos Demográficos **54**, 57–107 (2015)
5. Paúl, C.: Envelhecimento ativo e redes de suporte social. Sociologia **15**, 275–287 (2005)
6. Villas-Boas, S., Oliveira, A.L.D., Ramos, N., Montero, I.: Social support and generation diversity: the potential of the LSNS-6. Pedagogía Social: Revista Interuniversitaria **31**, 177–189 (2017)
7. Gomes, C.A., et al.: VIAS | Viseu InterAge stories: developing an app to foster social inclusion and healthy lifestyles. In: International Symposium on Computers in Education on Proceedings 2017, pp. 1–5. IEEE, Lisboa (2017)
8. Leedahl, S.N., Brasher, M.S., Estus, E., Breck, B.M., Cory, B.D., Clark, S.C.: Implementing an interdisciplinary intergenerational program using the Cyber Seniors® reverse mentoring model within higher education. Gerontol. Geriatr. Educ. **40**(1), 71–89 (2019)
9. Morganti, L., Scaratti, C., Cipresso, P., Gaggioli, A., Bonfiglio, S., Riva, G.: How can technology help intergenerational reminiscence? A pilot study. Int. J. Web Based Commun. **12**(1), 35–54 (2016)
10. Drigas, A., Papagerasimou, Y.: Intergenerational learning for the e-inclusion of senior citizens through the prism of the GRANKIT project. Int. J. Comput. Sci. Issues **12**(6), 64–71 (2015)
11. Fricke, A., Marley, M., Morton, A., Thomé, J.: The mix@ges Experience. How to promote Intergenerational Bonding through Creative Digital Media. Remscheid: Mix@ges (2013)
12. Stephanidis, C., Salvendy, G.: Seven HCI grand challenges. Int. J. Hum.-Comput. Interact. **35**(14), 1229–1269 (2019)
13. Shneiderman, B., Plaisant, C., Cohen, M., Jacobs, S., Elmqvist, N., Diakopoulos, N.: Grand challenges in HCI. ACM Interact. **23**(5), 24–25 (2016)
14. Scaife, M., Rogers, Y., Aldrich, F., Davies, M.: Designing for or designing with? Informant design for interactive learning environments. In: Proceedings of the ACM SIGCHI Conference on Human Factors in Computing Systems, pp. 43–350 (1997)
15. Bodker, S., Ehn, P., Sjogren, D., Sundblad, Y.: Cooperative design – perspectives on 20 years with the Scandinavia IT design model. In: Proceedings of NordiCHI, pp. 22–24 (2000)

16. Yip, J.C., et al.: Examining adult-child interactions in intergenerational participatory design. In: Proceedings of the CHI Conference on Human Factors in Computing Systems, pp. 5742–5754 (2017)
17. Rogers, Y.: HCI Theory: Classical, Modern, and Contemporary. Synthesis Lectures on Human-Centered Informatics. Morgan & Claypool Publishers (2012)
18. Robertson, T., Leong, T.W., Durick, J., Koreshoff, T.: Mutual learning as a resource for research design. In: Proceedings of the 13th Participatory Design Conference: Short Papers, Industry Cases, Workshop Descriptions, Doctoral Consortium papers, and Keynote Abstracts, PDC 2014, vol. 2, pp. 25–28. ACM, New York (2014)
19. Leong, T.W., Robertson, T.: Voicing values: laying foundations for ageing people to participate in design. In: Proceedings of the 14th Participatory Design Conference: Full Papers, PDC 2016, vol. 1, pp. 31–40. Association for Computing Machinery, New York (2016)
20. Iversen, O.S., Halskov, K., Leong, T.W.: Values-led participatory design. J. CoDes. **8**(2–3), 87–103 (2012)
21. Cozza, M., Tonolli, L., D'Andrea, V.: Subversive participatory design: reflections on a case study. In: Proceedings of the 14th Participatory Design Conference: Short Papers, Interactive Exhibitions, Workshops, PDC 2016, vol. 2, pp. 53–56. Association for Computing Machinery, New York (2016)
22. Rogers, Y., Paay, J., Brereton, M., Vaisutis, K., Marsden, G., Vetere, F.: Never too old: engaging retired people inventing the future with MaKey MaKey. In: Proceedings of the SIGCHI Conference on Human Factors in Computing Systems, CHI 2014, pp. 3913–3922. Association for Computing Machinery, New York (2014)
23. Gomes, C., Araújo, L., Figueiredo, M., Ribeiro, E., Felizardo, S., Ferreira, S.: Interchanging memories and meanings of places in the city of Viseu: an intergenerational and digital experience? In: ECER 2018, Bolzano (2018)
24. Gomes, C.A., Ferreira, S., Gouveia, T., Rito, P., Morais, N., Sousa, B.: Intergenerational participatory design: contributions to the development of an app. In: Proceedings of International Symposium on Computers in Education (SIIE), Jerez (Cadiz), Spain, pp. 1–6. IEEE (2018)

Technology Development with Older People: The Role of "Unfettered Design"

Björn Fischer[(✉)] [iD] and Britt Östlund [iD]

Department of Biomedical Engineering and Health Systems,
Royal Institute of Technology KTH, Stockholm, Sweden
bjorfisc@kth.se

Abstract. This article introduces a new method to design with older people: unfettered design. We discuss three points of concern with existing methods of involving older users: unspecific design outcomes, prejudiced views on older users, and underlying power asymmetries, which can diminish the innovative capacities of the older adults involved. To overcome these issues, we argue for the benefits of adopting unfettered design. Through unfettered design, the users involved are given the space to explore design ideas on their own terms, and unusual and unsolicited responses are explicitly desired and listened to. This, in turn, may help designers to elicit novel design ideas and identify potentials for innovative technologies. Thereby, designers may learn about the concerns and potentials for which older adults would find technologies particularly helpful - a crucial aspect considering rather low levels of technology uptake in this population segment. We illustrate our approach by means of examples from our own design experiences, and we formulate four core principles of unfettered design: ongoing reflection, retained impartiality, a distinct focus on the participants' view and remaining flexible throughout the procedure. Having undergone several waves of both technological and social change, older adults possess unique experiences and tacit knowledge that can serve as valuable inspirations for designers. Unfettered design can be particularly helpful to benefit from these competences during design projects.

Keywords: Involving the elderly in HCI methodology · Older people · User involvement · Participatory design

1 Introduction

Given our current knowledge, how could older people be appropriately involved during design procedures? To derive possible ways forward, we will begin the article with a critical examination of current practices of involving older people during design procedures. In particular, we argue that these are problematic for both designers and older people due to three important concerns: First, the existing literature includes various procedures and methodologies to involve older users, but their link to any specific outcomes is neither clear nor sufficiently differentiated. Second, procedures involving older people are prone to our particular views on older users. Thirdly, and perhaps most crucially,

© Springer Nature Switzerland AG 2020
Q. Gao and J. Zhou (Eds.): HCII 2020, LNCS 12207, pp. 18–33, 2020.
https://doi.org/10.1007/978-3-030-50252-2_2

user involvement is affected by underlying power dynamics, design agendas, assumptions and values, which in turn circumscribe the scope of potential contributions that the involved older participants may offer.

Based on this critical review, we then introduce our idea of unfettered design as an attempt to tackle these challenges. In doing so, we draw and expand on previous work in critical HCI research and science and technology studies. Using examples from our own design workshops, we show how we aimed at achieving unfettered design in practice, and highlight our own experiences and struggles. We end by concretizing our approach, and articulate four core principles of unfettered design that can help guide designers to implement this procedure: ongoing reflection, retained impartiality, a distinct focus on the participants' view and remaining flexible throughout the procedure. In that way, we contend, novel ideas and relevant aspects may surface that would otherwise not be considered during design procedures.

2   Current Methods of Older User "Involvement"

Our first point of skepticism refers to the variety of existing methods and outcomes of involving older people. Including older adults in design processes has become the focus of a large amount of studies recently (e.g. [1–3]). The benefit normally associated with this approach is that integrating older people in design projects will enable the designers to better cater for the expectations and requirements of older adults. An additional aspect sometimes put forward is that involving older people in the process may evade possible ageist stereotypes. Generally, the anticipation is that the inclusion of older people – in some way – will yield insights to create more suitable technologies for the older population.

Indeed, the experiences of older adults are of great relevance for designers. For example, Essén and Östlund [4] have shown how older people collaborated as creative innovators identifying potential service solutions for their specific life circumstances. Similarly, Peine and colleagues [5] have outlined the adoption and usage of e-bikes in the Netherlands, and demonstrated how older people were in fact early adopters of this novel technology. Other studies also highlight how older adults variously engage with technologies in their homes, for example by configuring DIY-gerontechnologies [6], adapting technologies to their needs [7], or rejecting technologies that they do not find meaningful for themselves [8]. Together, these studies bring to the fore the richness of older people's specific life situations and experiences; - an understanding of which surely would greatly benefit designers.

Although important and promising, however, the optimistic perspective outlined above is misleading, for it does not sufficiently specify what precisely "involvement" might entail. The concept of user involvement has enjoyed a considerable amount of attention over the past decades, and has been taken up by a range of disciplines, including software engineering [9], information systems [10] and health care [11]. As a result, there exists a panoply of different methods, such as user-centered design [12], participatory design [13], and prototyping [14], to name a few. Approaches to user involvement are diverse, and they can be differently interpreted. For example, we might further ask ourselves what we mean when we involve older people by adopting "participatory design", "user centered design" and so forth. And within each of those approaches, we might again be able to specify, for example, at which level we involve older people [15], or what the purpose of participation actually is [16]. Given this wide spectrum and depth of user involvement methods, it is difficult for designers to specify what method precisely they adopted.

The complexity of involving older people as a method is further compounded by the possibility that different procedures of involving older people may yield different results. Depending on how, where and when designers choose to involve older people, the outcome can refer to, amongst others, increased learning, design adjustments or a general sense of participation [17]. And again, even if the involvement projects yielded apparently similar outcomes, these outcomes could still be distinguished by means of different degrees. For instance, two projects that report increased learning may still distinguish themselves as to the ratio of what and how much was learned, compared to what could have been learned. The same could be the case for the other dimensions mentioned above.

Generally, it appears to us that current procedures and methodologies to involve older people are so overtly diverse and intricate that a clear understanding of the links between them and the various possible outcomes, including their degrees, is still lacking. Hence, a refined method of older user involvement is needed if we wish to specify how a *particular* outcome can be obtained.

3   Views on "Older Users"

A second point of critique is that any endeavor aiming at involving older users in design projects is susceptible to whom we consider "older users". This refers to two aspects: first, what designers believe "older" means; and, second, who designers believe "users" could be.

3.1 Old Age

First, the category of "old age" itself is multifaceted and contentious. Historically, the view on ageing and growing older has generally been complicated. Whether through magazines, government organizations or other types of public sources, questionable images of ageing have been perpetuated throughout recent decades. Stereotypical images about older people may be rooted in a culturally embedded fear of death, illnesses and physical decline and a consequential adoration of youthfulness [18, 19]. Furthermore, they may be linked to other contextual factors, such as the rise of consumerism and changes in consumption behaviors viewing older people as a new target group [20, 21]. Moreover, ageing populations are increasingly perceived as a challenge to existing care and social welfare systems, re-framing older people negatively as a 'tsunami' [22, 23].

What is important to note is that design projects involving older people are not unaffected by such images and views about old age. When choosing whom to involve, designers must inevitably identify and define whom they consider as belonging to the "older" population segment. In other words, older user involvement as a method itself encourages the designers to include *their* particular view on old age *into* the design project.

Thereby, common views and prejudices about older people may enter our involvement procedures without us even noticing, something that Neven [24] has referred to as "age scripts". Such common ideas may refer to the intention to design technology in order to compensate for the deficits that occur with age, such as loneliness or declining physical capabilities [25]. While there clearly is a considerable and valuable potential of technologies to tackle certain age-related diseases, this preoccupation runs the risk of narrowing the portrayal of older people into a lopsided focus onto their deficiencies: as fragile, passive receivers of technology [26]. The undesired consequence is that many older people may oppose such a portrayal [24]. In some cases, older people may even choose to not participate in technology projects at all if they do not identify with certain presumptions of these projects [27]. In fact, they have good reasons to do so, as they are far more diverse, creative and innovative than the most common portrayals suggest [28]. Despite this understanding, however, the overwhelming amount of design studies involving older people merely as test persons suggests that underlying prejudices about older people's creativity and technological literacy appear to persist [4, 17].

Against this background, it seems sensible to us that, when involving older users, we should be reflective of the possibility of stereotypical views about older people. Different views would likely encourage different attempts at involving them.

3.2 The Users

Second, the method of older user involvement not only requires that designers identify and define old age, but also that designers have to find appropriate user representatives. As such, designers need to identify and define characteristics of who "the user" actually is. A plethora of research efforts has been dedicated to explore how certain characteristics can be best extracted and isolated, particularly within the tradition of HCI design and user experience design (e.g. [29–31]). Amongst others, such characteristics may refer to different identities (such as race, gender, age or class), or socio-economic features (such as educational background, income, living situation). Moreover, different typologies for categorizing users have been developed. For example, Friedman (1989) distinguishes between patrons (users taking initiative), clients (target users), design interactors (involved users), end users (those who operate), maintenance interactors and secondary users (i.e. those lacking skills). Furthermore, various techniques can be adopted, such as marketing surveys or consulting experts to represent the user more or less accurately [32]. Generally, there appears to be the widespread idea that some neatly separable characteristics exist that designers can identify in order to define "the right user" [33].

Taken together, the studies above highlight how designers may choose to differently define and identify "the user". Thereby, however, the identity and role of an individual is described in relation to a specific technology that the designer envisions. Hence, the "user" appears as a more passive, restricted individual, with needs often merely in relation to the type of functionality a technology may offer. Such a view on "users" may disregard the more active and embodied nature of these individuals called "users", learning and interacting with their environments as they continuously engage with novel technologies [34]. Furthermore, particularly in the context of ageing populations, studies have emphasized the intricate nature of older people's life experiences as heterogenous and diverse [35, 36]. The term "user" bears the risk of discounting these varied and diverse life experiences to sets of requirements and impairments that can easily be met by the utilities and functionalities offered by a technology [37]. Involvement, thus, is prone to take place in the subtle light of a paternalistic view on users.

In sum, current procedures involving older people are vulnerable with regard to two aspects: First, the particular views of designers on old age, and second, the controversial term of "users". In light of our broader argument, we would like to stress that our ambition is by no means to eradicate this vulnerability, or to suggest that such an eradication could easily be possible at all. However, we do wish to emphasize the need for an increased awareness and reflexivity.

4   Conceptual Challenges to Older User Involvement: Assumptions, Values and Design Agendas

In the previous section, we briefly touched upon that involvement procedures may be impacted by how "older users" are framed. Our third point of critique is that, beyond discursive preconceptions and dubious terminologies, user involvement procedures are more broadly affected by underlying power dynamics, values and assumptions, which – as we will argue – may circumscribe the innovative potential of involving older users.

An example of the power dynamics underlying user involvement procedures is offered by Woolgar's [38] seminal ethnographic study of usability trials of a new range of microcomputers in a British computer manufacturer. In his study, he showed how the usability trials he observed entailed a set of design activities and negotiations that ulti-mately aimed at "configuring" the user. Woolgar argued that we could view the machine as working as a "text" that the designers "write" and "rewrite", setting parameters to achieve the "correct" interpretation by the users. In that sense, during involvement proce-dures, the designer can use the machine to enable and constrain the users' actions. Along similar lines, Akrich [39], based on an anthropological study of the implementation of three electrical technologies in Africa, developed the notion of a "script" to refer to the way designers may implement their representations about users into technology design, and thereby influence the users' actions and interactions. In particular, she noted how engineers can hold images of prospective users, which may work like a "film script": they ascribe particular roles and frames of action to both users and technologies. Such images can become "inscribed" into the technology, and thereby enable and constrain the actions of the future users. However, Akrich also noted that users may have the agency to deviate from the prescriptions and values embedded by the designers and "de-inscribe" previously included scripts. Combined, the studies by Akrich [39] and Woolgar [38] shed light on the power that designers may have during involvement procedures and technology development projects, in configuring users and inscribing their assumptions and values into technological objects[1].

---

[1] Of course, the role and influence of designers may itself be limited by other contextual influences as well as the agency of users [33, 34]. However, while designers themselves may have to deal with a multiplicity of constraints, in any single involvement procedure, the positions of designers and users are not perfectly equal [40]. Design actions relate to the perceptions, notions and ideas designers have about possible users, both consciously and unconsciously.

In this context, several studies exist that problematized the possibility for power imbalances that occur as part of design procedures (e.g. [40–44]). For example, Clarke [44] coined the notion of "implicated actors", referring to those individuals that are impacted by an action but relatively powerless when the decisions for these actions are taken. This notion is particularly relevant for user involvement procedures: Normally, the objectives and indicators of user involvement procedures are defined by the designers, while the users are required to conform to pre-determined design goals [42]. The designers decide on what the goal of the procedure is, and how the success of this goal is measured. In other words, the designers establish, already at the outset, a *design agenda*, which explicates a set of goals with respect to a particular technology that is deemed relevant to the users, and whose relevance is not particularly questioned during the design process. It is then expected that the users' involvement should squarely contribute to these goals and assumptions set by the designers. In the development and agreement of such design agendas, in contrast, the users rarely play a role in actual practice.

The setting of this design agenda is possible as designers have the privilege to begin the design procedure, by choosing to define and identify the users (as discussed in Sect. 3.2). It is hard to imagine that users could select and identify themselves beforehand. Hence, when adopting user involvement as a method, designers are, of necessity, in charge when deciding whom to involve, how and why. In turn, this initial privilege lends the designers a certain authority and legitimacy *throughout* the design procedure [42, 43]. Statements and interpretations made by designers may silently gain significance and preference over those made by users, and the designers may exert considerable influence on the users through making the central design decisions and choices [41]. Thereby, the established design agenda is particularly powerful, as it entails a normative dimension: The older participants and users are confronted with the imperative that the development agenda *should* be accepted, and their actions are situated within the boundaries that are envisioned for them.

In this regard, participatory design (e.g. [13]) is often mentioned as a method to account for the politics of design practices and to adhere to the democratic value of including multiple stakeholders as equals. However, we caution that power asymmetries might exist even for the noblest attempts of involving older people as equal partners (e.g. in participatory or co-design). As much as we appreciate attempts to position both users and designers as experts on their own life experiences, we need to be aware that this view masks subtle power imbalances existing between users and designers. Users *still* need to be selected and chosen by the designer, based on certain characteristics that are, again, selected and chosen by the designer, and they *still* need to be guided by the designer through the procedure, where important steps and decisions can be made at the will of the designer. The nature of older user involvement requires us to consider that, already from the outset, the positions of designers and older users are not absolutely equal.

Crucially, the power asymmetry outlined above bears the risk of missing promising potentials for technology development and innovation. In particular, following an established design agenda, the older users involved might feel obliged to tailor their suggestions to the expectations set by the design project. Thereby, instances of older adults not wanting and not wishing a particular feature may remain unnoticed if their replies might be ignored, sidelined or not evoked at all [45]. Neven [24], for example, showed how the designers' understanding of older test users of health robots clashed with the identities expressed by the older adults themselves, as the older adults did not identify as a potential user group. The designers, however, did not further consider the feedback by older adults, as their predominant focus was on evaluating the interaction between the older test users and the robots. Another example is the study by Compagna and Kohlbacher [46], who described how, during the introduction of a robot into a care facility for elderly people, the needs of the residents were ignored to make place for knowledge more relevant from a technical perspective.

In sum, frictions can occur between pre-established design agendas and the inputs older people can offer during involvement procedures. When a specific design agenda is followed, the older participants may (intentionally or unintentionally) be coerced to respond to designers' own pre-set technological ambitions and ideas. In such instances, the designers' assumptions about design-relevant characteristics may unwittingly delimit the scope of potential contributions that can be obtained from the involved older participants, and some of their needs and wishes may remain unattended to.

5 Our Proposal: Unfettered Design

5.1 Background and Definition

In response to the challenges outlined above, we propose a new approach to design when involving older people, which we term "unfettered design". We define unfettered design as *design where the users involved are given the space to explore design ideas on their own terms, and where unusual and unsolicited responses are explicitly desired and listened to.* Our proposal draws and expands on previous work, in particular reflective design [47] and critical perspectives on participatory design [41–43].

Reflective design has been introduced as a more profound method to account for the unconscious choices made by designers during HCI design projects [47]. Sengers and colleagues [47] proposed that ongoing critical reflection itself should be the core value of design. To do so, they built on and combined a range of different design disciplines (e.g. [48]), and introduced six main principles for reflective design, i.e. that designers should:

- reflect on the limitations of their design practices,
- reflect on their own roles in the procedure,
- empower users to reflect on their roles and backgrounds,
- allow technologies to be open for skepticism,
- include reflection as a central part into their design procedure,
- and foster mutual engagement between themselves and users [47].

In short, reflective design helps guide designers to critically deal with and rethink the prominent assumptions and values underlying their design, and to encourage users to participate in this reflective practice. Its design strategies and techniques have also been taken up in the context of designing technologies for older people specifically (e.g. [49]).

Our approach of unfettered design builds on this approach, specifically the insight that ongoing reflection throughout the design procedure is crucial to make visible and modify the values and limitations underlying current design practices [47, 49]. Through continuous reflection, designers are able to become more aware of their views on older users, and – most crucially – the intricacies of user involvement methods including their implicit values, assumptions, agendas and roles. However, reflective design and its principal techniques have mostly been directed towards reflecting on the values and assumptions underlying the *technical content* of design (i.e. the technological object). Unfettered design intends to expand the focus of reflective design, to reflect on the very *execution* of the *design methods* (i.e. involvement procedures and the roles of designers and users). It aims to not only reflect, but also use this reflection to *tackle* accompanying power asymmetries as we discuss in the next section.

Critical studies on participatory design have raised considerable questions regarding power asymmetries and the roles of designers during participatory design procedures (e.g. [42, 43]). In different shades, these studies derived guiding principles for designers to more closely attend to the democratic ideal of equal collaboration. Sanders and Stappers [43], for example, re-conceptualized the role of designers into facilitators supporting a creative collaboration between designers and users. Their argument is that designers have valuable knowledge other stakeholders do not possess, and they should use these insights to support non-designers to codesign. Vines et al. [42] critically discussed how designers may "configure" participation, and highlighted four main strategies to respond to these existing challenges:

- Be more transparent with regards to the design agenda
- Explore own preconceptions and assumptions
- Configure several forms of participation at different levels
- Participants may reconfigure the process and re-define design process

Together, these studies have brought forward more nuanced perspectives on how power is distributed among designers and users, and how this issue could be addressed in the future. Participation can be re-configured to counteract prejudices and power asymmetries. Largely, however, these perspectives are still not sufficiently considered within the HCI literature.

Our proposal of unfettered design builds on this earlier work, in particular on the recognition that designers may act as facilitators to enable a different type of collaboration with the users involved. Unfettered design specifically advocates that users should experience fewer constraints from pre-existing design agendas, preconceptions and assumptions. It also highlights the need to empower the older participants during the procedure.

However, our approach also expands on this earlier work, as it specifically aims to put the insights and contributions provided center stage. That is, unfettered design challenges designers to remain focused on, and open to, what matters to the older participants, i.e. what they consider relevant. This necessity for this "openness" requires that designers actively encourage and listen to the experiences uttered by older adults, and adjust the design procedure accordingly. It also involves removing constraints such as delimiting design agendas and prejudices. The promise of this approach is that thereby, designers may potentially explore areas of knowledge that otherwise would remain unknown. The older participants would be able to more broadly disclose their life experiences, their daily joys and struggles. It are these insights we are looking for in design, as these build the anchor points for innovative solutions that really target the needs and desires of older people [4].

By implementing unfettered design, designers may come to grips with the three main concerns we discussed before: First, by aiming at the specific outcome that the older adults' contributions form the central focus for design, unfettered design creates certainty about the outcome that should be achieved by involving older people. Second, it includes reflection about the roles and assumptions of designers as an integral part into design, thereby addressing the concern that problematic views on older users could unconsciously influence the design procedure. Thirdly, it requires the creation of an environment in which older participants are able to freely articulate their own experiences and ideas (without any prior prejudice or restrictions), and that these contributions form the basis for the ongoing design procedure. This speaks to our third criticism by encouraging designers to shape the existing power dynamics and design agendas in such a way that they are beneficial for an unfettered involvement of older participants.

5.2 Design Cases: Our Own Experiences with Unfettered Design

Above, we have described why unfettered design is a relevant approach to involve older adults, how we built on earlier work and how unfettered design seeks to expand this. To further elaborate this approach, we will now discuss how we ourselves aimed at implementing "unfettered" design in practice, and confide our own struggles and obstacles during that procedure. The design cases elaborated here are part of work in progress that includes an ongoing set of design workshops conducted with different types of participants, including older adults. In this section, our focus is on our experiences in organizing these workshops in an unfettered manner.

In line with our notion of "unfettered design", our central ambition was to build design workshops that foreground the experiences and contributions offered by the involved participants. To enable such an unfettered collaboration, we strove to overcome the design-related issues we have previously discussed: a certain view on older users, pre-existing design agendas, and underlying power-asymmetries, values and assumptions. To begin with, we constantly reflected on our own view on the capabilities of older users. We adopted an image of an older adult as a life-experienced expert, having witnessed multiple periods of technological change and transitions, and knowledgeable about their own personal life circumstances and lived realities. We saw the older people as equal partners, whose voice and views should form the integral part of the workshops. Throughout the procedure, we kept in mind the significance of our perspective on the older participants, and that our actions should correspond with this treatment [48].

Another aspect referred to is the recognition that, as we have argued before, any design workshop requires some type of agenda. Hence, to enable unfettered design, we built elements of this 'unfettered' approach into that very agenda. That is, we set out specifically to explore what mattered to our co-designers, and thereby identify possibilities for new innovative technologies. In practice, this agenda meant that we specifically focused on asking open questions, such as: What technology would you choose? How could it best be adapted to the needs of older people? Why? The participants were encouraged to work in groups and discuss and develop their ideas, and use examples from their own life worlds to illustrate where a certain technology could be useful, meaningful or enjoyable to them (and where not). We received a vast array of responses, ranging from issues with existing smartphones in terms of letter size and autocorrect to the possibility to combine smart home assistants with the ability to order laundry support.

Perhaps the most challenging aspect of implementing unfettered design was to tackle the concern that we, as workshop organizers, would dominate the procedure too much. We sought to deal with this, particularly by encouraging our participants from the beginning, at the idea creation phase, to explore their ideas, independent of how different they first seemed from our design agenda. This yielded a set of very interesting inputs, such as ethical issues with existing technology as some members uttered concerns about technologies that could run in the background and monitor their actions without their agreement, and the proposal to distinguish between different type of ringtones, depending on whether people call that they want to answer or not. It also proved especially helpful to attend to the aspects that our participants found interesting and potentially relevant, in contrast to those that they did not further engage with. Smartphones and smart homes seemed much more relevant to the realities of our participants, than did robots.

However, we also encountered certain limitations that unfettered design may not easily eradicate. In particular, design procedures are populated by different technological materials and workshop tools that both stimulate and restrict the imaginative landscapes of older participants. Examples are paper materials [50], prototype applications [51] and technology toolkits [52]. These different objects and tools are a central part of design procedures; and their benefits have been widely accepted, in particular their ability of fostering creativity among the participants [53, 54]. Our own workshops were no exception to this tradition, as we made available a range of simple design materials to our participants. These included papers and pens in various colors, post-it notes and PowerPoint slides to help explain our design procedure.

While these materials were certainly helpful to implement our design procedures, they may (at first) seem to clash with our initial ambitions to implement "unfettered" design. Did the presence and usage of certain tools not come at the cost of the absence and non-usage of others? Clearly, by offering our participants a menu of tools, we created a situation in which they could select certain dishes, but they could not choose a different menu. However, the central focus of unfettered design is not to remove all that may structure or constrain design actions and perceptions. Human actions are always situated within existing structures, both inevitably existing and mutually constituting each other [55]. Against this background, we did not aim to remove structures entirely, but to adjust them in such a manner that our participants' views formed the central concern for design. We engaged in an ongoing reflection about how we, as designers, could shape those structures in such a way that they enabled our participants to contribute freely during the procedure. Following this reflection, we chose to include tools and objects that can be combined and used for very different purposes, and we specifically asked for open and uncommon responses.

We admit, though, that different executions of our procedures might have been possible. For example, we could have provided a larger array of tools and thereby increased the scope for possible contributions. On the other hand, we could also have refrained from using any tools and presentations altogether, and make the participants the sole people responsible for driving the design procedure. This comparison makes it clear that different degrees of unfettered design exist, as, by different designers, and, on different days, design workshops can be very differently organized. Despite these varying contextual factors, however, we have seen how a focus on unfettered design can be maintained, by reflecting on our own roles as designers, and by shaping the design setting such that our participants are encouraged to contribute on their own terms.

5.3 Core Principles of Unfettered Design

The examples above show how unfettered design can matter in practice, and they illustrate how we sought to follow this approach and its central facets. Below, we outline four core principles to summarize how unfettered design can be achieved. They can be applied both to older participants particularly, or more broadly to various user groups in general.

1. **Ongoing reflection on own role and assumptions as integral part to design**
   Design does not occur in a vacuum, but is affected by differential distributions of power, the setting of certain agendas, the selection of participants, available tools, different individual backgrounds etcetera. The roles, practices and assumptions of designers may have a considerable impact on how the design procedure unfolds. Unfettered design requires designers to raise and maintain an awareness of their own roles and actions, and of how these may relate to certain design outcomes. This reflection should not be a separate activity, but become integral to the very design procedure itself (cf. [47, 48]). As reflection on underlying assumptions and roles becomes part of design, it guides designers to adjust future actions in present time.

2. **Retain impartiality throughout the design procedure**
   Unfettered design expects that unusual suggestions are given as much consideration as are more conservative ones; that participants are given the space necessary to explore design ideas on their own terms. All contributions and ideas should be given equal consideration during the design procedure, no matter how obscure they may seem at first. This should be facilitated by the ongoing reflection mentioned above: designers constantly check and reflect on whether the participants have the environment required for them to openly express themselves. It is the task of the designer to work as facilitators of this open exploration and contributions and avoid distorting the procedure into any particular (possibly personally favored) directions. This involves to engage in prejudice-free consultation and dialogue, and to remain impartial as the participants elaborate on their own lived realities and perspectives. Thereby, unfettered design may allow designers to uncover potentially new, innovative possibilities for technology development that they would else not have considered. Retaining impartiality is additionally advantageous, for it prevents designers from influencing the design procedure too much. By building impartiality into the

design agenda itself, designers commit to not *a priori* ascribe any particular "image", "need" or "requirement" to the user (that could be met by a certain technology), but instead develop their understanding of the peoples' lives as the procedure unfolds.

3. **Have a distinct focus on understanding the participant's points of view**
   Based on their own interests, designers may be tempted to steer away the design procedure from the concerns of users towards more practical or technical issues (cf. [24, 45, 46]). Unfettered design encourages the designers to maintain a distinct focus on the topics that matter to the people involved throughout the design process. The procedure should be built based on the views and concerns of the users involved in the project, and be modified in accordance as the design project progresses. This includes working closely together with the users and putting effort into understanding the perspectives of the people involved. We should note that this does not mean that designers should not be critical with the responses or suggestions uttered by the participants. Rather, we wish to highlight the importance of thoroughly engaging the participants' contributions, so as to focus on identifying opportunities that refer to their lived realities.

4. **Remain flexible**
   As we have argued before, unfettered design can occur to varying degrees. This is not a problem, as long as the focus is on that the participants can express themselves openly. To ensure this, we suggest designers to remain flexible, to be able to respond to the direction in which participants take the design procedure, and to remain open to alter parts of the procedure or the design focus if responses by participants suggest to do so. This involves critically engaging with the suggestions and descriptions by the participants, and, if deemed necessary, to follow up on them even though, at first, they seem absurd or irrelevant. Unfettered design supports that designers consider all avenues that become visible during the design procedure.

6   Conclusions

We have introduced "unfettered design" as a new approach to involve older people. By providing examples from our own experiences, we have shown what it means to implement unfettered design in practice, and what challenges exist. In particular, unfettered design addresses three main shortcomings of existing involvement practices: first, the lacking link between involvement procedure and outcome; second, preconceptions about older users and; thirdly, the impact by power imbalances, underlying values, assumptions and design agendas. Through ongoing reflection, retained impartiality, a distinct focus on the participants view and remaining flexible throughout the procedure, designers may be able to give older users the space to explore design ideas on their own terms, and to specifically attend to their contributions (both usual and unusal). This, in turn, may help designers to elicit novel design ideas and identify potentials for innovative technologies. Thereby, designers may learn about the concerns and potentials for which older adults would find technologies particularly helpful - a crucial aspect considering rather low levels of technology uptake in this population segment. Having undergone several waves of both technological and social change, older adults possess unique experiences and tacit knowledge that can serve as valuable inspirations for designers. Unfettered design can be particularly helpful to benefit from these competences during design projects.

Acknowledgements. Our proposed approach has emerged out of several design workshops conducted during an ongoing EU project: BConnect@Home, which focuses on co-designing technologies that may support older people as they maintain connected at home. This work is funded by the Swedish Research Council for Health, Working Life and Welfare [grant number: 2017-02301] as part of the More Years, Better Lives Joint Programme (MYBL). Furthermore, we are thankful to the many people that participated during our workshops.

References

1. Sjölinder, M., Scandurra, I., Nöu, A.A., Kolkowska, E.: To meet the needs of aging users and the prerequisites of innovators in the design process. In: Zhou, J., Salvendy, G. (eds.) ITAP 2016. LNCS, vol. 9754, pp. 92–104. Springer, Cham (2016). https://doi.org/10.1007/978-3-319-39943-0_10
2. Battersby, L., Fang, M.L., Canham, S.L., Sixsmith, J., Moreno, S., Sixsmith, A.: Co-creation methods: informing technology solutions for older adults. In: Zhou, J., Salvendy, G. (eds.) ITAP 2017. LNCS, vol. 10297, pp. 77–89. Springer, Cham (2017). https://doi.org/10.1007/978-3-319-58530-7_6
3. Doroudian, A., Hausknecht, S., Kaufman, D.: Creating an online escape room game for older adults: needs assessment, design process, and usability testing. In: Zhou, J., Salvendy, G. (eds.) ITAP 2018. LNCS, vol. 10927, pp. 516–525. Springer, Cham (2018). https://doi.org/10.1007/978-3-319-92037-5_36
4. Essén, A., Östlund, B.: Laggards as innovators? Old users as designers of new services & service systems. Int. J. Des. **5**(3), 89–98 (2011)
5. Peine, A., van Cooten, V., Neven, L.: Rejuvenating design: bikes, batteries, and older adopters in the diffusion of e-bikes. Sci. Technol. Hum. Values. **42**(3), 429–459 (2017). https://doi.org/10.1177/0162243916664589
6. Bergschöld, J.M., Neven, L., Peine, A.: DIY gerontechnology: circumventing mismatched technologies and bureaucratic procedure by creating care technologies of one's own. Sociol. Health Illn. **xx**(xx), 1–15 (2019). https://doi.org/10.1111/1467-9566.13012
7. Joyce, K., Loe, M.: A sociological approach to ageing, technology and health. Sociol. Health Illn. **32**(2), 171–180 (2010). https://doi.org/10.1111/j.1467-9566.2009.01219.x
8. Bailey, C., Foran, T.G., Ni Scanaill, C., Dromey, B.: Older adults, falls and technologies for independent living: a life space approach. Ageing Soc. **31**(5), 829–848 (2011). https://doi.org/10.1017/S0144686X10001170
9. Abelein, U., Paech, B.: Understanding the influence of user participation and involvement on system success – a systematic mapping study. Empir. Softw. Eng. **20**(1), 28–81 (2015). https://doi.org/10.1007/s10664-013-9278-4
10. He, J., King, W.R.: The role of user participation in information systems development: implications from a meta-analysis. J. Manag. Inf. Syst. **25**(1), 301–331 (2008). https://doi.org/10.2753/MIS0742-1222250111
11. Shah, S.G.S., Robinson, I.: Benefits of and barriers to involving users in medical device technology development and evaluation. Int. J. Technol. Assess. Health Care **23**(1), 131–137 (2007)
12. Gulliksen, J., Göransson, B., Boivie, I., Blomkvist, S., Persson, J., Cajander, Å.: Key principles for user-centred systems design. Behav. Inf. Technol. **22**(6), 397–409 (2003). https://doi.org/10.1080/01449290310001624329

13. Greenbaum, J., Kyng, M. (eds.): Design at Work: Cooperative Design of Computer Systems. Lawrence Erlbaum Associates, Hillsdale (1991)
14. Floyd, C.: A systematic look at prototyping. In: Budde, R., Kuhlenkamp, K., Mathiassen, L., Züllighoven, H. (eds.) Approaches to Prototyping, pp. 1–18. Springer, Heidelberg (1984). https://doi.org/10.1007/978-3-642-69796-8_1
15. Östlund, B.: The benefits of involving older people in the design process. In: Zhou, J., Salvendy, G. (eds.) ITAP 2015. LNCS, vol. 9193, pp. 3–14. Springer, Cham (2015). https://doi.org/10.1007/978-3-319-20892-3_1
16. Hickey, S., Mohan, G. (eds.): Participation: From Tyranny to Transformation? Exploring New Approaches to Participation in Development. Zed Books, London (2004)
17. Fischer, B., Peine, A., Östlund, B.: The importance of user involvement: a systematic review of involving older users in technology design. Gerontologist X(X), 1–11 (2019). https://doi.org/10.1093/geront/gnz163
18. Estes, C.L., Binney, E.A.: The biomedicalization of aging: dangers and dilemmas. Gerontologist 29(5), 587–596 (1989). https://doi.org/10.1093/geront/29.5.587
19. Featherstone, M., Wernick, A. (eds.): Images of Aging: Cultural Representations of Later Life. Routledge, London (1995)
20. Katz, S., Marshall, B.: New sex for old: lifestyle, consumerism, and the ethics of aging well. J. Aging Stud. 17(1), 3–16 (2003). https://doi.org/10.1016/S0890-4065(02)00086-5
21. Higgs, P.F., Hyde, M., Gilleard, C.J., Victor, C.R., Wiggins, R.D., Jones, I.R.: From passive to active consumers? Later life consumption in the UK from 1968–2005. Sociol. Rev. 57(1), 102–124 (2009). https://doi.org/10.1111/j.1467-954X.2008.01806.x
22. Stauner, G.: The future of social security systems and demographic change. Eur. View 7(2), 203–208 (2008). https://doi.org/10.1007/s12290-008-0052-8
23. Mort, M., Roberts, C., Callén, B.: Ageing with telecare: care or coercion in austerity? Sociol. Health Illn. 35(6), 799–812 (2013). https://doi.org/10.1111/j.1467-9566.2012.01530.x
24. Neven, L.: 'But obviously not for me': robots, laboratories and the defiant identity of elder test users. Sociol. Health Illn. 32(2), 335–347 (2010). https://doi.org/10.1111/j.1467-9566.2009.01218.x
25. Vines, J., Pritchard, G., Wright, P., Olivier, P., Brittain, K.: An age-old problem: examining the discourses of ageing in HCI and strategies for future research. ACM Trans. Comput. Interact. 22(1), 1–27 (2015). https://doi.org/10.1145/2696867
26. Peine, A., Rollwagen, I., Neven, L.: The rise of the "innosumer"—rethinking older technology users. Technol. Forecast. Soc. Change. 82(1), 199–214 (2014). https://doi.org/10.1016/j.techfore.2013.06.013
27. Waycott, J., Vetere, F., Pedell, S., Morgans, A., Ozanne, E., Kulik, L.: Not for me: older adults choosing not to participate in a social isolation intervention. In: Proceedings of the 2016 CHI Conference on Human Factors in Computing Systems, CHI 2016, pp. 745–757. ACM Press, New York (2016). https://doi.org/10.1145/2858036.2858458
28. Durick, J., Robertson, T., Brereton, M., Vetere, F., Nansen, B.: Dispelling ageing myths in technology design. In: Proceedings of the 25th Australian Computer-Human Interaction Conference: Augmentation, Application, Innovation, Collaboration, OzCHI 2013, pp. 467–476. ACM Press, New York (2013). https://doi.org/10.1145/2541016.2541040
29. Shneiderman, B., Plaisant, C., Cohen, M., Jacobs, S., Elmqvist, N., Diakopoulos, N.: Designing the User Interface: Strategies for Effective Human-Computer Interaction. Pearson, Hoboken (2016)
30. Cooper, A.: The Inmates are Running the Asylum: Why High Tech Products Drive Us Crazy and How to Restore the Sanity. Sams Press, Indianapolis (2004)
31. Pruitt, J., Adlin, T.: The Persona Lifecycle: Keeping People in Mind Throughout Product Design. Morgan Kauffmann, San Francisco (2006)

32. Akrich, M.: User representations: practices, methods and sociology. In: Rip, A., Misa, T.J., Schot, J.W. (eds.) Managing Technology in Society. The Approach of Constructive Technology Assessment, pp. 167–184. Pinter, London (1995)

33. Mackay, H., Carne, C., Beynon-Davies, P., Tudhope, D.: Reconfiguring the user: using rapid application development. Soc. Stud. Sci. 30(5), 737–757 (2000). https://doi.org/10.1177/030 631200030005004

34. Stewart, J., Williams, R.: The wrong trousers? Beyond the design fallacy: social learning and the user. In: Howcroft, D., Trauth, E. (eds.) Handbook of Critical Information Systems Research: Theory and Application, pp. 195–221. Edward Elgar, Cheltenham (2005)

35. Kuoppamäki, S.: Digital home: life transitions and digital domestic practices in later life. In: Zhou, J., Salvendy, G. (eds.) HCII 2019. LNCS, vol. 11593, pp. 393–404. Springer, Cham (2019). https://doi.org/10.1007/978-3-030-22015-0_31

36. Righi, V., Sayago, S., Blat, J.: When we talk about older people in HCI, who are we talking about? Towards a 'turn to community' in the design of technologies for a growing ageing population. Int. J. Hum. Comput. Stud. 108, 15–31 (2017). https://doi.org/10.1016/j.ijhcs. 2017.06.005

37. Frennert, S.: Older people meet robots: three case studies on the domestication of robots in everyday life (Doctoral dissertation), Lund University, Lund, Sweden (2016)

38. Woolgar, S.: Configuring the user: the case of usability trials. In: Law, J. (ed.) A Sociology of Monsters: Essays on Power, Technology and Domination, pp. 57–99. Routledge, London (1991)

39. Akrich, M.: The description of technical objects. In: Bijker, W.E., Law, J. (eds.) Shaping Technology/Building Society: Studies in Sociotechnical Change, pp. 205–224. MIT Press, Cambridge (1992)

40. Oudshoorn, N., Pinch, T.: Introduction: how users and non-users matter. In: Oudshoorn, N., Pinch, T. (eds.) How Users Matter: The Co-construction of Users and Technology, pp. 1–25. MIT Press, Cambridge (2003)

41. Bratteteig, T., Wagner, I.: Disentangling power and decision-making in participatory design. In: Proceedings of the 12th Participatory Design Conference: Research Papers 1, pp. 41–50. ACM, Roskilde (2012). https://doi.org/10.1145/2347635.2347642

42. Vines, J., Clarke, R., Wright, P., McCarthy, J., Olivier, P.: Configuring participation: on how we involve people in design. In: Proceedings of the SIGCHI Conference on Human Factors in Computing Systems, CHI 2013, pp. 429–438. ACM Press, New York (2013). https://doi. org/10.1145/2470654.2470716

43. Sanders, E.B.-N., Stappers, P.J.: Co-creation and the new landscapes of design. CoDesign 4(1), 5–18 (2008). https://doi.org/10.1080/15710880701875068

44. Clarke, A.E.: Disciplining Reproduction: Modernity, American Life Sciences and "the Problems of Sex". University of California Press, Berkeley (1998)

45. Peine, A., Faulkner, A., Jäger, B., Moors, E.: Science, technology and the "grand challenge" of ageing - understanding the socio-material constitution of later life. Technol. Forecast. Soc. Change 93, 1–9 (2015). https://doi.org/10.1016/j.techfore.2014.11.010

46. Compagna, D., Kohlbacher, F.: The limits of participatory technology development: the case of service robots in care facilities for older people. Technol. Forecast. Soc. Chang. 93, 19–31 (2015). https://doi.org/10.1016/j.techfore.2014.07.012

47. Sengers, P., Boehner, K., David, S., Kaye, J.: "Jofish": reflective design. In: Proceedings of the 4th Decennial Conference on Critical Computing Between Sense and Sensibility, CC 2005, pp. 49–58. ACM Press, New York (2005). https://doi.org/10.1145/1094562.1094569

48. Schön, D.A.: The Reflective Practioner: How Professionals Think in Action. Basic Books Inc., New York (1983)

49. Cozza, M., De Angeli, A., Tonolli, L.: Ubiquitous technologies for older people. Pers. Ubiquit. Comput. 21(3), 607–619 (2017). https://doi.org/10.1007/s00779-017-1003-7

50. Çarçani, K., Mörtberg, C.: Enhancing engagement and participation of seniors in society with the use of social media – the case of a reflective participatory design method story. IxD&A. **36**(SI), 58–74 (2018)

51. Waycott, J., et al.: Older adults as digital content producers. In: Proceedings of the SIGCHI Conference on Human Factors in Computing Systems, CHI 2013, p. 39. ACM Press, New York (2013). https://doi.org/10.1145/2470654.2470662

52. Rogers, Y., Paay, J., Brereton, M., Vaisutis, K.L., Marsden, G., Vetere, F.: Never too old: engaging retired people inventing the future with MaKey MaKey. In: Proceedings of the SIGCHI Conference on Human Factors in Computing Systems, CHI 2014, pp. 3913–3922. ACM Press, New York (2014). https://doi.org/10.1145/2556288.2557184

53. Rice, M., Carmichael, A.: Factors facilitating or impeding older adults' creative contributions in the collaborative design of a novel DTV-based application. Univers. Access Inf. Soc. **12**(1), 5–19 (2013). https://doi.org/10.1007/s10209-011-0262-8

54. Camburn, B., et al.: Design prototyping methods: state of the art in strategies, techniques, and guidelines. Des. Sci. **3**(e13) (2017). https://doi.org/10.1017/dsj.2017.10

55. Giddens, A.: The Constitution of Society: Outline of the Theory of Structuration. University of California Press, Berkeley (1984)

A Study of Green Printing Technology Application for Product Value-Added Design

Yu-Shi Huang, Jui-Hung Cheng$^{(\boxtimes)}$, and An-Jen Yang

Department of Mold and Die Engineering, National Kaohsiung University of Science and Technology, No. 415, Jiangong Road, Sanmin District, Kaohsiung City 80778, Taiwan
{f108147114,rick.cheng,1105192110}@nkust.edu.tw

Abstract. Nowadays, the trend of green environmental protection consumption has become an important issue for the public. When buying products, consumers will consider how to minimize the impact on the environment. From the analysis of sales of the scooter in Taiwan in recent years, riding electric scooters has gradually become the mainstream. Take the well-known brand in Taiwan, Gogoro smart scooter as an example. When the consumer group chooses the product from Gogoro smart scooter, they have different experiences in purchasing a scooter. Most of the traditional commercial accessories products are designed and sold by the original factory, but the type is fixed and the selection is low, while other subsidiary products are limited by cost or technical capabilities, and can only be monochrome spray paint, screen printing, etc. Traditionally, the coating used for printing or spraying on the surface of the product needs to be coated multiple times and taking several hours with the baking process. If defective products are produced during the printing or spraying process, the surface coating cannot be directly removed, and the product materials can be recycled for reuse. Moreover, the barrel coating material cannot be refilled after being opened, causing a lot of environmental pollution and waste. Therefore, the customer who chooses Gogoro to tend to choose non-original standard accessories that have green design style, uniqueness, differentiation, diversity, and low environmental impact. In this research combines green printing technology with the electric vehicle accessories market, and develops dual green products through Print Art, Product Value-Added, and Green Design as the concept of design. The product will be integrating diverse design-oriented elements such as art, materials, and technology, applying special environmentally materials and digital printing technology to achieve waste reduction goals, improve overall process efficiency, achieve green product production models, and create circular economy models. Judging from the sales results of these accessories with both design and functionality, the new blue ocean market for electric vehicles has been successfully established. The diversified products and added value created can also extend the upstream and downstream supply chains of products in the future, and integrate product design across cross-skilled areas.

Keywords: Green design · Printing technology · Visual design · Product design · Value-added

© Springer Nature Switzerland AG 2020
Q. Gao and J. Zhou (Eds.): HCII 2020, LNCS 12207, pp. 34–44, 2020.
https://doi.org/10.1007/978-3-030-50252-2_3

1   Introduction

Green consumption has become an important public concern. Considering the environmental impact and the growing awareness of environmental protection, consumers' choice of Gogoro, a driving force in the electric scooter market, indicates that they have changed their consumption patterns and switched to buying products that are less harmful or more beneficial to the environment. Nowadays, consumers tend to consider how they can reduce the impact to the environment when they buy products. The analysis of scooters sales in Taiwan in recent years shows that buyers of Gogoro electric scooters have accounted for 23.11% of the market share, indicating that the brand has gradually become the mainstream of the scooter market. This group of consumers act differently from the conventional scooter buyers in that they prefer customized and personalized products to make their vehicle stand out.

2   Literature Reviews

This study is to explore the relationship between "product value-added" and "green printing" and try to find the best strategic model to improve product quality and market differentiation. The literature review summarizes the electric scooter market, green design and digital printing. The first part discusses the development trends of electric scooters. The second part introduces product design and eco-friendly inks. The third part compares and analyzes the differences between UV printing and the traditional printing, and then the three parts are used to sum up the differentiation strategy for product design and profit strategy.

2.1   Development Trends of Electric Scooters

According to survey, the population of 23 million in Taiwan owns 13 million motorcycles, averaging 378 vehicles per square kilometer and making it the country with the highest density of motorcycles in the world. This unique culture of commuting by motorcycles makes Taiwan seen by companies and the government the best potential market for developing electric scooters [1]. In Taiwan, the transportation needs of people lead to a high density of motorcycles, which are convenient but can also cause serious air pollution. The air pollution caused by motorcycles' exhaust gas affects the quality of the living environment and people's health. As a result, people's awareness of environmental protection gradually grows. By speeding up the retirement of traditional scooters and switching to electric scooters, the air pollution may be greatly reduced and the environmental quality can be improved, further making the health conditions of people and quality of life better. The development of electric scooters can achieve the benefits of energy conservation and carbon reduction [2, 3]. Gogoro is the largest brand in Taiwan's electric scooter market (showed as Fig. 1), it has changed people's old perception of the conventional electric scooters, such as quick power consumption, slow traveling and charging speeds and others, with improvements. The brand also offers smart technology functions (for example: charging station App, Gogoro App, starting scooters or storage compartment with mobiles phones, and others). In order to reduce air pollution, the government has encouraged people to buy electric scooters by offering subsidies. The retirement of older scooters with two-stroke engines can help people to obtain more subsidies. These measures are to reduce carbon dioxide emissions [4].

Fig. 1. Gogoro electric scooters [Gogoro website]

2.2 Green Design Lifecycle

Green design refers to the process which fully considers products' functions, quality, development cycle and cost to optimize all design factors, so that the overall impact on the environment and resources consumption of products during their manufacturing and life-cycle can be minimized [5, 6]. Green design can help us potentially reduce the future environmental impact from products. In the early stages of product design, incorporating the environmental performance as part of the design goals is what makes green design different from the conventional design [7–9].

The purpose of green design is to make products meet the requirements of environmental protection, further reducing the impact on the environment. There are many factors related to environmental impact, such as materials selection, reuse, recycling, reduction design, easy disassembly, low toxicity and others. It is unlikely to incorporate all factors of environmental impact into product design to achieve a total green design. Therefore, the purpose of green design is the emphasis on meeting the requirements of environmental protection and selecting factors related to environmental impact, while retaining the functions, quality and life-cycle of products [10]. Green products have the following characteristics:

1. Extended life-cycle.
2. Energy-saving.
3. Recyclable and reusable, it can be reasonably put to sustainable use to protect the limited mineral resources of Earth.
4. Avoid waste generation, reduce the amount of waste and the difficulty with disposal.
5. Reduce the use of harmful substances, beneficial to environmental protection, and maintain the balance of the ecosystem.

2.3 Digital Printing for Product Design

According to the statistics from 2018 Future of Digital Printing, the global market for digital printing will grow from US$131.5 billion in 2013 to US$187.7 billion in 2018, at an average annual compound growth rate of 7.4%. With the rapid development of inkjet technology, the use of digital printing in the entire printing market is to grow from 9.8% in 2008 to 20.6% in 2018 [11]. The market for traditional lithography is bound to shrink further. The future industry should be based on smart technology, green manufacturing, integrated service innovation and value creation. According to Konica Minolta, the global digital printing market is expected to grow from US$22.18 billion to US$28.85 billion from 2017 to 2023. For Taiwan's printing industry, the future industry niche and outlook will be optimistic if it can keep up with advanced technology research to meet the demand of different industries and provide diverse innovative services [12, 13]. The UV ink printing technology description as follows:

1. UV curing concept: Lights in the field of printing are commonly used for drying. Once 4-color overprinting is completed, the colorants are absorbed by paper materials, and additional drying system is needed. UV printing is the process which uses ultraviolet light, as known as UV curing, to dry the printing ink. UV printing dries quickly and can be applied to a wide range of materials. UV printing ink or materials contain photoinitiator which reacts to specific wavelengths of ultraviolet light. Once the UV light of the curing system actives the photoinitiator of UV ink, they start to generate photopolymerization reactions, forming a hardened film tightly adhered to the surface of the printed materials. This process offers excellent print drying effects for special materials with abnormally smooth surfaces and low absorption and are difficult to dry. UV curing can be used for various types of traditional printing, such as letterpress, flexography, lithography and screen printing. As long as UV ink is used, the main part can be competed with a UV light source.

2. UV curing ink is also known as UV ink. The ink layer can be completely cured after being irradiated with UV rays. UV rays with different wavelengths and energy levels can form films on ink and make the ink dry. Different UV spectra can generate different levels of energy and polymerize monomers in different ink binders into polymers, so the color films of UV ink have good mechanical and chemical properties. UV ink consists of binders, pigments, reactive diluents, photoinitiators and auxiliaries. Binders are one of the main ingredients and they account for 30% to 50% of the content of ink, and they are the main substance for ink to form films. Many types of ink with special effects need to be thick to offer good performance, and they are foaming ink, wrinkle ink and others. As screen printing ink tends to be thick, there are many special UV screen printing inks, which have characteristics such as containing no volatile solvents, no odor, quick curing speed, tough cured films, strong water resistance, resistance to solvent scrubbing, good adhesion and many colors.

3 Integration of Marketing and Technology of Printing Applications

This research aims at the current combination of parts and UV printing in the domestic electric vehicle market, discusses its development profile and process application, summarizes its advantages and disadvantages and market potential, and analyzes the energy of existing technologies. Likelihood and direction.

3.1 Market Segmentation of New Digital Printing Applications

With the continuous improvement in productivity, reliability and cost efficiency of digital printing, the simplification of plate making further enables digital printing to produce highly customized accessories. The innovation of inkjet technology and the adoption of environmentally friendly materials drive the strong growth of digital printing. In the future, more industry operators and resources will be committed to optimize the production scale and reduce unit costs. Maintaining competitive advantages becomes future challenge for manufacturers. Digital printing provides printing solutions for more diverse materials and non-planar objects and can be widely used in daily life. The signs of market demand show that buyers' demand for customized and fast-printing accessories will continue to rise, and the market of personalized prints also continues to expand, so the market opportunities for digital printing will be rosy. The printing industry nowadays, whether it involves traditional crafts or the infusion of digital and multimedia communication technologies, certainly has much room for more exploration. he product supply chain to other industries and develop accessories products that are different from the past. The target design purpose of this study is to focus on the accessories design for Gogoro 1, 2, 3 and VIVA, Aeon Ai-one, PGO UR1, etc. (showed as Fig. 2). And it including two requirements: 1) customization design to attract users 2) customization market is growing, as follows:

Fig. 2. Target electric scooters: Gogoro 1, 2, 3 and VIVA, Aeon Ai-one, PGO UR1 (from left to right)

1. The customization design to attract users: The relationship between cross-domain technology and printing is becoming more and more inseparable. In the aspect of market development, the increasing popularity of digital printing enables prints buyers to not follow the minimum order quantity requirements to keep a large inventory. The print quantity can be more flexible, and there is room for more customization, which leads to the increasing demand for further processing after personalized printing. The shrinking quantity of traditional printing in the prints market has become a common trend around the world. Prints incorporating design, such as soft packaging, color boxes, metal inkjet and its post-processing and others, continue to grow due to economic growth and the active consumer activities.

2. The customization market is growing: It is an innovation that emphasizes individ-ualization, sophisticated taste, environmental protection and differentiation through materials, manufacturing process and product design. It also has the following digital printing technology characteristics which create product segmentation and differen-tiation to meet the market demand for small orders and customization. There are three reasons included a) high production efficiency b) universality of materials c) Print and cut capabilities, as follows:

a) High production efficiency: With the characteristics of UV ink, which can be immediately cured after being irradiated by UV lamps, products can be applied with protective films, cutting and other post-processing procedures to meet orders with a short lead time. No drying is required, which can greatly reduce the production time.

b) Universality of materials: Non-processed paper or fabric materials that cannot be printed with solvent-based inks can be used now, expanding the types of materials available. Non-processed and inexpensive materials now can be used, which reduces production costs.

c) Print and cut capabilities: The ID cut function reduces cutting errors. The con-tinuous positioning and reading functions reduce the number of procedures for operators. There are full positioning and zero-positioning cutting which empha-sizes productivity, zero blank space positioning which prioritizes precision or center positioning, and a variety of positioning points can be selected to meet the requirements of different tasks.

3.2 Digital Printing

The generation of pollutants is a problem for almost every industry. For the sustain-ability of the living environment and industries, the prevention and control of industrial pollution are key topics for discussion among industries. Therefore, understanding the sources of industrial pollution and the characteristics and components of pollutants is the priority for improving the pollution conditions. Printing ink is currently the biggest source for pollution in the printing industry. The global emissions of pollution by volatile organic compounds (VOCs) from printing ink have reached hundreds of thousands of tons every year. These VOCs can form greenhouse effects more serious than that of carbon dioxide. Under sunlight, the VOCs can form oxides and photochemical smog. Using the traditional screen-printing method as an example, the pollution of ink or the waste ink discharged from the cleaning of screens can cause serious pollution impacting the environment. For the purpose of reducing pollution to the environment, the develop-ment of environmentally friendly printing is gradually being valued by the public, and consumers are also leaning toward buying products printed with eco-friendly ink. Many printing-related regulations have been added to the environmental regulations in many countries to limit the VOCs released by the printing industry. This goes to show that the government and industry have paid more and more attention to the pollution and human health related to printing inks. So, this study applied the UV printing technology of UV curing inkjet and soft ink, as follow:

a) UV Curing Inkjet

1. Shorten process and improve efficiency: UV curable ink can be cured instantly when it is exposed to ultraviolet (UV light) rays. This omits the drying procedures after the printing, and other post-processing tasks can immediately start (showed as Fig. 3).

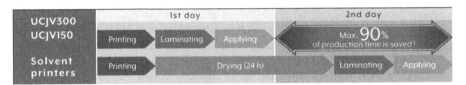

Fig. 3. Can reduce 90% of manufacturing time

2. Use of eco-friendly ink: The newly developed nickel-free ink (LUV-175) produces almost no VOCs and emits less chemicals indoors.
3. Suitable for diverse materials: UV curable ink, which does not require drying time, can be printed on PVC materials, tarpaulins, fabrics on which solvent-based inks or latex printing cannot be applied, paper without an absorbing layer and PET films.

b) Soft Ink

1. Solvent-based inks: Ink is secured by impregnating PVC-based materials and being dried by evaporating organic solvents. Solvent components need to be evaporated, which requires drying time. If the substrate is not PVC or does not contain PVC, the ink cannot be secured.
2. UV ink: Ink is cured by the exposure to UV (ultraviolet) light. As the ink can get cured immediately, protective films and other post-processing works can be applied on after printing. Specialized substrates must be used for the printing to be applied on a variety of materials (Fig. 4).

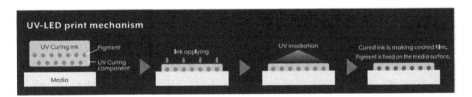

Fig. 4. UV-LED print mechanism

3.3 Product Value-Added

Products all pass the cross-cut adhesion test and are EU eco-certified (certificates attached). In order to meet the needs of various industries, product design and UV digital inkjet printing technology are incorporated to provide a full range of soft and hard printing. The core technology includes mold development and sheet metal applications. Product development has covered both the appearance and functionality. Mainly focusing on electric scooters, the design aims to achieve personalized components without damaging vehicle body structure. Besides retaining the original shape, the approach can add varieties to the appearance and functions, so consumers can enjoy the benefits of unique and personalized components. The abovementioned core technologies add product breadth and improve the added value via UV eco-friendly ink and clear ink.

1. The Eco-friendly ink products that have obtained GREENGUARD GOLD certification, GREENGUARD is a certification implemented by a US-based third-party safety science UL company, and it operates environmental certification related to chemical substances emitted in indoor spaces. It is based on fair empirical scientific data, and products that emit fewer chemicals in indoor spaces and are more eco-friendly can obtain the certificate. There are two types of certificates, regular and Gold, and the criteria for Gold certification are a lot more rigorous than that of the regular certification. VOC-free UV ink can be immediately cured with a UV lamp, so it does not emit VOCs and is more friendly to the environment (VOCs stand for volatile organic compounds, which can cause air pollution) (Fig. 5).
2. Use UV clear ink can improve the added value of printed materials. It can produce two kinds of printing effects: "Gloss surface" to enhance vividness and sophistication and "Matte surface" to have a understated and no-gloss effect. The gloss printing makes printed materials look sophisticated and more eye-catching. It can give a surface different texture effects and undulations to show its uniqueness. Products can be presented in many ways. Products can be presented in many ways. For example, the overlay printing with color and clear inks, using only clear ink to print on black and clear materials or printing on materials with a matte surface. There is no need to use other equipment for clear ink printing. This UV clear ink had some benefits, such as: a) The process is about 20% faster than the existing machine. b) Receive orders to produce at the industry's highest productivity. c) Support the creation of higher added value. d) High performance inks realize a wider range of product applications. e) Clear ink printing demonstrates sophistication and good design sense. f) Glossy printing, matte printing and thick film printing (Fig. 6).

3.4 Product Design Results

According to the above instructions, combined with printing art, product value-added, and green design, the integration of art, materials, technology and other multi-oriented design elements, the application of special environmental protection materials and digital printing technology, to achieve the goal of reducing waste, improve the overall process efficiency, to achieve green product production mode, and create a circular economy model. To do not hurt the locomotive, retain the body-based, design a variety of motor car spare parts, such as color spray to stop the slide pedal, car front modeling trim, color spray cylinder head, license plate protection base plate, color spray car cover… and so on, bring into today's consumer favorite customer design, increase uniqueness, enhance product value (show as Fig. 7).

CERTIFICATE
OF COMPLIANCE

Mimaki Engineering Co. Ltd.

UV ink LH-100

Restrictions:Certified for Decorative Wall Applications

67176-410
Certificate Number

03/27/2015 - 03/27/2020
Certificate Period

Certified
Status

UL 2818 - 2013 Standard for Chemical Emissions for Building Materials, Finishes and Furnishings

Decorative wall are determined compliant using an Offline Environment with an air change of 0.68 h⁻¹ and a loading of 12.44 m².
Products tested in accordance with UL 2821 test method to show compliance to emission limits in UL 2818, Section 7.1.

UL certification represents a sample of the plaintiffs Product's in the plaintiffs' Standards in effect. Improvements in UL's Internment Management and any applicable program which conveys a part between UL and the Certificate shown in this body "Agreement". The Certificate Holder is authorized to use the UL Mark on the identified Product(s) manufactured at the production site(s) covered by the UL Test Report, in accordance with the terms of the Agreement. This certificate is valid for the identified plaintiffs through valid compliance with the Agreement.

GREENGUARD Certification Criteria for Building Products and Interior Finishes

Criteria	CAS Number	Maximum Allowable Predicted Concentration	Units
TVOC(A)	-	0.50	mg/m³
Formaldehyde	50-00-0	61.3 (50 ppb)	µg/m³
Total Aldehydes (B)	-	0.10	ppm
Particle Matter less than 10 µm (C)	-	50	µg/m³
4-Phenylcyclohexene	4994-16-5	6.5	µg/m³
Individual VOCs (D)	-	1/10th TLV	-

(A) Defined to be the total response of measured VOCs falling within the C₆ – C₁₆ range, with responses calibrated to a toluene surrogate. Maximum allowable predicted TVOC concentrations for GREENGUARD (0.50 mg/m³) fall in the range of 0.5 mg/m³ or less, as specified in CDPH Standard Method v1.1.

(B) The sum of all measured normal aldehydes from formaldehyde through nonanal, plus benzaldehyde, individually calibrated to a compound specific standard. Heptanal through nonanal are measured via TD/GC/MS analysis and the remaining aldehydes are measured using HPLC/UV analysis.

(C) Particle emission requirement only applicable to HVAC Duct Products with exposed surface area in air streams (a forced air test with specific test method) and for wood finishing (sanding) systems.

(D) Allowable levels for chemicals not listed are derived from 1/10th of the Threshold Limit Value (TLV) industrial work place standard (Reference: American Conference of Government Industrial Hygienists, 6500 Glenway, Building D-7, and Cincinnati, OH 45211-4438).

Fig. 5. Certificate of compliance

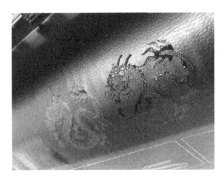

Fig. 6. UV clear ink

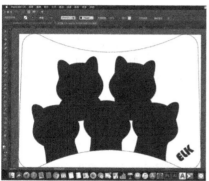

Step1: Using illustrator to make drawings

Step 2: Make color drawings

Step3: Preview

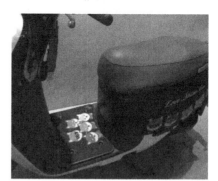

Step4 Design results and application

Fig. 7. Design process

4   Conclusion

The implementation of this study can enhance the benefits of digital economy, smart process management and provide speedy customization to meet customer demand and the needs of heterogeneous markets. It can create more output value, refine the design and development of prints and reinforce the mastery of the suitability of different substrates. The introduction of technology in image color processing, UV printing, specialized printing and digital printing can add value to the functional innovation in the domain of electric scooters and their related products and improve the friendliness of developed products in the market. Connections between the academic research and development and the industry's practical needs can be made. The study can define the rights, obligations and division of labor, share and integrate the results to engage in commercialization, further connecting the supply chains of diverse industries and customer needs. The innovative technologies and eco-friendly raw materials of digital printing, combined with visual aesthetics, personalized printing and functional design of industrial components, can be extended to other businesses outside the electric scooters market by adopting the cross-domain applications and other commercialization technologies. The product development incorporating the joint efforts of industry practitioners can help both students and practitioners to develop more job skills in the areas of printing, design, production and e-commerce activities through this program. The value-added design for metals can improve the value of components and develop products that could not be realized in the consumer market of the past, which emphasizes market differentiation to have personalized parts that can attract consumers.

References

1. Liu, A.S., Hsu, K.J.: Assessment of the electric motorcycle policy. J. Environ. Prot. **29**, 57–69 (2006)
2. Suen, S.H., Lin, B.M., Jang, S.C.: Strategy and construction of electric refueling system for electric scooter in Taiwan (2013)
3. Wu, H.C., Wang, P.W.: Facilities and service models for electric scooter recharge stations. MIS REV. Int. J. **18**, 1–18 (2013)
4. Peng, U.: Reconstruction of the dawn of the electric motor industry. Ind. Mater. 68–69 (2010)
5. Fullerton, D., Wu, W.: Policies for green design. J. Environ. Econ. Manag. **36**, 131–148 (1998)
6. Smith, S.S., Chen, W.-H.: Rule-based recursive selective disassembly sequence planning for green design. Adv. Eng. Inform. **25**, 77–87 (2011)
7. Paul, I.D., Bhole, G.P., Chaudhari, J.R.: A review on green manufacturing: it's important, methodology and its application. Procedia Mater. Sci. **6**, 1644–1649 (2014)
8. Radford, S.K., Bloch, P.H.: Linking innovation to design: consumer responses to visual product newness. J. Prod. Innov. Manage. **28**, 208–220 (2011)
9. Khan, B.E.: Using visual design to improve customer perceptions of online assortments. J. Retail. **93**, 29–42 (2011)
10. Kress, G.R., van Leeuwen, T.: Reading Images: The Grammar of Visual Design. Psychology Press, London (1996)
11. Hartmann, J., Germain, R.: Understanding the relationships of integration capabilities, ecological product design, and manufacturing performance. J. Clean. Prod. **92**, 196–205 (2015)
12. Nguyen, V.D., Martin, P.: Product design-process selection-process planning integration based on modeling and simulation. Int. J. Adv. Manuf. Technol. **77**(1–4), 187–201 (2015)
13. Liu, J., Cheng, Z., Ma, Y.: Product design-optimization integration via associative optimization feature modeling. Adv. Eng. Inform. **30**(4), 713–727 (2016)

Using Academic Work Places to Involve Older People in the Design of Digital Applications. Presentation of a Methodological Framework to Advance Co-design in Later Life

Britt Östlund[1]([✉]), Björn Fischer[1], Barbara Marshall[2], Nicole Dalmer[2], Mireia Fernandez-Ardévol[3], Andrea Garcia-Santesmases[3], Daniel Lopez[3], Eugene Loos[4], Fangyuan Chang[1], Xin Chen[1], Louis Neven[5], Alexander Peine[5], Andrea Rosales[3], and Sanna Kuoppamäki[1]

[1] Department of Biomedical Engineering and Health Systems, Royal Institute of Technology, KTH, Stockholm, Sweden
`{brittost,bjorfisc,fancha,xinchen3,sannaku}@kth.se`
[2] Sociology Department, Trent University, Peterborough, ON, Canada
`{bmarshall,nicoledalmer}@trentu.ca`
[3] Internet Interdisciplinary Institute (IN3), Universitat Oberta de Catalunya/ Open University of Catalonia, Barcelona, Spain
`{mfernandezar,agarcia_santesmases,dlopezgo,arosalescl}@uoc.edu`
[4] Utrecht University School of Governance, Utrecht University, Utrecht, The Netherlands
`e.f.loos@uu.nl`
[5] Copernicus Institute of Sustainable Development, Utrecht University, Utrecht, The Netherlands
`lbm.neven@avans.nl, a.peine@uu.nl`

Abstract. Methods to involve users in design have long been used to create relevant content and increase the accuracy of product development. Demographic trends have raised the issue of the needs and demands of older people, especially with regard to digitization. In contrast to the high number of publications discussing the importance of involving people in the design of their daily life, very few publications suggest *how* to do it. While participatory design is used with older people, there is no common understanding about which methods are used for what purposes. This paper presents a framework methodology that further advances the opportunity to involve older people in the design process and increase understanding of old people's subjective experience of getting their lives digitized and how to involve them in design. Given that digitalization, with its systemic complexity, requires an understanding of how technology is contextualized, the need to understand what it means to age in today's digital society is part of successful design. One objective is to go beyond stereotypes that often characterize generalizations of older people. We are using the concept of co-design, which is well established but not specifically adapted to older users. The goal is a matrix of tested co-design methods to be used by citizens, researchers, businesses or anyone who is interested in increasing the impact of old people on the design of new technologies.

Keywords: Digitization · Co-design · Old people

© Springer Nature Switzerland AG 2020
Q. Gao and J. Zhou (Eds.): HCII 2020, LNCS 12207, pp. 45–58, 2020.
https://doi.org/10.1007/978-3-030-50252-2_4

1 Introduction

Co-design, defined as a collaboration between users and designers, is one of the concepts used to increase a user's impact on the design of technological artefacts or modification of already-existing artefacts by involving them in the design process. This conceptual thinking has its origin in the democratic ideal of giving people a voice and opportunities to influence functions and forms of new applications as well as gaining more control over the user's situation [1]. Idea of involvement deeply rooted both in the democratisation of society and in the development of consumer markets. In Northern Europe, democratisation of working life and demands for improved working environments, including the Codetermination Act (Medbestämmandelagen – MBL) and the negotiations between partners in the labour market, have for decades had participation and involvement at the core of their collaborations. This development has contributed to the enhancement of methods such as action research and the development of research circles with the aim of educating employees on how they can exert influence over the work, especially the influence over technology developments [2, 3]. Architectural research carries an important piece of the puzzle to understand the move to democratisation and the involvement of users. Planning people's living environments and urban planning contributed to early reflections and methods on how people can be involved [4–6]. Today there are experiences of how community-based design fosters increased participation and ownership of projects among older people [7, 8].

The identification of needs and configuration of users became of particular importance in the development of human computer interaction research. Interface usability and interactions in IT systems became crucial to achieve success in this area and accelerated the development of different methods of understanding the user, for example, human-centered design, experience-centered design, participatory design, and co-design [9]. Several of these conceptual methods are used in design research, such as co-design and participatory design.

Design research, applied in industrial design, aiming at designing for the production of consumer products as well as for procurement of public goods, has generated considerable interest in recent years. Within the design community, there has long been a discourse on design as research and design by using research that points out the close relationships between research and design and the design-like empirical processes used in engineering sciences and theories used in social science [10–12]. In understanding practice, design sciences make use of authors that explain any design, being social design, as not deterministic; scientific laboratories as reconfigurations of natural and social orders; and practice as situational and contextual [13, 14]. With this discourse and the spread of interest in design practices in the broader research community, methods that directly involve users have grown in number such as participatory design, user involvement, mutual learning and action-oriented design [15–18]. One particular kind of participatory method is "Universal design", also known as "Design for all" or as used in the European context, strive to include all citizens in IT-society: "Inclusive design" [18–20]. The concept of inclusive design has similarities and differences with universal design. Inclusive design is seen as a progressive, goal-oriented process while the universal design is more like a genre of design or a performance measure [21, 22].

Universal design builds on the idea that products, buildings and environments should be accessible, as far as possible, to as many people as possible, not least focusing older adults [23]. Universal design guidelines were developed to create a holistic relation between the product and the user covering seven principles, including equitable access, flexibility, simple and intuitive use, perceptible information, tolerance for error, low physical effort and appropriate size and space for approach and use [18, 24]. The holistic relation by Olander in 2011 proved that there is more to this relation beyond physical and functional properties of the product covered by the guidelines, such as emotional experiences, self-identity and strategies to use products that the users didn't choose themselves [25].

Hence, according to previous publications, appropriate design requires access to users and their own articulation of experiences, needs and preferences, them being experts of their own life situation. A critical aspect is to what extent users should be involved. Arnstein [26] suggests five levels of involvement corresponding to how much influence we can or want to give to users. The highest level representing the most optimal influence is when people themselves are in control, initiating and driving design to accomplish something. The second highest level is when people participate as experts on their own life situation, negotiating and collaborating with designers in partnership. The third level is when people allow commenting on already made-up plans or design. The fourth level is when people receive information and/or are subject to different types of efforts. The lowest level is simply manipulation, where people are objects of other people's actions.

Awareness of the level of user involvement and the consequences it has for designing different solutions is important. There is a tendency for engineers and designers to configure users by scripting appropriate user interaction with technology into its design [27–29]. But we also know that users, in turn, can challenge such scripts and reconfigure technologies when they are interacting with the "lived realities" of users [28] and can become eventful figures in the practice of design [30], also in involvement of different set of practices and practitioners [31]. This paper is based on a social science perspective, drawing from both Design Sciences, Science and Technology Studies (STS) and Critical Gerontology [37, 55]. The ambition with this perspective is to contribute to a richer understanding of how technologies are contextualized and made meaningful and over time become domesticated and embedded in people's lives [32, 33, 56]. In doing this, unnecessary restrictions can be avoided. Technologies being artefacts - man-made - reflect relations, values and norms, not only in the interplay with users but also from the very start of designing and engineering technological artefacts. Whether we are aware of it or not, the image of the user is fundamentally included as we create and design the technology. That image represents our understanding of who that person is and what assumptions we make about their abilities and preferences [34].

2   Purpose

The purpose of developing the design framework presented in this paper is to advance the opportunities to involve older people in the design processes and increase understanding of older people's subjective experience of getting their lives digitised, inviting them to participate as co-designers, allowing them the role of being consultants and experts of their own lives. In doing so, the design framework methodology contributes to closing the gap between the extensive and rapid digitalisation of our societies and the lack of methods to confidently involve older people in the design. The goal is a matrix of tested co-design methods accessible for the research community, including designers and involved stakeholders. The long-term goal is to provide older people with access to relevant digital resources through methods where they own the interpretation of their own needs and expectations, as a way to emancipate from the stereotypes and limitations underlying design and innovation for older users.

Older people as users of technology and inhabitants of today's digital society are at the centre of the methodological framework presented in this paper. Demographic trends with growing older populations have raised the issue of design related to the needs and demands of old people, especially with regard to digitisation [35]. Despite major investments and efforts to develop digital applications with older people as a target group, the uptake of some digital interventions has proved disappointing [36, 37]. In contrast to the high number of publications, convincing readers that involvement of older people is both important and possible, very few publications suggest *how* to do it [32, 38, 39]. In this paper, older adults are resources for design, sharing their lifelong experiences from technology use and technological change in the societies they endured. Regarding age, this research analyzes cohorts that were born between 1939 and 1963, a group that spans a period of 25 years.

To be involved is to be responsible for the result of the design. Since older people, voluntarily or involuntarily, may depend on other people in some way, they become exposed to the attitudes and expectations of others. The technology today discussed in connection with increased needs for health care and social services, risks limiting their social roles to only patients and care receivers and forgetting that they are also citizens, consumers and fellow human beings, not least experienced ones. For these reasons the framework methodology presented in this paper also includes older people's social resources such as friends, families, caregivers and others that have an influence on technologies used by old people, for example, engineers, designers and planners.

Focusing on older adults in this project, mainly contributes to increased knowledge and method development about co-design with older users but also to general knowledge about user involvement. First, it contributes to concretise the user concept by defining whom we are talking about, not generalising human aspects but, as universal design states, as far as possible, designing for as many people as possible. To select older people as a target group also raises issues, since older people are far from a homogenous group of people with similar needs and demands. As shown in the methodology section below, we solve this by carefully defining which groups of older people we work with in co-design [47].

Second, involving older users, we are challenging an area that is still driven by outdated perceptions of older people. Technology development and design for older users are still guided by stereotypes and outdated images [33, 40–42]. A co-design approach can in this regard prevent misleading design and take the edge off patronising attitudes to user groups such as older people, describing ageing as merely a downhill process. While physical losses may well be expected, too little attention has been given to the growing experience that comes from lifelong learning [53].

Third, despite the fact that participatory design is well established, very few attempts have been made to involve older people in co-design. The notion that adoption of new technologies among older people is constantly lower than for younger age groups has for a long time perpetuated images of older users as less innovative and in need of more support [43]. Recent studies are questioning these notions by reporting on the great potential to include older adults as sources of innovations [32, 33, 44]. Including older people and their experiences of their daily life have contributed both to innovations and to an increased knowledge of the older people's preferences and the conditions of ageing in digitised societies. These examples encompass designing buildings [45], bikes [46], telerobots [54], furniture [48], digital communications [49], digital games [50, 51, 57, 58], as well as methodological developments [39] and using daily experiences [50, 59].

The technology in focus for this paper are digital applications and systems, especially smart home technologies, for example, "voice smart speakers", smart phones or any other digital application to be used for communication and information transfer in the home or between the home and the world outside the home. Being artefacts, technologies are part of sociotechnical systems shaped by the actors being involved in design. We are not solely focusing on singular applications but the interplay between artefacts, later life and digitised societies.

3 Methodology

The methodological framework presented in this paper is part of the BCON-NECT@HOME project, (https://www.jp-demographic.eu/wp-content/uploads/2017/01/BCONNECT_2017_conf2018_brochure.pdf), which is an international collaboration within the European programme, More Years Better Life, between Trent University in Peterborough, Canada, Utrecht University Netherlands, Open University of Catalonia in Barcelona, Spain and the Royal Institute of Technology, KTH, in Stockholm, Sweden. Establishing "Academic Work Places" (AWP) aiming "at bringing academics and practitioners together, on a continuous basis, to work on a common project, in order to make practice more evidence-based as well as to make academic evidence more practice-based" (Van Woerkum and Renes 2010, p. 573), are located at these universities, we have systematically investigated which types and methods are most suitable to involve older participants and stakeholders. With this set-up, workshop procedures are tested and compared. AWP are resources and there are networks available in every partner country. Some universities collaborate with social movements organising old people or older citizens who form opinion in order to bring about political change. Other universities collaborate with businesses.

The Canadian AWP has mobilized a variety of resources and networks to facilitate their research, including technology and aging networks, such as AGE-WELL NCE (Aging Gracefully across Environments using Technology to Support Wellness, Engagement and Long Life NCE Inc.) and more local research centres, including TCAS (The Trent Centre for Aging & Society). Additionally, the Canadian AWP has intentionally sought to reach and engage with older people not always accessible through organized groups.

In Netherlands workshops are taken place in the GET-Lab (health technology lab), Academie for Health Care, Avans University of Applied Sciences, Breda. The focus is older people's smart phone everyday practises and about the creative things our respondents did with their smart phones.

In Barcelona (Catalonia, Spain), the focus of study was a real-life participatory design activity that involved young and older participants. The observation comprised the design activities in their different stages (from instruments of data collection to answers, the results and the final design implementations). The real-life project observed is an EU-supported project conducted at the Open University of Catalonia, entitled "Decentralised Citizens Owned Data Ecosystem (DECODE) (https://www.decodepro ject.eu/). One technology was selected, a mobile app that allows petitions to be signed anonymously but with authentication requirements, which should provide any citizen control over their data.

In Sweden this project is tied into KTH's long-term partnership with a number of businesses designing digital technologies and joint public projects such as Stockholm Digital Care.

A preliminary design workshop procedure was tested at a BCONNECT@HOME project meeting in 2018 in Stockholm. The purpose was to test the procedure and discuss how to apply this procedure developed as part of the Swedish team's AWP to the social and cultural context in the four participating countries. The pilot workshop was a combination of product design described above and a modification of the procedure presented by Joshi and Bratteteig [39].

Older adults are defined as a heterogeneous group of people aged 55 and over, which reflects the objective to include older people not yet at the very end of life. At the same time the groups of older people who will be involved and carefully described differ between the four countries involved. In Canada, older citizens, care providers and designers are involved in a series of focus groups to understand: what are older adults' understandings and insights regarding the use of technologies in their daily lives; where, how, and why are these technologies used (or not used); and in what ways do the stakeholder groups' understandings of technological design and applications coincide with or differ from older adults' experiences? In the Netherlands, experiments about the resourceful and creative daily use of smart phones by older people is ongoing. In Barcelona, the focus is to observe participatory design methods in action, in particular how designers/engineers implement usability test, to evaluate a prototype of a digital platform to control personal data on the Internet. In Sweden, design workshops are conducted with retired engineers and other retired citizens, teachers of a health care college, producers and designers. These activities will be completed and presented in 2020.

This project has combined focus groups and design workshops to more fully explore insights from older people, which have collectively contributed to the team's development of the methodology for their own AWP co-design workshops. The purpose of focus groups, organised in a variety of ways, is to listen, interact with, learn from and gather information on a defined area of interest, not to design artefacts [32]. Design workshops, on the other hand, are aiming at creating or modifying design ideas, mock ups (prototypes or physical models of ideas) or modifications of already existing technologies. Both models are used in this project and part of the framework methodology. The Canadian team has held a series of four focus groups with 29 older adults. These focus groups were intentionally advertised in less-conventional spaces and as a result, researchers were fortunate to recruit and speak with older people from a wide array of life experiences. Researchers facilitated focus groups lasting between 90–105 min in length. Focus groups started with a question asking what digital technologies older participants use. Conversations covered topics covered topics including the place of technology itself in everyday living, the costs, breakdowns, age-neglectful design, and what kinds of technologies might be desirable and (in)appropriate.

The pilot workshop held in Stockholm in September 2018 was an attempt for the project partners to become part of a design procedure themselves and evaluate its usefulness for developing a methodological framework among the four partner countries. The pilot was a simulation of what a design process can be about. Observations of the evolving social process that took place was documented by the second author of this paper. The social process evolved as three phases. First, a phase of discomfort among the participants in order to get started. Second, finding a way to collaborate in spite of different backgrounds: scientifically and culturally. Third, a phase of slowly socialising with each other.

The scientific and cultural differences were reflected in the set-up of the AWP and in the design ideas that came out of the pilot workshop. Infrastructures, payment models and organisation of welfare services are different in the four partner countries and are expected to influence old people's access to digital technologies and use of digital services. Different stakeholders are available to varying degrees depending on what the collaboration looks like between ageing communities, researchers and business. Cultural values was discussed during the design workshop in Stockholm, for example ongoing transitions from a marriage culture to a divorce/single culture. The personas selected during the workshop were partly based on the nuclear family and traditional values, even though they were divorced and single. Being an older foreigner was one aspect. Technology was associated with being either connected with family as in Spain and Sweden, or to connect with family as in Canada. Scientific differences also became evident during the design workshop and reflect the project participants' scientific background that comes from Design Sciences, Critical Gerontology and Science and Technology Studies (STS).

4   Towards a Co-design Framework

Building on insights from all four AWP, the Swedish team model has developed as outlined in the following three sections:

4.1   Workshop Participants and Stakeholders

Three kinds of workshop participants are defined. First, older participants with lifelong experience and experience of later life. Second, stakeholders involved in the production of technological artefacts: engineers, designers, and business. Third, stakeholders involved as employees to provide home health care or home help services to older people.

One reason behind this selection is to make it possible to make comparisons between the three stakeholder groups, to see if participation in design workshops makes any difference. If such a comparison is planned, one recommendation from the pilot workshop was to hold the workshop with older participants last to give them the opportunity to comment on the result from previous workshops.

4.2 Procedure for Co-design Workshops

The co-design workshop was developed out of the Joshi and Bratteteig [39] four step procedure: create choices; select among choices; concretise choices; and evaluate choices added two steps of importance: introduction and closing the workshop. This procedure is estimated to last two hours, which includes a break for refreshments. The introduction considered as important for the participants to feel socially comfortable and to make sure that they get appropriate and enough information about the workshop. One aspect is ethical issues that should be raised and discussed, i.e. will sensitive data be collected that might run the risk of violating the personal integrity; how to sue the result of the workshop and how to get feedback from the workshop organisers to the participants. The closing of the workshop is important for the same reasons. The proposed six steps are illustrated in Table 1.

Table 1. Procedure for co-design workshops

Steps	Content	Milestone
1. Introduction	Presentation of the purpose of the workshop Presentation of the participants and time limits	Participants informed and socially comfortable
2. Creating alternatives	The workshop leader presents a number of digital applications (pictures or gadgets). Participants can add more alternatives Take time to look at them and discuss	Alternatives on the table
3. Priorities of digital applications	Participants select alternatives that seem to be useful and meaningful to modify or that are creating new ideas Discuss why	A few alternatives selected

(continued)

Table 1. (*continued*)

Steps	Content	Milestone
4. Concretise	Participants discuss how the selected alternatives or the new ideas can be developed and modified to be of use Elaborate in small groups Illustrate and motivate	Alternatives to be modified or invented, concretized and illustrated
5. Evaluation	Participants jointly evaluate every alternative a) General question: Why is this alternative important? Meaningful? Enjoyable? b) Question on preferred changes: How to make the most out of the usefulness? c) Question for this particular user group: Why is this useful for you?	Alternatives evaluated
6. End of workshop	The workshop ends Inform participants how to get feedback from the project	Content participants

4.3 Documentation and Analysis

During and after the co-design workshop, notes should be taken about how each of the groups contributed in each decision. If the results of the design workshops will be compared, this will sort the data with sufficient detail, see Table 2.

Table 2. Organisation of the matrix

	Stakeholder group 1	Stakeholder group 2	Stakeholder group ....etc.
A. *Inputs provided when creating alternatives* 1. How did the group contribute? 2. What are the suggested alternatives provided by the group? 3. What are the reasons put forward for these suggestions? 4. What level of participation was the group in according to Arnstein? 5. What can be said about the influence of this group in this choice? Did it matter what they said?			

(*continued*)

Table 2. (*continued*)

	Stakeholder group 1	Stakeholder group 2	Stakeholder group ....etc.
B. Inputs provided when selecting alternatives 1. How did the group contribute? 2. What are the alternatives prioritised by the group? 3. What are the reasons put forward for these priorities? 4. What level of participation was the group in? 5. What can be said about the influence of this group in this choice? Did it matter what they said?			
C. Inputs provided when modifying or concretising ideas 1. How did the group contribute? 2. What are the modifications or concrete ideas provided by the group? 3. What are the reasons put forward for these modifications and ideas? 4. What level of participation was the group in? 5. What can be said about the influence of this group in this choice? Did it matter what they said?			
D. Inputs provided for evaluating the preferred alternatives 1. How did the group contribute? 2. What is the feedback provided by the group? 3. What are the reasons put forward for this feedback? 4. What level of participation was the group in? 5. What can be said about the influence of this group in this choice? Did it matter what they said?			

It is important for the researchers and designers to realise their role in facilitating and empowering the users to encourage them to participate [1]. This means that we need to critically examine at which level the different groups are actually involved in the co-design workshop and critically examine the organizers' participations.

The result, the experiences working with the design workshop procedure and with the focus group model will be published in future publications.

5 Concluding Remarks

This paper discusses a preliminary design framework methodology aiming at giving older people experiencing digitisation a voice and possibilities to take part in design workshops or interviews. This is an attempt both to learn more about their situation in digitised societies and the role of technology in their daily life. Does it make a difference? Does involving users increase their influence in any way? If the design framework methodology discussed in this paper will increase older people's influence over digitization will show in the evaluation of the trials in 2020. Since there is no actual engineering or design competence involved in the project, a direct influence is not part of the project goal. However, it definitely is an impact goal. The AWPs that are tied into the project are networks and organisations with older people that have great opportunities to create political opinions and businesses with designers and engineers that have old people as target groups for their products and services. With these connections, the project results expect to increase older people's influence of design. Also, the result – the design framework methodology – is supposed to be useful and usable for any stakeholder.

Comparisons of the results from design workshops and with different stakeholders will also add to the knowledge of where the gaps are between old people and stakeholders trying to articulate needs and preferences of older populations. Do they agree or how big are the differences between old people and other stakeholders?

The development work described in this paper is unique in that it allows social scientists to use their knowledge to improve older people's possibilities to make their voice heard. Having competence in social practices, later life and its conditions and combining this with established design procedures and design research will give a new flavour to technology developments, not least critical perspectives on how society's norms and values affect the situation of old people in connection with digitalisation. Should later life be digitised and to what extent? What are their needs, problems, visions and dreams and what is the role of technology in accomplishing this? What makes them becoming wired into technology in an unfamiliar way or more comfortable [52]?

Acknowledgements. The research project BConnect@Home – Making use of digital devices in later life (https://www.researchgate.net/project/) is funded by the JTP 2017 - JPI More Years, 12 Better Lives (Grant Agreement 363850), FORTE (ref. 2017-02301).

References

1. Bratteteig, T., Wagner, I.: Disentangling Participation. Power and Decision-Making in Participatory Design. Springer, Heidelberg (2014). https://doi.org/10.1007/978-3-319-061 63-4
2. Brydon-Miller, M., Greenwood, D., Maguire, P.: Why action research? Action Res. 1(1), 9–28 (2003)

3. Gunnarsson, L., Perby, M.-L.: Forskningscirklar: en metod i facklig kunskapsuppbyggnad (Research circles: a method in trade union knowledg buidling). Report 33. Arbetslivscentrum, Stockholm (1982)
4. Schön, D.A.: The Reflective Practitioner. How Professionals Think in Action, 4th edn. Ashgate, Aldershot (1999)
5. Arnstein, S.R.: A ladder of citizen participation. J. Am. Plan. Assoc. **35**(4), 216–224 (1969)
6. Dreyfuss, H.: Designing for People. Allworth Press, New York (1955)
7. Righi, V., Sayago, S., Ferreira, S., Rosales, A., Blat, J.: Co-designing with a community of older learners for over 10 years by moving user-driven participation from the margin to the centre. CoDes. Int. J. CoCreation **14**, 32–44 (2018)
8. Botero, A., Hyysalo, S.: Ageing together: steps towards evolutionary co-design in everyday practices. CoDes. Int. J. CoCreation Des. Arts **9**(1), 37–41 (2013)
9. Wright, P., McCarthy, J.: The politics and aesthetics of participatory HCI. Interact. Mag. **22**, 26–31 (2015)
10. Grand, S., Jonas, W.: Mapping Design Research: Positions and Perspectives (Board of International Research in Design) Birkhäuser Verlag GmbH (2012)
11. Zimmerman, J., Forlizzi, J., Evenson, S.: Research through design as a method for interaction design research in HCI. In: Proceedings of the SIGCHI Conference on Human Factors in Computing Systems, pp. 493–502. ACM (2007)
12. Frayling, C.: Research in art and design. R. Coll. Art. Res. Pap. **1**(1), 1–5 (1993)
13. Latour, B.: Science in Action: How to Follow Scientists and Engineers Through Society. Harvard University Press, Cambridge (1987)
14. Knorr, C.K.: Epistemic Cultures: How the Sciences Make Knowledge. Harvard University Press, Cambridge (1999)
15. Munoz, S.-A., Macaden, L., Kyle, R., Webster, E.: Revealing student nurses' perceptions of human dignity through curriculum co-design. Soc. Sci. Med. **174**, 1–8 (2017)
16. Östlund, B.: The revival of research circles: to meet the needs of modern ageing and the third age. Educ. Gerontol. **34**(4), 255–266 (2017)
17. Swann, C.: Action research and practice of design. Des. Issues **18**(2), 49–61 (2002)
18. Story, M., Mace, R., Mueller, J.: The Universal Design File, Designing for All Ages and Abilities. The Center for Universal Design North Carolina State University, Raleigh (1998)
19. Waller, S., Bradley, M., Hosking, I., Clarkson, J.: Making the case for inclusive design. Appl. Ergon. **46**, 297–303 (2015)
20. Preiser, W., Ostroff, E.: Universal Design Handbook. McGraw-Hill Companies, Inc., New York (2001)
21. Persson, H., Åhman, H., Yngling, A.A., Gulliksen, J.: Universal design, inclusive design, accessible design, design for all: different concepts—one goal? On the concept of accessibility—historical, methodological and philosophical aspects. Univ. Access Inf. Soc. **14**(4), 505–526 (2015)
22. Clarkson, P.J., Coleman, R., Keates, S., Lebbon, C.: Inclusive Design: Design for the Whole Population. Springer, Heidelberg (2013). https://doi.org/10.1007/978-1-4471-0001-0
23. Demirbilek, O., Demirkan, H.: Universal product design involving elderly users: a participatory' design model. Appl. Ergon. **35**(4), 361–370 (2004)
24. Olander, E.: Emotional principles for a holistic approach to Universal Design. Licentiate thesis. Division of Industrial Design, Department of Design Sciences, Lund University, Sweden (2007)
25. Olander, E.: Design as reflection. Dissertation. Division of Industrial Design, Department of Design Sciences, Lund University, Sweden (2011)
26. Akrich, M.: The description of technical objects. In: Bijker, W., Law, J. (eds.) Shaping Technology/Building Society, pp. 205–224. MIT Press, Cambridge (1992)

27. Pinch, T.: Giving birth to new users: how the minimoog was sold to rock and roll. In: Oudshoorn, N., Pinch, T. (eds.) How Users Matter: The Co-construction of Users and Technology (Inside Technology), pp. 247–270. MIT Press, Cambridge (2003)
28. Akrich, M.: User representations: practices, methods and sociology. In: Managing Technology in Society. The Approach of Constructive Technology Assessment, pp. 167–184. Pinter, London (1995)
29. Woolgar, S.: Configuring the user: The case of usability trials. In: Law, J. (ed.) A Sociology of Monsters. Routledge, Abingdon (1991)
30. Wilkie, A.: Prototyping as event: designing the future of obesity. J. Cult. Econ. **7**, 476–492 (2013)
31. Hyysalo, S.: Representations of use and practice-bound imaginaries in automating the safety of the elderly. Soc. Stud. Sci. **36**(4), 599–626 (2006)
32. Östlund, B.: The benefits of involving older people in the design process. In: Zhou, J., Salvendy, G. (eds.) Human Aspects of IT for the Aged Population-Design for Aging, pp. 3–14 (2015)
33. Peine, A., Rollwagen, I., Neven, L.: The rise of the "innosumer"—rethinking older technology users. Technol. Forecast. Soc. Chang. **82**(2014), 199–214 (2014)
34. Oudshoorn, N., Pinch, T. (eds.): How Users Matter, The Co-construction of Users and Technology. Cambridge (2003)
35. European Commission: Blueprint Digital Transformation of Health and Care for the Ageing Society (2016). http://bit.ly/2j4gxCg
36. Östlund, B., Björling, G., Sahlström, M., Mattsson, J.: Digitizing health care in collaboration between nursing and engineering. Int. J. Adv. Life Sci. **10**(1–2), 11–22 (2018)
37. Peine, A., Faulkner, A., Jaeger, B., Moors, E.: Science, technology and the grand challenge of ageing – understanding the socio-material constitution of later life. Technol. Forecast. Soc. Chang. **93**, 1–9 (2015)
38. Merkel, S., Kucharski, A.: Participatory design in gerontechnology: a systematic literature review. Gerontologist **59**, e16–e25 (2018)
39. Joshi, S.G., Bratteteig, T.: Designing for prolonged mastery. On involving old people in participatory design. Scand. J. Inf. Syst. **28**(1), 1–34 (2016)
40. Ayalon, L., Tesch-Römer, C. (eds.): Contemporary Perspectives on Ageism. IPA, vol. 19. Springer, Cham (2018). https://doi.org/10.1007/978-3-319-73820-8
41. Kuijer, L., de Jong, A.: Practice theory and human centered design: a sustainable bathing example. Nordes (4), 607–619 (2011)
42. Rosales, A., Fernández-Ardèvol, M.: Structural ageism in big data approaches. Nordicom Rev. **40**(s1), 51–64 (2019). https://doi.org/10.2478/nor-2019-0013
43. Chen, K., Chan, A.H.: Gerontechnology acceptance by elderly Hong Kong Chinese: a senior technology acceptance model (STAM). Ergonomics **57**(5), 635–652 (2014)
44. Essén, A., Östlund, B.: Laggards as innovators? Old users as designers of new services & service systems. Int. J. Des. **5**(3), 89–98 (2014)
45. Sixsmith, J., Lan Fang, M., Woolrych, R., Canham, S.L., Battersby, L., Sixsmith, A.: Ageing well in the right place: partnership working with older people. Work. People **21**(1), 1–9 (2017)
46. Peine, A., Cooten, V., Neven, L.: Rejuvenating design: bikes, batteries, and older adopters in the diffusion of e-bikes. Sci. Technol. Hum. Values **42**(3), 429–459 (2017)
47. Fischer, B., Peine, A., Östlund, B.: The importance of user involvement: a systematic review of involving older users in technology design. Gerontologist (2019). https://doi.org/10.1093/geront/gnz163
48. Jonsson, O.: Furniture for later life. Dissertation. Lund University, Department of Design Sciences, Industrial Design (2013)
49. Lindén, K., Östlund, B.: Turning old people's experiences into innovations: IPPI, as the example of mobile services and TV viewing. Gerontechnology **10**(2), 103–109 (2011)

50. Subasi, Ö., Malmborg, L., Fitzpatrick, G., Östlund, B.: Reframing design culture and aging. Interactions. ACM (2014). 1072-5520/2014/

51. Krueger, R.A., Casey, M.-A.: Focus Groups. A Practical guide for Applied Research. Sage Publications, London (2009)

52. Turkle, S.: Alone Together. Why We Expect More from Technology and Less from Each Other. Basic Books, New York (2011)

53. Graff, J.: Career as an experiential learning voyage. Development of experiential assessment methodology in a lifelong learning context. Dissertation. Umeå University, Umeå School of Business, Sweden (2008)

54. Frennert, S.: Older people meet robots. Three case studies on the domestication of robots in everyday life. Lund University. Faculty of Engineering, Department of Design Sciences, Doctoral dissertation (2016)

55. Katz, S., Calasanti, T.: Critical perspectives on successful aging: does it "appeal more than it illuminates"? Gerontologist **55**(1), 26–33 (2015)

56. Haddon, L.: Roger Silverstone's legacies: domestication. New Media Soc. **9**(1), 25–32 (2007)

57. De la Hera, T., Loos, E.F., Simons, M., Blom, J.: Benefits and factors influencing the design of intergenerational digital games: a systematic literature review. Societies **7**(3), 18 (2017)

58. Loos, E., de la Hera, T., Simons, M., Gevers, D.: Setting up and conducting the co-design of an intergenerational digital game: a state-of-the-art literature review. In: Zhou, J., Salvendy, G. (eds.) HCII 2019. LNCS, vol. 11592, pp. 56–69. Springer, Cham (2019). https://doi.org/10.1007/978-3-030-22012-9_5

59. Mannheim, I., et al.: Inclusion of older adults in the research and design of digital technology. Int. J. Environ. Res. Public Health **16**(19), 3718 (2019)

Services for Cognitive Health Co-created with Older Adults

Mihoko Otake-Matsuura[1,2]([⊠]), Yoshie Taguchi[1,2], Katsutoshi Negishi[1,2], Mitsuteru Matsumura[1,2], Kiyomi Shimizu[1,2], Eiko Nagata[1,2], Hideko Nagahisa[1,2], Akane Uotani[1,2], Akira Suzuki[1,2], Mieko Yoshida[2], and Norihisa Miyake[1,2]

[1] Center for Advanced Intelligence Project, RIKEN, Nihonbashi 1-Chome Mitsui Bldg. 15F, 1-4-1 Nihonbashi, Chuo-ku, Tokyo 103-0027, Japan
mihoko.otake@riken.jp
[2] Fonobono Research Institute, Tokyo, Japan

Abstract. In super aged society, healthy older adults are expected to serve as service providers rather than receivers. Through participation of healthy older adults to cognitive health research, the results are expected to be practical for use in daily life. We have been conducting participatory research towards society without preventable dementia. At first, older adults are participants of the service for cognitive health so as to prevent cognitive decline and dementia. Then, some of the participants become providers of the services by participating the research on the service. The key technology for the service is named Coimagination method, which is designed for the active use of cognitive functions through interactive conversation. The platform for this participatory research was founded, whose name is Fonobono Research Institute (FRI). Healthy older adults affiliated with FRI have been engaged in the research through designing, providing, and improving services. This paper reports the designed services and major findings through practices.

Keywords: Healthy aging · Dementia prevention · Participatory research · Service design

1 Introduction

Cognitive health is one of the hot issues in this aging world [1]. Not only developed countries, developing countries face rapid aging which cause increase of dementia patients [2]. Recommendations for prevention of cognitive decline and dementia have been published based on the currently available evidences [3]. However, the knowledge for maintaining cognitive health is not recognized among older adults. Most of the older adults are unaware of cognitive health or worry about cognitive health but do nothing for it. Even if they have some knowledge on cognitive health, it is rare that good practices are incorporated in their everyday lives. We are convinced that we can reduce the occurrence of cognitive decline and dementia dramatically by the knowledge for maintaining cognitive health is to become prevalent and by good practices are adopted as daily habits among

© Springer Nature Switzerland AG 2020
Q. Gao and J. Zhou (Eds.): HCII 2020, LNCS 12207, pp. 59–72, 2020.
https://doi.org/10.1007/978-3-030-50252-2_5

older adults. We assume that there exists preventable dementia which is caused by such ignorance and no action. It is possible to realize society without preventable cognitive decline and dementia where services for cognitive health are available, accessible, and applicable to older adults. If the services for cognitive health are delivered by healthy older adults, the knowledge on cognitive health may become popular among older adults. If the services for cognitive health are studied by healthy older adults, the services are expected to become practical and usable for older adults since they make use of the services by themselves. Therefore, we adopt participatory approach to study services for cognitive health.

Goal of this study is to develop services which may contribute to realize society without preventable dementia when such services become ubiquitous in the society. Through practice, we aim to investigate frameworks for developing services for cognitive health. Towards the goal, we propose and provide services based on Coimagination method [4, 5], which is a conversation support method for cognitive health to embody the idea. Through regular participation, cognitive functions which tend to decline with age are actively utilized. The service which provide Coimagination session regularly intend participants to acquire habit of utilizing cognitive functions in everyday life. The platform for participatory research to study services for cognitive health is non-profit organization named Fonobono Research Institute [6].

Research questions of this study is summarized as:

RQ1) Can healthy older adults deliver novel services for cognitive health?
RQ2) Can healthy older adults work together with professional researcher and create novel services?
RQ3) What kind of activities are applicable to provide services for cognitive health?

The methods and platforms adopted in this study is described in the next section, followed by the results, discussions, and conclusion sessions.

2 Method

2.1 Key Technology for Cognitive Health: The Coimagination Method

The Coimagination method was designed to serve as effective intervention method through social interaction [4, 5]. The method was proposed by Otake in 2006. Since there are evidences that social interaction is associated with cognitive health [7], it is expected that cognitive health may be maintained through intervention of social interaction. Although association are not necessarily causal association, it should be possible to engage cognitive functions through carefully designed stoical interaction. Target cognitive functions to be engaged are episodic memory, division of attention [8], planning and executive functions [9] which tend to decline with age and severely impaired when dementia progresses. Even if the pathological change may occur, higher level of cognitive function before pathological change may compensate its decline [10].

The Coimagination method is defined with the following two rules:

1) Each participant has equal allocated time and period for talk, questions and answers.

2) Participants prepare topics and photos beforehand according to the themes of the conversation sessions.

The purpose of the first rule is to utilize divided attention function. The purpose of the second rule is to utilize episodic memory, planning and executive functions. Once the participants understand the tips to utilize cognitive functions, they are able to apply them to other situations. The good practice of interactive group conversation during Coimagination session is expected to be transferred to conversations in everyday lives. If the person listens carefully to other people talking, thinking about questions and comments in parallel, then divided attention function may be used actively. The strict evaluation of the method via randomized controlled trial is on the way while fundamental effectiveness and safety are confirmed through practices.

2.2 Platform for Participatory Research: Fonobono Research Institute

Fonobono Research Institute is a platform for participatory research. The institute was established as a research project in 2007 and was incorporated into a non-profit organization in 2008. Otake founded and serves as a director of the institute jointly appointed at a national research institute. Healthy older adults are the members of the institute called citizen scientists who are involved in participatory research. They were participants of Coimagination service at first, got interested in activities so as to become practitioners and researchers of the services. The age of citizen scientists ranges from 60s to 90s whose average is 70s. The services and activities stated in this article have been designed and delivered by them under supervision of the director according to the service design method [5]. Starting from service design, conceptual design and evaluation of the systems and business models are explored at the platform while systems and methods are studied and developed at universities and a national research institute where the director have been affiliated in the course of the study.

3   Results

3.1   Outline of the Activities

The activities which have been developed and implemented are classified into five categories: 1) practice of services, 2) public relations, 3) collaborations, 4) training programs and 5) researches, as shown in Fig. 1. 2) Public relations activities recruit participants and practitioners of 1) services in practice. 2) Public relations activities also trigger 3) collaborations since the collaborators contacted us through press reports or publications. Then, the needs for 4) training programs emerged to support start-up and operate services for 3) collaboration, and accelerate 1) practice of services. 5) Research activities are to design and improve all these activities as well as to explore systems and business models derived from these activities.

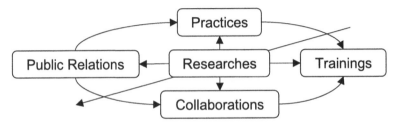

Fig. 1. Categorized activities and their relationships

3.2 Practice: Continuing and Introductory Coimagination Services

Continuing and introductory Coimagination services have been delivered. We have explanatorily tested several types of services. Services have been delivered for figuring out sustainable way of providing services for both participants and practitioners to maintain cognitively active life styles. At the time of 2020, the developed sustainable service in action are "Continuing Coimagination Service" and "Introductory Coimagination Service".

"Continuing Coimagination Service" started in 2011 and has been continuously provided for about 10 years. Frequency and themes of sessions were figured out and whether participants can continue participating services without getting tired of them, rather, enjoying them through practice. The service consists group conversation sessions based on Coimagination method. Adequate frequency was found: the sessions are held once a month, 12 times a year. Some of the participants have been participating the service from the beginning for about 10 years and got 10 years older maintaining their health. They say that they could maintain their cognitive health and could improve quality of life through participation. Explored themes are based on the theories including but not limited to: advanced care planning, cognitive behavioral therapy, and acceptance and commitment therapy so as to improve quality of life. The themes include things which you cannot discard, favorite things, favorite colors, things which you found 10 min' walk.

"Introductory Coimagination Service" also started in 2011 and evolved in the current form in 2016 under the sponsorship of local government, Kashiwa city. Times and curriculum of the service was figured out so as to make participants can continue participating "Continuing Coimagination Service" after taking introductory service. The service consists three classes whose length are about two hours. Classes are delivered three times with two weeks intervals. On the first day, the lecture on the fundamental idea on maintaining cognitive health and themes for Coimagination sessions are assigned to the participants. Typical themes for the beginners are favorite things or favorite foods. Practitioners demonstrate the Coimagination session so that participants can prepare topics and photos according to them. On the second day, half of the participants may experience in Coimagination sessions as well as tips for effective way of preparing and participating the sessions. On the third day, rest of the participants may experience in Coimagination sessions, and all participants are invited to participate in "Continuing Coimagination Service". Some of the participants who wish to employ continuing service for maintaining their cognitive health have been participating successfully.

Figure 2 (a) shows the "Continuing Coimagination Service" delivering Coimagination sessions. Figure 2 (b) shows the "Introductory Coimagination Service" delivering lectures on maintaining cognitive health.

(a)   "Continuing Coimagination Service" delivering Coimagination sessions

(b) "Introductory Coimagination Service" delivering lectures

Fig. 2. Practice: continuing and introductory coimagination services

Major findings on practicing services are summarized as follows.

- Frequency of Coimagination Sessions for continuing Coimagination service is once a month, 12 times a year to maintain cognitively active life styles.
- Participants never get tired of attending series of sessions by changing the themes.
- Themes which improve quality of life have been explored based on the theory for successful aging.
- Times and Curriculum of introductory Coimagination service is three times for two hours with two weeks intervals.

- Some of the participants subsequently participated in continuing Coimagination service successfully.
- Curriculum consists lectures, demonstrations, and experiencing the sessions.

3.3 Public Relations: Lecture Meetings, Newsletters, Blogs

Public relations activities have been conducted from the beginning to find potential participants and practitioners of the services, supporters and partners. The tools for public relations are lecture meetings, newsletters, and blogs. We exploratory figured out reasonable pace to deliver lecture meetings or publish newsletters and blogs.

We have been held lecture meetings once or twice a year. The lecture meetings are composed of invited lectures by specialists, keynote lecture by the organizer, and party. We learned cutting edge of the researches and practices on dementia prevention and care prevention by invited lectures and shared the knowledge with participants. We reported the state of the art of our activities as well as findings of each time through keynote lecture. Parties were held after the lecture meeting, providing networking opportunities among who have common interests and needs. We recruited potential participants and practitioners through the series of events. We also positioned these activities as services for supporting members. We sent invitation letters to the supporting members on these events. The typical time for lecture meetings are June or July as anniversary lecture meetings and December as Christmas lecture meetings.

Newsletters have been published after the lecture meetings reporting the lectures and other service activities [11]. The newsletters are published in January after Christmas lecture meetings and in August after anniversary lecture meetings. Each article of newsletters are edited by blog articles.

Blog articles have been posted once a week, reporting the activities as well as topics with photos presented at Coimagination sessions [12]. The roster system was operated for blog postings. A pairs of rosters collected and posted articles once a week for each month. The authors of activity reports are people in charge of each activity. The authors of the topics with photos presented at Coimagination sessions are presenter themselves with comments followed by the rosters of the posting.

Through active public relations activities, we received massive media coverage of more than 100 newspapers, magazines and TV programs.

Figure 3 (a) shows the photo of one of the lecture meetings delivering an invited lecture. One of the newsletters is shown in Fig. 3 (b), one of the blog articles is shown in Fig. 3 (c).

Major findings on public relations activities are summarized as follows.

- Lecture meetings, newsletters, and blogs are used for public relations.
- Lecture meetings have been held twice a year.
- Newsletters reporting the lectures and other activities have been published twice a year after the lecture meetings.
- Blog articles have been posted once a week, reporting the activities as well as topics with photos presented at Coimagination sessions.
- We received massive media coverage through the above voluntary activities.

(a) One of the lecture meetings delivering an invited lecture

(b) Front cover of one of the newsletters   (c) One of the blog articles

Fig. 3. Public relations: lecture meetings, newsletters, blogs

3.4 Collaborations: Working with Care Facilities and Hospitals

Collaborations with care facilities and hospitals have been done. Collaborations were triggered by public relations activities where people got interested in delivering Coimagination services at their sites. The participants range from healthy older adults to older adults who need care, and older adults with dementia. Although Coimagination method was originally proposed for healthy older adults to maintain their cognitive functions, applications and limitations of the method were explored through applying the methods to older adults in diverse conditions [12]. Practitioners were also diverse including care givers, nurses, occupational therapists, clinical psychologists, nursery staffs. Figure 4 (a) shows a Coimagination service at the care facility in Ibaraki prefecture. There, the Coimagination services have been provided as activity programs for older adults who need care. The average age of participants is over 90 years old, most of them use wheelchairs. Figure 4 (b) shows a Coimagination service at the care facility in Saitama prefecture. There, the Coimagination services have been provided as community programs for older adults living at home who are willing to maintain cognitive functions. The age of the participants ranges from 60 to 70s. Figure 4 (c) shows a Coimagination service provided at the hospital in Nagasaki prefecture. There, Coimagination services were provided as brain rehabilitation program for patients with dementia. Figure 4 (d) shows a Coimagination service at the care facility in Osaka prefecture. There, Coimagination services have been provided as training programs for care givers to improve communication skill with older adults as well as community programs for older adults living at home.

(a) Service at the Care Facility in Ibaragi   (b) Service at the Care Facility in Saitama

(c) Service at the Hospital in Nagasaki   (d) Service at the Care Facility in Osaka

Fig. 4. Collaborations: working with care facilities and hospitals

We supported start-ups and operations of Coimagination services. We found that the conditions for successful collaborations is that both employers and employees of the organizations have passion to start and continue to provide novel services and increase the values in addition to their routine works. We visited the sites at first and discussed possibilities and difficulties for delivery of the services. We provided user accounts for the

Coimagination support system to practitioners so that the sessions are smoothly guided and at the same time, session data are accumulated. We monitor the practices by reviewing the session data. We have been consulting the practitioners mainly through emails, sometimes on site. We explored implementation of the Coimagination services adapted to the needs and the participants' capabilities. Training programs for practitioners were delivered which are described in the next subsection.

Major findings on collaborations are summarized as follows.

– Coimagination services could be provided at care facilities and hospitals.
– Coimagination services could be provided by care givers, nurses, occupational therapists, clinical psychologists, and nursery staffs.
– Coimagination services could be provided as activity programs for older adults who need care, community programs for older adults living at home, brain rehabilitation program for patients with dementia, training programs for care givers.

3.5 Trainings Programs: On-site, Off-site, and Annual Meetings

We have developed training programs. The programs aim to train practitioners providing Coimagination services. The needs to train beginners for a short period emerged since people working in different areas tried to start services at their care facilities or hospitals. New practitioners who were originally participants of the Continuing Coimagination Services also need training. The training course for collaborators at different sites consists on-site, off-site, and annual mutual learning. Firstly, we visit the site and discuss the needs and seeds, potential problems and solutions for implementing the service. Secondly, we invite potential practitioners for off-site training. The length of the typical program is two days: lectures and demonstrations for the first day, exercises and discussions for the second day. Then, we visit the site again for on-site training. There, the trained practitioner run Coimagination sessions to their candidate colleagues or participants. After they start their own services, they are invited to participate in annual mutual learning program. The practitioners of all sites get together, report their own practices at their sites, give comments with each other. The program is not one-way. Findings, problems and solutions are shared in order to improve services. The photo of the off-site training doing group discussion is shown in Fig. 5 (a). The photo of the annual mutual learning program is shown in Fig. 5 (b).

Major findings on training programs are summarized as follows.

– Training programs consist on-site, off-site, and annual learning program.
– Basic training program for practitioners with lectures, demonstrations, exercises, and group discussions was developed.
– Annual mutual learning programs provide opportunity to share findings at all sites.

3.6 Researches: Development and Improvement of Services, Systems, and Business Models

Services, systems, and business models based on Coimagination method have been explored towards society without preventable dementia where services for cognitive

(a)   One of the off-site trainings doing group discussion

(b)   One of the annual mutual learning programs

Fig. 5. Training practitioners: on-site, off-site, and annual meetings

health are available and accessible to older adults. The services are the results of the participatory research. All these services have been designed and improved through series of practices. One of the explored services which have not described above and was invented is the Coimagination with expedition service [13]. Here we describe the existed problems and how the service solves the problems as well as developed system to support the service and examined business model of the service.

The needs for services in which participants can grasp the essence of Coimagination service in one day emerged. In order to participate in Coimagination session, the participants are required to prepare photos and topics beforehand. The assignment to prepare them are informed at the time of recruitment. Some participants find difficulty for preparation. Then, orientation sessions were introduced in order to remove difficulty. The participants have to participate at least two days sessions in this case. In order to experience in one day to improve accessibility, the Coimagination with expedition service was invented. The service is provided as a workshop style in four steps.

Firstly, participants get together in the meeting place. It starts from the orientation session. Themes for taking photos and finding topics are assigned. Secondly, both participants and practitioners go out for expedition. They are grouped according to their walking speeds. Thirdly, after the expedition, groups get back to the meeting place, and select photos to be used during conversation for each. Finally, the participants and practitioners share the episodes during expeditions looking at photos and talking about it. Coimagination with expedition services have been provided at different places, ranging from park in the neighborhoods, museums, to sightseeing places with historical buildings and streetscapes.

The system for Coimagination with expedition services was developed based on the emerged needs. Coimagination support system have been developed from the beginning of the study. Before the Coimagination with expedition service was invented, the photos need to be registered by the practitioners. Since photos are required to be registered to the system immediately to start Coimagination session after expedition, the application which runs on smartphones or tablets was developed. The system was developed at the university where the first author was affiliated at that time with a help of companies. The system was evaluated by the participants and practitioners through the usage of it. With a help of practitioners, participants can take photos and upload them to the Coimagination contents management system [14]. They can select the photo to be displayed on the screen for describing during the session. Usability was confirmed that both participants and practitioners could use it in the course of the service, and the services have been held smoothly with a help of the developed system.

Business model of the service was also explored. The Coimagination with expedition services have been held through collaboration. One of the services was provided with a help of travel-planning company in which meeting place and courtesy bus were arranged to examine whether the service can be positioned as a one-day tour. Other services were also delivered through collaborating with local government and hospitals in which meeting place were provided by the collaborators. We have been exploring business models for other services as well aiming at sustainable delivery of the services. The expedition session at the Coimagination with expedition services are shown in Fig. 6 (a). Figure 6 (b) shows older adults taking photos during expedition by utilizing the application which runs on smartphones or tablets.

Major findings on researches are summarized as follows.

– Services, systems, and business models based on Coimagination method have been explored.
– Coimagination with expedition service was invented through practices.
– The system for Coimagination with expedition services was developed based on the emerged needs.
– Business model of Coimagination with expedition was explored collaborating with travel-planning company, local government, and hospitals.

(a)   The expedition session at the Coimagination with expedition services

(b) The older adults taking photos during expedition by utilizing the application which runs on smartphones or tablets

Fig. 6. Researches: development and improvement of services, systems, and business models

4   Discussion

We discuss the results by answering to the research questions which are stated in introduction session.

Answer to RQ1) Yes, they can. The services reported in this paper have been designed, provided, and improved by healthy older adults. Through practice, we proved that services for cognitive health can be delivered by healthy older adults.

Answer to RQ2) Yes, they can. We showed that healthy older adults can be involved in participatory research and have capability for generating values. The processes have been supervised by the professional researcher based on the theory of service design.

Research activities have been conducted with a picture of society without preventable dementia where services for cognitive health are installed.

Answer to RQ3) Through implementation, we identified that activities are classified into five categories: practices, public relations, collaborations, trainings, and researches.

Application of this study could be applied to the similar community where retired healthy older adults are densely populated with passionate researcher who are dedicated to work together with healthy older adults. Types of activities could be universal regardless of the key technologies of services. Limitation of this study is that the conditions for successful co-creation needs to be investigated. Implementation of the classified activities could be specific to the key technologies of services.

5   Conclusion

This paper reported the services for cognitive health co-created with older adults. We demonstrated that co-creation of service with older adults is feasible. Coimagination method are adopted for key technology of service for cognitive health. Activities for running services for cognitive health based on Coimagination method are identified thorough participatory research whose platform is named Fonobono Research Institute. The conclusion of this study is summarized as:

1. Healthy older adults can provide services for cognitive health.
2. Healthy older adults can work together with professional researchers to create novel services.
3. Activities for running services are classified into five categories: practices, public relations, collaborations, trainings, and researches.

Future work include but not limited to investigate conditions for successful co-creation of services through practices as well as comparing other participatory research involving healthy older adults.

This research is partially supported by USPS KAKENHI Grant Number JP 18KT0035, JP19H01138.

References

1. Grayson, M.: Cognitive health. Nature **531**(7592), S1 (2016)
2. Prince, M., Bryce, R., Albanese, E., Wimo, A., Ribeiro, W., Ferri, C.P.: The global prevalence of dementia: a systematic review and metaanalysis. Alzheimers Dementia **9**, 63–75 (2013)
3. Livingston, G., et al.: Dementia prevention, intervention, and care. Lancet **390**(10113), 2673–2734 (2017)
4. Otake, M., Kato, M., Takagi, T., Asama, H.: The coimagination method and its evaluation via the conversation interactivity measuring method, pp. 356–364. IGI Global (2011)
5. Otake, M., Nergui, M., Otani, T., Ota, J.: Duplication analysis of conversation and its application to cognitive training of older adults in care facilities. J. Med. Imaging Health Inform. **3**(4), 615–621 (2013)

6. Otake, M., Kato, M., Takagi, T., Iwata, S., Asama, H., Ota, J.: Multiscale service design method and its application to sustainable service for prevention and recovery from dementia. In: Onada, T., Bekki, D., McCready, E. (eds.) JSAI-isAI 2010. LNCS (LNAI), vol. 6797, pp. 321–330. Springer, Heidelberg (2011). https://doi.org/10.1007/978-3-642-25655-4_31

7. Kuiper, J.S., Zuidersma, M., Oude Voshaar, R.C., et al.: Social relationships and risk of dementia: a systematic review and meta-analysis of longitudinal cohort studies. Ageing Res. Rev. **22**, 39–57 (2015)

8. Rentz, D., Weintraub, S.: Neuropsychological detection of early probable Alzheimer's disease. In: Scinto, L.F.M., Daffner, K.R. (eds.) Early Diagnosis and treatment of Alzheimer's disease, pp. 69–189. Humana Press, Totowa (2000)

9. Barberger-Gateau, P., Fabrigoule, C., Rouch, I., et al.: Neuropsychological correlates of self-reported performance in instrumental activities of daily living and prediction of dementia. J. Gerontol. Ser. B: Psychol. Sci. Soc. Sci. **54**(5), 293–303 (1999)

10. Stern, Y.: Cognitive reserve in ageing and Alzheimer's disease. Lancet Neurol. **11**, 1006–1012 (2012)

11. Fonobono Research Institute: Fonobono Research Institute Website (2020). http://www.fonobono.org/

12. Otake, M.: Application of co-imagination method to healthy older adults, older adults who need care, and older adults with dementia. Gerontechnology **13**(2), 119–120 (2014)

13. Khoo, E., Otake, M.: Comparison of mental time of older adults during conversations supported by coimagination method and coimagination method with expedition. In: Well-Being Computing: AI Meets Health and Happiness Science, AAAI Spring Symposium, pp. 356–361 (2016)

14. Otake-Matsuura, M.: Conversation assistive technology for maintaining cognitive health. J. Korean Gerontol. Nurs. **20**(Suppl. 1), 154–159 (2018)

Enhancing Self-efficacy as a Part of
the Design Process

Marie Sjölinder[✉]

RISE, Box 1263, 164 29 Kista, Sweden
marie.sjolinder@ri.se

Abstract. The overall aim with the paper is to create a starting point for a design framework that incorporates elements that support the participants', in this case older adults, feeling of social belonging, being knowledgeable and able to contribute. The paper describes different aspects of ageism and stereotypes related to older adults and the design and use of digital technology. The paper also places these stereotypes in relationship to self-efficacy and how degrading and internalized stereotypes affect motivation to learn and use new technology. Further, the paper presents examples from conducted projects where co-operation and co-creation have reduced the impact of negative stereotypes in the design process; and highlights design guidelines aiming at reducing the impact of negative stereotypes. Finally, the paper elaborates on elements that could be included in the design process to enhance self-efficacy alongside with developing meaningful digital tools that are motivating to use.

Keywords: Older adults · Technology · Design

1 Introduction

With digitalization, interest is growing around the topic of ageing, and what it may mean for society to have an increased number of older people in Europe. This has influenced research related to older people and technology [1–3]. It has also generated a lot of worry related to how older people will manage in future society, since a high degree of digital literacy will be required [4].

There are many assumptions regarding ageing that are deeply rooted in our culture [5]. Older adults are often targets for age-based prejudice, and they are often perceived as less attractive, more forgetful and less dynamic than younger adults. Age related presumptions are also used to explain older adults' lower interest and usage of Information and Communication Technologies (ICT). This assumption has been questioned, and the age-related negative stereotypes in terms of being less competent and less interested in learning and using ICT have been discussed in terms of internalized stereotypes resulting in a "self-fulfilling prophecy" [6].

The overall aim with the paper was to create a starting point for a design framework that incorporates elements that support the participants', in this case older adults, feeling of social belonging, being knowledgeable and able to contribute. In Sect. 2 the paper

© Springer Nature Switzerland AG 2020
Q. Gao and J. Zhou (Eds.): HCII 2020, LNCS 12207, pp. 73–83, 2020.
https://doi.org/10.1007/978-3-030-50252-2_6

describes different aspects of ageism and stereotypes related to older adults and the design and use of digital technology; and in Sect. 3 the paper places these stereotypes in relationship to self-efficacy and identity. In Sect. 4 the paper discusses the design process and how user involvement can be conducted in a way where negative stereotypes are avoided. In Sect. 4 the paper also highlights design guidelines aiming at reducing the impact of negative stereotypes. Finally, in Sect. 5, the paper elaborates on elements that could be included in the design process to enhance self-efficacy alongside with developing meaningful digital tools that are motivating to use.

2 Ageism and Stereotypes

Ageism is defined as negative attitude or behavior towards individuals based on their age [7]. It is a way of using stereotypes to discriminate against older adults [8], using prejudice in terms of societal norms that marginalize and make older adults feel unwelcome [9]. The stereotypes rely on a perception of older people as generally unattractive, frail, useless, dependent, forgetful, lacking agency [7], inflexible and cannot learn new things [9]. These negative stereotypes also affect social encounters and how people communicate with each other. They affect speech, voice and gestures and communication are adjusted in such a way as to reinforce and confirm stereotypes [6].

Old-age stereotypes are powerful, they get integrated into the individuals self-concept and affect the way older adults perceive themselves [7, 9], which in turn conforms the stereotypes [7]. The internalized ageist stereotypes have a detrimental impact on older adults' perceptions of their own competencies [10], they generate feelings of disengagement and they could lower self-esteem and self-efficacy [7, 11]. Self-efficacy in turn, has shown to be a determinant of older adults' perception of internet use [12], and the more seniors endorse ageist stereotypes, the less they use ICT [7].

Due to the stereotype that older adults are unwilling and unable to learn how to use new technologies, older adults are often excluded and feel excluded from social issues related to the information society [7, 13]. The negative stereotypes may also affect the perceived ease of use of the internet due to the assumptions that older adults are lacking the ability to adapt to new things such as using internet. If the stereotypes convey the message that internet is difficult to use for older adults, the threshold for start using it becomes higher and the perceived risk of failing becomes larger [9].

As a way of dealing with or protecting the self-image due to the internalized age-related stereotypes about Internet and technology use, older adults might underestimate the usefulness of the internet. They may rationalize in terms of that they have managed well without before and will continue doing so. This negative loop with a negative self-image and an underestimation of usefulness of the Internet are likely to further affect attitudes and willingness to engage with new technology [9].

3 Performance and Self-efficacy

Self-esteem is complex and has been brought up from many perspectives in the literature. From a hierarchical perspective Self-esteem has been described in terms of three sub-concepts: *performance* self-esteem, *social* self-esteem, and *physical* self-esteem.

Performance self-esteem is related to general competence including intellectual abilities, self-confidence and efficacy [14]. Self-efficacy is related to personal capabilities while self-esteem is the broader concept and related to judgments of self-worth [15]. According to Bandura, people with high self-efficacy believe they can perform well and are more likely to view difficult tasks as something to be mastered rather than something to be avoided [14, 15].

The self-concept is the view of one-self that is formed through direct experience and evaluations adopted from significant others. The self-concept contributes to an understanding of people's attitudes toward themselves are how they are perceived by others. Theories related to self-concept often addresses self-image from a global perspective while self-efficacy can vary between different domains [15].

Self-efficacy has been suggested to play an important role in technology acceptance and use, and ageism may lead to a reduction in self-efficacy among older adults if they internalize negative stereotypes of older adults in terms of lacking the ability to use new technology [9]. Computer self-efficacy has been shown to be an important predictor of technology usage. Self-efficacy has also shown to be a predictor of computer anxiety which in turn was shown to be related to interest in computers and usage of computers. The belief in the own ability is likely to explain, at least to some extent, age differences in computer interest [16, 17].

4 Design and Introduction of New Technology

Based on findings where beliefs about the own ability is related to how we approach new technology it becomes crucial how technology is presented and introduced. It is also important how the individual is treated as a possible user of the technology. As described previously, when encountered with the age-related stereotypes there is a risk of decreased engagement and interest. However, several studies have shown that age-differences related to technology usage can be reduced depending on how the older adults are encountered or involved. Below, in Sect. 4.1, insights from own previous projects are described, with a focus on outcomes that have decreased the impact of age-related stereotypes and/or supported the feeling of being included and knowledgeable. The second part in this Sect. 4.2, describe guidelines, to avoid ageism and exclusion of older adults, suggested by Mannheim et al. [13].

4.1 Content and Communication

It is often claimed that it is more difficult for older adults to learn how to use technology. Studies have shown that the learning process is longer [18], and that more time is needed to solve different tasks [19–21]. However, the effect of these age-related differences might be overestimated. Studies reporting difficulties for older adults who are learning and using technology have often failed to provide the appropriate context for introduction and learning [22]. This again reiterates the importance of not contributing to a degrading self-image but, instead, providing a supportive environment [22]. This could be, for example, through the design of products and services, and the instructions that belong to the devices or services [4]. When designing new technology, stereotypes of frail older adults often affect designers and might shape how the technology targeted towards older adults are designed [13].

Getting Beyond the Stereotype. In a project presented by Sjölinder and Scandurra [23], a new communication device was developed together with older adults living at a nursing home and the personnel. In a study, conducted in the beginning of the project, both the older adults and the personnel were asked about the technology experience of the older adults. The answers given by the older adults themselves were compared with ones given by the personnel. The care personnel underestimated the older adults' technology experience and overlooked that many of the older adults once had worked with technology in different environments. When a few months of the project had passed, the personnel participated in a task where the aim was to get descriptions of different subgroups of users. They created a number of Personas [24] that represented older adults living at the nursing home. This turned out to be an eye-opener for the personnel since it forced them to reflect about their residents and their relationship to technology. To think of a person as he or she used to be was useful, as well as to reflect upon the entire person in a salutogene manner, beyond the medical conditions. The task contributed to gaining a new perspective of the elderly since the care personnel was forced to think about them as possible users of new technology. This, also increased the personnel's understanding for possibilities with the technology, and they started to suggest new ways of using the technology at the nursing home [23].

Communication and Social Context. Communication and working together in cross-generational groups may increase understanding and reduce negative stereotypes [6]. This was also shown in the project described above [23] where a communication device targeting older adults was developed. Based on ideas from older adults and the care personnel quizzes, riddles and a memory game were developed and introduced at the nursing home. These mini games were mainly used when the older adults and the personnel were gathered at common meetings. The meetings where appreciated and they contributed to further increase the personnel's understanding of the older adults within the context of technology usage. Another functionality that was developed for the communication device supported social interaction with friends and family. This functionality made it possible to send messages and pictures and communicate in different ways. However, this functionality was not used due to far too small social networks. When the personnel suggested the devices to be moved to the common areas, the older adults started to use the functionality as something to gather around and, for example, show each other pictures of friends and family. The technology became a support in conveying identity and showing other residents' important things in their lives outside the nursing home.

The importance of close involvement of users in the design process has been stated in many contexts, however being a part of the design process may also increase the feeling of belonging to a social context or to a group. Co-design could be conducted in a way where the participants get a positive experience, feel like partners and engage in the design process between the sessions [13]. The development of the communication tool described above also gained feed-back from a second user group consisting of older adults living on their own (not in a nursing home). This group of older adults participated in design workshops at an activity centre (see Fig. 1). Besides valuable input to the design process, the importance of a social context around such work was clear. The users were very engaged throughout the project and workshops were frequently visited and the participants became friends [26]. The high amount of input from the participants could be explained in terms of social inclusion; they belonged to a group and each member was considered important for the work.

Fig. 1. A design workshop with the older adults

In another project a Kinect™ sensor tool for stroke rehabilitation at home was developed [25]. As a part of this project a study was conducted that aimed at exploring whether or not usage could be broadened to other user groups than stroke patients [26]. The system was installed at three activity centres for older adults with the aim of supporting general exercising and for having fun. Each centre had responsible care personnel doing observations during the tests. After the session both the older adults and the care professionals filled out a questionnaire about usage of the system and the exercises. The older adults answered from their perspective and the care professionals based their answers on the support given to the users when using the system. When evaluating the questionnaires, there were no direct contradictions between the answers given by older users and the care professionals. However, the care professionals provided a deeper insight since they had a more holistic perspective on the situation. They provided valuable information about how and why features and interaction should be changed. The shared experience between care professionals and the older adults contributed to a similar view of the situation and of the usage of the technology, and it also created a cross-generational common ground for communication and understanding with respect to technology usage [27].

Becoming Lead-Users and Teaching Others. The importance of technology ambassadors has been pointed out, both with respect to older adults and care personnel [13, 23]. Mannheim et al. [13] showed that networks supported by technology-literate mediators, for example older adults could create digital support circles and act as agents for enhancing wider inclusion. In the work with developing the communication tool described above [23], the care personnel had the responsibility of user involvement. They took on different roles; recruiting elderly, information to the relatives, display of food or menus, information about activities for the residents, teaching activities to the rest of the care personnel as well as medication and technology experts. The entire setting was prominent and cheerful and all involved care personnel was appointed as ambassadors for the technology in relation to the residents or their relatives. This was also a contributing factor to that the personnel step by step understood different user needs and possible usage contexts, and as a result of that started to suggest new services and ways of using the technology.

In another study conducted by Sjölinder et al. [28] focus groups where held with older adults living at nursing homes and their care personnel. At some of the nursing homes they had explicitly defined technology ambassadors. The aim with the focus groups were to discuss the need for new technology and new digital services. From a co-creation perspective, this project generated two main outcomes. One of these were the advantage of having both the older adults and the personnel in the same focus group. In the beginning of the focus groups, many of the older adults and the caregiving personnel were convinced that new technology was not their area and that they could not contribute. As the focus groups proceeded, the participants became more and more engaged and they realised that they had many ideas that could be turned into new technical solutions. At the end of the sessions, both the older adults and the personnel left in a state of mind where they, at least to some extent, perceived themselves as ambassadors for new technical solutions. To some extent, the sessions had bridged the gap between the older adults and the personnel with respect to understanding each other's need for technology, and the personnel had realised that that the older adults actually could use and benefit from new technology. At one of the nursing homes, where they explicitly worked with technology ambassadors among the personnel, we got insights in further positive outcomes with using technology ambassadors. The ambassadors among the personnel showed a great engagement and described how they constantly suggested new ways of using the technology. For example, to support social interaction and communication between both the older adults living at the nursing home, and between the older adults and their relatives.

4.2 Co-creation with Older Adults – Guidelines for the Design Process

Mannheim et al. [13] suggest that ageism in the design process of digital technology might play a role as a possible barrier of adopting technology. They argue that much of the development of digital technology and the research are not focused on what the older adults really need and want. Ageism and stereotypes where older adults are perceived as weak and less capable has led to that much of the development has been in the area of health and/or care taking. They also argue that the stereotypes affect involvement in the design process and exclusion both on a general level but also in particular of the oldest and the disabled. Further, Mannheim et al. [13] point out the need for more inclusion in the design process and co-creation. The design process has to be set up in a way that it does not convey stereotypes and make it difficult for older adults to participate in an equal way. With this as a foundation, they suggest a number of guidelines to be used in the co-creation process together with older adults, see Table 1.

Table 1. The design guidelines suggested by Mannheim et al. [13].

Ethical Aspects and Considerations	Guidelines for Inclusion
Awareness of Stereotypes and Ageism	Pay attention to appearance and aesthetics. Older adults should be included in developing the external attributes of DTs to minimize possible stigmatization caused by them. Prefer disguising technology as an everyday device. Adoption of a "universal design" which can be conceived as making more products usable by a wide range of people, not just older adults or people with disabilities
Consent and Re-Consent	Use a broader and more holistic conceptualization of competence beyond cognitive ability. Simplify consent forms by cognitively adapting language and using corrective feedback. Account for the setting. Choose a time and place convenient for the person with noise levels that are appropriate
Autonomy, Trust and Respect	Assess the person's needs and wants at the particular time and place. Provide an optional "exit" or possibility to withdraw using a specific DT (such as surveillance and monitoring technologies). Establish trust and respect the older person's choices
Research Methods and Tools	On the individual level, take into consideration and control for sensory decline. Adapt the use of fonts, contrast and visibility of materials. Furthermore, pay attention to sound amplification and reducing background noises. When using DT as part of a study or design, notice that adequate instruction is provided on how to use the devices, charge and maintain them. On the societal level, pay attention to possible cues (e.g., in trail instructions or setting) that can prime negative age stereotypes. Consider the most suitable method. Qualitative methods are often more suitable when involving older adults with cognitive decline. Prefer to ask about experiences and feelings rather than 'factual' information
Privacy and Confidentiality	For DTs that are invasive, older adults should be included in their development to decide how much privacy loss is acceptable. Provide control as to who has access to sensitive information about the older adult

(*continued*)

Table 1. (*continued*)

Ethical Aspects and Considerations	Guidelines for Inclusion
Safety and Security	Prefer to design and study DTs in a natural environment so that issues of safety can be addressed. Include older adults with different conditions and health statuses in order to adapt and account for various situations

5   Enhancing Self-efficacy and Identity as a Part of the Design Process

In this paper insights from different projects have been described, alongside with design guidelines for avoiding stereotypes and stigmatization. The next step is to, in a more active way, incorporate elements in the design process that increase the feeling of belonging and of being capable. Below the elements of the design process are described based on the insights they are based upon. In Table 2, a summary of the design elements is presented as possible features to include in the design process.

5.1   Increasing the Feeling of Being Able to Contribute

The guidelines suggested by Mannheim et al. [13] proposes a holistic view of the person, that goes beyond cognitive ability and that takes sensory decline into consideration. This relates to the feeling of being capable, instead of creating a feeling of not being able or not being able to participate. The work described by Sjölinder et al. [28] shows how the feeling of being able to contribute increased step by step during a focus group. Based on this insight, focus groups could intentionally be planned with the aim of creating insights about the own ability to contribute. This could for example be achieved by 1) gather knowledge about the participants before the focus group and 2) based on the gathered knowledge select and phrase questions in a way that makes it easy to share information and to contribute. The overall aim with the focus group could be approached stepwise starting at level where all participants feel that they can contribute with something. Another possibility is to make use of is the dynamics when two different user groups participate in the same focus group. The importance of communication between different age groups are supported by the work conducted by Lagace et al. [6]. This approach could be facilitated by asking about experiences and needs based on the perspectives of the different groups. It would also be possible to take this one step further and let the participants discuss their different perspectives. This could both generate new ideas and increase the understanding for each other's situation and needs.

5.2   Contributing by Teaching and Supporting Others

Previous work has described positive effects of being able to teach others and the usage of ambassadors or lead users, both among older adults and among care giving personnel

Table 2. Elements to include in the design process

Concepts	Suggested elements in the design process
Increasing the feeling of being able to contribute	Support communication and discussions between different user groups – make it possible to share different perspectives of the need for new technology Gather knowledge about the participants before the focus group and based on the gathered knowledge select and phrase questions in a way that makes it easy to share and contribute
Contributing by teaching and supporting others	Create situations where participants can teach and support each other Engage older adults in leading the design process and provide possibilities to get basic skills in methods for user involvement
Identity and being a part of a group	Provide the possibility to be a part of a social context, both within and outside the design process Try to incorporate the possibility to be seen by others and to get appreciation Make the participation something to be proud of Aim for universal products and services that could convey identity for all user groups

[13, 23]. These roles convey both a feeling of having knowledge and the feeling of being able to contribute in a meaningful way. One way of incorporating this in the design process or as a part of a focus group is to involve older adults in being a part of leading the focus groups. For example, by engaging retired designers in leading parts of the design process. Another possibility is to give introduction courses about methods for user involvement to the older adults. After this introduction, they could be a part of leading the focus groups. Such an approach could have several advantages since it will create a further social context, provide the possibility to learn new skills and convey these skills further when leading the focus groups. These introduction sessions about how to work with user involvement could also include other age groups and students which further will increase possibilities for discussions between different age groups.

5.3   Identity and Being a Part of a Group

Social belonging and being a part of a group is an important aspect of our lives. This aspect could actively be incorporated in the design process [26]. By creating the possibility for the same participants to meet on a frequent basis they will get to know each other and have the possibility to plan activities outside the focus groups. The participation in this social context and in the involvement of developing new technology could also be something to be proud of and talk about with friends and family. The importance of being seen and appreciated by others is also crucial to consider when developing services targeted towards older adults [23], since many services are just addressing physical and practical needs.

In the guidelines suggested by Mannheim et al. [13], the authors point out the importance of avoiding stigmatizing external appearance of products [4]. This relates to concept of self-image, social interaction with others and how we are perceived by others. Mannheim et al. [13] suggest the adoption of universal design, which enhances the feeling of inclusion and being a part of a group or a social context. New technology could target all user groups, but it could be used in different ways in different phases of life. For example, devices for measuring physical activity could be used in a variety of ways depending on context and need, and there is no need to target some devices and services specifically towards older adults.

6   Conclusions and Future Work

The overall aim with the paper was to create a starting point for a design framework that incorporates elements that support the participants' feeling of social belonging, being knowledgeable and able to contribute. This work was mainly targeted towards older adults, however the suggested elements of the design process could be relevant regardless of the participants' age. A next step is to describe the elements in a more concreate way; and also incorporate and evaluate them in a coherent design process.

References

1. Longhurst, B., Smithe, G., Bagnall, G.: Introducing Cultural Studies. Routledge, London (2017)
2. Nikou, S.: Mobile technology and forgotten consumers: the young-elderly. Int. J. Consum. Stud. **39**(14), 294–304 (2015)
3. Turkle, S.: Life on Screen. Identity in the Age of Internet. Simson & Schuster, New York (1995)
4. Eriksson, Y., Sjölinder, M.: The role of designers in the development and communication of new technology. In: Sayago, S. (ed.) Perspectives on Human-Computer Interaction Research with Older People. HIS, pp. 37–48. Springer, Cham (2019). https://doi.org/10.1007/978-3-030-06076-3_3
5. DeFalco, A.: Uncanny Subjects. The Ohio State University Press, Columbus (2009)
6. Lagace, M., Charmarkeh, H., Zaky, R., Firzly, N.: From psychological to digital disengagement: exploring the link between ageism and the 'grey digital divide'. J. Commun. Public Relat. **18**(1(37)), 65–75 (2016). ISSN 1454-8100/E-ISSN 2344-5440
7. Lagacé, M., Charmarkeh, H., Laplante, J., Tanguay, A.: How ageism contributes to the second-level digital divide: the case of Canadian seniors. J. Technol. Hum. Usability (2015). www.techandsoc.com, ISSN 2381-9227
8. Butler, R.N.: Why Survive? Being Old in America. Harper & Row, New York (1975)
9. McDonough, C.C.: The effect of ageism on the digital divide among older adults. J. Gerontol. Geriatr. Med. 2(008) (2016). https://doi.org/10.24966/ggm-8662/100008
10. Cherry, K.E., Allen, P.D., Denver, J.Y., Holland, K.R.: Contributions of social desirability to self-reported ageism. J. Appl. Gerontol. **34**, 712–733 (2015)

11. Kotter-Grühn, D., Hess, T.M.: The impact of age stereotypes on self-perceptions of aging across the adult lifespan. J. Gerontol. Ser. B: Psychol. Sci. Soc. Sci. **67**(5), 563–571 (2012). https://doi.org/10.1093/geronb/gbr153

12. Zhang, Y.: Age, gender, and Internet attitudes among employees in the business world. Comput. Hum. Behav. **21**, 1–10 (2005). https://doi.org/10.1016/j.chb.2004.02.006

13. Mannheim, I., et al.: Inclusion of older adults in the research and design of digital technology. Int. J. Environ. Res. Public Health **16**, 3718 (2019). https://doi.org/10.3390/ijerph16193718

14. Heatherton, T.F., Polivy, J.: Development and validation of a scale for measuring state self-esteem. J. Pers. Soc. Psychol. **60**, 895–910 (1991)

15. Bandura, A.: Self-Efficacy: The Exercise of Control. W H Freeman/Times Books/Henry Holt & Co., New York (1997)

16. Czaja, S.J., Charness, N., Fisk, A.D., Hertzog, C., Nair, S.N.: Factors predicting the use of technology: findings from the Center for Research and Education on Aging and Technology Enhancement (CREATE). Psychol. Aging **21**, 333–352 (2006)

17. Ellis, D., Allaire, J.C.: Modeling computer interest in older adults: the role of age, education, computer knowledge, and computer anxiety. Hum. Factors **41**, 345–355 (1999)

18. Kelly, C.L., Charness, N.: Issues in training older adults to use computers. Behav. Inf. Technol. **14**(2), 107–120 (1995)

19. Kubeck, J.E., Miller-Albrecht, S.A., Murphy, M.D.: Finding information on the World Wide Web: exploring older adult's exploration. Educ. Gerontechnol. **25**, 167–183 (1999)

20. Mead, S.E., Sit, R.A., Rogers, W.A.: Influences of general computer experience and age on library database search performance. Behav. Inf. Technol. **19**(2), 107–123 (2000)

21. Sjölinder, M., Höök, K., Nilsson, L.-G.: The effect of age-related cognitive differences, task complexity and prior internet experience in the use of an on-line grocery shop. Spat. Cogn. Comput. **3**(1), 61–84 (2003)

22. Broady, T., Chan, A., Caputi, P.: Comparison of older and younger adults' attitudes towards and abilities with computers: implications for training and learning. Br. J. Educ. Technol. **41**(3), 473–485 (2010). https://doi.org/10.1111/j.1467-8535.2008.00914.x

23. Sjölinder, M., Scandurra, I.: Effects of using care professionals in the development of social technology for elderly. In: Zhou, J., Salvendy, G. (eds.) ITAP 2015. LNCS, vol. 9194, pp. 181–192. Springer, Cham (2015). https://doi.org/10.1007/978-3-319-20913-5_17

24. Cooper, A.: The Inmates Are Running the Asylum. Macmillan Publishing Co., Inc., Indianapolis (1999). ISBN 0672316498

25. Sjölinder, M., et al.: A multi-disciplinary approach in the development of a stroke rehabilitation tool. In: Kurosu, M. (ed.) HCI 2014. LNCS, vol. 8512, pp. 351–362. Springer, Cham (2014). https://doi.org/10.1007/978-3-319-07227-2_34

26. Sjölinder, M., Scandurra, I., Avatare Nõu, A., Kolkowska, E.: To meet the needs of aging users and the prerequisites of innovators in the design process - lessons learned from three pilot projects. In: Proceedings of HCI International 2016, Toronto, Canada, 17–22 July 2016 (2016)

27. Sjölinder, M., Scandurra, I., Avatare Nou, A., Kolkowska, E.: Using care professionals as proxies in the design process of welfare technology – perspectives from municipality care. In: Zhou, J., Salvendy, G. (eds.) ITAP 2017. LNCS, vol. 10297, pp. 184–198. Springer, Cham (2017). https://doi.org/10.1007/978-3-319-58530-7_13

28. Sjölinder, M., Avatare Nöu, A., Fristedt, J.: ICT services for nursing homes – a needs analysis. In: The 11th World Conference of Gerontechnology, St. Petersburg, Florida, USA, 7–11 May 2018 (2018)

Active Participation of Older Adults in the Development of Stimulus Material in an Storytelling Context

Torben Volkmann[✉], Deniz Akyildiz, Nikolas Knickrehm, Fabian Vorholt, and Nicole Jochems

Institut für Multimediale und Interaktive Systeme, Universität zu Lübeck, Ratzeburger Allee 160, 23562 Lübeck, Germany
{volkmann,jochems}@imis.uni-luebeck.de,
{deniz.akyildiz,nikolas.knickrehm,fabian.vorholt}@student.uni-luebeck.de

Abstract. Information and communication technology is of great importance in our society an became an integral part of our every day life. However, older adult's acceptance and technology adoption rate still lacks behind. To address this issue, older adults have to be actively involved as co-authors in the development process to ensure that products meet the right requirements. The Historytelling project relies heavily on the integration of older adults in the whole human centered design projects and aims to compensate age-related deficits and addresses their strengths such as life-experience. It offers the possibility to document and share personal life stories. In addition to content-related aspects, such as the design of stimulus material for stories inspiration, the project aims at using participatory methodological aspects. Thus, this paper presents two workshops with 14 participants which dealt with the evaluation of stimulus material and a web-based prototype. The evaluation served as a good method for gathering the required information regarding stimulus material and the evaluation of the prototype. We could show that pictures, concise questions and unfamiliar stories worked best to stimulate personal stories, especially if they are personalized to the authors.

Keywords: Older adults · Participatory design · Storytelling · Stimulus material

1 Introduction

Information and communication technologies have never pervaded society more and thus have become an integral part of everyday life. However, the acceptance and usage of technology of older adults still lacks behind, which leads to social exclusion, making it imperative to consider older adults in the development process to achieve the best possible accessibility and usability [3,5,10]. To ensure that products meet the right requirements, it is essential to actively integrate the older age group as co-authors to technology [8,22].

© Springer Nature Switzerland AG 2020
Q. Gao and J. Zhou (Eds.): HCII 2020, LNCS 12207, pp. 84–95, 2020.
https://doi.org/10.1007/978-3-030-50252-2_7

The Historytelling (HT) project remains heavily on the integration of older adults in the whole human centered design process and engages them from early on in the project to cooperatively create technology [20]. It aims to compensate age-related deficits and addresses strengths such as life-experience. Thus, HT is a social networking site, offering older adults the possibility to document and share personal life stories and categorize them regarding their historical, temporal and local context. HT has influence on a personal, family and group as well as on a societal level. On the personal level it provides, for instance, the possibility for biographical work, cognitive training, life long learning and confrontation with the own past. On the family and group level it fosters the connection between family and friends, creates new bonds between people and promotes inter-generational knowledge transfer. On a societal level, HT offers a tool for multi-perspective history and active participation in the society.

There are always two aspects relevant in the HT development process: In addition to content-related aspects, such as the design of stimulus material, we are invested in participatory methodological aspects. Thus, this paper presents two workshops which dealt with evaluation of stimulus material and evaluation of prototypes. The workshops used guidelines regarding recruiting, procedure and atmosphere and methods acting as a practical example of this approach [16].

One important aspect for the success of HT is the question of how to engage older adults to tell their personal life stories. Remembering and sharing autobiographic life stories is different than telling fictional stories and the "autobiographic memory" is essential to access these information. These information are stored in three layers of specificity [4]. These are called the layer of life periods, the layer of general events and the layer of event specific knowledge [12]. An important role in this regards are stimulus materials. If the person has a personal connection to a stimulus material, it can be used as a trigger to provoke mental images. Stimulus material can be of various forms, such as photos, pieces of music or objects [2,9]. Research on stimulus material focuses mostly on the health sector or fictional storytelling, but lacks of research in regard of autobiographical stories [13,14,17,18]. First findings in triggering memories for HT were already published. There, it could be shown that there has to be a strong emphasize on stimulus material and first design indications were found [19]. Further insights are necessary to provide better guidelines for presenting stimulus material and media usage.

2   Method

Two workshops were conducted to get insights regarding stimulus material and to evaluate a prototype based on the learnings in [19]. Particular attention was paid to ensure compliance with the guidelines published by [16] regarding the active involvement of older adults in the human centered design process. See Table 1 for an overview of the guidelines. The stimulus material was tested regarding the appeal, inspirational power and emotionality. Different types of stimulus material were provided: images, unfamiliar stories, questions, dates and audio. Additionally, a web based prototype was tested, which included the tested stimulus material, based on the HT style guide [21].

Table 1. Guidelines for active participation of older adults. The table is based on [16]. A more detailed version can be found there.

Recruitment	
Engage with group leaders	G1
Emphasize reciprocity when recruiting	G2
Procedure and Atmosphere	
Plan for social engagement	G3
Overestimate the scheduled time	G4
Methods	
Accommodate participants' wishes	G5
Establish fallbacks	G6
Use abstract description of technology	G7

2.1 Procedure

Recruiting and communication with participants was done indirectly via the group leaders of the "Deutscher Frauenring e.V." and the German Association of RuralWomen on a telephone interview, in which the procedure was also discussed in advance (G1). The "Deutscher Frauenring" is an independent, nonpartisan and interdenominational nation wide women's association and a member organisation of international women's associations [6]. The German Association of RuralWomen is the largest women's association in Germany and represents the interests of all women and their families in rural areas [7].

The workshops were divided into five parts:

- Presentation of the topic and introduction of the participants
- Filling in questionnaires
- Open question and answer session
- Stimulus material evaluation
- Prototype evaluation
- Discussion

There was planned time between each section to leave room for further questions and social interaction between the participants as well as between participants and workshop facilitators (G3 & G4).

First, a round of introductions was held with cards from a game called "Dixit" which help with creative thinking and idea generation [11]. Participants were encouraged to use images on these cards to introduce the other participants to an event in their past (G3). See Fig. 1 for exemplary cards.

Fig. 1. Picture of exemplary Dixit cards used to stimulate participants' creative thinking.

Second, questionnaires were provided regarding demographic data and affinity for technology interaction (ATI, [1]). After that, an open question and answer session was held. The topics were:

- In what situations do you tell stories?
- Who are you telling stories to?
- What motivates you?
- What stops you from telling certain stories?

While the methods mentioned above were carried out in the groups, the following methods were conducted individually.

For designing the stimulus material, various materials were prior printed out and glued on a large wrapping paper (G7). The topics of the stimulus materials were childhood and family (personal stimulus material), GDR and the attacks on 9/11 (historical stimulus material) as well as holidays and wedding (general stimulus material) [15]. The offered media were images, unfamiliar stories of the topic, questions, dates and audio.

Every participant got his or her own wrapping paper of material to avoid group effects and the arrangement of themes was randomized. The participants had the task to label the stimulus material based on different categories with sticky dots:

– Is it appealing? (red)
– Can I come up with a story about that? (blue)
– Is this material emotionally moving? (green)

Each participants individually chose three items which were appealing (pink), he could tell a story about (purple) and that he found emotionally moving (green).

The aim of the prototype evaluation was to evaluate initial concepts and identify first usability problems. In particular, information regarding navigation, use of stimulus material and saving stimulus collections was gathered. The prototype was not fully functional, only some areas were clickable. Thus, the participants had to carry out a task and no deeper exploration was possible. Comments and interactions were recorded through the think aloud method, note taking and screen capturing. See Fig. 2 for a screenshot of the evaluated prototype.

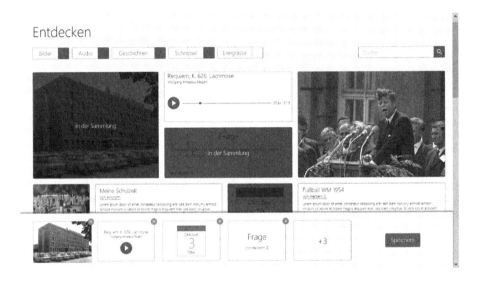

Fig. 2. Web based high fidelity prototype used in the evaluation with filter options at the top, personal collection at the bottom and public stimulus material in between.

Lastly, the results of all participants regarding the stimulus material evaluation were compiled on another wrapping paper and were open for discussion. Answers were recorded in writing by the workshop facilitators.

3 Results

The first workshop lasted 3 h and was carried out in rooms of the university. The second workshop lasted 8 h and was carried out at the home of the group leader of the "Landfrauen". The results concern especially the preferred topics of the presented stimulus material and the evaluation of the media. Also, the results regarding the prototype evaluation can help in the further development and refinement of the prototype.

3.1   Participants

At the first workshop 5 older adults (2 male, 3 female) aged from 66 to 77 (M = 72.4, SD = 4.2) from the social environment of "Deutscher Frauenring" took part. At the second workshop 9 older adults (1 male, 8 female) aged from 51 to 78 (M = 67.4, SD = 8.7) from the German Association of RuralWomen were participating. The first group scored 3.9 (SD = 0.4, N = 4) on the Affinity for Technology Interaction on a scale from 1 to 6 (ATI, [1]). The questionnaire of one person could not be evaluated because one value was missing. The second group scored 3.5 (SD = 0.8).

3.2   Question and Answer Session

The open question and answer session resulted in various contributions that are summarized by the posed question in the following.

Situation to Share Stories. The frequency in which participants shared stories were very diverse, ranging from "hardly ever" to "non-stop". Obstacles to telling stories may be the fear to tell anything not interesting. Most participants answered that storytelling depends on the context they are in and that stories often emerge from conversations with friends and family in more intimate situations or situations that remind of the past.

Persons to Share Stories with. Like the situations to share stories, also the persons to share stories with were diverse, but children and grandchildren were mentioned most frequently. Also, colleagues, friends and relatives of the same age were mentioned. Two persons mentioned that not the person is the most relevant aspect but the situation they are in.

Motivation to Share Stories. Three topics regarding the motivation to share stories emerged. The participants stated that the exchange, especially about mutual travel and events on which everyone in a discussion can participate in are a key motivation to share stories.

Second, the participants acknowledge the rise in self-esteem, when they can pass on knowledge, insights and old stories. Thus, they can make contributions on particular topics and can also learn from other experiences.

Situation and context is, again, key for sharing stories. Stories often develop through a conversation and questions can push a story in various directions, even single keywords may be sufficient.

Obstacles to Share Stories. Participants stated, there are three obstacles to share stories: Particular themes, particular people and particular atmospheres. Topics that prevent people from passing on are stories that drag them down emotionally, such as stories about diseases, war, childhood traumata or those which are too private, intimate or embarrassing. If there are persons present, participants do not sympathise with, they are not likely to tell their stories. A lack of trust also hinders storytelling. Likewise, the willingness to share stories is depending on the right discussion atmosphere. One participant stated that there must be a certain sentiment that a story is "is in good hands".

Selection of Topics. Based on the sticky dots distribution, the preferred topics were childhood (12), family (10) and the terror attacks of 9/11 (9). See Fig. 3 for a graphical comparison. In open discussions, further ideas came apparent, in particular offering stimulus material regarding hobbies and occupations were wishes of the participants.

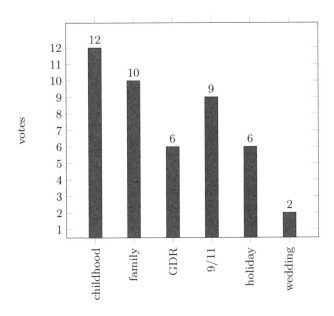

Fig. 3. Votes regarding topics of presented stimulus material. Each participant voted three times.

Figure 4 shows the arrangement of the stimulus material for one participant. The sticky dots indicating the participants preferences are also in this picture.

Afterwards, the point distribution suggestions for further topics were discussed within the group. Most important for their rating was their personal connection to a topic. A lack of connection often resulted in the selection of other materials. Challenges in the selection of materials are diverse. The participants declared that there may be no connection to a particular topic due to relatedness, such as the GDR or participants were too young or too old to have knowledge about a topic. But also personal preferences regarding topics influence the rating of stimulus material. One participant stated that she liked the topic

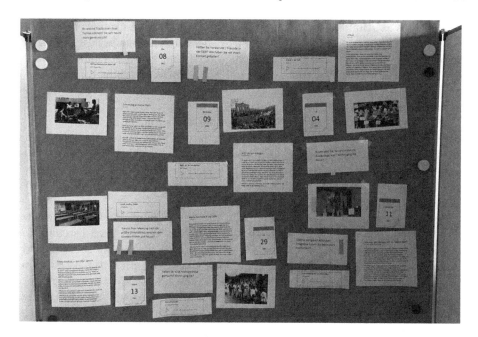

Fig. 4. Stimulus material was pinned to wrapping paper. Each participant individually chose three items he found appealing (pink), he could tell a story about (purple) and that he found emotionally moving (green). (Color figure online)

"school" and "holiday" and another participant disliked the topic "marriage". Emotional relevancy was also a discussed aspect, since participants stated that they need a emotional connection to the topic. On the other hand, participants reported that some topics may have a general relevance. They would like to share stories which have a reference to an historic event these are the stories that the next generation is more interested in, but have to be careful, because the stimulus material must not be too general either. Participants also shared suggestions for further topics, they would like to see in HT. Among these were school time, family feasts, birth of (grand)children, exams, comparisons of then and now, work, friendship, animals and regional topics.

Choice of Medium. In addition to the preference of topics, the effects of certain types of media were evaluated and classified. The results are presented according to appeal, inspirational power and emotionality. The provided questions scored highest on all three categories followed by stories and pictures. See Fig. 5 for more detailed information. A lot of comments focussing on the differences of several media types were collected. Only one participant stated that the presented media are nearly equivalent and that the topics are of more importance when telling stories.

Questions as stimulus for telling and writing stories were liked overall which is also reflected in the distribution of points. Especially, the conciseness was rated positively. On the other hand, participants stated that the particular questions used in the study lacked of conciseness did not address the right topics. Questions should acknowledge personal and emotional preferences to really inspire the participants.

The participants did not like Dates. Neither their appeal nor their inspirational or emotional characteristics were appreciated. They stated that there are only some specific dates that would work as inspiration, such as marriage dates and birthday but other than that there is no emotional connection to specific dates. As an improvement, participants suggested that a combination of texts and dates could be helpful to match dates and events.

Like dates, audio was rated low among the participants. Although the low rate of appeal, the participants commented that they overall liked listening to the audio, especially to short snippets such as "goal calls" at the soccer world championships 1954. Using audio presented two dilemmas. First, the used audio did not trigger emotions in the participants and thus did not work as a trigger for stories and second, participants stated that they rather use audio for collecting thoughts. Again, participants reported that the specific selection of audio was not appealing.

Pictures were liked among most of the participants. They stated that they are very appealing, of high relevance and can be more expressive than any other type of media. On the other hand, some of the selected pictures did not inspire the participants because the personal connection was missing.

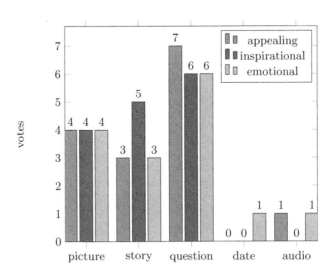

Fig. 5. Votes regarding the preferred media representation of the stimulus material.

Stories of events were rated as inspirational among the participants but lacked in the appeal and emotion. Regarding the appeal, especially the length and the style of the texts were commented as in need of improvement. They suggested to focus on headings and short text passages instead.

Prototype Evaluation. For the evaluation of the interface, it became apparent that especially the clear structure of the interface was assessed positively. Also, the participants rested their attention on images a long time. Half of the participants stated that pictures were most appealing, the other half stated that questions images were more important. Stimulus material was often not clicked and thus the detailed view with further information was not assessed.

4 Discussion

Due to the wishes of the second group, the workshop took part at the group leader's home and the timetable of the workshop had to be adjusted (G5, G6). The participants arrived with time delays in groups of two. Thus, no introductions of the participants were carried out and the group discussions were executed in every small group.

It could be shown, that concise questions, pictures and unfamiliar stories worked best for stimulating personal stories, but the participants still had improvement proposals, especially regarding the presented topics. They stated, that they disliked some of the presented material, because they did not have an emotional connection to it. Thus, they could not tell a story inspired by these materials. Additionally, since the personal preferences of each participant was of high importance, for further HT development ways must be explored how data can be collected from users without making them feel insecure or exploited.

The low interest in the media type audio may be due to the presentation of the medium. Representative audio stimulus material in the form of an audio player was glued on the wrapping paper and then played externally by the workshop facilitators when selected.

Participants stated multiple times that atmosphere and people are important factors for sharing personal life stories and they would share particular stories only with particular people. Thus, there must be a strong emphasis on a user interface that offers a warm and welcoming atmosphere. This also shows us that a system that can be used on different devices at any time, such as Historytelling, is a good way to support telling and sharing personal life stories.

5 Conclusion

The conducted workshops served as a good method for gathering the required information regarding the type of stimulus material and the evaluation of the high fidelity prototype. In particular the combination of open discussions with the target group and individual task-based evaluation worked well. Also, the guidelines proposed by [16] supported the planning phase and the conduction of the workshops.

Further research must be conducted for example in terms of the reliability of outcomes of workshops held following the guidelines presented. The question arises as to whether the location of a workshop and thus the necessary adaptation has an effect on the results. Thus, we see this workshop as a good starting point for the practical implementation of the suggested guidelines. Nevertheless, further research is needed to identify more advanced guidelines which are relevant to the planning and conducting of workshops for older adults.

Currently, the individual components of HT are further refined and new input methods such as voice user input are implemented and tested, so that the HT system can be tested in a field study soon.

Acknowledgements. We would like to thank all participants of the Historytelling project. Without them, this research could not be done.

References

1. Attig, C., Wessel, D., Franke, T.: Assessing personality differences in human-technology interaction: an overview of key self-report scales to predict successful interaction. In: Stephanidis, C. (ed.) HCI 2017. CCIS, vol. 713, pp. 19–29. Springer, Cham (2017). https://doi.org/10.1007/978-3-319-58750-9_3
2. Butler, R.N.: Successful aging and the role of the life review. J. Am. Geriatr. Soc. **22**(12), 529–535 (1974)
3. Coelho, J., Rito, F., Luz, N., Duarte, C.: Prototyping TV and tablet Facebook interfaces for older adults. In: Abascal, J., Barbosa, S., Fetter, M., Gross, T., Palanque, P., Winckler, M. (eds.) INTERACT 2015. LNCS, vol. 9296, pp. 110–128. Springer, Cham (2015). https://doi.org/10.1007/978-3-319-22701-6_9
4. Conway, M.A., Pleydell-Pearce, C.W.: The construction of autobiographical memories in the self-memory system. Psychol. Rev. **107**(2), 261–288 (2000). https://doi.org/10.1037/0033-295X.107.2.261
5. Demirbilek, O., Demirkan, H.: Universal product design involving elderly users: a participatory design model. Appl. Ergon. **35**(4), 361–370 (2004). https://doi.org/10.1016/j.apergo.2004.03.003
6. Deutscher Frauenring e.V.: Deutscher frauenring - website des deutscher frauenring e.v. (2019). https://deutscher-frauenring.de/. Accessed 02 Jan 2020
7. Deutscher LandFrauenVerband e.V.: deutscher landfrauen verband e.v. (2019). https://www.landfrauen.info/. Accessed 02 Jan 2020
8. Eisma, R., Dickinson, A., Goodman, J., Syme, A., Tiwari, L., Newell, A.: Early user involvement in the development of information technology-related products for older people. Univers. Access Inf. Soc. **3**(2), 131–140 (2004). https://doi.org/10.1007/s10209-004-0092-z
9. Hölzle, C., Jansen, I.: Ressourcenorientierte Biografiearbeit. Springer, Heidelberg (2011)
10. Kopeć, W., Nielek, R., Wierzbicki, A.: Guidelines towards better participation of older adults in software development processes using a new spiral method and participatory approach. In: Proceedings of the 11th International Workshop on Cooperative and Human Aspects of Software Engineering, CHASE 2018, pp. 49–56. ACM, New York (2018). https://doi.org/10.1145/3195836.3195840

11. Kwiatkowska, J., Szóstek, A., Lamas, D.: (Un)structured sources of inspiration: comparing the effects of game-like cards and design cards on creativity in co-design process. In: Proceedings of the 13th Participatory Design Conference: Research Papers, PDC 2014, vol. 1, pp. 31–39. ACM, New York (2014). https://doi.org/10.1145/2661435.2661442
12. Maercker, A., Forstmeier, S.: Der Lebensrückblick in Therapie und Beratung. Springer, Heidelberg (2012)
13. Mergler, N.L., Faust, M., Goldstein, M.D.: Storytelling as an age-dependent skill: oral recall of orally presented stories. Int. J. Aging Hum. Dev. **20**(3), 205–228 (1985). https://doi.org/10.2190/31UP-QEPE-24A0-E46G
14. Park, D.C., Puglisi, J.T., Sovacool, M.: Memory for pictures, words, and spatial location in older adults: evidence for pictorial superiority1. J. Gerontol. **38**(5), 582–588 (1983). https://doi.org/10.1093/geronj/38.5.582
15. Rubin, D.C., Rahhal, T.A., Poon, L.W.: Things learned in early adulthood are remembered best. Mem. Cogn. **26**(1), 3–19 (1998). https://doi.org/10.3758/BF03211366
16. Sengpiel, M., Volkmann, T., Jochems, N.: Considering older adults throughout the development process-the HCD+ approach. In: de Waard, D., et al. (eds.) Proceedings of the Human Factors and Ergonomics Society Europe Chapter 2018 Annual Conference, HFES, pp. 5–15 (2019). http://hfes-europe.org
17. Steiner, K.E., Moher, T.G.: Graphic storywriter: an interactive environment for emergent storytelling. In: Proceedings of the SIGCHI Conference on Human Factors in Computing Systems, CHI 1992, pp. 357–364. Association for Computing Machinery, New York (1992). https://doi.org/10.1145/142750.142831
18. Stone, T.E., Levett-Jones, T.: A comparison of three types of stimulus material in undergraduate mental health nursing education. Nurse Educ. Today **34**(4), 586–591 (2014). https://doi.org/10.1016/j.nedt.2013.07.014. http://www.sciencedirect.com/science/article/pii/S0260691713002657
19. Volkmann, T., Grosche, D., Sengpiel, M., Jochems, N.: What can I say?: presenting stimulus material to support storytelling for older adults. In: Proceedings of the 10th Nordic Conference on Human-Computer Interaction, NordiCHI 2018, pp. 696–700. ACM, New York (2018). https://doi.org/10.1145/3240167.3240256
20. Volkmann, T., Sengpiel, M., Jochems, N.: Historytelling: a website for the elderly a human-centered design approach. In: Proceedings of the 9th Nordic Conference on Human-Computer Interaction, NordiCHI 2016, pp. 100:1–100:6. ACM, New York (2016). https://doi.org/10.1145/2971485.2996735
21. Volkmann, T., Unger, A., Sengpiel, M., Jochems, N.: Development of an age-appropriate style guide within the historytelling project. In: Zhou, J., Salvendy, G. (eds.) HCII 2019. LNCS, vol. 11592, pp. 84–97. Springer, Cham (2019). https://doi.org/10.1007/978-3-030-22012-9_7
22. Xie, B., et al.: Connecting generations: developing co-design methods for older adults and children. Behav. Inf. Technol. **31**(4), 413–423 (2012)

A Study of the Rubber Mat Product Design for Electric Scooter

An-Jen Yang, Jui-Hung Cheng$^{(\boxtimes)}$, and Yu-Shi Huang

Department of Mold and Die Engineering, National Kaohsiung University of Science and Technology, No. 415, Jiangong Road, Sanmin District, Kaohsiung City 80778, Taiwan
{1105192110,rick.cheng,f108147114}@nkust.edu.tw

Abstract. Taiwan is one of the countries with the highest density of motorcycles in the world. However, under the trend of environmental protection awareness, more people are riding electric scooters. They like personalized and unique accessories, but the original design didn't provide many choices, lots of restrictions, and high prices, so the demands for personalized style accessories in the aftermarket parts had greatly increased and had multiple choices for customers. The scooters are the most common means of transportation in Taiwan metropolitan areas. Besides the convenience and mobility for short transportation, carrying goods is also this local unique demand. The structure of motorcycles is generally divided into two different models: the motorcycle with clutch and the scooter without the clutch. The motorcycle mainly uses the rear shelf to carry items, while most of the scooter uses the footrest area. For the different appearance of electric scooters with the same rubber mat design, this research is mainly to integrate Gogoro2, Gogoro3, and Aeon Ai-1 Sport. Due to the shape of the existing foot pedal is designed as a curved surface for aesthetic appearance, but it will cause instability for the placement of items and affect riding safety. In terms of design integration, this research will improve the flatness of the footrest surface, the joint ability of the curved surface of the pedal, the addition of drainage design, and the improvement of anti-staining by rubber molding. During the research process, market survey, user analysis, usability engineering, product design, and other methods were used to increase user riding comfort, shipping safety, meanwhile, a simple and intuitive design also improved the human-machine interface problems. From the feasibility research results, this new product has obvious effects no matter whether it is improving user satisfaction, increasing sales volume, etc. This research result can provide an academic or industry based on this new product design process to develop a related series of products.

Keywords: Electric scooter · Aftermarket · Usability engineering · Product design · Rubber molding

1   Introduction

Today, Taiwan is one of the countries with the highest scooter density in the world; with a population of about 23 million, the number of scooters has reached 13.99 million. With

Q. Gao and J. Zhou (Eds.): HCII 2020, LNCS 12207, pp. 96–108, 2020.
https://doi.org/10.1007/978-3-030-50252-2_8

the growing awareness of environmental protection, more and more motorcycle riders are opting for electric scooters. This study mainly integrates Gogoro Taiwan Limited and Aeon Motor scooter models, which are unstable when loaded due to the curvature of the body foot section. The study is designed to explore the need for the use of the footrest. The design and the market of electric scooter accessories and the introduction of shared designs to increase model usage were discussed, leading to the development of a design proposal for electric scooter accessories. Integrating the above-mentioned, the main motivations for the study are as follows:

1. Discuss what is the current market demand for electric scooters in Taiwan.
2. Understand out the factors the electric scooter community considers when choosing the footrest.
3. How to design a footrest that meets various design needs and aesthetics.

2 Literature Review

Focusing on the electric scooter industry, product design, thermoforming, documents on these various aspects were collected for examination purposes and to proceed with the discussion of this research, divided into a total of four phases - Phase 1 Overview of the Electric Scooter Industry, Phase II Discussion on Product Design Principles, Phase III Thermoforming Technology.

2.1 The Market of Green Electric Scooters

According to statistics compiled by the Taiwan Ministry of Transportation, Taiwan currently has a total of 139.92,000 scooters registered, the highest density in the world. In the small and densely populated Taiwan, scooters have become the first choice of transportation, they have high mobility, low maintenance costs, convenient parking, and so on. These advantages reveal the factors that have increased sales of scooters in Taiwan year on year. In recent years, with growing environmental awareness, green issues have continued to rise and environmental protection regulations have, also, become more stringent [1]. The Government has constantly been promoting electric scooters, increasing subsidies for the purchase of motor vehicles, and encouraging the public to purchase electric motorcycles [2]. However, before Gogoro was launched, Taiwan had only light electric scooters to choose from and their performances were only comparable to gasoline-fueled scooters with 50 cc engine displacement. However, their durability, indeed, was not as good as that of gasoline-fueled scooters, which led to a low purchase intention from the general public. After the introduction of Gogoro in 2015, on account of Gogoro's capability and dynamic performance being the standards for general motorcycles, coupled with the introduction of smart technology and the use of non-rechargeable primary cell replacement methods [3]. As soon as it made its appearance on the market, it has been a constant subject discussion. Although the high cost of research and development has resulted in higher pricing than the average general motorcycle, but the market share of Gogoro in the electric scooter market has reached 23.11% as at today. Moreover, with the continuous launch of various models of the Powered by Gogoro Network (PBGN), the electric scooter product range is gradually being made comprehensive to meet different types of consumers, and the vehicle models are becoming more affordable [4, 5]. The purchase threshold has also been lowered, and the wave of electric scooters is expected to continue to expand.

2.2 The User Product Design Discussion of Principles

User engineering differs from traditional design concepts and is a design process from the user's perspective [6]. If the user-focused consideration can be taken, the impact of individual subjective awareness is reduced. The important concepts and demonstrated user-centric design principles [7–9], as follows:

1. User both knowledge in the world and knowledge in the head
2. Simplify the structure of tasks
3. Make things visible: bridge the gulfs of execution and evaluation
4. Get the mapping right
5. Exploit the power of constraint, both natural and artificial
6. Design for error
7. When all else fails, standardize.

2.3 Thermoforming Technology

Since everyone is now striving for speed and efficiency, most plastic and rubber products are mainly injection molded. The main reason is that injection molding has high-production efficiency to the extent that it is widely used in our country. However, injection molding is not likely for manufacturing large-area products, because high pressure is required to completely inject the material into the die core of the product with a high ratio. If it is easy to cause filling shortages, short shots will occur [10]. Thermoforming has the advantage of being suitable for large-area products but has a slower manufacturing process cycle time than injection molding, mainly due to the heating and cooling process. The molding temperature is supplied by the machine heating installation unit and the entire mold must be at the average machining temperature to process thermoforming. After the hot pressure process is complete, it is also necessary to return from the machining temperature to the ejection temperature; therefore, the integral heating and cooling process greatly reduces the production efficiency of thermoforming [11]. The advantages of thermal pressure formation are no runners. The line temperature and pressure are low. Because there is no runner, the material is heated first in the mold. Therefore, the material flow is short during the molding process. And since the molding temperature is low, the contraction ratio of the product is low when it is cooled, and it is suitable for forming this product with a high, deep, wide-ratio size, low pressure, no risk of damage to the platform or mold, and a relatively longer machine life [12]. The thermoforming process showed in Fig. 1.

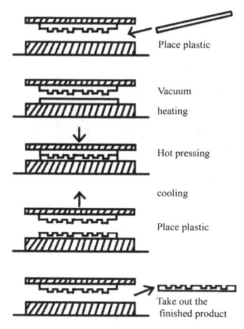

Fig. 1. Thermoforming process

3 Case Study Methodology

The previous chapter discussed the overview of the electric scooter industries in Taiwan, the product design principles and the thermoforming technology. The case study methodology is focused on market analysis of electric scooter, mat product design process, EPDM material selection, 3D printing prototype, mold engineering.

3.1 Market Analysis of Electric Scooter

In small but densely populated Taiwan, scooters have become the preferred transportation tools of the people in Taiwan. In recent years, with the influence of environmental awareness and backed by government subsidies, the number of electric scooters has continued to rise. This study selected to use Taiwan's largest electric scooter brand, Gogoro's (Gogoro Taiwan Limited) Gogoro 2, Gogoro 3 and PBGN Alliance's Aeon Ai-1 smart electric scooter (Aeon Motor), these vehicles are designed with the footrest partially curved for esthetic reasons (showed as Fig. 2 & Fig. 3), which can cause instability to the items and indirectly affect the safety of the vehicle. Users also indicated that the original factory products had low practicality and could not be smoothly loaded (showed as Fig. 4), the price was not affordable, they had poor abradability, had no anti-slip effect, the drainage performance was poor, they easily hid dirt resulting in appearance problems.

Fig. 2. The red area is footrest (Color figure online)

Fig. 3. The body part is curved

Fig. 4. The original product by Gogoro

3.2 Mat Product Design Process

All products are designed for a special purpose, so the primary function of product design is "practicality". This study follows the user engineering principles for product design and with user-centric consideration, focuses on user experience to understand the real needs of users, and sets up design solutions. The requirements, therefore, surface flattening, foot deck surface joint, an additional drainage system and a product appearance design. Common designs are also introduced, which, in addition to making more models available, can significantly reduce the cost of developing the products [13]. The shared design takes into account not only the user's usage situation but also the psychological feelings of the user. This design is easy to understand and use regardless of the user's experience, knowledge, and language skills.

The initial conceptual design of the creation's sketch (showed as Fig. 5), which was explored above, is easy to review and confirm the design direction, using Solidworks to validate the design and with 3D printing to verify whether the design meets the needs of the users. Figure 6 below shows a size 1 reduction in the appearance, the main purpose is to make more vehicles available for sharing. A size 2 increase in the appearance, the main purpose of the increase is to make the foot deck more spacious, and in addition to riding comfortably, the load is also more secure.

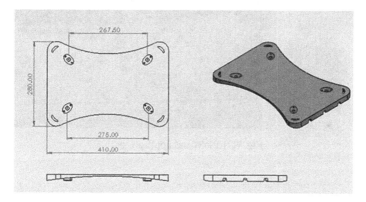

Fig. 5. Concept of mat product design

3.3 EPDM Material Selection

Before selecting materials, you must first understand the environment in which the product is used. The foot deck is exposed to sun, wind and rain every day, so its weather resistance needs to be very good. Materials suitable for the outdoor environment must be chosen and we, later, found that that most of the common sports tracks today are made of laid EPDM rubber granules (showed as Fig. 7). For automotive, truck and bus tires and non-tire components, including car radiators and heating hoses, seal strips are all made of EPDM. EPDM has excellent ozone resistance, superior to CR rubber and IIR rubber. It has, also, better weather resistance, suitable for the outdoor environment and

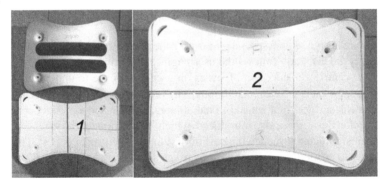

Fig. 6. Comparison of case study with original product

a good vibration absorption effect. This is a big improvement in comfort level for those users who ride long distances.

Fig. 7. EPDM and applications

3.3.1 3D Printing Prototype

3D printing is mainly used in the proofing process, where before printing, the heating section heats the materials (plastics, resin, nylon and so on) to a critical state so that it appears in a semi-fluid state. The semi-fluid material is then squeezed out, the extruded material is instantaneously solidified, and when one layer is completed, it moves into the next layer of extrusion until the entity is achieved. Since the machine is too small and the printing cannot be integrated, the pattern must be disassembled before proofing. We divided the product into 6 pieces and designed a double-top snap to prevent rotation and limit the freedom of the product (showed as Fig. 8). The prototype was assembled in the Aeon Ai-1 & Gogoro scooter that showed as Fig. 9, and confirmed function showed as Fig. 10.

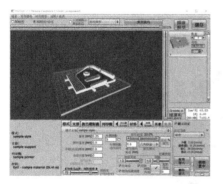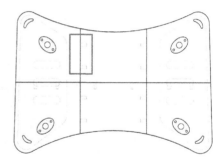

Fig. 8. 3D printing and divide drawings

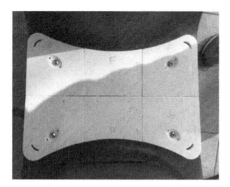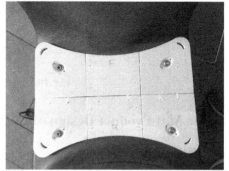

Fig. 9. Assembled in Aeon Ai-1 & Gogoro scooter

3.4 Mold Engineering

The mold design process must undergo design justification, design rationale, analysis of open-die, mechanism conception, design execution operations, take into account the background of processing technology and so on in order to produce results that meet customer expectations. Each mold set is the result of a new and independent design development process, and the quality of the product depends on the mold design. Molds are a critical tool in the production of various industrial products. Under competitive pressure, manufacturers must continuously upgrade their mold technical capabilities. The mold industry attaches great importance to technology, capital and high-added value. It is also the basic tool for the mass production of various products; therefore, molds have always had the title of Mother of the industry. The mold industry can be said to be the most important basic industry to promote the development of manufacturing industries.

Fig. 10. Confirm function

4   The Mat Product Design of Case Study

4.1   Design Idea Explanation

After discussing the above-mentioned sketch designs with the entrusted manufacturer, it was decided to use the third version as the final choice and the following 3D models were subsequently established to provide a clearer picture of the details. The following describes each of the detailed design features:

Step 1: Plane modeling
In order to accommodate steady carriage load for the user's needs, the first version of the sketch is drawn in the modeling feature with a focus on flatness showed as Fig. 11.

Step 2: Structural reinforcement
To increase the strength of the product structure, an additional wall structure is added to prevent the product from warping and deforming when the mold is formed (showed as Fig. 12).

Step 3: Non-slip function
In addition to using streaks in the non-slip sections, the surface of the product is protruded (on the mold surface) to increase the electric discharge spark erosion texture to make the non-slip effect more visible (showed as Fig. 13 & Fig. 14).

Step 4: Alleviated design
Remove unnecessary thickness from the back, in addition to allowing the product to shrink and stabilize the thicker areas evenly, the most important thing is to alleviate. The lighter a product for the user, the more energy conservation it can have on a vehicle, and for the manufacturer, the fewer materials used, the greater will be the reduction in costs (showed as Fig. 15).

Fig. 11. First sketch

Fig. 12. Second Sketch

Fig. 13. Third sketch

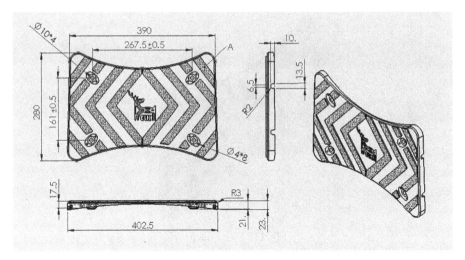

Fig. 14. Third plane figure

Fig. 15. Third back side

5 Conclusion

This creation is a collection of the views and needs of all parties via literature review and market survey, it is a case of academia-industry cooperation. As a result, the needs of the manufacturers, mold processing factories, dealers and end-users were arranged through interviews with them as a basis for discussion and history of the various design changes. And, in accordance with the user-centered design and various design principles, a complete design plan is proposed.

This study, as an academia-industry cooperation case, will not only enhance students' technical skills but also to put in practice what they have learned. It will also reduce the gap between the academic and industrial circles. The implementation of the study has so far been characterized by a number of problems, which are summarized as follows:

1. First, when designing products, you should not design only for existing problems and needs, you should create a list of requirements that will allow you to discuss products more quickly, and you will be able to provide a more accurate reference to design requirements for other future case designs.
2. After the design proposal, the mold processing factory has to review the engineering drawing several times before processing the mold. If the mold processing factory finds any suspicious problem, it should immediately enquire and communicate with the designer. In this case, the engineering drawings were sent to the mold processing plant without any proofreading before the trial mold, resulting in the first trial mold bearing defects in the product.
3. Designers need to be more careful and precise when drawing. In this case, several meetings were held with the mold processing factory to confirm the drawing, which not only increased the time for product development, but also tends to generate more problems for the product to hit the market.

After the completion of this research design, mass production and market launch will be carried out. The current product feedback is evaluated to meet a wide range of needs in various aspects including steady carriage loading, non-slip, inter-brand usage, and improved drainability. The research results are both, user and sales volume, have increased, proving that this study has achieved its goals and the project is feasible. The above provides reference for future designers, when designing products.

References

1. Hartmann, J., Germain, R.: Understanding the relationships of integration capabilities, ecological product design, and manufacturing performance. J. Clean. Prod. **92**, 196–205 (2015)
2. Hwang, J.J.: Sustainable transport strategy for promoting zero-emission electric scooters in Taiwan. Renew. Sustain. Energy Rev. **14**(5), 1390–1399 (2010)
3. Suen, S.H., Lin, B.M., Jang, J.S.C.: Strategy and construction of electric refueling system for electric scooter in Taiwan. In: 2013 World Electric Vehicle Symposium and Exhibition (EVS27), pp. 1–6. IEEE (2013)
4. Dombrowski, U., Engel, C., Schulze, S.: Scenario management for sustainable strategy development in the automotive aftermarket. In: Hesselbach, J., Herrmann, C. (eds.) Functional Thinking for Value Creation, pp. 285–290. Springer, Heidelberg (2011). https://doi.org/10.1007/978-3-642-19689-8_50
5. Dobrican, O.: Forecasting demand for automotive aftermarket inventories. Informatica Economica **17**(2) (2013)
6. Demirbilek, O., Sener, B.: Product design, semantics and emotional response. Ergonomics **46**(13–14), 1346–1360 (2003)
7. Sohaib, O., Khan, K.: Integrating usability engineering and agile software development: a literature review. In: 2010 International Conference on Computer Design and Applications, vol. 2, p. V2-32). IEEE, June 2010

8. Iqbal, H., Khan, M.F.: Assimilation of usability engineering and user-centered design using agile software development approach. Int. J. Mod. Educ. Comput. Sci. **6**(10), 23 (2014)

9. Norman, D.A., Draper, S.W.: User Centered System Design: New Perspectives on Human-Computer Interaction. CRC Press, Boca Raton (1986)

10. Martin, P.: Product design-process selection-process planning integration based on modeling and simulation. Int. J. Adv. Manuf. Technol. **77**(1–4), 187–201 (2015). https://doi.org/10.1007/s00170-014-6446-7

11. Yang, C.C., et al.: Control of hot runner type micro injection molding module. In: IECON 2007-33rd Annual Conference of the IEEE Industrial Electronics Society, pp. 2928–2933. IEEE (2007)

12. Stanek, M., Manas, D., Manas, M., Javorik, J.: Simulation of injection molding process. In: Proceedings of 13th WSEAS International Conference on Automatic Control, Modelling & Simulation, vol. 231, p. 234 (2011)

13. Liu, J., Cheng, Z., Ma, Y.: Product design-optimization integration via associative optimization feature modeling. Adv. Eng. Inform. **30**(4), 713–727 (2016)

Value and Values in Inclusive Design

Haiou Zhu[(⊠)], Thorsten Gruber, and Hua Dong

Loughborough University, Loughborough, UK
{H.Zhu,T.Gruber,H.Dong}@lboro.ac.uk

Abstract. As an ethical design approach embedding with the human value of inclusiveness, inclusive design could contribute to economic value creation. However, research on the relationship between economic value and human values in inclusive design has seldom been explored. This preliminary literature review focuses on how value and values have been discussed in inclusive design research. The findings first present the evolving conceptions of inclusive design that formulate and transform the understanding of value and values. Then, existing literature on the economic value of inclusive design, and inclusive design for human values at both individual and social levels are reviewed respectively. We categorize these disparate discussions into 'value creation' and 'value distribution' and propose opportunities for an integrated approach that would bridge discussions on the economic value and human values in future research.

Keywords: Inclusive design · Economic value · Human values · Value creation · Value distribution

1 Introduction

The value concept occupies a central position across all the social sciences [1] and its definition differs according to several disciplines. Rokeach [1] describes that 'The value concept has been employed in two distinctively different ways in human discourse. We will often say that a person has a value but also that an object has value'. While sociologists may be concerned with the origins of human values, economists may focus on the creation of economic value. In this paper, we adopt Rokeach's definition that a person's value means 'an enduring belief that a specific mode of conduct or end-state of existence is personally or socially preferable to an opposite or converse mode of conduct or end-state of existence'. In an economic paradigm, an object's value can be understood as value inherent in an object, which can be further interpreted from both the production perspective and the usage perspective [2]. From the production perspective, value is added through different stages of production [3]. The economic value of an artifact consists of profit and cost of producing it. From the usage perspective, value is perceived value [4] by users at the stage of use, which consists of consumer surplus and the sacrifice a user is willing to pay for. Then, the exchange value in monetary form, the price, is the reconcile between producers and users in the marketplace. In this paper, we use the term 'human values' to refer to a set of values that a person may have, the term

© Springer Nature Switzerland AG 2020
Q. Gao and J. Zhou (Eds.): HCII 2020, LNCS 12207, pp. 109–122, 2020.
https://doi.org/10.1007/978-3-030-50252-2_9

'economic value' to refer to the value of an object in the production context, and the term 'perceived value' to refer to the value assessed by users in the usage context.

Inclusive design was first coined as a term to promote social inclusivity towards the ageing and disability population [5]; it has extended well into a business setting where mainstream products are designed more inclusively to reach a wider market [6]. As an ethical design approach embedding with the human value of inclusiveness, inclusive design could contribute to economic value creation. Although there exists research on the economic value of design [2], design for the value of inclusiveness [7] would involve discussions on human values. However, little research has looked at inclusive design from the perspective of value. How economic value or human values have been discussed in inclusive design should be made explicit to better understand the value concept in inclusive design.

This preliminary literature review includes studies focusing on conceptions of inclusive design and research examining the relationship between economic value, human values, and inclusive design. Regarding the conceptions of inclusive design, there is an expanding from the inclusion of physical and/or cognitive diversity to the inclusion of pluralistic human values [8]. Regarding inclusive design for economic value creation, existing studies are striving to build business cases and facilitate inclusive design to speak the language of business [9] for its value to 'be proven to decision-makers' [10]. Moreover, inclusive design for human values at both personal and social levels are explored from different perspectives. Based on the literature reviewed, this paper identifies that in addition to value creation through inclusive design, there exists a value distribution issue, which adds another dimension to the value discussion. Then, research questions are outlined for further investigation. This preliminary review presents:

a) the methodology of literature search and analysis;
b) the existing conceptions of inclusive design and the understandings of value and values in inclusive design;
c) results synthesizing theories from the above fields;
d) research questions that need further investigation.

2   Methodology

2.1   Data Collection

Table 1 summarizes three categories of data sources. The first category is eight prominent design journals, which were selected based on the ranking by Gemser et al. [11], considering both weighted index and popularity. The second category consists of six conference proceedings that were closely related to inclusive design research. Besides, three general academic databases (Web of Science, Scopus and Google Scholar) were used as complementary sources for literature not published in the above journals and proceedings. Instead of using the narrowed terms 'economic value', 'human values', 'value creation' or 'value distribution', we used more general terms such as 'value', 'values', 'economy/economic' and 'business case' to enlarge the searching space. These were searched with different combinations of 'inclusive design', 'universal design' and 'design for all' (we use inclusive design to refer to the three adjacent fields in this paper). We also included book chapters because they lay the groundwork for theoretical and conceptual discussion.

Table 1. List of literature review sources.

Category	Name
Design journals	Design Studies
	Design Issues
	Human-Computer Interaction
	Applied Ergonomics
	Journal of Engineering Design
	International Journal of Design
	The Design Journal
	Journal of Design Research
Conference proceedings	Cambridge Workshop on Universal Access and Assistive Technology (CWUAAT)
	The Include Conference
	Design Research Society (DRS)
	International Conference on Engineering Design (ICED)
	International Conference on Human-Computer Interaction (HCI)
	International Conference on Applied Human Factors and Ergonomics (AHFE)
Academic databases	Web of Science
	Scopus
	Google Scholar

However, the initial searching results showed that studies directly discussing the relationship between value and values and inclusive design were rare. Then, a 'snowball' approach was adopted to seek papers in the reference lists from the first search. Three aspects of selection criteria were considered: number of citations, correlation of study and year of publication.

2.2 Data Analysis

We found 118 results from the above search, including 64 papers from design journals, 33 papers from conference proceedings, 12 papers from complementary searches and 9 published books. After reading the abstract and keywords of these papers, 76 papers and 4 published books were eliminated mainly because of two reasons: replicated ones and those mentioned value or values but not as the core purpose of discussion in their papers. Then, 33 papers and 5 published books were selected for further reading.

A summarization of the title, keywords, abstract, and key points that directly related to value and values was conducted. By identifying links to this review and writing down the critique, insights were generated effectively for further analysis. Another imperative we found during data analysis was to better understand the definitions and core concepts of inclusive design. Although the focus of this review is to investigate the discussion of value and values, the evolving conceptions would formulate and transform our understanding of them. Therefore, the following findings start with the evolving conceptions of inclusive design and continue with the core discussions of value and values.

3   Findings

3.1   Conceptions of Inclusive Design

Four constructs about conceptions of inclusive design are identified (see Table 2): sample definitions, from margins to mainstream, redefining ageing and disability, and diversity beyond ageing and ability. They cover the definitions, especially those defined by influential organizations in the field, and core concepts such as ageing, disability, and diversity.

The terms inclusive design, universal design, and design for all are used in the design field to call for the inclusion of various forms of human differences, including age, ability, gender, ethnicity, lifestyle, and culture. These definitions seem straightforward and not difficult to understand. However, as a practice-based activity, methods and processes to design and realize those inclusions could be intricate. For example, the i~design program [12] set out to explore standards and metrics to measure inclusivity directly, which was proved to be problematic at first [9]. But the reversing concept of design exclusion was developed to measure the number of people who would be excluded when the demand for using a particular product or service exceeds the capabilities of the user.

The evolving conceptions have pushed the boundaries of inclusive design and have advanced the understanding of its core concepts. The theme 'design for our future selves' [18] in the first special issue of Applied Ergonomics in 1993 is still applied to contemporary context, but there has been a shift of thinking from designing assistive technology for the margins, i.e. the ageing and disabled population, to designing mainstream products that everyone can use [6]. Discussions on redefining ageing and disability revealed reflections and improvement of design methods and processes. For example, Raghavendra et al. [21] question who is 'an older person' and suggest looking at cognitive abilities instead of chronological age. Dankl [22] explores the transformation of preconceptions on ageing and old age using design anthropology, participatory and speculative design. In terms of disability, Clarkson and Coleman [9] emphasize a change from the medical model to the social model in which people are disabled by designs and environments. Sørensen Overby and Ryhl [23] further propose a Bio-Psycho-Social Model to understand disability.

Furthermore, Nickpour and Dong [19] highlight the need to extend definitions and dimensions of 'inclusion beyond the conventional age & ability axes'. Other than the ability variation, Waller et al. [24] suggest an understanding of diversity could be broadened to real-world contexts, lifestyle, aspirations, gender, and past experiences. Lim, Giacomin and Nickpour [8] emphasize the non-physical inclusivity, the psychosocial

Table 2. Conceptions of inclusive design.

Construct	Authors	Conceptions
Sample definitions	British Standards Institute [13]	Inclusive design: design of mainstream products and/or services that are accessible to, and usable by, as many people as reasonably possible on a global basis, in a wide variety of situations and to the greatest extent possible without the need for special adaptation or specialized design
	Keates and Clarkson [12]	Design exclusion: arises when the demand for using a particular product or service, within a given environment, exceeds the capabilities of the user
	Design Council [14]	Inclusive design: a general approach to designing in which designers ensure that their products and services address the needs of the widest possible audience, irrespective of age or ability
	Inclusive Design Research Centre [15]	Inclusive design: considers the full range of human diversity with respect to ability, language, culture, gender, age and other forms of human difference
	Centre for Universal Design [16]	Universal design: design and composition of an environment so that it can be accessed, understood and used to the greatest extent possible by all people regardless of their age, size, ability or disability
	European Institute for Design and Disability [17]	Design for all: design for human diversity, social inclusion and equality
From margins to mainstream	Coleman [18]	designing for our future selves
	Clarkson, Coleman, Keates and Lebbon [6]	from designing specifically for disability and ageing towards the integration of them in mainstream society, from designing assistive technology to mainstream products
	Nickpour and Dong [19]	moving from 'physicality' to overall 'quality' of life, exploring nonphysical and psychosocial elements of inclusivity
	Dong [20]	The core of inclusive design is human-centred design for products that are useful, usable, desirable and sustainable

(*continued*)

Table 2. (*continued*)

Construct	Authors	Conceptions
Redefining ageing and disability	Raghavendra et al. [21]	looking at cognitive abilities instead of chronological age
	Dankl [22]	using design anthropology, participatory and speculative design to support a transformation of preconceptions on ageing and old age
	Clarkson and Coleman [9]	from medical model to social model in which people are disabled by designs and environments
	Sørensen Overby and Ryhl [23]	a Bio-Psycho-Social Model to understand disability
Diversity beyond ageing and ability	Nickpour and Dong [19]	inclusion beyond the conventional age & ability axes
	Waller et al. [24]	broadening diversity to different real-world contexts, lifestyle, aspirations, gender, and past experiences
	Lim, Giacomin and Nickpour [8]	non-physical inclusivity: the psychosocial dimensions, including 'cognitive', 'emotional', 'social', and 'value' factors
	St John [25]	a cultural inclusion between non-Indigenous and Indigenous people in Australia using creative participation design
	Boess [26]	designing for self-inclusion and supporting emotional capability
	Nicholl et al. [27]	integrating inclusive and sustainable design to holistically cover 'people', 'profit' and 'planet'
	Evans [28]	to consider the role of aging population in addressing climate change

dimensions, including 'cognitive', 'emotional', 'social', and 'value' factors. Boess [26] adds self-inclusion as an additional component by designing for emotional and experiential elements. These explorations broaden the understanding of diversity from different perspectives, but still with a focus on human beings. Another dimension of diversity and inclusivity, the environment, has been proposed. The Designing Our Tomorrow initiative [27] at the University of Cambridge intends to integrate inclusive and sustainable design to holistically cover 'people', 'profit' and 'planet'. Evans [28] also argues that the disparate inclusive design and sustainable design approaches would result in 'unsustainable inclusivity' and 'deterministic sustainability' outcomes. The two forces should work together to consider the role of the ageing population in addressing climate change.

The definitions of inclusive design are promoted to raise awareness and to re-configure the role of design in addressing social issues. This, however, 'to some degree downplays inclusive design as a distinct design movement' [29] on the one hand, and labels it as a moral driven design approach on the other hand. We argue that inclusive design can contribute to economic value creation. Working as a design methodology and a value orientation synchronously, inclusive design guides the design process to maximize the number of design beneficiaries. It is not an idealized ideology but a human-centred design approach that needs the participation of multi-stakeholders to co-create value [20]. Therefore, it is necessary to look at how both human values and economic value are discussed in the existing literature.

3.2 Inclusive Design for Economic Value Creation

One of the economic driving-forces to adopt an inclusive design approach is the ageing population with significant disposal income [30]. With the strengthening of government legislation and the increasing industry awareness of the market potential, the promotion of inclusive design has become a global phenomenon, but barriers remain due to economic, societal and cultural factors.

The Japanese industries, especially large corporations such as Toyota, Panasonic, TOTO and Fujitsu, are 'quickly awakening to the value of universal design' [31] in a super-aged society. But a study conducted by Kose [32] reveals that schemes of financial assistance for aged residents are not enough in the housing industry because of the lack of economic incentives. In the US, Fletcher et al. [33] identify two factors constraining the growth of universal design: attitudinal barriers from a defining individualism in the US society and legal mandates for accessibility. There are fewer design companies that adopt inclusive design out of their business awareness. While the 'design for all' concept in Scandinavia has moved 'from a purely social dimension to its business potential and in relation to Corporate Social Responsibility' [34]. Similarly, inclusive design emerged in the UK in the 1990s to challenge the ageing and disabled stereotypes, but the UK adopted a market-driven approach to address these design challenges at the beginning [9]. The term 'inclusive design' was first coined in 1994 by Coleman in the paper 'The case for inclusive design-an overview' [5] to exemplify its commercial benefits. Later, UK academia has focused on building business cases to help business decision-makers to see the commercial benefits for their businesses. Table 3 are selected business cases that featured the application of inclusive design in various industries.

The benefits that business organizations can obtain include wider market reach and revenue growth [30]; customer satisfaction and loyalty [24, 36]; product and service innovation [30, 35]; competitive advantages such as fulfilment of company social responsibility and better brand image [34]; and risk mitigation such as disability rights lawsuits and costly rectification work [24, 37]. What these business cases share is that the uptake of inclusive design depends on strategic design management, including the support from board members, a user-centred design process, and knowledge transfer to design practitioners. The BS 7000-6 [13] guide is a comprehensive document developed by the British Standards Institution to offer a start point for organizations to adopt inclusive design management for their businesses. Waller et al. [24] establish a set of success

Table 3. Selected business cases.

Authors	Company	Industry	Case descriptions and insights
Coleman, Topalian, Clarkson and Dong [30]	OXO Good Grips	Cookware	Develop new products with design consultancies constantly; not branded as inclusive design but for its easy to use by everyone; the annual growth rate of 30% since 1991; with over 50 staff but generated turnover more of a company ten times of its size
Chamberlain et al. [35]	British Telecommunications plc (BT)	Telecommunications	Senior management support is vital; inclusive design is better design other than just corporate social responsibility; adopted user-centered design part of business as usual and direct contact with a diverse range of end-users to inform the design
Benoit et al. [36]	Ferrari Enzo	Car Manufacturer	The average buyer of a Ferrari road car is nearing 50 and set to get older; better access and egress without compromising the sportiness
Fleck [37]	London 2012 Olympic and Paralympic Games	Architecture	Disabled people still face environmental, attitudinal and organizational barriers; experience of delivering the 2012 Games should be promoted to the built environment and business

criteria for an inclusive product: people (utility, usability and desirability), profit (commercial viability, technical viability and compatibility) and planet (resource consumption, waste control and energy efficiency). These criteria extend the understanding of inclusive design beyond profit, taking into consideration the user and the environment.

Another stream of research introduces social entrepreneurship or social innovation to address the issue of inclusivity [38–40]. These are committed mainly by non-profit organizations and government sectors to offer creative solutions for social issues. A further step is to explore an integrated way to solve social inclusion problems and to realize commercial success. For example, Rogers, Gill and Alley [40] propose a sustainable social innovation model to design and commercialize a product intended for inclusive use. It opens another opportunity for value co-creation through inclusive design in entrepreneurial activities.

The above research mainly focuses on the role of inclusive design in creating economic value from the perspective of production, either at the industrial level or at the firm level. An opposite position is from the users' perspective. Although the user-centred design has been constantly emphasized as the core principle of inclusive design [20], there exist few studies looking at value as perceived or created by users themselves. The same issue exists in the designers' perspective. Clarkson and Coleman [9] point out that knowledge transfer 'added a whole new dimension' to inclusive design research. Indeed, both business organizations and design practitioners are knowledge users, and what they need to know about foremost is the users, their characteristics, preferences, behaviours and decision-making. Together the value creation problem becomes a value co-creation between users, designers and business organizations. Further efforts should be made to demonstrate how value is co-created among stakeholders and how metrics can be set up to measure it, both qualitatively and quantitively.

3.3 Inclusive Design for Human Values

Understanding human diversity is the starting point of inclusive design and is the key approach that differentiates it from other design approaches. As discussed at the conception part, beyond age and ability, diversity can be broadened to users' personal preferences and lifestyle, social and cultural factors, and even the environment. According to Rokeach [1], 'values that are internalized as a result of cultural, societal and personal experience are psychological structure that, in turn, have consequences of their own…values are determinants of virtually all kinds of behaviour that could be called social behaviour'. Therefore, we may conclude that these efforts are moving toward understanding the diversity of human values, in which all dimensions of human diversity are internalized and then exhibited in human behaviour.

Although there are few studies directly addressing design for diverse human values, we identify one study from Lim, Giacomin and Nickpour [8] that explores the psychosocial dimensions, in which 'value' is one of the dimensions, parallel with 'cognitive', 'emotional', and 'social' dimensions. The value dimension consists of three sub-themes: satisfaction, happiness and self-esteem, which are further broken down into multiple codes. This paper contributes to the conceptual construct of inclusive design for human values, but further research should explore how these diverse values can be revealed. An example is Briggs and Thomas' [41] discussion on an inclusive, value sensitive design perspective on identity technology management to allow individuals to discuss and express values in their own terms. Inclusive design for human values is to elicit and report, not interpret or represent, users' values. It raises questions such as: if there are a limited number of individual values and how to identify them? or if it is numerous, is it possible to include all kinds of human values?

These answers may be answered by sociologists. Both Rokeach [1] and Schwartz [42] identify a limited number of universal values that humans share by conducting empirical research worldwide. For inclusive design research, a further direction may be to explore ways of revealing these universal values by drawing on findings from sociology. However, contradictions remain between the diversity of values and the universality of values since inclusive design is supposed to recognize and celebrate the full range of human values.

Another stream of research conducted by Bianchin and Heylighen [43] explores the relationship between ethics and values in inclusive design. There exists a paradox in inclusive design philosophy between 'addressing the needs of the widest possible audience' and 'considering human differences' [44]. Bianchin and Heylighen [45] develop the theory of just design by recruiting Rawls' theory of justice as fairness [46] to address this paradox. By converting it into the question of how design can be fair, to design inclusively means to match users' choices with the condition sketched. However, they also point out that this can hardly be realized at the individual level but at the social level when the 'overall usability for the offs is maximized' [44]. They answer the question partially since the fair issue can only be addressed at the social level. Li and Dong [47] offer another explanation by using theories from economics, especially welfare economics and institutional economics. At the individual level, the goal of inclusive design is about how to distribute the freedom of choice in a free competition market. They point out user sensitive design may be an effective approach to respond to the diversity of specific users in a specific context.

4   Discussion and Further Research

4.1   Discussion

There are two clusters of research focusing on value and values in inclusive design (see Fig. 1). The first cluster is the economic contribution of inclusive design driven by profit, both at individual (firm/user) level and social level; the second cluster views inclusive design as a value-embedded approach that needs to be addressed at both individual and social levels.

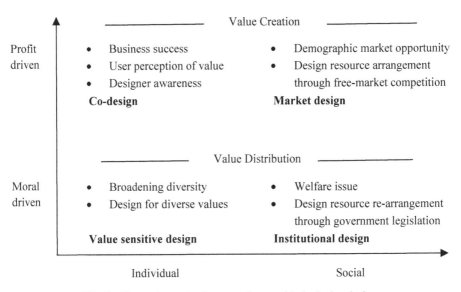

Fig. 1. How value and values are discussed in inclusive design

The discussion of economic value is, in essence, a value creation perspective. Industries driven by profit have increasingly realized the market opportunity for designing for the ageing and disability population with mainstream products. Inclusive design can be defined as an arrangement of design resources by the means of free-market competition [47]. Value is created at the social level through market design. At the individual level, value creation through inclusive design is a co-design approach, either it is to make business cases to board members, to develop methods and processes for designers through knowledge transfer, or to deliver inclusive products and services that are of perceived value to end-users. Together, it is a value co-creation process among all stakeholders, but with users as the source and subject of value creation.

The discussion of design for human values can also be categorized into the individual level and the social level. At the individual level, design for human values is to understand and respond to the diversity of personal values through value sensitive design [41] or contextualized user-sensitive design [48]. At the social level, a moral driven approach to inclusive design can be viewed as a design resource re-arrangement by government legislation and/or institutional design. The intersection and conflicts of personal values and social values becomes a value distribution issue.

4.2 Further Research

The value creation and value distribution are issues interrelated. If business organizations lack the incentive to adopt inclusive design in their business activities, it would rely on government legislation and mandatory regulation. If value created cannot be allocated fairly among stakeholders, both economic and social issues would arise. A possibility is an integrated approach to address value creation and value distribution in future research. Based on what reviewed above, we summarize further research questions that need to be answered:

- How do business organizations, users and designers define value respectively? How could value be co-created among all stakeholders in an inclusive design process?
- How to establish intersubjective objectivity to assess the value of inclusive design among different stakeholders?
- How to design for diverse personal values? How to deal with conflicting values?
- What is the relationship between economic value and human values?
- How could both value creation and value distribution be considered to enrich the discourse of value in inclusive design research?
- How to integrate the profit driven approach and moral driven approach to realize value congruency, taking into consideration both value creation and value distribution?

5 Conclusion

From redefining ageing and disability to designing beyond these two conventional axes, conceptions of inclusive design have moved from designing for the marginalized group, i.e. the ageing and disabled population, to designing for the full range of human differences. This paper discusses value and values in inclusive design and serves as an initial understanding of the value concept. Further research should be conducted to investigate an integrated approach that unifies these two different discourses of value. We focus on literature from the field of inclusive design for this preliminary literature review. Further research should expand to value and values in other fields of design research, such as design management and value sensitive design. Furthermore, notions of economic value and human values and their intertwined relationships should be examined beyond the discipline of design, extending to philosophy, economics, management and sociology.

References

1. Rokeach, M.: The Nature of Human Values. The Free Press, New York (1973)
2. Heskett, J.: Design and the Creation of Value. Edited by Dilnot, C., Boztepe, S. Bloomsbury Academic, London (2017)
3. Porter, M.E.: Competitive Advantage: Creating and Sustaining Superior Performance. Free Press, New York (1985)
4. Zeithaml, V.A.: Consumer perceptions of price, quality and value: a means-end model and synthesis of evidence. J. Mark. **52**(3), 2–22 (1988)
5. Coleman, R.: The case for inclusive design - an overview. In: 12th Triennial Congress, International Ergonomics Association and the Human Factors Association of Canada, Toronto, Canada (1994)
6. Clarkson, P.J., Coleman, R., Keates, S., Lebbon, C. (eds.): Inclusive Design: Design for the Whole Population. Springer, London (2003). https://doi.org/10.1007/978-1-4471-0001-0
7. Keates, S.: Design for the value of inclusiveness. In: van den Hoven, J., Vermaas, P.E., van de Poel, I. (eds.) Handbook of Ethics, Values, and Technological Design, pp. 383–402. Springer, Dordrecht (2015). https://doi.org/10.1007/978-94-007-6970-0_15
8. Lim, Y., Giacomin, J., Nickpour, F.: Beyond accessible aisles? Psychosocial inclusivity of shopping experience: an ethnographic investigation. In: Proceedings of the DRS2018, Limerick, Ireland (2018)
9. Clarkson, P.J., Coleman, R.: History of inclusive design in the UK. Appl. Ergon. **46**, 233–324 (2015)
10. Mieczakowski, A., Hessey, S., Clarkson, P.J.: Inclusive design and the bottom line: how can its value be proven to decision makers? In: Stephanidis, C., Antona, M. (eds.) UAHCI 2013. LNCS, vol. 8009, pp. 67–76. Springer, Heidelberg (2013). https://doi.org/10.1007/978-3-642-39188-0_8
11. Gemser, G., de Bont, C., Hekkert, P., Friedman, K.: Quality perceptions of design journals: the design scholars' perspective. Des. Stud. **33**(1), 4–23 (2012)
12. Keates, S., Clarkson, P.J.: Countering Design Exclusion: An Introduction to Inclusive Design. Springer, London (2003). https://doi.org/10.1007/978-1-4471-0013-3
13. BS 7000-6.: Design Management Systems: Managing Inclusive Design. British Standard Institution, London (2005)
14. Design Council: Inclusive Design Education Resource. Design Council, London, UK. http://www.designcouncil.info/inclusivedesignresource/. Accessed 21 Jan 2020
15. Inclusive Design Research Centre: What is inclusive design? OCAD University, Toronto, Canada. https://idrc.ocadu.ca/resources/idrc-online/49-articles-and-papers/443-whatisinclusivedesign. Accessed 21 Jan 2020
16. Centre for Universal Design: What is Universal Design? NC State University, North Carolina, US. https://projects.ncsu.edu/ncsu/design/cud/index.htm. Accessed 21 Jan 2020
17. EIDD Design for All Europe: Stockholm Declaration. www.designforalleurope.org. Accessed 21 Jan 2020
18. Coleman, R.: Editorial: designing for our future selves. Appl. Ergon. **24**(1), 3–4 (1993)
19. Nickpour, F., Dong, H.: Editorial: designing for diversity: inclusive design as a catalyst for change? In: Proceedings of 2018 Design Research Society Conference, vol. 5, pp. 1814–1815 (2018)
20. Dong, H.: Inclusive design: the Chinese archive. Tongji University Press, Shanghai (2019)
21. Raghavendra, R.G., et al.: Designing for older people: but who is an older person? In: Proceedings of 2016 Design Research Society Conference, vol. 8, pp. 3251–3262 (2016)
22. Dankl, K.: Design age: towards a participatory transformation of images of ageing. Des. Stud. **48**, 30–42 (2017)

23. Sørensen Overby, R., Ryhl, C.: Responding to diversity including disability. In: Proceedings of 2018 Design Research Society Conference, vol. 5, pp. 1894–1907 (2018)
24. Waller, S., et al.: Making the case for inclusive design. Appl. Ergon. **46**, 297–303 (2015)
25. St John, N.: Towards more culturally inclusive communication design practices: exploring creative participation between non-Indigenous and Indigenous people in Australia. In: Proceedings of 2016 Design Research Society Conference, vol. 8, pp. 3349–3372 (2016)
26. Boess, S.: Design for self-inclusion: supporting emotional capability. In: Proceedings of 2018 Design Research Society Conference, vol. 5, pp. 1908–1918 (2018)
27. Nicholl, B., Hosking, I.M., Elton, E.M., Lee, Y., Bell, J., Clarkson, P.J.: Inclusive design in the key stage 3 classroom: an investigation of teachers' understanding and implementation of user-centred design principles in design and technology. Int. J. Technol. Des. Educ. **23**(4), 921–938 (2012). https://doi.org/10.1007/s10798-012-9221-9
28. Evans, G.: Ageing and climate change: a society-technology-design discourse. Des. J. **16**(2), 239–258 (2013)
29. Luck, R.: Inclusive design and making in practice: bringing bodily experience into closer contact with making. Des. Stud. **54**, 96–119 (2018)
30. Coleman, R., Clarkson, P.J., Dong, H., Cassim, J.: Design for Inclusivity: A Practical Guide to Accessible, Innovative and User-centred Design. Gower, London (2007)
31. Kawahara, K., Narikawa, M.: The unique achievements of Japanese industries in the super-aged society. Appl. Ergon. **46**, 258–266 (2015)
32. Kose, S.: How can the exploding senior population be accommodated? Japanese struggle towards inclusive design. J. Eng. Des. **21**(2–3), 165–171 (2010)
33. Fletcher, V., et al.: The challenge of inclusive design in the US context. Appl. Ergon. **46**, 267–273 (2015)
34. Bendixen, K., Benktzon, M.: Design for all in Scandinavia - a strong concept. Appl. Ergon. **46**, 248–257 (2015)
35. Chamberlain, M., et al.: BT's adoption of customer centric design. Appl. Ergon. **46**, 279–283 (2015)
36. Benoit, B., Hall, B., Roberts, D.: Ferrari's Greatest Design Challenge. Press article. Appeared in Financial Times, 20 January (2004)
37. Fleck, J.: Inclusive design - a lasting Paralympic Legacy? Embedding inclusive design knowledge and skills into architectural education. Charette **2**(1), 92–105 (2015)
38. Donahue, S.: Inclusive design: meeting the challenges of the 21st century. In: Proceedings of the Include Conference, London, UK (2011)
39. Franz, J., Bitner, G.: Is social entrepreneurship the way forward? The case of the living in collective. In: Proceedings of the Include Conference, London, UK (2011)
40. Rogers, P., Gill, C., Alley, K.: A sustainable social innovation model: challenges and opportunities for collaboration in an academic setting. In: Proceedings of the Include conference, London, UK (2011)
41. Briggs, P., Thomas, L.: An inclusive, value sensitive design perspective on future identity technologies. ACM Trans. Comput.-Hum.-Interact. **22**(5), 1–28 (2015)
42. Schwartz, S.H.: Universals in the content and structure of values: theoretical advances and empirical tests in 20 countries. Adv. Exp. Soc. Psychol. **25**, 1–65 (1992)
43. Bianchin, M., Heylighen, A.: Ethics in design: pluralism and the case for justice in inclusive design. In: Proceedings of 2018 Design Research Society Conference, vol. 1, pp. 86–97 (2018)
44. Bianchin, M., Heylighen, A.: Fair by design: addressing the paradox of inclusive design approaches. Des. J. **20**(sup1), 3162–3170 (2017)
45. Bianchin, M., Heylighen, A.: Just design. Des. Stud. **54**, 1–22 (2018)
46. Rawls, J.: Justice as fairness. Philos. Public Aff. **14**(3), 223–251 (1985)

47. Li, F., Dong, H.: The economic explanation of inclusive design in different stages of product lifetime. In: Proceedings of the 22nd International Conference on Engineering Design (ICED19), Delft, The Netherlands (2019)
48. Li, F., Dong, H.: Achieving inclusion with contextualized user-sensitive design. In: Antona, M., Stephanidis, C. (eds.) HCII 2019. LNCS, vol. 11572, pp. 113–132. Springer, Cham (2019). https://doi.org/10.1007/978-3-030-23560-4_9

User Experience and Aging

Use of Augmented Reality by Older Adults

Jessyca L. Derby and Barbara S. Chaparro$^{(\boxtimes)}$

Department of Human Factors and Behavioral Neurobiology,
Embry-Riddle Aeronautical University, 1 Aerospace Blvd, Daytona Beach, FL 32114, USA
derbyj1@my.erau.edu, Barbara.Chaparro@erau.edu

Abstract. Augmented Reality (AR) is an emerging technology that is gaining in popularity as it becomes more affordable. AR applications superimpose computerized objects on top of the users' physical world. Through the use of mobile devices or AR glasses, users can see their physical environment around them as well as the digital artifacts. AR has been touted as the next technology to replace our current smartphone and desktop experiences for everyday activities. For example, online shopping, examination of health information, interior decorating, and family communication are activities that have the potential to be enhanced by AR. Older adults, in particular, stand to benefit from this technology. This paper discusses the usability and user experience (UX) of AR applications among older adults. In addition, it explains the heuristics that have been suggested for AR applications and how they can be applied to older adult populations. Such heuristics allow providers of AR solutions to more quickly and reliably assess usability and UX, which in turn facilitates informed iterative design/development, resulting in more satisfying, efficient, and effective solutions.

Keywords: Older adults · Augmented Reality · Heuristics · Heuristic evaluation

1 Older Adults and Technology

Smartphones, smart home devices such as Amazon Alexa and Google Home, and even our personal vehicles include technology that aim at making our daily routines easier. As these technologies become more mainstream, more populations such as older adults begin to adopt these technologies. According to a recent study of older adults' technology usage, 67% of adults aged 65-year-old or older stated that they use the internet, 42% owned a smartphone, and 32% owned a tablet computer [1]. All of these technologies have shown an increase in use since 2013 within the older adult population, especially smartphone use which more than doubled [2]. It is projected that older adults will continue to increase their use of technology as they see it to be useful and perceive it to have a positive impact on society [1].

New technologies have begun to emerge and have been deemed the next innovation to replace our current smartphone and desktop experience for everyday activities. They are known as virtual, augmented, and mixed reality. Virtual Reality (VR) is commonly implemented using a head-mounted display (HMD) device, like the HTC Vive, Oculus Rift, or

© Springer Nature Switzerland AG 2020
Q. Gao and J. Zhou (Eds.): HCII 2020, LNCS 12207, pp. 125–134, 2020.
https://doi.org/10.1007/978-3-030-50252-2_10

Oculus Quest where the user is immersed in a virtual environment. The user's environment, objects around them and their interactions are digitized while the user is immersed in the virtual world. Augmented reality (AR) superimposes computerized objects on top of the users' physical world. Through the use of mobile devices or AR glasses, users can see their physical environment around them as well as the digital artifacts. Mixed Reality (MR) fills the gap between VR and AR by creating virtual elements that adapt to the user's physical environment. MR can be experienced through mobile devices as well as head-mounted displays, such as the Microsoft HoloLens and Magic Leap One. While VR remains a popular technology for gaming and immersive activities, it is limited in its portability and applicability to workplace settings since users are unable to view their surrounding environment. AR and MR have been used for more everyday activities. For example, online shopping, examination of health information, and interior decorating have been demonstrated to be enhanced by these technologies [3–6, 8]. The use of VR, AR, and MR is widespread, and expected to grow exponentially in the coming years. The global augmented and virtual reality market value is approximated around 26.7 billion dollars and has been projected to reach 814.7 billion dollars by 2025 [9].

For older adult populations, AR is a technology that has the potential to enhance their mental, physical, and social wellbeing. It has been proposed that use of this technology may allow them to become more independent and less dependent on their caregivers. For example, small and hard to read instructions and prescription labels can be augmented through a smartphone to produce larger, bolder text or even translated to a different language [10]. In another example, wayfinding directions could be given to an older adult using augmented step-by-step directions on a screen. AR applications could also be connected to health apps, like MyFitnessPal, allowing older adults to scan food labels and receive recommendations based on salt, iron, or other dietary requirements in real time. AR applications have also been used to promote hydration habits in older adults with dementia and have shown promise for medical uses, cognitive aids, education, and promotion of spiritual beliefs [11].

1.1 AR Medical Applications for Older Adults

Within the medical domain, AR applications are often focused on rehabilitation, encouraging a healthy lifestyle, and medication management. Papegaaij and colleagues described the benefits of an AR app for rehabilitation exercises such as balance and gait training by providing instant feedback, external cues for corrections, easily adjustable variation and intensity of trainings, and increased motivation through games [12]. AR game applications have also been shown to be useful for early cognitive screening for dementia and cognitive training [13]. CogARC, an application with AR cube mini-games helped physicians with cognitive screening of older adults and was reported to be fun and engaging by users [13]. AR has also been applied to medication management. By pairing it with intelligent assistive systems, researchers were able to create a projection-based AR prototype that focused on older adults' and caregivers' needs and abilities [10]. Older adults were able to dispense their own medication and receive instructions on how to take the prescription through the use of gesture commands [10]. This technology allowed older adults to take their medication correctly, without the need of a caregiver's assistance.

AR game applications also has been used to motivate older adults to lead a more active and independent lifestyle. In one example, an AR game was projected onto the floor and older adults could sit in a wheelchair or stand and use their arms to play the game and, as a result, exercise their arms [14]. Researchers found that this game was easy for nursing home staff to set up and usable for those with cognitive deficits. It also promoted physical and cognitive rehabilitation and allowed personalization by adapting to the physical and cognitive abilities of the user through game selection and changing the height of the device [14]. AR also has been used to assist older adults who have Alzheimer's disease and their caregivers. Through this system, caregivers could easily tag everyday objects with auditory or visual information that people with Alzheimer's disease could use to assist in everyday tasks through the combination of a smartphone device, headphones, and a video camera [15].

In addition to motivating older adults to become more physically active, AR applications have been used to encourage them to play a more prominent role in medical decision-making. Falls, unfortunately, are a common occurrence that many older adults face. In order to prevent falls, home modifications such as the installation of handlebars are often suggested by healthcare professionals. When planning these home modifications, older adults can become compliant. As one older adult user stated, "I could have designed it better… but I didn't think that it was my place. You know when people are doing things for you go along with what they say" [16]. AR applications can help older adults visualize home modifications during the planning process and empower them to take a more active role in the decision making.

1.2 AR Applications as Cognitive Aids

AR also has been developed to help people perceive and react to situations that they may otherwise miss. For example, a prototype of an AR car windshield heads-up display has been used to assist older adults with recognizing roadway hazards [17]. Older adults are more at risk for roadway accidents due to worsening visual acuity and slower reaction times. This AR application assisted older adult drivers in a driving simulation by making important roadway signs and hazards more salient by encapsulating them with an outline of a virtual rhombus, referred to as an AR cue. AR cuing enabled the older adult participants to increase their response rates and decrease response times, specifically with low visibility hazards such as warning signs and pedestrians [17]. One concern when using AR heads up displays, however, especially when driving, is that the AR display could distract the driver from the roadway. While this may occur with some applications, Schall et al. demonstrated that older adults could still identify secondary objects on the opposite side of the roadway after the AR heads-up display had been triggered [17]. Another study investigating AR cues for gap estimation for left-turns found a similar result. AR cueing involving a transparent sign, when placed in a fixed region that was important to the driver such as the traffic lane, helped drivers perform better in a simulator and drivers reported that the cue was not distracting [18]. AR displays such as this and similar applications developed by Porsche and GMC are helping drivers become more aware of hazards to decrease the potential for roadway accidents [19, 20].

1.3 AR Applications for Education and Spiritual Beliefs

Educational AR applications have been developed to work alongside magazines, such as Time and National Geographic, as well as museum experiences. They can be designed to give the user supplemental information, such as videos [21]. User scan the magazine within the application and it triggers a video that would provide the same information as the magazine article. This is beneficial for people who are blind or older adults who have a more difficult time reading, as they can experience the content without struggle [21]. Content can also be added through AR. A museum application at the Svevo Museum in Italy was able to pair statues with external links containing narrations, historical audio recordings, and interactive animations on smartphone devices [22]. Participants in these studies enjoyed the applications and recognized the benefits. However, it was challenging for older adults to hold the mobile devices in place for longer periods of time, which is necessary to interact with these applications, and they stated this would be increasingly difficult for those who suffer from Parkinson's disease [21, 22].

AR has also been shown to help support a persons' spiritual beliefs. For example, a Qibla AR application was developed to assist in finding a Qibla prayer direction towards Mecca. The application scanned the users' location and pointed out the direction of Qibla based on where the phone was being held [21]. Older adults found the application overall to be useful. However, they also stated that it was difficult to use at first due to a lack of clear instructions during the application start-up [21]. AR can be extremely beneficial to older adults, however, for it to be useful, it is essential that these AR applications are designed so this population can easily understand and enjoy this technology.

1.4 Barriers to Technology Adoption

As seen from these previous examples, there are many uses of AR that can be targeted for older adults, however it is a concern that older adults will not accept the technology, or even feel comfortable trying it. This stereotype stems from the idea that older adults do not want to use new technology because it is too difficult to learn to use. Davis's technology acceptance model does state that the perceived ease of use correlates to continued system use [23]. However, this model as well as others also mentions that perceived usefulness plays a larger role in technology adoption [23–25]. Some people can overcome difficult and time-consuming technologies if it gives them great benefit, but adoption can be increased by making a system easier to use [23]. As older adults see benefits and usefulness in technology, they are more willing to spend time to learn and adopt it [23, 24].

2 Developing Technology for Older Adult Users

If technology is not designed with the user in mind, it can quickly turn from a thing of value to a complicated hindrance. One way to create a positive interaction between technology and the user is through usability evaluation. Usability is defined in ISO 9241-11 as, "the extent to which a product can be used by specified users to achieve specified goals with effectiveness, efficiency and satisfaction in a specified context of use" [26].

For AR to be accepted, it should be assessed through usability technique. One effective technique is a heuristic evaluation.

Heuristic evaluations are conducted by evaluators' scoring a product using a set of validated guidelines or best practices, called heuristics. Through this scoring process, websites, applications, devices, or other products can be rated on a variety of dimensions based on the set of heuristics. Some heuristic lists are short and generic with five simple rules to follow, while others are very specific with over a hundred detailed checklist items. Based on the score from these heuristics, suggestions for redesign of the product can be proposed.

One set of heuristics that is commonly used are the Nielsen's 10 usability heuristics for user interface design [27, 28]. These heuristics include 10 generalizable principles that can apply to any user interface: visibility of system status, match between system and real world, user control and freedom, consistency and standards, error prevention, recognition rather than recall, flexibility and efficiency of use, aesthetic and minimalist design, help users recognize, diagnose, and recover from errors, and help and documentation [28]. These heuristics consider people's cognitive and perceptual limitations as well as their expectations in order to design the best experience for the user. For example, people have an easier time recognizing something that they have seen before rather than trying to recall where or what that item was, so it is important to design with recognition rather than recall. This can be done through the creation of a menu structure on a website with important key actions or providing a search term for a user rather than requiring them to recall it from memory [29]. People's expectations also influence how they interact with interfaces. People tend to expect that an interface will work in a specific way. For example, if a user selects a menu button, they expect that an action will occur that will bring them to a new page that is relevant to the menu item they selected, and that it will have a similar theme to the previous page. This is where the heuristics of visibility of system status and match between the system and the real world are relevant. Nielsen's 10 heuristics are useful, but generic, ambiguous, and do not account for issues specific to special populations like older adults.

Due to the perceptual changes that adults develop as they age, such as a decline in visual acuity, contrast sensitivity, auditory detection thresholds, reaction time, and cognitive processing, special considerations should be factored into the design process. The National Institute on Aging and National Library of Medicine created specific senior-friendly guidelines for developing websites for older adults to tackle this issue [6]. Many of the specifications could be easily applied and useful for AR applications. For example, to address visual acuity and contrast sensitivity issues, they suggest designers use fonts that are easy to read such as sans serif font types and larger sizes set at least 12–14 point font, to avoid specific color combinations or patterns that may be difficult to discriminate text information from [6]. It is also important to include simple language, positive statements, consistent layouts, large buttons, and subtitles to any videos or audio instructions to accommodate for users who may have cognitive or motor deficits [6]. When designing an AR application for older adults, all of these factors must be considered – as Evans and Koepfler accurately stated, "we need to apply user-centered design when it comes to AR, rather than technology-driven design, so that we don't augment reality with a bunch of stuff no one needs" [30]. Standardized and validated

AR heuristics can help providers design AR applications that are both easy to adopt and beneficial to older adults [7].

2.1 Perceptual and Cognitive Considerations

When designing for older adults, it is important to keep in mind the decline of perceptual and cognitive abilities that many in this age group experience. Age-related changes to the eye, such as the development of cataracts, yellowing of the lens, lessened visual acuity due to the hardening of the lens, and a decline in contrast sensitivity can make using technology with small text or low contrast difficult [24]. This is important when creating menu structures, instructions, or any text in an AR application that could be difficult for some older adults to read. Some design recommendations that could alleviate this include customizable font sizes, sans serif fonts, and high contrast ratios between the background and text colors [24, 31]. Hearing loss is also common, affecting about 40% of older adults [27]. As a result, designing applications with customizable volume and the capability to work with hearing aids is important. Perceptual speed, working memory capacity, attention, and some executive functioning also have been shown to decline with age [24, 32]. This becomes important to consider when developing instructions for applications or asking for a user's input. Typically, it is a recommended to keep auditory options below 7 items, minimize cluttered screens, give adequate amount of time if a user needs to shift their attention, and stress the use of consistency when developing applications for older adults [24, 31]. Perceptual and cognitive declines are common for this population, and it is important to keep these in mind in order to design usable interfaces and AR enhancements to combat these deficits.

3   Heuristics for Older Adults

Generic heuristics, such as Nielsen's 10 are based on a general population and does not fully address the perceptual and cognitive differences of older adults. As a result, research has been conducted to developed heuristics aimed to address these issues. Researchers have combined general heuristics, such as Nielsen's 10, alongside with W3C accessibility recommendations for older adults, and usability checklists developed by the National Institute of Aging [24, 33–35]. This has been done for smartphone applications targeted to older adults, social media platforms such as Facebook, and website design (see Table 1) [33, 35–37].

AR heuristics for older adults have not been as prevalent in the literature. In fact, a recent publication by Dey and colleagues revealed that less than 10% of AR research studies published between 2005 and 2014 included any kind of user study or analysis [38]. Of those that did, only a handful used heuristic evaluation. To our knowledge, there is currently only one study that has been designed to create design principles for AR applications for older adult users [34].

Table 1. Heuristics and guidelines commonly used for older adults

Heuristic or guideline name	Area of focus	Number of items
Nielsen's 10 Usability Heuristics for User Interface Design [27]	UI Design	10
National Institute on Aging (NIA) and the National Library of Medicine (NLM) Making your web site senior-friendly: A checklist [6]	Web sites for older adults	25
Web Content Accessibility Guidelines (W3C/WAI) [31]	Web sites for older adults	~62
Harari, Diaz, & Baldasarri's Usability Heuristics [33]	Social networks for older adults	66
Silvia et al.'s Heuristics for Smartphone applications targeted at older adults [35]	Smartphone apps for older adults	33
Chisnell et al.'s Web site heuristics for older adults [36]	Web sites for older adults	~67
Liang's Design Principles for Augmented Reality for Older Adults [34]	AR applications for older adults	10

Using iterative design and focus group testing, Liang adapted five AR heuristics and created an additional five design principles that applied to older adults [34] (see Table 2). For example, the Layer-focus augmentation (LA) design principle describes how large quantities of information should be organized into easy to understand groupings or layers to minimize clutter [34]. This helps older adults who may have declining eyesight or cognitive capabilities navigate through the application, but also benefits younger users by making the application simpler to use. These design principles are a good starting point for AR designers; however, they are only limited to mobile devices such as iPads and smartphones and do not include wearable AR devices such as head-mounted devices and/or glasses [34]. It can be difficult for some older adult users to use mobile AR due to physical limitations, Parkinson's disease, decreased hand grip strength, or arthritis. Mobile AR applications require the user to hold the device to interact with the application [21, 34]. Since this population may find it easier to use a wearable AR application, guidelines should be developed to apply to both wearable and mobile AR. Wearable AR, however, introduces its own challenges related to interaction gestures, comfort, and visual integration of physical and virtual elements.

Table 2. Liang's design principles for older adult AR applications [34]

Design principle name	Recommendation
Affordability (AF)	A clear physical indicator should show that virtual content is available
Familiarity-focus augmentation (FA)	Familiar interactions such as scrolling and tapping as well as using icons that the user can easily recognize should be used
Privacy augmentation (PA)	Privacy needs should be considered
Physical-focus augmentation (PFA)	Minimize physical load and the amount of steps a user must take to complete a task
Reducing cognitive overhead (RCO)	Minimize cognitive load
Accurate Augmentation (AA)	Virtual elements shown in a way that users expect
Hidden Reality (HR)	Virtual content should not hide real content that is related to user goals
Instantaneous augmentation (IA)	Quick and useful feedback should be provided if virtual content cannot be displayed immediately
Layer-focus augmentation (LA)	Virtual content should be organized in layers that are based on user goals to avoid clutter and confusion
Modality-focus augmentation (MA)	Virtual content should be provided in different modalities (i.e., visual, auditory, vibration)

4   Next Steps

For older adults to accept AR applications, they must be designed in a way that is easy to use and deemed useful by this population. Heuristic evaluation is one method that can be used during the design process along with traditional usability testing. However, heuristics for older adults that cover the wide range of AR applications still need to be validated. To maximize the effectiveness of older adult AR heuristics, new heuristics should include information from guidelines such as those presented by the National Institute on Aging and National Library of Medicine and W3C Accessibility guidelines, the latest research considering older adult capabilities, and also be in the form of easy-to-use checklists that can be used by both developers and practitioners [6, 31]. It is also important to be able to generalize to different AR hardware such as head-mounted displays (HMDs), mobile AR (smartphones, iPads, etc.), and marker-based AR.

AR technology is still in its infancy of development. Proper attention to human factors principles and the validation of heuristics to evaluate the applications in the design and development process will help in the acceptance and realization of AR potential to enhance older adults' quality of life.

References

1. Anderson, M., Perrin, A.: Technology use among seniors. Pew Research Center for Internet & Technology, Washington, DC (2017)
2. Smith, A.: Older adults and technology use. Pew Research Center for Internet & Technology, Washington, DC (2014)
3. Dacko, S.: Enabling smart retail settings via mobile augmented reality shopping apps. Technol. Forecast. Soc. Change **124**, 243–256 (2017)
4. Phan, V.: Interior design in augmented reality environment. Int. J. Comput. Appl. **5**(5), 16–21 (2019)
5. Monkman, H., Kushniruk, A.: A see through future: augmented reality and health information systems. In: Courtney, K., Kuo, A., Shabestari, O. (eds.) Driving Quality in Informatics: Fulfilling the Promise, pp. 281–285. ISO Press, Amsterdam (2015)
6. National Institute on Aging and National Library of Medicine: Making your web site senior friendly: A checklist, US Government Printing Office, Washington, DC (2001)
7. Quiñones, D., Rusu, C., Rusu, V.: A methodology to develop usability/user experience heuristics. Comput. Stand. Interfaces **59**, 109–129 (2018)
8. Wang, C., Chiang, Y., Wang, M.: Evaluation of an augmented reality embedded on-line shopping system. Procedia Manuf. **3**, 5624–5630 (2015)
9. Zion Market Research: Global Augmented and Virtual Reality Market Will Reach USD 814.7 Billion By 2025 (2019). https://www.globenewswire.com/news-release/2019/02/21/1739121/0/en/Global-Augmented-and-Virtual-Reality-Market-Will-Reach-USD-814-7-Billion-By-2025-Zion-Market-Research.html
10. Guerrero, E., Lu, M., Yueh, H., Lindgren, H.: Designing and evaluating an intelligent augmented reality system for assisting older adults' medication management. Cogn. Syst. Res. **58**, 278–291 (2019)
11. Lehman, S., Graves, J., Mcaleer, C., Giovannetti, T., Tan, C.C.: A mobile augmented reality game to encourage hydration in the elderly. In: Yamamoto, S., Mori, H. (eds.) HIMI 2018. LNCS, vol. 10905, pp. 98–107. Springer, Cham (2018). https://doi.org/10.1007/978-3-319-92046-7_9
12. Papegaaij, S., Morang, F., Steenbrink, F.: Virtual and augmented reality based balance and gait training [White Paper] (2017)
13. Boletsis, C., McCallum, S.: Augmented reality cubes for cognitive gaming: preliminary usability and game experience testing. Int. J. Serious Games **3**(1), 3–18 (2016)
14. Simão, H., Bernardino, A.: User centered design of an augmented reality gaming platform for active aging in elderly institutions. In: icSPORTS, pp. 151–162 (2017)
15. Quintana, E., Favela, J.: Augmented reality annotations to assist persons with Alzheimers and their caregivers. Pers. Ubiquit. Comput. **17**(6), 1105–1116 (2013). https://doi.org/10.1007/s00779-012-0558-6
16. Bianco, M., Pedell, S., Renda, G.: Augmented reality and home modifications: a tool to empower older adults in fall prevention. In: Proceedings of the 28th Australian Conference on Computer-Human Interaction, pp. 1–11. ACM, Lauceston (2016)
17. Schall Jr., M., Rusch, M., Lee, J., Dawson, J., Thomas, G., Aksan, N., Rizzo, M.: Augmented reality cues and elderly driver hazard perception. Hum. Factors **55**(3), 643–658 (2013)
18. Rusch, M., Schall Jr., M., Lee, J., Dawson, J., Rizzo, M.: Augmented reality cues to assist older drivers with gap estimation for left-turns. Accid. Anal. Prev. **71**, 210–221 (2014)
19. Bruce, C.: Porsche makes big investment in augmented reality windshield tech (2018). https://www.motor1.com/news/266480/porsche-augmented-reality-windshield-investment/
20. Cooley, B.: Augmented reality is coming to your car (2019). https://www.cnet.com/roadshow/news/augmented-reality-is-coming-to-your-car/

21. Malik, S., Azuddin, M., Abdullah, L., Mahmud, M.: Exploring older people's experience with augmented reality (AR) applications. J. Eng. Appl. Sci. **10**, 18004–18011 (2015)
22. Fenu, C., Pittarello, F.: Svevo tour: The design and the experimentation of an augmented reality application for engaging visitors of a literary museum. Int. J. Hum.-Comput. Stud. **114**, 20–35 (2018)
23. Davis, F., Davis, G., Morris, M., Venkatesh, V.: Technology acceptance model. J. Manag. Sci. **35**, 982–1003 (1989)
24. Pak, R., McLaughlin, A.: Designing Displays for Older Adults. Taylor & Francis Group, Boca Raton (2011)
25. Schlomann, A., et al.: Augmented reality games for health promotion in old age. In: Geroimenko, V. (ed.) Augmented Reality Games II, pp. 159–177. Springer, Cham (2019). https://doi.org/10.1007/978-3-030-15620-6_7
26. ISO: Ergonomic requirements for office work with visual display terminal (VDT's)–Part 11: Guidance on usability (ISO 9241-11(E)), Geneva, Switzerland (1998)
27. Nielsen, J.: Enhancing the explanatory power of usability heuristics. In: Proceedings of the SIGCHI Conference on Human Factors in Computing Systems. CHI, Boston, Massachusetts, pp. 152–158 (1994)
28. Nielsen, J., Molich, R.: Heuristic evaluation of user interfaces. In: Proceedings of the SIGCHI Conference on Human Factors in Computing Systems, pp. 249–256. AMC (1990)
29. Budiu, R.: Memory recognition and recall in user interfaces (2014). https://www.nngroup.com/articles/recognition-and-recall/
30. Evans, K., Koepfler, J.: The UX of AR: Toward a Human-Centered Definition of Augmented Reality (2017). https://uxpamagazine.org/the-ux-of-ar/
31. W3C WAI: Web Accessibility and Older People: Meeting the Needs of Ageing Web Users (2010). http://www.w3.org/WAI/older-users/
32. Harada, C., Love, M., Triebel, K.: Normal cognitive aging. Clin. Geriatr. Med. **29**(4), 737–752 (2013)
33. Harari, I., Diaz, J.F., Baldasarri, S.: Adapting usability heuristics to evaluate Facebook according to elderly. Hum. Factors Des. **7**(13), 203–226 (2018)
34. Liang, S.: Establishing Design Principles for Augmented Reality for Older Adults. Sheffield Hallam University, Sheffield (2018)
35. Silva, P., Holden, K., Jordan, P.: Towards a list of heuristics to evaluate smartphone apps targeted at older adults: a study with apps that aim at promoting health and well-being. In: 2015 48th Hawaii International Conference on System Sciences (HICSS), pp. 3237–3246 (2015)
36. Chisnell, D., Redish, J., Lee, A.: New heuristics for understanding older adults as web users. Tech. Commun. **53**(1), 39–59 (2006)
37. Petrovčič, A., Taipale, S., Rogelj, A., Dolničar, V.: Design of mobile phones for older adults: an empirical analysis of design guidelines and checklists for feature phones and smartphones. Int. J. Hum.-Comput. Interact. **34**(3), 251–264 (2018)
38. Dey, A., Billinghurst, M., Lindeman, R., Swan, J.: A systematic review of 10 years of augmented reality usability studies: 2005 to 2014. Front. Robot. AI **5**, 37 (2018)

Age-Related Differences in Takeover Request Modality Preferences and Attention Allocation During Semi-autonomous Driving

Gaojian Huang$^{(\boxtimes)}$ (ID) and Brandon Pitts (ID)

Purdue University, West Lafayette, IN, USA
{huan1186,bjpitts}@purdue.edu

Abstract. Adults aged 65 years and older are the fastest growing age group worldwide. Future autonomous vehicles may help to support the mobility of older individuals; however, these cars will not be widely available for several decades and current semi-autonomous vehicles often require manual takeover in unusual driving conditions. In these situations, the vehicle issues a takeover request in any uni-, bi- or trimodal combination of visual, auditory, or tactile alerts to signify the need for manual intervention. However, to date, it is not clear whether age-related differences exist in the perceived ease of detecting these alerts. Also, the extent to which engagement in non-driving-related tasks affects this perception in younger and older drivers is not known. Therefore, the goal of this study was to examine the effects of age on the ease of perceiving takeover requests in different sensory channels and on attention allocation during conditional driving automation. Twenty-four younger and 24 older adults drove a simulated SAE Level 3 vehicle under three conditions: baseline, while performing a non-driving-related task, and while engaged in a driving-related task, and were asked to rate the ease of detecting uni-, bi- or trimodal combinations of visual, auditory, or tactile signals. Both age groups found the trimodal alert to be the easiest to detect. Also, older adults focused more on the road than the secondary task compared to younger drivers. Findings may inform the development of next-generation of autonomous vehicle systems to be safe for a wide range of age groups.

Keywords: Autonomous driving · Older adults · Takeover · Multimodal displays · Attention · Preferences

1 Introduction

Interest in autonomous transportation has grown steadily in recent years. In fact, several auto manufacturers are testing autonomous vehicles in many U.S. states, such as California, Texas, Nevada, and Florida [1]. These vehicles, which can control various driving functions without continuous input from human drivers' [2], are being designed to provide various benefits to society, such reducing drivers' workload and lowering the number of traffic accidents [3–7]. They are also expected to support the mobility

© Springer Nature Switzerland AG 2020
Q. Gao and J. Zhou (Eds.): HCII 2020, LNCS 12207, pp. 135–146, 2020.
https://doi.org/10.1007/978-3-030-50252-2_11

of populations, particularly older adults, who might have experienced difficulties being mobile prior to this technology.

Aging is becoming a major concern for many countries. In the United States alone, by the year 2030, the baby boomer generation, i.e., individuals born between the years 1946 and 1964, will account for approximately 17–29% of the general population [8, 9]. The root of many concerns regarding older adult populations is that perceptual, cognitive, and physical declines are often associated with an increase in age [10, 11]. These changes are likely to create challenges in performing common daily tasks, such as personal care, home chores, and transportation (e.g., [10]). With respect to driving, a daily task that is considerably more complex than most, age-related biological changes can result in driving performance decrements, and Eby et al. [12] concluded that older drivers had higher fatal crashes rates compared to younger adults. Given that the majority of older adults assign a high level of importance to maintaining independence and autonomy throughout later stages of life [13, 14], limiting driving privileges does not represent a feasible solution for this age group.

Autonomous vehicles may help to mitigate some of the problems faced by older adults. Yet, in their current state, these vehicles have their own set of challenges. The Society of Automotive Engineers (SAE) International [15] defines 6 levels of vehicle automation (see Fig. 1). Levels 0–2 require manual input, as well as continuous monitoring of the driving environment. However, for Levels 3 & 4, drivers will be allowed to disengage (to some extent) from driving and perform non-driving related tasks (NDRTs), such as watching a video, reading a book, or resting [15]. For Level 5, drivers will not need to control the vehicle. It will take several decades before SAE Level 5 vehicles makeup the majority of vehicle fleet on roadways. In the interim, Levels 2–4 will likely remain the focus of many research efforts [2, 7]. Specifically, Levels 3 and 4 automated driving systems can reach their design limits, when faced with difficult or unusual conditions, such as encountering road construction, poorly visibility, or loss of GPS connection, and require drivers to resume driving. In these cases, the vehicle will issue a takeover request to signify the need for manual intervention [16–19]. However, age-related declines may limit elderly drivers' abilities to quickly notice and interpret takeover alerts, and successfully resume control of the vehicle [10]. For this reason, it will be critical to ensure that takeover warning alerts are designed considering age-related differences in perception and cognition.

Research studies have evaluated the effectiveness of different types of multimodal warning signals as takeover requests, particularly, different combinations of visual (V), auditory (A), and tactile (T) signals during Level 3 autonomous driving. Many have found bi- and trimodal alert requests to result in the fastest braking response time [21, 22], hands-on steering response time [23], and/or automation disengagement time (captured by button presses) [23]. However, most of these studies involved younger adults only and did not confirm their findings with respect to older groups. But in manual driving, Pitts and Sarter [24] showed that older adults have more difficulty in noticing a tactile signal when it is combined with visual and auditory cues. While this work highlights potential limits in older adults' abilities to recognize and respond to different types of multimodal stimuli, little is known about how drivers subjectively perceive these warning signals. This knowledge is important because it will determine how drivers interpret and

SAE AUTOMATION LEVELS

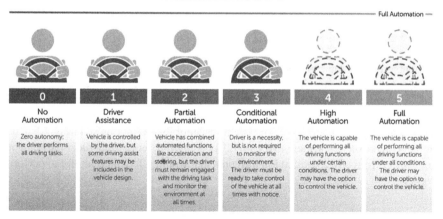

Fig. 1. SAE levels of automation [15] (taken from [20])

respond to notifications. For example, if alarms appear annoying, drivers may decide to ignore them overtime [25, 26]. Therefore, examining the ease of detecting multimodal warning takeover alerts warrants more investigation. Here, perceived ease is defined as the extent to which a system is used without effort [27]. One particular study asked younger drivers to rate all singles, pairs, and triplets of multimodal cues (i.e., V, A, T, VA, VT, AT, and VAT) while using conditional automation and found higher evaluation scores, in terms of usefulness and satisfaction, for bi- and trimodal warnings compared to unimodal warnings [23]. However, it is not clear whether older adults have the same or similar preferences.

In addition, the allocation of attention during semi-autonomous driving between younger and older drivers is also likely to affect the perception of warning signals. For example, Lee, Kim, and Ji [28] found older adults to pay more attention to the road during manual driving, even when instructed to engage in secondary tasks. This behavior may increase their overall readiness to perceive in-vehicle warnings. Currently, it is unclear if older drivers will employ this same strategy (compared to younger adults) during Level 3 autonomous driving operations, when engagement in NDRTs is more tolerated. At the same time, however, this engagement may alter their perception of ease in detecting takeover alerts.

Therefore, the goals of this study were to determine if age-related differences exist in a) the perceived ease of detecting multimodal takeover requests, and b) attention allocation in SAE Level 3 conditional automation. Based on previous studies [21–23, 28], we expected that both age groups would rate multimodal alerts as easier to perceive compared to single signals, and that older adults would focus more on the road (and less on NDRTs) compared to younger drivers.

2 Methods

2.1 Participants

Twenty-four younger and 24 older adults participated in this study. Younger adults were all students from Purdue University and older adults were residents of the Lafayette/West Lafayette, Indiana community. Table 1 provides demographic information about each group. Requirements for participation in the study included: a) possession of a valid U.S. driver's license, b) normal/corrected-to-normal vision; c) no impairments to the sense of hearing and touch, and d) no self-reported susceptibility to motion sickness. Also, the Montreal Cognitive Assessment (MoCA) [29] was used to ensure that older participants did not suffer from any cognitive impairments that would affect their ability to perform our tasks.

Table 1. Demographic information of participants for both age groups. (Data are mean ± standard error of the mean)

	Age	Driving hours per week	Years of driving
Younger adults	21.9 ± 1.4	5.2 ± 5.8	5.3 ± 2.3
Older adults	71.7 ± 4.9	9.8 ± 9.1	54.1 ± 4.8

2.2 Apparatus

Driving Simulation. The experiment used a medium-fidelity driving simulator (min-iSim developed by the National Advanced Driving Simulator - NADS) (see Fig. 2), which consisted of three 48-inch LED monitors that displayed the driving environment and one 24-inch LCD screen that simulated the in-vehicle dashboard. Other system hardware included a steering wheel, foot pedals, and a standard-sized leather seat.

Stimulus. Visual (V) warning signals were red circles (200 × 200 pixels) displayed in the center of the main monitor. Auditory (A) signals were 400 Hz beeps. Tactile (T) warnings were presented using two C-2 tactors (i.e., vibration apparatuses) developed by Engineering Acoustics, Inc. They delivered vibrations signals at 250 Hz. As seen in Fig. 3, the tactors were attached to a waist belt and attached to participants' low-back center. The duration of all signals was 1 s.

2.3 Driving Scenario and Study Design

A 2 (age group: younger and older) × 7 (signal type: V, A, T, VA, VT, AT, and VAT) full factorial design was employed. Participants experienced three different driving conditions, i.e., baseline (B), performing a non-driving-related task (NDRT), and performing a driving-related task (DRT), on a simulated 4-lane highway (with two lanes in each direction). Specifically, in condition B, participants were asked to monitor Level 3 automation. They were told that at any time, any of the 7 warning signal types would be presented

Fig. 2. MiniSim driving simulator

Fig. 3. C-2 tactors (Color figure online)

randomly and would represent 'takeover' requests. In the NDRT condition, participants were required to perform the same task as in condition B. However, now, a (technical talk) video played on the right-hand lower corner of the main display. This task was designed to simulate an in-vehicle (non-driving-related) interaction that drivers can expect to experience in the future. Participants were asked to pay attention to the content of the video. Finally, in the DRT condition, drivers monitored the automation as in condition B, while also performing a driving-related headway estimation task. The purpose of this task was to measure how accurately drivers could estimate the time-to-collision (TTC) with respect to a lead vehicle. This task presented participants with a scenario that could happen right after a takeover request. The researcher randomly probed participants about TTC judgements throughout the drive (12 times in total). At the end of the study, participants were simply asked to rate their perceived ease of detecting the signals.

After the experiment, participants completed a structured questionnaire where they were asked to rate, on a scale from 1 to 10, the ease of detecting each type of warning signal (with 1 being the easiest; 10 being the most difficult). They also answered open-ended questions related to their driving behavior in all three driving conditions, such as the allocation of their attention and headway gap preferences. Questions are listed below:

1) *Based on your ratings of the ease of detecting the signals, explain if any of the seven signals were more difficult to detect compared to others?*
2) *Please describe where your attention was mostly concentrated during the driving while watching a video condition*
3) *In real-life driving, what distance do you feel most comfortable keeping between you and a vehicle in front of you?*

2.4 Procedures

Participants first signed the experimental consent form. Then, a pre-experiment questionnaire was administered to gather information about participants and their driving experiences. After completing this questionnaire, participants completed a 10-min training session. This training introduced them to the experimental equipment, including the driving simulator and warning signal stimuli, reviewed experimental procedures, and provided a sample driving scenario for participants to become familiar with the driving environment and conditions.

For the experiment, the presentation of the three simulated conditions was counterbalanced for each participant, and each condition lasted about 15 min. Also, the 7 warning signals were randomly presented (4 times each) throughout the trials. No actually takeover action was required. A 5-min break was given between each driving condition. After the experiment, the post-experiment questionnaire was conducted.

2.5 Data Analysis

For perceived ease of detecting warning signals, a two-way mixed Analysis of Variance (ANOVA) was conducted to compare differences between age groups and signal types. In this case, independent variables were age (between-subject) and signal type (within-subject), and the dependent variable was the rating score selected by participants. Results were considered statistically significance where p < 0.05. Partial eta squared (η_p^2) was used as a measure of effect size. In addition, analysis of the qualitative data from the open-ended questions included summary statistics, such as the number (or percentage) of people who shared common responses.

3 Results

3.1 Perceived Ease of Detecting Warning Signals

The scores for the ease of detecting warning signals were significantly affected by age ($F(1, 42) = 7.915, p = .007, \eta_p^2 = .159$) and signal type ($F(6, 252) = 18.686, p < .001, \eta_p^2 = .308$). With respect to age, older adults ($2.007 \pm .197$) perceived all signals to be significantly easier to detect compared to younger adults (2.923 ± .180). For signal type, post-hoc comparisons revealed that the VAT trimodal signal (1.379 ± .126) was easiest to detect, followed by bimodal signals (VA (2.096 ± .163), VT (2.429 ± .170), and AT (2.004 ± .172)), followed by unimodal signals (V (3.488 ± .277), A (2.671 ± .213), and T (3.188 ± .293)). No significant differences were found between bimodal and unimodal signals (i.e., $p > .05$). See Fig. 4.

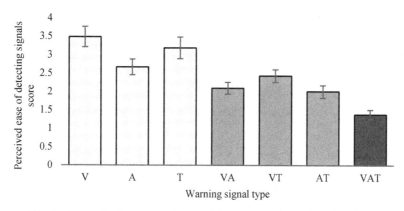

Fig. 4. Scores for the perceived ease of detecting each warning signal type

There was also a significant age × signal type interaction (F (6, 252) = 7.149, p < .001, η_p^2 = .145) on the scores for the perceived ease of detecting warning signals. According to post-hoc comparisons, younger adults had significantly higher scores for V, T, VA, and VT (i.e., V = 4.875 ± .448; T = 3.875 ± .483; VA = 2.542 ± .255; VT = 2.958 ± .244) compared to older adults for the same signals (i.e., V = 2.100 ± .280; T = 2.500 ± .276; VA = 1.650 ± .182; VT = 1.900 ± .228). Also, older adults rated the single tactile signal (T = 2.500 ± .276) as being more difficult to perceived compared to all other signals. Finally, for younger adults, V (4.875 ± .448) and T (3.875 ± .483) had the highest scores, followed by A (3.042 ± .304), VA (2.542 ± .255), VT (2.958 ± .244), and AT (1.958 ± .204), followed by VAT (1.208 ± .104) (Fig. 5).

3.2 Open-Ended Questions

For the question, *Based on your ratings of the ease of detecting the signals, explain if any of the seven signals were more difficult to detect compared to others?*, 9 out of 24 (37.5%) younger adults felt that the visual signal was the hardest to detect, compared to 4 out of 24 (16.7%) older adults. Here, participants commented that performing secondary tasks impacted the detection of visual signal and also felt that the size of the visual signal made it less salience. For the tactile signal, the same number of younger and older adults (that is, 5) stated that it was more difficult to detect compared to other signals. They explained that the vibration from the driving simulator influenced their perception of the tactile signal. Only 3 participants (i.e., 1 younger adults and 2 older adults) felt that the auditory signal was the hardest to perceive.

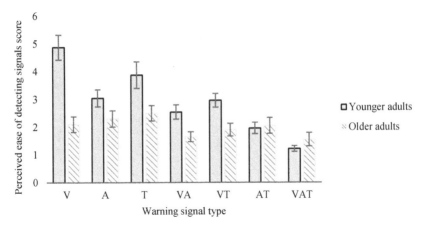

Fig. 5. Scores for the perceived ease of detecting each warning signal type between age groups

For the question, *Please describe where your attention was mostly concentrated during the driving while watching a video condition*, 84.2% of younger drivers reported that they focused mainly on the video in the NDRT (non-driving related task) video watching condition. In contrast, 78.6% of older adults explained that they focused on the road and only seldomly listened to the video.

For the question, *In real-life driving, what distance do you feel most comfortable keeping between you and a vehicle in front of you?*, four options were provided to participants: 1) 1–2 s, 2) 4–5 s, 3) 7–8 s, or 4) if other, please specify. Numerical responses were given by participants. An independent-sample t-test was conducted to compare the mean differences between younger and older adults. The results indicated that older adults preferred a larger headway, $6.43 \pm .524$ s, compared to younger drivers, $4.73 \pm .456$ s ($p = .018$).

4 Discussion

The goal of this study was to investigate the effects of age on a) the ease of perceiving takeover requests in different sensory modalities and b) attention allocation during SAE Level 3 conditional autonomous driving. Overall, both age groups perceived the trimodal (VAT) signal to be the easiest to detect, followed by bimodal signals. Also, when engaging in non-driving related tasks (NDRT), most of older adults focused on the road, while younger drivers paid more attention to the NDRT.

4.1 Signal Perception

For overall score comparisons between the seven types of signal, trimodal warnings were perceived to be the easiest, followed bimodal signals. This finding is very much consistent with the results of other studies on multimodal warning signal deign, even though the dependent measure is different. In particular, studies that found the same trend with respect to trimodal and bimodal signals often measured response times to cues (e.g., [23, 24, 30, 31]). This consistency may be explained by the notion that multimodal warning signals are often perceived to convey a higher level of urgency [32, 33]. In addition, as many participants mentioned, when visual attention was consumed by watching the video, or when tactile attention was consumed by perceiving the vibration produced by the simulator, it was difficult to detect single signals presented in single modalities. In this case, multimodal signals that used more than one sensory channel (i.e., redundant cues) made it easier to perceive the warnings.

For the observed age-related differences in sensory perception, older adults had the most difficulty in perceiving tactile signals, while younger adults struggled more with visual signals. This phenomenon may be the result of older adults having less exposure to technologies with tactile feedback. Younger adults, on the other hand, thought that visual signals were hardest to detect. This rating is consistent with their subjective responses in the first open-ended question. One possible explanation for this finding may have been captured by the second open-ended quesiton. Here, younger drivers explained that they focused more of their attention on the video watching task. This likely reduced their ability to detect the visual signals, which were located in the peripheral field-of-view, when they were engaged in the video.

4.2 Attention Allocation

The responses from the open-ended questions about the attention allocation in the non-driving related task condition were in accordance with our expectations, as well as previous studies [28] that found that older adults emphasize safety over entertainment compared to younger drivers. This was even further supported by the third open-ended question about the preference of time-to-collision. Here, older adults preferred to have longer headway distances. One possible explanation for this preference could be that older drivers moderate their driving behaviors/patterns (i.e., employ self-regulatory strategies) to compensate for age-related declines in abilities that are critical for driving [34–36]. Alternatively, less exposure to, and thus a general lack of knowledge regarding the capabilities of next-generation autonomous vehicles [37], may create hesitation in senior populations [38].

5   Conclusion

This study examined the effects of age on the ease of perceiving takeover requests in different sensory modalities, as well on the allocation of attention during SAE Level 3 conditional autonomous driving. Overall, trimodal warning signals were perceived easiest to be detected. Also, compared to younger participants, older adults rated the tactile signal as the most difficult unimodal signal to detect. They also focused more on the road even when asked to engage in a non-driving related task. Future work should investigate the perceived ease of detecting multimodal stimuli of different intensities. The findings of this usability study may help to inform the development of next-generation of autonomous vehicle systems that seek to achieve inclusive design.

Acknowledgement. The authors would like to acknowledge the support of funds from the National Science Foundation (NSF grant #1755746; Program Manager: Dr. Ephraim Glinert).

References

1. Favarò, F., Eurich, S., Nader, N.: Autonomous vehicles' disengagements: trends, triggers, and regulatory limitations. Accid. Anal. Prev. **110**, 136–148 (2018). https://doi.org/10.1016/j.aap.2017.11.001
2. Wan, J., Wu, C.: The effects of lead time of take-over request and nondriving tasks on taking-over control of automated vehicles. IEEE Trans. Hum.-Mach. Syst. **48**, 582–591 (2018). https://doi.org/10.1109/THMS.2018.2844251
3. Anderson, J., Kalra, N., Stanley, K., Sorensen, P., Samaras, C., Oluwatola, O.: Autonomous Vehicle Technology: A Guide for Policymakers. Rand Corporation (2014). https://doi.org/10.7249/rr443-2
4. Bishop, R.: Intelligent vehicle applications worldwide. IEEE Intell. Syst. Their Appl. **15**, 78–81 (2000). https://doi.org/10.1109/5254.820333
5. Young, M.S., Stanton, N.A.: What's skill got to do with it? Vehicle automation and driver mental workload. Ergonomics **50**, 1324–1339 (2007). https://doi.org/10.1080/00140130701318855
6. Saffarian, M., de Winter, J.C.F., Happee, R.: Automated driving: human-factors issues and design solutions. Proc. Hum. Factors Ergon. Soc. Annu. Meet. **56**, 2296–2300 (2012). https://doi.org/10.1177/1071181312561483
7. Litman, T.: Autonomous Vehicle Implementation Predictions: Implications for Transport Planning (2019)
8. Erber, J.T.: Aging and older adulthood, p. 466. Hoboken, Wiley-Blackwell (2012)
9. Czaja, S.J., Boot, W.R., Charness, N., Rogers, W.A.: Designing for Older Adults: Principles and Creative Human Factors Approaches. CRC Press, Boca Raton (2019). https://doi.org/10.1201/b22189
10. Anstey, K.J., Wood, J., Lord, S., Walker, J.G.: Cognitive, sensory and physical factors enabling driving safety in older adults. Clin. Psychol. Rev. **25**, 45–65 (2005). https://doi.org/10.1016/j.cpr.2004.07.008
11. Lemke, U.: The challenges of aging – sensory, cognitive, socio-emotional and health changes in old age. In: Hearing Care for Adults 2009—The Challenge of Aging. Proceedings of the 2nd International Adult Conference, pp. 33–43. Phonak AG, Stäfa (2009)
12. Eby, D., Molnar, L.J., Zhang, L., St Louis, R.M., Zanier, N., Kostyniuk, L.P.: Keeping older adults driving safely: a research synthesis of advanced in-vehicle technologies. AAA Foundation for Traffic Safety (2015)
13. Molnar, L.J., Eby, D.W., St Louis, R.M., Neumeyer, A.L.: Promising approaches for promoting lifelong community mobility, Ann Arbor (2007)
14. Hassan, H., King, M., Watt, K.: The perspectives of older drivers on the impact of feedback on their driving behaviours: a qualitative study. Transp. Res. Part F: Traffic Psychol. Behav. **28**, 25–39 (2015). https://doi.org/10.1016/J.TRF.2014.11.003
15. SAE International: Automated driving: levels of driving automation are defined in new SAE international standard J3016, no. 1. SAE International (2014)
16. Eriksson, A., Stanton, N.A.: takeover time in highly automated vehicles: noncritical transitions to and from manual control. Hum. Factors **59**, 689–705 (2017). https://doi.org/10.1177/0018720816685832
17. Llaneras, R.E., Salinger, J., Green, C.A.: Human factors issues associated with limited ability autonomous driving systems: Drivers' allocation of visual attention to the forward roadway. In: Proceedings of the Seventh International Driving Symposium on Human Factors in Driver Assessment, Training, and Vehicle Design, pp. 92–98 (2013). https://doi.org/10.17077/drivingassessment.1472

18. Zhang, B., de Winter, J., Varotto, S., Happee, R., Martens, M.: Determinants of take-over time from automated driving: A meta-analysis of 129 studies. Transp. Res. Part F: Traffic Psychol. Behav. **64**, 285–307 (2019). https://doi.org/10.1016/j.trf.2019.04.020

19. Mcdonald, A., Alambeigi, H.: Towards computational simulations of behavior during automated driving take-overs : a review of the empirical and modeling literatures (2019)

20. National Highway Traffic Safety Administration: Automated Driving Systems 2.0: A Vision for Safety (2017)

21. Politis, I., Brewster, S., Pollick, F.: Using Multimodal Displays to Signify Critical Handovers of Control to Distracted Autonomous Car Drivers. Int. J. Mob. Hum. Comput. Interact. **9**, 1–16 (2017). https://doi.org/10.1016/j.bbapap.2014.08.013

22. Huang, G., Steele, C., Zhang, X., Pitts, B.J.: Multimodal cue combinations: a possible approach to designing in-vehicle takeover requests for semi-autonomous driving. Proc. Hum. Factors Ergon. Soc. Annu. Meet. **63**, 1739–1743 (2019)

23. Yoon, S.H., Kim, Y.W., Ji, Y.G.: The effects of takeover request modalities on highly automated car control transitions. Accid. Anal. Prev. **123**, 150–158 (2019). https://doi.org/10.1016/j.aap.2018.11.018

24. Pitts, B.J., Sarter, N.: What you don't notice can harm you: age-related differences in detecting concurrent visual, auditory, and tactile cues. Hum. Factors **60**, 445–464 (2018). https://doi.org/10.1177/0018720818759102

25. Baldwin, C.L.: Verbal collision avoidance messages during simulated driving: perceived urgency, alerting effectiveness and annoyance. Ergonomics **54**, 328–337 (2011). https://doi.org/10.1080/00140139.2011.558634

26. Edworthy, J., Stanton, N.: Human Factors in Auditory Warnings. Routledge, Abingdon (2019). https://doi.org/10.4324/9780429455742

27. Venkatesh, V., Davis, F.D.: Theoretical extension of the technology acceptance model: four longitudinal field studies. Manag. Sci. **46**, 186–204 (2000). https://doi.org/10.1287/mnsc.46.2.186.11926

28. Lee, S.C., Kim, Y.W., Ji, Y.G.: Effects of visual complexity of in-vehicle information display: age-related differences in visual search task in the driving context. Appl. Ergon. **81**, 102888 (2019). https://doi.org/10.1016/j.apergo.2019.102888

29. Nasreddine, Z.S., et al.: The Montreal cognitive assessment, MoCA: a brief screening tool for mild cognitive impairment. J. Am. Geriatr. Soc. **53**, 695–699 (2005). https://doi.org/10.1111/j.1532-5415.2005.53221.x

30. Lundqvist, L.M., Eriksson, L.: Age, cognitive load, and multimodal effects on driver response to directional warning. Appl. Ergon. **76**, 147–154 (2019). https://doi.org/10.1016/j.apergo.2019.01.002

31. Petermeijer, S., Bazilinskyy, P., Bengler, K., de Winter, J.: Take-over again: investigating multimodal and directional TORs to get the driver back into the loop. Appl. Ergon. **62**, 204–215 (2017). https://doi.org/10.1016/j.apergo.2017.02.023

32. Politis, I., Brewster, S., Pollick, F.: Evaluating multimodal driver displays of varying urgency. In: Proceedings of the 5th International Conference on Automotive User Interfaces and Interactive Vehicular Applications, AutomotiveUI 2013. pp. 92–99 (2013). https://doi.org/10.1145/2516540.2516543

33. Suied, C., Susini, P., McAdams, S.: Evaluating warning sound urgency with reaction times. J. Exp. Psychol. Appl. **14**, 201–212 (2008). https://doi.org/10.1037/1076-898X.14.3.201

34. Meng, A., Siren, A.: Cognitive problems, self-rated changes in driving skills, driving-related discomfort and self-regulation of driving in old drivers. Accid. Anal. Prev. **49**, 322–329 (2012)

35. Gwyther, H., Holland, C.: The effect of age, gender and attitudes on self-regulation in driving. Accid. Anal. Prev. **45**, 19–28 (2012). https://doi.org/10.1016/j.aap.2011.11.022

36. Molnar, L., Eby, D., Zhang, L., Zanier, N., Louis, R., Kostyniuk, L.: Self-regulation of driving by older adults: a synthesis of the literature and framework. Aging (Albany. NY) **20**, 227–235 (2015)
37. Rovira, E., McLaughlin, A.C., Pak, R., High, L.: Looking for age differences in self-driving vehicles: examining the effects of automation reliability, driving risk, and physical impairment on trust. Front. Psychol. **10** (2019). https://doi.org/10.3389/fpsyg.2019.00800
38. Abraham, H., Lee, C., Mehler, B., Reimer, B.: Autonomous Vehicles and Alternatives to Driving: Trust, Preferences, and Effects of Age Learning to Use Technology View project. In: Transportation Research Board 96th Annual Meeting (2017)

Older People and Technology Use: The Importance of Using Video Stimuli in Group Discussions

Loredana Ivan[✉] and Florinela Mocanu[✉]

National University of Political Studies and Public Administration, Bucharest, Romania
loredana.ivan@comunicare.ro, florinela.mocanu@gmail.com

Abstract. Current work aims to discuss the importance of using short video materials when investigating technology practices and meanings in older people's lives. We gathered data through the means of focus groups and we employed an innovative methodology, using a short movie: "The Yellow Smiling Face", directed by a young Romanian director Constantin Popescu– already distributed in several film festivals. Introducing a short movie in the focus group allowed a reflection on everyday practices with communication technologies. We used this movie as a trigger for older people, asking them to relate their experience with learning different ICTs with the movie. Our findings suggest that some emergent topics are triggered by the context of the movie, such as the learning process, learning from the partners, whereas other topics were indirectly triggered by movie, such as the history of using communication technologies and the interference between technology use and gender roles. Based on these findings, we discuss, in the current article, the importance of learning from the partners to use new technologies, from the spouses, challenges of the learning process at this age group: namely the active role of women and the relatively passive role of the men and the stereotypically gender roles.

Keywords: Older people and technology use · Innovative methodology and ICT use · ICT learning in family and older adults

1 Introduction

Research studies on ICT use at older people often includes individual or group discussions regarding patterns of use, advantages and disadvantages, habits, motivations, and generally speaking the way technology is integrated in their lives; and meanings they attribute to different ICTs [1, 2]. As information and communication technologies are becoming intrinsic part of our lives, people's discourses about technology use convey aspects on social practices, social learning processes, inequalities and exclusion [3]; also on integration and cohesiveness, conflicts and cooperation [4]. The way people talk about technology use reveals their anxieties, expectations, skills and cognitive mechanisms by which they interpret the role of technology [5].

© Springer Nature Switzerland AG 2020
Q. Gao and J. Zhou (Eds.): HCII 2020, LNCS 12207, pp. 147–163, 2020.
https://doi.org/10.1007/978-3-030-50252-2_12

Moreover, conversations about technology use with older people is part of an approach which is starting to grow in usage and value: a collaboration and empowerment approach [6, 7], advocating for the inclusion of the older adults in each step of the research: formulation of the research problem, data collection and data analysis. Most of the time, when we talk about the role of communication technologies in older people's lives, collaboration and empowerment, this comprises creative techniques such as photovoice activities, exploring picture collages, creative techniques during interviews and group discussions, workshops and forums [6].

However, when discussing about technology use, older people might feel reluctant to talk from different reasons.

(1)   Their familiarity and skills in using different ICTs might not be very similar. Several studies [8, 9] have underlined the fact that older people are not a "homogeneous" group in the way they use communication technologies.
(2)   Older people could experience stereotype threat, as they might perceive themselves poorer in using different technologies than then actually are [10].
(3)   Negative experience in using different devices is probably difficult and generally speaking not easy to share [11], unless people perceive that such situations are common to others. Typical instances in which people might feel reluctant to talk are the dependence of others who are called as assistants, the frustration in handling new applications or the social pressure to accommodate them in everyday life. In this respect, using video stimuli might trigger older people's answers and their willingness to share positive and negative feelings in using communication technologies.

In previous studies in which we interviewed older people on the role of communication technologies [12–15] in their everyday life, we noticed that some topics are recurrent:

(1)   The relative positive views of older people over the impact of ICT– a kind of techno-optimism, accompanied by the perception that they do not have the necessary skills to handle different devices and applications.
(2)   Perceived risks regarding health, dependency, particularly when they talk about children and grandchildren and in some instances perceived risks regarding privacy an decency – especially when using Social Media Sites.
(3)   Perceived advantages and dis-advantages of technology use – particularly the possibility to be in contact with family members living far away and share daily life experiences with them; also conflicts that might emerge during family gatherings over the (mis)use of communication technologies.
(4)   Intergenerational aspects: learning from grandchildren, difficulties and discomfort in asking for help to their adult children or to younger family members/acquaintances or friends.
(5)   The fact that family members push them to use different devices they do not necessary want or need, and the constant "pushing" factor to master different new

applications – including here the dominant role of their adult children – who some-times decide what "it is best" for them to use, purchase different devices or pay for some of the Internet-based services.

(6) The imperative asking for courses, guidelines, organised activities, which could fill their need to learn and get updated in an independent way and according to their particular needs.

Having these extensive findings in mind, we looked for a creative approach that might explore other facets of ICT appropriation and use at older people. Vignettes, stories, short movies are rarely used to stimulate such discussions, though focus groups for example are techniques in which such tools are recommended [16, 17]. Also, for some sensitive topics, as for example partners' conflicts when using different technologies, topics been partially identified before, video materials might be a way to activate the discussion without making people feel un-comfortable. The same argument is valid when we talk about their "in-abilities" to handle different applications [18] – we noticed people being not comfortable talking about this topic and feeling more willing to discuss it in groups that in the individual interviews.

From this point of view, using characters (as in vignettes or in short movies) could help people open some topics they feel less comfortable with, as they could relate with the behaviours or situations in which characters are presented.

2 Using Video Materials to Discuss with Older People About ICT Use

In this section we will present some studies that use videos, visual or graphic materials for data collection on older people and ICT use. The video or visual stimuli may facilitate the experience sharing of old participants and stimulate discussions that may not be top of mind when directly asking them about their life happenings, especially for topics related to the new technologies and their influence over daily life activities. Topics like gender roles, family connections and anxiety towards new media can be much easier approached in this way. The below studies involved video or visual materials helping in data the collecting phase of the research.

Newell, Arnott, Carmichael and Morgan [19] were focused on creating a user-friendly computer interface for older people and use the theatrical interaction in order to activate the discussion. Short plays described how the system worker, errors and emo-tions caused by the errors of the system or participants' errors; the play could be live or recorded. This technique is efficient because participants can imagine themselves in that situation and provide the experience details. Wherton, Sugarhood, Procter and Green-halgh [20] were engaged in creating a gadget to enhance digital communication among older adults. Wherton et al. [20] created a prototype of a touchscreen phone with handset and speakers for improving the social interaction through devices for the older people who might try to overcome loneliness. As a starting point they analysed the current state of the social interaction and the loneliness management techniques of the participants using graphic and visual methods to gather information. The participants received maps, photo camera and an album, conceptual lists, body outline, postcard, relationship maps and a diary to fill in and used them over a certain period, then send these materials back filled with content. Afterwards, to gather feedback about the application, Wherton et al. [20] designed together with the participants the interface by analysing visual aids, story boards, and cardboard cut-outs for selecting the most suitable item for the new gadget.

Muñoz et al. [21] started from the observation that social media is not used at its best capacity by older people, which may result in isolation and loneliness, idea mentioned also by Wherton et al. [20]. Social Connector was projected to be a social media application which may increase the adults' interactions with their families. The first part of the study comprises data gathering about this prototype through semi-structured interviews. A recorded video call with a family member was used as the main material for the analysis. A feedback interview as organized to share the experience and the usefulness of the application. Both the time spent and the number of errors were influenced by the adults' age and their level of technology adoption, together with the self-confidence. Similarly to Muñoz et al. [21], Gonzalez, Ramirez and Viadel [22] started from the observation that attitudes towards technology in general and the self-confidence may affect the outcome in technology adoption at older people. Gonzalez et al. [22] focused their study on older people's attitudes regarding computer use and how their attitudes influence the ICT learning. They organized a skill training of 20 h, followed by 30 h for consolidation including video tutorials, to better explain the terms. The researchers had as graphic materials a manual of instructions. Survey was taken pre-training and post-training and group interview were organized post-training. The results show that attitudes toward computers were influenced by the basic skills of older adults.

The above-mentioned studies included the digital adoption theme as a problem solver for loneliness and isolation, attitudes towards technology and self-confidence being a factor in the learning process and people's level of digital skills. Such approaches have not only been used in Human Computer Interaction (HCI), as in the examples listed above, but also in the health care domain, as improving digital skills of older people is a way to facilitate the health monitoring and well-being communication to the care-givers and family. Cozza, De Angeli, and Tonolli [23] conducted a research focused on how a smart home for older people can increase the efficiency of the provided healthcare services. The data collection included both visual elements and hands-on experience. Participants were asked to keep a personal diary, recording daily activities, a techniques used also by Wherton et al. [20]. They also added Problem Mapping – a visual technique to relate problems with solution and semi-structured interviewers. The data collection included also a scenario-based design incorporating 11 different scenarios, one facilitator and one ethnographer who took pictures and notes of the whole process. The hands-on experience involved the actual utilization of the prototype under researcher's observation and feedback interviews afterwards.

The visual stimuli can be in different forms and formats; some researcher used for data collection theatrical representations [19], some used video formats, as recordings, tutorials or clips [19, 21, 22]. Some authors prefer the data gathering under printed or written graphic materials format, as diaries, scenario-based design, vignettes, problem solving maps, postcards, photo-albums [20, 23]. Those studies recommended a combining the visual methods in order to enlarge the data. Still the purpose of the studies presented here had the scope to create or enhance the technology use for older adults via different application and prototypes in order to reduce loneliness, increase social media interactions, or family's liaisons and for health monitoring and health communicating purposes.

3 The Present Study

In the present study we engaged with older people from Bucharest, Romania (age 60 and older) in talking about the use of ICT in everyday life, using a video material to trigger the conversation. We select people 60 years and above, as this is the typical age limit considered by the official statistics (see Eurostat for example) when they present data on older people and technology use. We gather data though the means of focus groups and we employed an innovative methodology, using a short movie: "The Yellow Smiling Face", directed by a young Romanian director Constantin Popescu (https://www.you tube.com/watch?v=8HDM6ERbBKA) – already distributed in several film festivals. We used this movie as a trigger, asking participants to describe situations from their lives in which they experienced feelings, difficulties in using different types of communication technologies.

We aim to investigate the topics that could emerge when using such video material in a group discussion and in which way such topics are linked with the characters and the plot of the video we presented. Also, we explore whether using such technique could stimulate people to talk about more "sensitive" topics, as compare to the ones we identified in previous studies when we used interviews with older people, on the same topic.

Accordingly, we formulate the following research questions:

(1) What are the main topics people discuss about after watching the video material, and in which way the characters and the plot of the movie are linked with the emerging topics?
(2) To which extend the video material contribute to stimulate the discussion on topics people usually might feel uncomfortable talking about, as for example conflicts with partners on technology use and their poor technology skills? We have to qualify here that the both conflicts between partners and older people's poor technology skills are found in the movie we have selected.

Answering these questions yielded significant insights regarding the role of video stimuli in studies in which older people are asked to talk about the role of ICT in their lives. Moreover, it will open the discussion on creative techniques that could be used to approach more "sensitive" topics when investigating technology appropriation.

4 Methodology

Older people (60 and above) were invited to discuss the role of communication technologies in their life, using the focus group technique. Two focus groups were conducted, N = 17 participants (see Table 1) in Bucharest at the National University of Political Science and Public Administration. After participants have been introduced to each other and described the type of communication technologies they use (e.g. laptop, tablets, smart phones) and also some of the applications the use frequently (as Facebook, WhatsApp, and Skype), they were invited to see a 15 min movie: "The Yellow Smiling Face", directed by a young Romanian director Constantin Popescu (https://www.youtube.com/watch?v=8HDM6ERbBKA). The movie has been produced in 2008 and it is available from 2009, after been distributed in several film festivals. The movie presents an old couple (approximately 60 years of age) having trouble to open the computer to install Skype application, so that they will be able to communicate with their son, who is working in US. A tragic-comic series of actions occur in the movie when they try to read the instructions provided by the son on a piece of paper in the context of poor digital skills. The two characters impersonate the difficulties we found in our previous research studies conducted in Romania on older adults and ICT use and this is mainly the reason for which the movie has been selected. It brings into attention.

(1) the difficulties of reading English instructions and getting familiar with applications, when there are no proper training or guidelines
(2) the initial frustration when mastering a new application/device and the tendency to reject it or fear that "something will get broken"
(3) difficulties to handle devices which are not ergonomically tailored for older adults – as for example perceiving small letters on keyboards
(4) discomfort when thinking of the possibility of asking acquaintances or neighbours for help
(5) regret and frustration that they did not learn such things earlier in their lives, so that that they will be independent users. The movie is reduced to a domestic environment and the two characters (the old couple), so the movie might indirectly trigger aspects regarding the use of technology in family settings, particularly in interaction with the partner and subsequently gender aspects regarding technology use later in life.

4.1 Data Collection

Two focus groups were conducted in Bucharest during a period of one week (September 2019). We selected older people (see Table 1), who regularly use Internet, having at least one device which allows Internet access (mobile phone, computer, or tablet). These interviews were audio-recorded, with participants' informative consent, and then transcribed verbatim. Participation in the study was strictly confidential and any identifying information has been removed to ensure that confidentiality is maintained. Interviews lasted from 60–90 min and were translated from Romanian to English for analysis purposes.

Qualitative data analysis of the interpretive interviews employed the constant comparative method [24] as a mean to process the data. Data was stored and organized using the QSR NVIVO software package to facilitate the development of categories and comparison of codes applicable to each category. Analysis began with open coding, and then selective coding [25]. The interviews were coded inductively based on the research questions presented above.

Table 1. Participant socio-demographics

Code	Age	Family status	Highest education	Occupation	Current work status	What is your average annual household income?
Group 1	**20.09.2019 17:30**	**8 participants**				
P1.1	64	Widowed	Some college or university	Accountant	Retired	1201–2000 lei
P1.2	66	Widowed	Completed high school	expert in science of commodities	Retired	1201–2000 lei
P1.3	67	Married	Completed high school	Trade Manager	Retired	Less than 1200 lei
P1.4	75	Married	Completed college program	Not stated	Retired	1201–2000 lei
P1.5	60	Married	Completed high school	Not stated	Employed part-time	1201–2000 lei
P1.6	63	Widowed	Completed college program	Accountant	Retired	1201–2000 lei
P1.7	60	Widowed	Completed college program	Sociologist	Retired	1201–2000 lei
P1.8	65	Separated/divorced	Some high school	Electrician	Retired	1201–2000 lei
Group 2	**21.09.2019 10:00**	**9 participants**				
P2.1	62	Married	Completed high school	Sales person	Not Employed	Less than 1200 lei
P2.2	64	Married	Completed high school	Laundress	Retired	Less than 1200 lei

(continued)

Table 1. (*continued*)

Code	Age	Family status	Highest education	Occupation	Current work status	What is your average annual household income?
P2.3	83	Widowed	Some college or university	Not stated	Retired	1201–2000 lei
P2.4	67	Married	Completed high school	Technician	Retired	Less than 1200 lei
P2.5	69	Married	Completed high school	Foreman	Retired	2001–3000 lei
P2.6	64	Married	Completed high school	Cashier	Retired & Employed	2001–3000 lei
P2.7	68	Separated/divorced	Completed college program	Marketing Manager	Retired	3001–4000 lei
P2.8	66	Married	Completed high school	Accountant	Retired	2001–3000 lei
P2.9	66	Separated/divorced	Completed high school	Economist	Retired	Less than 1200 lei

4.2 Participants

Participants were selected by posting an announcement on Facebook regarding our research and they received a small gift for their participation. We recruited participants who declared they use Internet on their own devices. Our final sample included participants from 60 to 83 years of age, who signed an informative consent to participate in our study. Details about participants' demographics are presented in Table 1. Most of them were medium to high educated, pensioners, using several ICTs, with a socio-economic background above the average of people age 60+ in Romania.

5 Findings

The findings presented here represent the emerging themes of discussion, once the video has been shown to the participants. They were asked to discuss first thoughts coming to their minds after watching the movie. Consequently, the following topics appeared:

(1) history of using communication technologies.
(2) the progress of learning: old and new communication technologies
(3) older people learning from their partners;
(4) gender roles and gender interactions when using ICT.

In order to present the findings, we will use participants' codes as shown in Table 1. We note that some of the themes were directly triggered by the context of the movie: the learning process, learning from the partners, whereas others were indirectly triggered by movie, such as the history of using communication technologies and the interference between technology use and gender roles. Also, participants related their own experience with the one presented in the video and with the characters, in a self-reflective exercise in which they went back and forward from the movie to their own experience with ICT use.

5.1 History of Using Communication Technologies

As the movie dated ten years ago, when probably most of the participants were still on the labour market and they first got I contact with computers and Internet based technologies, it triggered participants to talk about "the beginnings", when they struggle to learn using the new technologies. Some remembered that it was a compulsory requirement at the work, whereas others remembered that they bought a computer for a younger family member who was in school.

> *P2.4: Yes. I worked in accounting immediately after the revolution. They comput-erized us and we were forced to learn on the go. I also did a computer course, but I didn't learn much from it, I was also with a job and caring for the children. They forced us to do it at that time. I have a clue, but I can't say that I'm great*
> *P1.6: I remember when the first computers where introduced, we were working the Salaries department, the manager wanted to make us learn, to do classes, what did mouse mean, did we know? We didn't know. When we were writing, to press A, we didn't know how to press 'space', we learned, exactly in the same way [like in the movie], I learn myself.*

Here we found consistent findings with previous research studies [12, 26] showing that there was a "push" factor in the way older people learnt to use the new technolo-gies: jobs which required basic computer skills (as for example accounting, engineering) forced them to appropriate some applications or devices, an aspect which had a signifi-cant influence on people's willingness to progress in learning and use other technologies also ones they retired. We showed that not age per se was a factor in generating computer anxiety, but rather familiarity with computers during work activities and the type of jobs people had [26]. The push factor appears in the conversations, people using the words as "forced", and "obliged" to describe the beginnings of their learning process. As dif-ficult and challenging was this process at the beginning, the work environment, through courses, training or learning by observation, determined people's attitudes towards tech-nology use once they retired. "Learning by heart" – without fully comprehend what they were doing was often described as a normal beginning in technology appropriation: "we all have been like this" – referring to the characters in the movie. Interesting enough, the movie does not present a working setting, but it triggers participants to place themselves at the beginning of their learning process, when they were pushed to learn at work how to use computers.

In the case of the participants from the transnational families – having children or grandchildren far away from home or experiencing in the past a separation from an important family member, mainly due to migration for work – the movie triggered them to think how they were learning to use new technologies by the necessity of communicating in such situations.

> *P2.5: I also find myself in this movie. My oldest son is on the boat and wherever he goes, through Japan through Vietnam, through Bombay, we can see him; and the same for the youngest son – he is traveling around the country with Petrom [work]*
> *Moderator: And what did you install? Did you install Skype or..?*
> *P2.5: Yes, my wife handles it better…*

Some participants recalled the begging of technology use by contrast with the movie: they were the ones who embraced technology as an opportunity, a pulling factor. They bought computers for their children to support their education in school and estimating that Internet-based technologies would be a factor of inequalities in skills and opportunities on the labour market. More educated, and probably more in contact with the evolution of technology, such participants used the opportunity to learn together with their children.

> *P1.3: Myself I remembered when I first bought a computer. None of us knew how to handle it. My daughter was in the first year of college. It was when we considered it was time for her to have a computer*
> *Moderator: And you and your husband bought a computer for her…*
> *P1.3: Yes, as a birthday present in January. But we didn't know how to set it up, we just had the object. And then, we asked a guy from the college to come in and he installed everything we needed, the Windows. I was next to them; I didn't leave them alone so that she would only know. I was there, once on their left side, once on their right side, and I memorized everything. We learned together to work on it.*

It is usually women who described pull situations, and the gender differences in the learning process are issues deserving a special analysis. Women described themselves as more willing to the take the opportunities offered by the new technologies and less reluctant to try different applications. They also appreciate more the fact that the working environment pushed them to learn using computers.

5.2 The Progress of Learning: Old and New Communication Technologies

Against the initial expectations, the movie shows that the unexperienced couple is finally successful in their attempt to install Skype application. Looking back, our participants remembered the challenges, but also the continuation in the learning process: overcoming the challenges gave them courage to approach new applications and confidence that eventually they would manage.

> *P1.3: When she was at school, I was discovering other things that she didn't know, like installing games. Well, step by step. One thing I did not know - "Mom you press on X and the page goes away, if you don't know what to do next".*

The "golden rule" of pressing the X button was mentioned by several participants. It gives them the feeling that "they can stop" the device when they wish to, a feeling of control and simplicity that was useful in the early stages of the learning process. These feelings accompanied them later, when learning to master new applications.

> *P1.7: Well, I knew Enter and how to press it. My children showed that to me. I wasn't doing so well with the keyboard options and that is why I preferred being taught. I had the fear not to break anything. My son was saying: You press on that X and then it shuts down.*

Taking notes on paper, memorizing everything was a way people described the learning process at the beginning. Patience of the trainer was important in this process, as well as the role of younger family members (children and grandchildren).

> *P1.1: It took a while, when I was looking for the letters, on the keyboard, until I found them.*
> *P1.3: The punctuation marks, as well*
> *P1.1: To write with capital letters, with pause, it was hard*
> *Moderator: How long it took until you got used to it?*
> *P1.1: A lot. We are still looking for them. We had the keyboard question also at the exam, we had to remember it.*
> *Moderator: You learned it by heart.*
> *P1.1: Yes, absolutely.*

The learning process was rather mechanic: "press this, press than" and participants recalled few moments when they had initiative to "try things". Instead, they relay and expected clear indications, and they use the same approach, when the new digital technologies appeared. During focus groups, participants repeatedly brought into discussion the importance of having a guide or a manual with instructions every time they buy a new smart phone, tablet or similar devices, but also when they use different applications, including the Social Network Sites.

In the process of relaying on guidelines, and not necessarily on try and error, older people acquired skills where to find these guidelines and who is reliable to provide them. Finding guidelines, reading instructions is how they learnt using old media (as TV or radio), but also how they managed domestic technologies (as washing or cooking machine). Few studies that we know about brought this aspect into discussion: the fact that younger generations, the so-called "digital natives" [27], born and raised with the digital technology, rarely used guidelines when they have new devices, and they simply just try to "figure out how does it work" [28], whereas older people rely on guidelines, as this is the way technology was handled in their formative years. Some of the participants in our study were familiar with the fact that devices have incorporated guidelines (as for example in the case of the smart phones), others were not aware of it, since this aspect is hardly advertised by the providers.

Moreover, even people who were aware that such guidelines should be offered by providers and they are incorporated in the devices, claimed for the usefulness of a "small book" – printed guidelines that could be easily used in the learning process. Some underlined the fact that when they purchased a specific device, they hardly had enough attention and instructions from the shop assistants or client service offices. This is an issue that it worth further exploration, as usually shop assistants are young people holding stereotypes on older people and technology use [29]. Technology is designed mostly by young people with the youth market in mind, creating prototypes that are more difficult for older people to use, and this aspect has already caught researchers' attention [30]. To a lesser extend such topic has been researched through the voices of older people, and we believe that the movie here triggered people to talk about the importance of guidelines and instruction in the learning process of using ICT.

> *P2.7: I saw myself many years ago, when my son-in-law brought me a computer, with a desktop. He installed some programs and because, at that time, it was only in English, I wrote everything on paper. Besides this, he installed YouTube and Google and newspapers. I liked reading a lot. The first thing I did was reading all the newspapers. Then I entered on Facebook, on YouTube, on various shows.*

Another aspect was related to English skills, as most applications, at least in the beginning, did not have the option of installing applications in Romanian. Older people learnt mechanically how to use computers and further how to use digital technologies. Most of the times, applications were in English, even when it was possible to be in be in their native language – usually because younger people were not the ones who initiated the learning process.

5.3 Older People Learning from Their Partners

The movie presents a scene in which a couple try to install and work with Skype. This will trigger participants to talk about how they learnt from and with their partners. Few studies that we know about have approached this topic. From this point of view the findings are interesting, as learning from the partners, at this age group, could be a more important phenomena compared to learning from peers or from younger family members: when people grow older and they retired in pension, the number of opportunities for peer learning decreases and this is valid also for learning to use the new communication technologies.

> *P1.3: It was very difficult until I taught my husband [to use Internet]. He wanted to access the sport programs. I showed him how to open it [the program] and to close it [program].*
> *Moderator: So, does he enter on Internet by himself?*
> *P1.3: Now he enters by himself.*
> *Moderator: What about before?*

P1.3: He would not enter [on the Internet], poor him, until I was next to him. He was afraid to damage something. He would think: 'If I broke something, she will kill me'

Participants described the learning process led and initiated by women, while men are rather the followers. Indeed, our focus groups consisted mainly in women participants, and they were more willing to respond to our announcements in this study and in previous studies conducted in Romania. However, even the two men participants admitted that "they were taught" to use Internet based applications by their female partners.

P1.6: My husband never knew how to use him phone agenda. And I was saving all the numbers. He used a notebook to write the number on the phone. When he wanted to call someone, he went to the phone and typed all the numbers. I was telling him: why are you struggling so much? Look you can press here. He would say: go away with your technology. It took so long for him to check there [the Agenda in his phone], to read it. I was telling him: check it out because this person called you, you need to talk with him. He was like: '- When did you dial?' '- Well, I only pressed here to see'.
Moderator: So, you also though of your husband when you saw the movie.
P1.6: I saved his numbers, I closed the phone, and I explained everything. My husband was not very fond of technology, I don't know why. He used his phone only to answer the calls or to dial.
P1.4: Usually the men are more retrograde.

Our findings indicate that, at least for this age group, women played a more active role in the learning process, whereas men remained passive. Yet, many studies conducted around the world on digital skills and digital literacy at older people show that women are, generally speaking, less technologically skilled than men. On contrary, in the current study women showed more openness to learn using new applications and they took a leading role in the relationship with their partners in setting them "the things they need to know" and constantly trying to persuade them to learn more about how to use ICT.

We believe that older women could play indeed a key role in the way old couples learn using new technologies, especially when we talk about urban areas and women from the middle-class (our focus group consisted mostly of women with medium to upper socio-economic status). In addition, we found, also in previous studies, that women tend to under-rate their technology skills, they are more affected by stereotype threat and this could be an explanation for their overall lower digital literacy in comparison with men. The way older people learn from the partners to use ICT is a process we intend to explore further.

5.4 Gender Roles and Gender Interactions When Using ICT

The movie triggered interesting discussion about technology use and gender roles at older people. Some participants would say that "men are more retrograde", while women are more progressive in approaching communication technologies.

P1.4: Any beginning is hard. My thinking is that after a certain age, you don't need the computer anymore.
P1.1: I think opposite (more voices)
P1.7: How can you stay updated?
P1.3: For socializing. We make time. No woman or person can say that she spends all her day doing chores in the house. Let's be realistic.
P1.3: Also, when we had a job, we didn't go from work directly to the bathroom and start washing clothes. Now, I spend my breaks doing something on the computer.
P1.2: If your wife cooks, maybe she finds a recipe online and cooks it (to P1.4)
P1.3: I would rather be without TV than without computer.

Male participants expressed more reluctance to technology use and the way this interfere with their partners' household duties. The rather conflictual discussions during focus groups between men participants and women participants over the traditional role of the women in the household and how this interfere with the continuous use of communication technologies requires more in-depth exploration. Men from this age group holds rather traditional views about the role of women in the families and they expect their partners to get engage intensively with doing chores, while women, by engaging with the new communication technologies depart themselves from this role. Conflicts between spouses emerged in families in the context of the pervasiveness use of Internet based-technologies are insufficient explored in the literature. Indeed, stereotypical gender roles attributed the technology mastery to men, and using different ICTs might not be consistent with the traditional role attributed to women. For many of these women, being active in adopting and using different applications could also be a sign of progress, a way to depart from their traditional roles. Our data suggest at least three aspects that need further exploration on gender roles and ICT use for this age group (60+). First, the relationship between the willingness of older women to actively engage with the ICT use and take a leading role in partners' learning process and their progressive values. Women who are more active in the learning process might share more progressive views about their gender roles in families and in society overall. Second, as people age 60 and above are a generation in which the traditional gender roles were dominant, at least in the Romanian society, the active role of women in engaging with the new technologies might result in tensions with their partners, frustrations, accompanied with men's views that the new technologies are waste of time and resources. This might explain their passive role in learning, but also their less optimistic views about incorporating new devices and applications. Third, traditional gender roles might interfere with women opportunities to learn, partially explaining their lower digital skills: especially in couples in which the gender roles are strictly negotiated in the traditional terms, women might feel like they are neglecting their family duties when they engage with technologies. We found support for this issue in our findings: older women in our focus groups kept mentioning that they continue to do household duties like they use to do before and that technology was mainly use in the breaks between different choirs.

6 Conclusions, Limitations and Suggestions for Future Research

6.1 Conclusions

In the current study we explore topics that could emerge when using short video in a group discussion regarding technology use in everyday live. We aimed to reveal the emergent topics and in which way the video material triggers different topics of discussions compared with the ones we already revealed in previous studies in which we explored the role of ICTs in older people lives.

Regarding the first research question on the potential of the video stimuli to stimulate new topics of discussion, our findings indicate that some of the emergent topics: the learning process and learning from the partners to use ICT were directly linked with the context of the movie. Other emergent topics – as the history of using communication technologies and the interference between technology use and gender roles – came rather unexpectedly, deepening the discussion of ICT use in family settings.

Indeed the video stimuli triggered participants to talk about situations in which they felt less comfortable with technology appropriation: the interpersonal conflicts with partners when they learnt to use different applications and the difficulties experienced at the beginning.

The beginning of the learning process is marked by a "push factor" – in most cases this constituted the working environment: people were force to learn by the job requirements. In other cases, they were pushed to learn when family members moved abroad, as the process of migration for work usually left older people behind. We also identify a "pull factor" in our conversations – older people who bought computers for their children, to support their children's education and training, when they went to college. In this case, some of the older people learnt with their children. The learning process, at such age group, was rather mechanic, they relayed on guidelines and written instructions and not or try and error or on observational learning. The importance of written guidelines and "small books" in which things will be explained shortly was repeatedly mentioned in the discussions: they continue to play an important role in acquiring new digital skills. We believe that this happens because it is a way in which they appropriate old media devices (TV, radio) and how they learnt using domestic technology. Moreover, the beginning of the learning process, when computers appeared, occurred in the same way: written instructions and things that they simply learn by heart.

6.2 Limitations

The research has some limitations regarding the socio-demographic characteristics of our sample and future research should consider more gender mix groups, from various socio-economic backgrounds. Also, our sample is gender unbalanced and we have to find ways to attract older men when conducting group discussion on the technology appropriation. We have noticed also in previous studies when posting announcements or selecting participants through the associations for older people, we got more women participants than men. Also the choice of the video has a direct impact on the topics of discussion and it would have been better to test the emergent topics when using several video stimuli.

6.3 Implications for Future Research

Our findings suggest two interesting directions to be further explored: learning from the partners and the interference between gender roles and ICT use in home settings. The video material has created the context for these topics to appear in the discussion, as they did not particularly emerge in our previous research studies conducted on older people. We found that women have a more active role in the learning process of ICT, whereas men remain passive. Learning from the partners is a process that could play a more important role in ICT appropriation for this age group, compared with learning from peers or for younger family members, also because, when we grow older and retire peers, learning becomes less important and children are moving from the house. In a future study we plan to approach this aspect in-depth. Also, learning from the partners to use ICT is shaped by people's views on gender roles and technology. Our findings indicate that, by taking a leading role in the learning process, women depart from their traditional gender role. They reinforced the fact that technology use in home setting did not interfere with their time spending doing different household duties, while men were reluctant to believe this. Whether the active role of women is appropriating communication technologies in the household is a sign of progressive views in relation to a stereotypical masculine domain – as technology is– it worth further explorations.

Acknowledgments. This work is supported by a grant from the Social Sciences and Humanities Research Council of Canada to the Ageing, Communication, Technologies project (actproject.ca).

References

1. Ma, Q., Chen, K., Chan, A.H.S., Teh, P.-L.: Acceptance of ICTs by older adults: a review of recent studies. In: Zhou, J., Salvendy, G. (eds.) ITAP 2015. LNCS, vol. 9193, pp. 239–249. Springer, Cham (2015). https://doi.org/10.1007/978-3-319-20892-3_24
2. Yusif, S., Soar, J., Hafeez-Baig, A.: Older people, assistive technologies, and the barriers to adoption: a systematic review. Int. J. Med. Inform. **94**, 112–116 (2016)
3. Francis, J., Ball, C., Kadylak, T., Cotten, S.R.: Aging in the digital age: conceptualizing technology adoption and digital inequalities. In: Neves, B.B., Vetere, F. (eds.) Ageing and Digital Technology, pp. 35–49. Springer, Singapore (2019). https://doi.org/10.1007/978-981-13-3693-5_3
4. Bailey, A., Ngwenyama, O.: Bridging the generation gap in ICT use: interrogating identity, technology and interactions in community telecentres. Inf. Technol. Dev. **16**(1), 62–82 (2010)
5. Nimrod, G.: Technophobia among older Internet users. Educ. Gerontol. **44**(2–3), 148–162 (2018)
6. Rémillard-Boilard, S., Buffel, T., Phillipson, C.: Involving older residents in age-friendly developments: from information to coproduction mechanisms. J. Hous. Older Pers. **31**(2), 146–159 (2017)
7. Walker, A.: Why involve older people in research? Age Ageing **36**(5), 481–483 (2007). https://doi.org/10.1093/ageing/afm100
8. Loos, E.: Senior citizens: digital immigrants in their own country? Observatorio (OBS*) **6**(1), 1–23 (2012)
9. Neves, B.B., Waycott, J., Malta, S.: Old and afraid of new communication technologies? Reconceptualising and contesting the 'age-based digital divide'. J. Sociol. **54**(2), 236–248 (2018)

10. Ivan, L., Schiau, I.: Experiencing computer anxiety later in life: the role of stereotype threat. In: Zhou, J., Salvendy, G. (eds.) ITAP 2016. LNCS, vol. 9754, pp. 339–349. Springer, Cham (2016). https://doi.org/10.1007/978-3-319-39943-0_33

11. Linhorst, D.M.: A review of the use and potential of focus groups in social work research. Qual. Soc. Work 1(2), 208–228 (2002)

12. Fernández-Ardèvol, M., Ivan, L.: Older people and mobile communication in two European contexts. Rom. J. Commun. Public Relat. 15(3), 83–98 (2013)

13. Ivan, L., Fernández-Ardèvol, M.: Older people, mobile communication and risks. Societies 7(2), 7 (2017)

14. Ivan, L., Fernández-Ardèvol, M.: Older people and the use of ICTs to communicate with children and grandchildren. Trans. Soc. Rev. 7(1), 41–55 (2017)

15. Ivan, L., Hebblethwaite, S.: Grannies on the net: grandmothers' experiences of Facebook in family communication. Rom. J. Commun. Public Relat. 18(1), 11–25 (2016)

16. Krueger, R.A., Casey, M.A.: Focus Groups. A Practical Guide for Applied Research, 3rd edn. Sage, Thousand Oaks (2000)

17. Sayago, S., Blat, J.: Older people and ICT: towards understanding real-life usability and experiences created in everyday interactions with interactive technologies. In: Stephanidis, C. (ed.) UAHCI 2009. LNCS, vol. 5614, pp. 154–163. Springer, Heidelberg (2009). https://doi.org/10.1007/978-3-642-02707-9_17

18. Sävenstedt, S., Sandman, P.O., Zingmark, K.: The duality in using information and communication technology in elder care. J. Adv. Nurs. 56(1), 17–25 (2006)

19. Newell, A., Arnott, J., Carmichael, A., Morgan, M.: Methodologies for involving older adults in the design process. In: Stephanidis, C. (ed.) UAHCI 2007. LNCS, vol. 4554, pp. 982–989. Springer, Heidelberg (2007). https://doi.org/10.1007/978-3-540-73279-2_110

20. Wherton, J., Sugarhood, P., Procter, R., Greenhalgh, T.: Designing technologies for social connection with older people. Aging Digital Life Course 3, 107–124 (2015)

21. Muñoz, D., Cornejo, R., Gutierrez, F.J., Favela, J., Ochoa, S.F., Tentori, M.: A social cloud-based tool to deal with time and media mismatch of intergenerational family communication. Future Gener. Comput. Syst. 53, 140–151 (2015)

22. Gonzalez, A., Ramirez, M.P., Viadel, V.: ICT learning by older adults and their attitudes toward computer use. Curr. Gerontol. Geriatr. Res. (2015). https://doi.org/10.1155/2015/849308. Article ID 849308

23. Cozza, M., De Angeli, A., Tonolli, L.: Ubiquitous technologies for older people. Pers. Ubiquit. Comput. 21(3), 607–619 (2017)

24. Glaser, B., Strauss, A.: The Discovery of Grounded Theory. Weidenfeld and Nicholson, London (1967)

25. Strauss, A., Corbin, J.M.: Grounded Theory in Practice. Sage, London (1997)

26. Fernández-Ardèvol, M., Ivan, L.: Why age is not that important? An ageing perspective on computer anxiety. In: Zhou, J., Salvendy, G. (eds.) ITAP 2015. LNCS, vol. 9193, pp. 189–200. Springer, Cham (2015). https://doi.org/10.1007/978-3-319-20892-3_19

27. Prensky, M.: Digital natives, digital immigrants part 1. Horiz. 9(5), 1–6 (2001)

28. Clarke, L., Abbott, L.: Young pupils', their teacher's and classroom assistants' experiences of iPads in a Northern Ireland school: "four and five years old, who would have thought they could do that?". Br. J. Educ. Technol. 47(6), 1051–1064 (2016)

29. Cutler, S.: Ageism and technology. Generations 29(3), 67–72 (2005)

30. Rosales, A., Fernández-Ardèvol, M.: Structural ageism in big data approaches. Nordicom Rev. 40(s1), 51–60 (2019)

Embodied Interaction Design to Promote Creative Social Engagement for Older Adults

Lina Lee[✉], Johanna Okerlund, Mary Lou Maher, and Thomas Farina

University of North Carolina at Charlotte, Charlotte, NC 28223, USA
llee52@uncc.edu

Abstract. This paper presents an embodied interactive system designed for older adults to promote creative and social engagement, called Move and Paint. We performed a study to investigate the engagement and behavior patterns of older adults as they used Move and Paint. We conducted a focus group and interview study to understand general attitudes towards this gesture-based interactive system. We used the results to develop an evaluation framework to identify engagement and behavior patterns of older adults and conducted pattern analysis. Our findings show that embodied interactive technology can offer creative engaging experiences that enhance opportunities for older adults to participate in social and community engagement in public spaces.

Keywords: Embodied interaction · Creative embodiment · Social engagement · Aging adults

1 Introduction

Embodied interactive technologies have the potential to offer playful and positive experiences to older adults and enhance opportunities for meaningful social connectivity and engagement in public space. Many studies pointed out that active participation and engagement in social activities are critical for maintaining a good quality of life for older adults [1–3]. Embodied interactive technology installed in a public space can facilitate engagement and connection with others, which can benefit older adults in maintaining psychological, physical and cognitive health. Embodied interactive systems also can offer playful and positive experiences to older adults [4–6]. Embodied interaction is interaction that recognizes and includes the use of our bodies. It means designing interaction such that the user can use their body in ways in which they are used to using it in the natural physical world. Embodied interaction requires certain actions and is compelling enough that users are willing to perform those actions to interact with the system. Not only is this an attractive approach for an aging population since it requires less time to learn how to use the system, it also requires them to move and participate in natural physical activity. In addition, providing opportunities to be creative can draw the attention of older adults.

Current studies of interactive technologies for older adults are limited because they focus on new technologies and usability [7–9] with little regard for the engagement

© Springer Nature Switzerland AG 2020
Q. Gao and J. Zhou (Eds.): HCII 2020, LNCS 12207, pp. 164–183, 2020.
https://doi.org/10.1007/978-3-030-50252-2_13

of older adult users. Efforts to conduct research on the elderly use of technology are often hampered by lack of understanding of the abilities, requirements, and preferences of this population. Human-computer interaction studies have emphasized the need to move beyond usability to understand and design for more engaging experiences [10–12]. Despite the fact that embodied interactive systems are likely to offer engaging experiences to older adults, there is relatively little research on embodied interaction for older adults.

The goal of our research is to discover behavior and usage trends and obtain insights about older adults' usage of an embodied interactive system. We believe that our design approach provides new opportunities for older adults to stay more connected and engaged with others, while participating in a creative experience. In this paper, we present our Move and Paint system, an embodied interactive painting application that converts full-body gestures detected by a Kinect sensor to drawings and adding color on a large screen. We conducted a qualitative analysis of focus groups and interviews with older adults to provide an understanding of how older adults interact with gesture-based interactive technology. We identified that emotional, physical, social, creative, and cognitive experiences act together to engage older adults when they interact with the Move and Paint system. We developed an engagement evaluation framework based on these five experiential factors to analyze the behavior and usage pattern of older adults. We deployed the system in the wild in an assisted living facility. Two motion-detecting cameras sat on a shelf at the base of the screen to record video of the people that engaged with Move and Paint from different angles. Through the application of this framework, each case interacting with Move and Paint system can be evaluated from a balanced and equalized perspective on engagement. Lastly, we conducted a pattern analysis to understand how social interaction that takes place while using Move and Paint has a positive influence on emotional, creative, physical, and cognitive experiences. The contribution of this paper is the insights about the impact of social engagement of older adults on the experience of using an embodied interactive system.

2   Related Research

2.1   Potential of Embodied Interactive Technologies in Older Adults

This section describes how recent embodied and tangible interactive systems are used by older adults, for what purposes they are designed and what challenges there are by searching and reviewing the current embodied interactive technologies designed for older adults. Embodied interactive systems are increasingly entering public spaces due to decreasing cost of large screens and the emergence of increasingly sophisticated sensing technologies. They are widely used in various areas as a means to engage people in public space [13, 14]. Embodied technologies such as robots [15–17], tangible user interface (TUI) [18, 19], mid-air gesture [5, 20, 21], mixed reality [22, 23], multi-touch display [24, 25] have been proposed as a way to support physical, social, and emotional wellness.

Many assisted living communities offer older adults physical therapy as part of the daily exercise options [4, 26, 27]. Many older adults are opposed to exercises that involve physical activity. Bruun-Pedersen et al. [4] described that some form of fun factors must be included in exercise to motivate people to engage in physical activity. They performed a study that involved placing exercise bikes in front of large screens. As the users pedaled, the screens displayed virtual landscapes that the participants rode through at speeds that were aligned with their output on the bike. This study showed positive indications that a recreational virtual environment augmentation and embodiment could motivate older adults to exercise more than before. The Eldergames project [22] is a gaming platform using a tabletop, tangible and mixed reality solution aimed specifically at preserving cognitive functions and providing pleasurable experiences to older adults. The Cognitive Augmented Reality Cubes (CogARC) system [18] presents a game-based cognitive training experience that uses an augmented reality-based approach through which people can interact with physical and tangible objects (in this case, cubes). These studies highlighted that it is important to motivate and engage older adults through the gaming factor. One example of embodied technology developed for older adults is Paro [6], a mental commit robot that provides social, physiological, and psychological effects to its users by means of physical interactions. Paro is designed to resemble animals, such as seals and cats. The mental commit robot [28] was used by older adults at a day service center to assist them with their daily activities. A study investigating the effects of the robot's influence on the participants' social and emotional well-being, including social interaction and depression, found that the mental robotic technology was widely accepted among the adults, as they did not show anxiety when using it.

Despite the fact that embodied technologies have the potential to improve the quality of life of older adults, there are few studies to understand engagement and behavioral characteristics of older adults. Embodied interactive systems are no longer unfamiliar and novel for many people, but this is not the case for many older adults due to differences in prior experience and knowledge of new technologies. Older adults face additional challenges because as people grow older, their cognitive, physical and sensory abilities change, causing older adults to show different attitudes towards technology when compared to the younger population [29, 30]. Generally, older adults are passive in using interactive technology. Several interactive systems have been developed with little consideration for older adults because the assumption has been that the aging population has little interest in the use of interactive technologies [31, 32]. Older adults tend to have negative, preconceived notions that new technology is difficult to use or unnecessary, and they do not trust their ability to have control over the systems [33–35]. These physical and cognitive characteristics could act as interference factors for older adults to be engaged in using the interactive technology. Researchers easily overlook that older adults have heterogeneous characteristics. They introduce bigger prompts, high contrast and simplified interactive functions etc. as design solutions for older adults. These factors could assist older adults to have smooth interaction, but also could reduce the interest of older adults. Recently, older adults are being exposed to technologies and increasing their experiences with the assistance of younger population. It is increasingly important to understand when, how and why older adults are engaged in using embodied interactive systems and their behavioral characteristics.

2.2   Creative Embodiment and Social Engagement of Older Adults

Designing embodied interaction is not just about designing new technologies, but is also about designing the human experience and anticipated human behavior [36]. Dourish [37] explores the physicality of embodied interaction and its effect on moving human computer interaction toward more social environments. He describes an approach to embodiment grounded in phenomenology, and claims that any understanding we have of the world is the result of some initial physical exploration. Interaction designers draw upon the idea of embodied interaction to design systems that take advantage of our prior understanding of the physical world and our ability to develop new understanding through interacting with it. Open research questions include figuring out the most intuitive and natural mapping functions as well as figuring out the impact that embodied aspect has on the experience [38–41].

Embodied interaction for creative expression has the potential to positively impact older adults' interactions with gesture based interactive technology. There are several angles from which to consider the body's role in artistic and creative endeavors. Creativity that includes emotions and movements, such as dancing, writing, or any creative art can place older adults in a situation to express themselves. Ryokai et al. [42] explore the role of body position in experiencing and appreciating art. There is a natural way we use our bodies to express ourselves, even in every day gestures and body language [43]. There is evidence of artists and musicians focusing on the synergy between body movements and natural emotional expression. For example, in the Dalcroze music expression teaching method, students explore how to use their bodies to mimic musical expression and thus learn how to make more expressive music. De Rooij et al. [44] explore the relationship between the body and expression of emotions by designing creative interaction and show how performing different physical actions can cause someone to exhibit different emotions. According to Van Rheden and Hengeveld [45], more embodied interaction has the potential to be more engaging. This study explores engagement and embodiment through the design of multiple kitchen blenders. Their motivation is to make food preparation more mindful and show that when interaction with appliances such as blenders is more embodied, people find it more engaging.

There are a few studies about the idea of fostering social inclusion through a community-engaged approach to art-making [46, 47]. Moody [47] found that older adults were able to expand their community connections through an art program. Embodied interaction for creative expression can help older adults build and strengthen meaningful social connections. For example, an art application can be used to connect people in social settings by gathering a group for talking, learning about the arts, or things relevant to the software [48]. However, little empirical evidence has been reported. In this study, we present a design of embodied interaction for creative expression for older adults. We expect to see increased social interaction not only as a result of this embodied system, but also as something that is required for older adults to interact successfully with it. We expect that social engagement influences engagement with the system and engagement with the system influences social engagement.

3 Move and Paint Design

System Embodiment. Move and Paint is an embodied interactive painting application that converts full-body gestures detected by a Kinect sensor to drawings and coloring book actions on a large screen. Move and Paint was implemented using a Kinect sensor, a Microsoft 55″ display, and a Mac Mini computer on a vertical mount, promoting group interaction. The software was developed using Processing with SimpleOpenNI for gesture tracking. Two motion-detecting cameras sit on a shelf at the base of the screen to record video of the people that engage with Move and Paint from different angles (Fig. 1).

Fig. 1. Left: Move and Paint in coloring book mode/ Right: Move and Paint in free draw mode

Engagement Modality. Our design concept emerged from interviews with senior residents and the evaluation of early prototypes of Move and Paint. We held these interviews in two stages of early prototyping for Move and Paint with 10 senior residents of an assisted living residence between the ages of 55 and 85. We found that many of them enjoy being creative, playing games, and being social. This information informed our decision to use full body gesture-based art in a social setting as the conceptual basis for the design. Our system is designed for older adults with the goal of encouraging individual creative expression and strengthening social connections.

Interface Design. The interaction design, shown in Fig. 2, uses a palette of colors to add color or a drawing to the canvas on the screen. The user changes the color by waving their hand to move the circle representing the cursor to a color at the top of the screen. Selecting icons on the screen allows the user to change the background, brush thickness, or color. A line on the floor indicates where the interaction area is.

Background Options. Move and Paint has two modes: coloring book and free draw. Each mode has two background options, which the user can switch between by hovering the circle controlled by their hand over the icons on the left side of the screen. In coloring book mode, a sketch of a famous work of art is displayed. The user moves their hand to a section on the sketch to add color. In drawing mode, users can draw lines and shapes anywhere on the screen by moving their hands.

Fig. 2. Illustration of instructions in Design 2

Brush Interaction. The user can choose between 2 different brushes, thick and thin. Users switch brushes by hovering the circle controlled by their hand over the brush menu icon on the right side of the screen. The picture is drawn on the screen as the hand moves, mimicking real-life painting. The user can stop the brush from drawing by bringing that hand close to their torso, mimicking the physical activity of removing the pen or brush from the paper.

Shadow Design Concept. The user's shadow is shown as grey pixels to provide feedback on the location of their body, and therefore the hand controlling the cursor. This mirror effect has been used to catch a user's attention as they pass by and encourage interaction [49]. The mirrored representation helps users position themselves within the system, understand that the system is interactive, and discover how to interact. The shadow visually represents the current state of the user's relationship to the system.

Instruction Design Concept. The Move and Paint system has three points at which it provides guidance, as shown in Fig. 3. The instruction "Come closer" is displayed when there is no one in range of the Kinect. When someone is too close to the screen, the instruction tells them to stand back behind the line on the floor. When there is someone standing in the correct place but is not interacting, an instruction tells them to raise their hand to draw. The instructions are performed by a humanoid figure to make the instructions more friendly. Providing instructions makes the behavior easier to do.

4   Understanding General Attitudes Toward the Move and Paint System

We conducted a qualitative analysis of focus groups and interviews with older adults to understand their general attitude toward the use of gesture-based interactive technology. This analysis will be a basic understanding of an engagement evaluation framework.

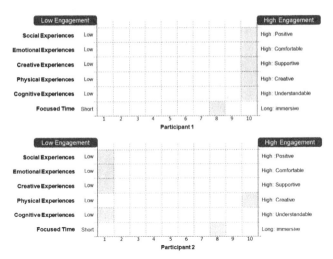

Fig. 3. Two examples of engagement and behavior pattern while using the Move and Paint system

4.1 Data Collection

We carried out focus group studies and interviews at a senior community, the [anon] Center. Participants signed a written informed consent. Questions for the focus group and in-person interview aim to understand user experiences and usability issues of older adults. The facilitator takes notes and records the conversations. The recordings were transcribed to facilitate analysis (Table 1).

Table 1. The semi-structured interview questions for the focus group discussion and in-person interview.

Interview questions
1) Have you ever used a gesture-based interactive system like Move and Paint, which remotely controls the system by using your body?
2) What did you think about this system at first glance?
3) When you first looked at this system, did you want to use it immediately? Or were you unwilling to use it? Explain why?
4) On a scale of 1 to 10, where 10 denotes the most difficulty, how difficult was to use the system?
5) What was your favorite part of this experience?
6) When you were using the system, did you discover the shadow of your body projected on the screen? What do you think the role of the shadow of your body?
7) When you were using the system, can you find an instruction? What do you think of the role of the instruction?
8) Have you used other functions such as modification of backgrounds or drawing modes, in using the system?
9) What did you plan to draw through this system?
10) Did the system properly respond as you intended?
11) What improvements would be required for you to have more interests in the system and continuously use it?

Focus Group Study. This senior community provides individuals 55 years and older various opportunities such as exercise and educational programs to improve their physical and cognitive health. In order to get more insights through an active discussion, we visited the aerobics class and recruited participants for a focus group discussion. Older adults who voluntarily participated in the exercise program are judged to be active. The recruited participants move to a space in which the Move and Paint system was installed separately for a focus group discussion. The focus group study comprised a one-hour group discussion and the same moderator conducted two focus group discussions. The total number of senior participants in this study was 16: the first group included 8 female participants and the second group included 2 male and 6 female participants. The researcher explained to older adults how to use the system prior to the discussion and induced them to use it as freely as they liked.

Semi-structured Interview. For the interview, the Move and Paint system was installed in the hallway towards the main lobby and gym. Older adults who showed interest in the Move and Paint system and approached it were recruited as participants. The interviews took place over two weeks with a total of 15 participants (3 males and 12 females) participated. The participants were encouraged to ask questions about the Move and Paint system while interacting with it. The participants were then asked to answer questions with the facilitator. An interview session takes approximately 20 min. The questions the study facilitator asked were the same as the questions from the focus group studies.

4.2 Analysis and Results

In the interview, the same questions were used as the focus group study. The responses to each question obtained through the interview and the focus group discussions were classified. This analysis is on both data sets together. We applied a thematic analysis [50] to identify the underlying meaning of the data set. We did an inductive approach by coding every single sentence. We did not have pre-set codes, but developed and modified the codes as we worked through the coding process. Initial themes were clustered such as "physical discomfort", "need support", "different needs", "lack of experience", "usability issues", "emotions", "communication with others", "multiple interaction", etc. In the next phase, initial codes were categorized into main themes, by mapping the relationships between codes. We identified five themes: "positive affect", "supportive environment", "creative expression", "comfortable usage", and "usability". We found that emotional, social, creative, physical, and cognitive experiences should be considered to design engaging experiences for older adults.

Emotional Experiences: Positive Affect. This section describes the emotions mentioned while older adults use the Move and Paint system. We found that our participants felt motivated to try something new. 15/15 of interview participants had not used a gesture based interactive system like Move and Paint before. 11/15 participants responded that they do not have many opportunities to access technology. They have difficulties using their mobile phones or computer and tend not to use them very often. 8/15 participants said that they have heard of the Wii but have never experienced it in person. 5/8 participants said they wanted to use the Wii system but had no opportunity. They looked very excited even before using the Move and Paint system. One participant mentioned "I've been wondering when you'd ask me for an interview, because I really wanted to try this one." For the interview, 5/15 participants said the first word that crossed their mind was 'curiosity', 'fun', or 'interesting'. Their initial approach and attitude towards the Move and Paint system was positive. In the first focus group study, they expressed an interest in the appearance of the system and showed curiosity when other people were using it. They found it very interesting that pictures can be drawn using a different method without pen and paper. We expected that older adults' lack of experience would cause them to resist the system, but surprisingly, older adults were curious to try Move and Paint even though they have never used an embodied interaction system. These reactions lead us to infer that embodied interactive technology has a potential to deliver new and positive emotions of older adults.

Social Experiences: Supportive Environment. We found that the older adults might be engaged when they can use the embodied interactive technology without any burden and feel support from others. In both focus group sessions, 16/16 participants agree that they need external help to figure out the system. When the participants encountered the system for the first time, they said they want to have someone to help them in the same way the focus group study was implemented. All participants said they would not attempt to use the system on their own without outside help. One participant expressed "Are you going to come every day and teach me how to use it? I am not like you. I am pretty sure I won't be able to use this system by myself." Personal support may be required as a supplement to the system as older adults connect differently with human beings than machines. Personal support may also be necessary not as instruction, but rather to increase confidence or reduce self-consciousness. This implies that interaction with other people is needed to encourage older adults to use the system. They also said that they would continue to use the system and maintain their interests if they could use it with their grandchildren. They made many comments about their family when the facilitator explained that the system supports multiple simultaneous interactions. For example, one participant said "Can multiple people use this simultaneously? Is there any way that I can have this system at my home? I am dying to show this to my grandchild and play with him." Using the Move and Paint system with others may be an accelerator that stimulates the interest of older adults. Through this, we infer that the role of the external environment is important for older adults to make a decision on whether to use the Move and Paint system.

Creative Experiences: Creative Expression. There were specific interactive elements the participants mentioned that would maintain their interest and engagement. In the second focus group study, participants discussed that the system could be designed in a more interesting way by using more diverse colors. 15/15 participants said that it is interesting to observe the drawings and the changing colors. 6/15 participants prefer to watch the varied movements of the colors other people are working on than to use the system personally. 15/15 participants said that they feel happy when they see various colors. 3/15 participants responded that they are grateful that the system makes them move. For example, one participant mentioned "It is really interesting to see the color change whenever the hand is moving." In the first focus group discussion, participants especially noted that there are too few options for the background and would like to see more images. A game format could be introduced for the coloring book, so that completion of each level can lead to a more complex picture. Participants also discussed that it would be nice to make Christmas cards using the system. In that case, they said they would expect additional features such as choosing cards, decorating cards with stamps, coloring, and inserting text, and that stamps would be much easier to use than brushes. We were unsure if older adults would have continued interest in the system after the initial novelty, but given the variety of use cases older adults proposed such as making cards and playing with grandchildren, we found that designing for creative activity and open-ended interaction is a worthwhile pursuit to ensure older adults do not prematurely lose attention and to sustain engagement with the system.

Physical Experiences: Comfortable Usage. Move and Paint requires constant active motion of the body. Large motions are required to choose a color or draw on the entire canvas. 5/15 participants reported physical shortcomings as the most major cause for hesitating to use the system. They answered they could not use it readily because standing a long time is hard for them. But, they also responded they would actively use the system if they can be seated to use it. We saw that older adults often did not succeed in reaching the color even though they were making a full stretch. One participant said "I am too short to reach the color." 6/15 participants commented that their arms and legs felt strained when they returned to their seats after using the system. 2/15 participants said that their vision problems made it hard for them to identify small icons or illustrations in the background. They pointed out that clear text feedback would be much more useful than illustrations. One participant also expressed that it will be good to listen to narrative instruction when she is standing in the designated position to use the system. A design that is more physically comfortable will be more likely to engage older adults. Since we found that differences in physical ability not only prevented some participants from performing certain actions, but also made participants feel discouraged, the system should be designed by correctly understanding the physical ability of older adults.

Cognitive Experience: Understanding Functions. The system should be designed to help them easily discover and perceive its functions. We found that older adults did not automatically know the functions of buttons and did not explore with gestures on their own unless prompted. This impacts the discoverability of the system for older adults when compared to other populations. We investigated that providing instructions has a positive effect on older adults' exploration (Fig. 2). Interview results found that only 5/15 participants were able to discover the instructions. They said they had difficulty finding the instructions, but it would be of great help in learning how to use the system once found out. These five participants said that different types of feedback such as a video or pop up image are necessary, and that consistent feedback can improve the usability of the system. Older adults had difficulty understanding the function of the Move and Paint system. For example, one participant commented "I've looked around the system for information on how to use it, but I couldn't find it. I only figured out that the video is being recorded. How do you expect me to use this without any information on it?" 11/15 participants responded they could not recognize the functions except for color palette.

For example, one participant mentioned "Is it possible to change the brush? I've never thought it possible until you told me about it" 2/15 participants pointed out interface layout. One participant said she faced a difficulty in discovering other drawing functions located edge of the screen because her attention was focused on the center of the screen.

In the focus group discussion, most participants expressed difficulty in understanding the concept of the shadow. 2/8 participants responded that the purpose of the shadow is to give feedback to the user about his/her current location but added that the element itself was not interesting at all. Rather, they commented that the shadow interferes with drawing. One person said "I thought the grey color (shadow) is me, because it followed me every time I moved. But it always got in my way whenever I colored it." In the interview, one participant mentioned it is difficult to recognize because the form of the shadow is not clear. Perceiving the shadow movement was difficult because more focus is on the color changing on the screen than the shadow. The shadow concept, which was originally designed to draw older adults' interest, may in fact distract them. Older adults lose interest when the system does not respond as they expected. One person said "Why on earth the color keeps changing. I didn't want this color." In both focus groups, participants discussed that the lower part of the screen did not sense their movements properly nor responded to their coloring. They said that the upper part of the screen was very responsive and that their interest would be sustained if the lower part of the screen would be as responsive and sensitive as the upper part to encourage their free movements. While using the system, 7/15 participants said they clearly had an object they wish to draw or color they wish to apply, but they could not execute it because they were unable to control the system as they intended. 11/15 participants pointed out this problem as a major issue and they said if this was not improved, they would not continue to use the system. Since the usability issue has a great effect on understanding system's functions, the gesture based interactive system should be designed to help older adults easily discover and perceive its functions.

5 Identifying the Importance of Social Engagement in the Use of Gesture Based Interactive Technology

The Move and Paint system has the potential to increase social connectedness and community engagement of older adults. In the qualitative study, it is difficult to observe natural interaction of users, and to observe what kind of social interaction takes place naturally around the system. We performed an in-the-wild user study to identify behavior and usage patterns using the Move and Paint system in a natural setting. We developed an evaluation framework to analyze the engagement and behavioral usage patterns of older adults while using Move and Paint. We conducted a pattern analysis to identify the importance of social engagement in the use of the Move and Paint system.

5.1 Data Collection

The location of the system in the retirement community was near the entry of a multi-purpose function room in which events, movies, exercise classes, and parties were held. Move and Paint was left unattended for several weeks for passersby to engage with.

All senior visitors were able to use it naturally as many times as they want. We did not prompt older adults to use it in any particular way or to try to accomplish any particular task. Two motion-detecting cameras were used to record video of the people that engaged with Move and Paint from different angles. This enables us to study the natural interactions that occur around the proposed system. We collected data from 66 instances of interaction. We only included older adults who engaged with the system voluntarily and stopped in front of the display either to look at it or to interact with it. We did not include people who looked at or gestured at the display as they were walking past.

Evaluation Framework. We classified evaluation factors affecting older adults to be engaged in using the Move and Paint system largely into 5 categories through the focus group discussions and interviews with older adults: Emotional, Physical, Social, Creative, Cognitive experiences. We added the factor 'Focused interaction time' to the evaluation framework even though there was no mention in the qualitative data analysis. By 'focused interaction time', we mean not only being in the vicinity of the system or showing interest in it, but actively acting or attempting to act upon it. This is an important factor in judging how much the user is engaged in the system [12]. Each of the 6 categories of the framework has something to measure and results in a value between 1–10 depending on where the measure falls within the predetermined range (Table 2). When we used this framework in our analysis, data were normalized so that a comparison could be made between the categories, and that each category could be set to the same range. These measures and ranges were determined by the ratio of the time for each category taking up as compared to the total time each user stayed in front of the system.

5.2 Engagement and Usage Pattern

We analyzed the 66 interaction cases of 47 older adults by using this evaluation framework that we developed (Table 2). Figure 3 shows how two individual users used the Move and Paint system differently. A lower numerical value of each factor corresponds to lower engagement with the system. For example, Participant 1 tried not only free drawing but also coloring mode with changing the background (Usage time: 5 min and 24 s). Moreover, she wanted to complete a coloring book with considering diverse colors. She maintained a positive vibe throughout her time using the system. In this case, all factors tend towards the high engagement side. On the other hand, Participant 2 is not interested in the system itself even though the condition of using the system is satisfied because independent mobility is possible (Usage time: 18 s). All factors except the physical factor tend towards the low engagement side.

Using this framework enables us to not only visualize the engagement and behavior pattern of each individual user, but find out the behavioral characteristics of older adults by aggregating the pattern of all participants who use the Move and Paint system. Overall, the use of the Move and Paint system by older adults shows a polarized pattern (Fig. 4). Individual user's scores fall on the low or high engagement side, with little distribution in the middle. Positive emotions and creative expressions are both low overall (highlighted in red, Fig. 4). On the other hand, physical comfort was generally high (highlighted

Table 2. Evaluation framework for analyzing engagement and behavior pattern

Category	Clarification
Emotional experience	We measure emotional changes that occurred during the interaction. The changes in facial expression were examined and the number of positive expressions (happiness) in the dialogue that naturally occurred during the interaction was counted. The total duration that a user stays in the Move and Paint system should be measured. The time revealing a positive emotion out of total duration is measured 1: When the time revealing a positive emotion is less than 10% … 5: More than 40% and less than 50% … 10: More than 90%
Physical experience	We measure when a user has difficulty in moving oneself or is assisted by an assist device. Count how many times a user experiences physical discomfort while using the Move and Paint system (For example, he/she can't stretch his/her hand higher, or can't maintain for a long time while stretching his/her hand) 1: Stand only with support and not able to reach to the system Or a user feels discomfort more than 6 times … 5: When an assistant device such as walker is needed, Or a user feels discomfort equal to or more than twice and less than four times … 10: When the movement is natural and there is no physical discomfort in using the system at all
Social experience	We measure social interaction occurring around the system. It includes cases of receiving help from an acquaintance to find out how to use the system, discussing how to use the system with other users, and connecting to the everyday conversation by using the system usage as a mediator. The time spent for social interactions compared to the total time spent in the system is measured 1: When the time revealing for social interactions is less than 10% … 5: More than 40% and less than 50% … 10: More than 90%
Creative experience	We measure when a user shows a creative intent. It includes cases of specifying the desired color to paint a picture, showing a clear purpose for painting or clear finality for a target, or finding and playing a shadow. The ratio of time showing creative expression to the total-duration should be measured 1: When the time revealing for creative expression is less than 10% … 5: More than 40% and less than 50% … 10: More than 90%

(*continued*)

Table 2. (*continued*)

Category	Clarification
Cognitive experience	We measure how well a user identifies the system at the first encounter. When another interaction modality is used instead of mid-air interaction, it includes cases of failing to find a suitable distance for using the system correctly. We measure the percentage of time that a system fails to interaction out of the total duration 1: When the time revealing for difficulty in understanding how to use the Move and Paint system is less than 10% … 5: More than 40% and less than 50% … 10: More than 90%
Focused interaction time	We measure the immersed time while using the system. The time of actually actively using the system out of the time staying in front of the system was calculated. If they were talking to someone, watching someone else interact, or simply staring at the system, this does not count as focused interaction time 1: When the focused interaction time is less than 10% … 5: More than 40% and less than 50% … 10: More than 90%

in blue, Fig. 4). There is a tendency that social experiences, cognitive experience, and focused interaction time are comparatively distributed evenly on both sides. The rate of the use of the system in cooperation with others (n = 38) is higher than that of the use of it alone (n = 28).

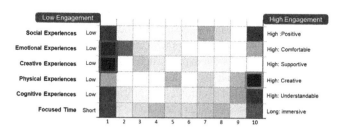

Fig. 4. Aggregate engagement and behavior pattern of 66 use cases in the use of the Move and Paint system (n = 66) (Color figure online)

In the following paragraphs, we explore 3 different cases: single-user interaction with no social interaction, user interaction with high social experience, user interaction with limited social interaction. The reason for looking at these categories of usage is to study the relationship between the amount of social interaction and the engagement factors.

Single-user interaction with no social connectedness while interacting with the system has 28 cases highlighted in blue in Fig. 5. Users in this category hardly showed any positive emotion. Five users out of 28 cases only smile once for a short time and they don't verbalize their emotions. Users in this category tended not to interact with the system in a creative way and did not react explicitly to their shadow image on the screen (highlighted in red, Fig. 5). The actual time of using the system is 43 s on average.

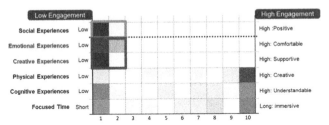

Fig. 5. Engagement and behavior pattern on cases with no social interaction while using the Move and Paint system (n = 28) (Color figure online)

High social engagement while interacting with the system has 27 cases, as shown in Fig. 6. Users in this case interact with others during the whole time they are in the vicinity of the system (highlighted in blue, Fig. 6). There are a few different cases within this category: the case in which multiple users find the system and try to use it together; the case in which one uses the system first, and does not figure out how to use it, and brings another person who may help; the case in which one uses the system first, finds it interesting and introduces it to another person; or the case in which one comes alone to try to use the system, which instantly calls attention to the people in the space and makes them involved in the use of it. There is social interaction for 197 s on average. The actual time of using the system is 82 s on average, which shows that they invest more time in interacting with people than using the system. Compared to the previous case of single-user, no social interaction, the most notable difference is the pattern that the emotional and creative factor is more distributed between low and high engagement (highlighted in red, Fig. 6). There are 5 users who exhibit creative intent while using the system, specifying the object they want to paint such as flowers, trees, sun, etc. Moreover, they tried not only free drawing but also coloring mode with changing the background. Moreover, users in this case wanted to complete a coloring book with considering diverse colors. Sometimes, they discussed design ideas to be more creative. They made many positive comments about the system. In this case, users used the system for a relatively long period (159.8 s on average).

Limited social interaction, when the participants are social only during a percentage of the total time while using the system, has 11 cases as shown in Fig. 7. The focused interaction time, a subset of the total time in front of the system, was 119 s on average. Even though a social interaction takes place naturally around the system, users in this case were not easily distracted by others. Users in this case needed help from the staff members or others who knew the system well then used it alone for the rest of the time. However, 9 users expressed negative feelings about the Move and Paint system.

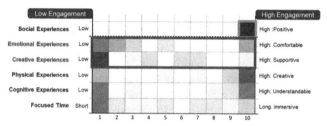

Fig. 6. Engagement and behavior pattern on cases with social interaction while using the Move and Paint system (n = 27) (Color figure online)

From this visualization, we see that when the elderly used the system with limited social interaction, the 6 factors of engagement are much more evenly distributed.

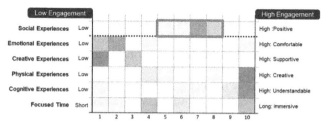

Fig. 7. Engagement and behavior pattern on cases that social interaction takes place only during a certain period of time (n = 11) (Color figure online)

6 Discussion and Conclusion

The contribution of this paper is the insight about the impact of social engagement of older adults on the experience of using an embodied interactive system. The insight we report is the consequence of the design and use of an embodied interactive system for older adults and the evaluation using an engagement framework. Move and Paint is designed to provide entertainment and exercise for each individual user and promote social engagement among older adults. Our design goals emerged from our discussions with the senior residents. Move and Paint was designed iteratively, focusing on exploration, engagement and creativity support. These design principles are the vehicle for promoting creative activity and social connectedness.

Generally, studies evaluating the user experiences of older adults using gesture-based interactive technology focus on usability issues. This study considers the emotional, physical, cognitive, social, creative characteristics of older adults to evaluate usage patterns of gesture based interactive system. To find the usability issues, many studies focus on qualitative analysis such as in-person interviews, surveys, or focus group discussions. The main challenge of self-report methods is that they rely upon users' recollections and self-interpretations. People tend to provide responses that are more positive or more frequent than reality. This study used self-report to identify the engagement factors and then collected behavioral data of older adults to investigate engagement based on actual usage. The evaluation framework of six engagement factors that we developed allowed us to analyze the behavioral characteristics of adults while using the Move and Paint system. The engagement and behavior evaluation framework is a valuable research tool for designers and researchers by providing guidelines for analysis and design of gesture-based interactive systems for any population.

Lastly, this study shows that embodied interactive systems have the potential to create a positive social experiences for older adults in a public space. In this study, we saw that as social interaction occurs around the system, older adults are more likely to express positive affect about the system and use the system in a creative way. Sixsmith [30] stated that older adults are often concerned that new technology will diminish the level of interaction among and between people. However, our study shows that elderly participants were less likely to figure out the interaction on their own. When another person showed a senior person how to use Move and Paint, they found it more interesting and stayed longer to interact with the system. A gesture-based interactive system installed in a public space can be a vehicle to improve on the existing social networks. When designing an embodied interactive technology, sustaining enhanced connections to others is an important consideration to increase engagement with the system.

One limitation of this study is that most of the users used the system only one time. Perhaps the one time users had a positive social experience because using Move and Paint was a special or unusual opportunity rather than it was due to their interactive experience. However, we found many cases where users who engaged in social interaction while interacting with Move and Paint also showed positive emotions, exhibited creative expressions and stayed more focused on using the system. As the social experience is an important part of the evaluation, future studies will measure how the system is being used by multiple users and how many social interactions occurred by explaining the system among the users. This study is in the initial stage, but is of significance in that embodied interaction can possibly be a vehicle to promote the social interaction of older adults and encourage their interest in technology.

References

1. Cacioppo, J.T., Cacioppo, S.: Social relationships and health: the toxic effects of perceived social isolation. Soc. Pers. Psychol. Compass **8**, 58–72 (2014)
2. Chopik, W.J.: The benefits of social technology use among older adults are mediated by reduced loneliness. Cyberpsychol. Behav. Soc. Netw. **19**, 551–556 (2016)
3. Czaja, S.J.: The role of technology in supporting social engagement among older adults. Public Policy Aging Rep. **27**, 145–148 (2017). https://doi.org/10.1093/ppar/prx034
4. Bruun-Pedersen, J.R., Serafin, S., Kofoed, L.B.: Motivating elderly to exercise-recreational virtual environment for indoor biking. In: 2016 IEEE International Conference on Serious Games and Applications for Health (SeGAH), pp. 1–9. IEEE (2016)
5. Chen, W.: Gesture-based applications for elderly people. In: Kurosu, M. (ed.) HCI 2013. LNCS, vol. 8007, pp. 186–195. Springer, Heidelberg (2013). https://doi.org/10.1007/978-3-642-39330-3_20

6. Kidd, C.D., Taggart, W., Turkle, S.: A sociable robot to encourage social interaction among the elderly. In: Proceedings 2006 IEEE International Conference on Robotics and Automation, ICRA 2006, pp. 3972–3976. IEEE (2006)

7. Alkhamisi, A.O., Arabia, S., Monowar, M.M.: Rise of augmented reality: current and future application areas. Int. J. Internet Distrib. Syst. **1**, 25 (2013)

8. Lawson, S., Nutter, D.: Augmented reality interfaces to support ageing-in-place. Draft paper (2005)

9. Liang, S.: Research proposal on reviewing augmented reality applications for supporting ageing population. Procedia Manufact. **3**, 219–226 (2015)

10. Hassenzahl, M., Tractinsky, N.: User experience-a research agenda. Behav. Inf. Technol. **25**, 91–97 (2006)

11. Jacques, R.: Engagement as a design concept for multimedia. Can. J. Educ. Commun. **24**, 49–59 (1995)

12. O'Brien, H.L., Toms, E.G.: What is user engagement? A conceptual framework for defining user engagement with technology. J. Am. Soc. Inf. Sci. Technol. **59**, 938–955 (2008)

13. Brignull, H., Rogers, Y.: Enticing people to interact with large public displays in public spaces. In: Proceedings of INTERACT. pp. 17–24 (2003)

14. Long, D., Jacob, M., Magerko, B.: Designing co-creative AI for public spaces. In: Proceedings of the 2019 on Creativity and Cognition, pp. 271–284. ACM (2019)

15. Fasola, J., Mataric, M.J.: Using socially assistive human–robot interaction to motivate physical exercise for older adults. Proc. IEEE **100**, 2512–2526 (2012)

16. Pripfl, J., et al.: Results of a real world trial with a mobile social service robot for older adults. In: 2016 11th ACM/IEEE International Conference on Human-Robot Interaction (HRI), pp. 497–498. IEEE (2016)

17. Šabanović, S., Bennett, C.C., Chang, W.-L., Huber, L.: PARO robot affects diverse interaction modalities in group sensory therapy for older adults with dementia. In: 2013 IEEE 13th International Conference on Rehabilitation Robotics (ICORR), pp. 1–6. IEEE (2013)

18. Boletsis, C., McCallum, S.: Augmented reality cubes for cognitive gaming: preliminary usability and game experience testing. Int. J. Serious Games **3**, 3–18 (2016)

19. Marques, T., Nunes, F., Silva, P., Rodrigues, R.: Tangible interaction on tabletops for elderly people. In: Anacleto, J.C., Fels, S., Graham, N., Kapralos, B., Saif El-Nasr, M., Stanley, K. (eds.) ICEC 2011. LNCS, vol. 6972, pp. 440–443. Springer, Heidelberg (2011). https://doi.org/10.1007/978-3-642-24500-8_61

20. Simor, F.W., Brum, M.R., Schmidt, J.D.E., Rieder, R., De Marchi, A.C.B.: Usability evaluation methods for gesture-based games: a systematic review. JMIR Serious Games **4**, e17 (2016)

21. Webster, D., Celik, O.: Systematic review of Kinect applications in elderly care and stroke rehabilitation. J. Neuroeng. Rehabil. **11**, 108 (2014)

22. Gamberini, L., et al.: Eldergames project: an innovative mixed reality table-top solution to preserve cognitive functions in elderly people. In: 2009 2nd Conference on Human System Interactions, pp. 164–169. IEEE (2009)

23. Saracchini, R., Catalina-Ortega, C., Bordoni, L.: A mobile augmented reality assistive technology for the elderly. Comunicar **23**, 65–74 (2015)

24. Leonardi, C., Albertini, A., Pianesi, F., Zancanaro, M.: An exploratory study of a touch-based gestural interface for elderly. In: Proceedings of the 6th Nordic Conference on Human-Computer Interaction: Extending Boundaries, pp. 845–850. ACM (2010)

25. Tsai, T., Chang, H.: Sharetouch: a multi-touch social platform for the elderly. In: 2009 11th IEEE International Conference on Computer-Aided Design and Computer Graphics, pp. 557–560. IEEE (2009)

26. Korn, O., Buchweitz, L., Rees, A., Bieber, G., Werner, C., Hauer, K.: Using augmented reality and gamification to empower rehabilitation activities and elderly persons. a study applying design thinking. In: Ahram, T.Z. (ed.) AHFE 2018. AISC, vol. 787, pp. 219–229. Springer, Cham (2019). https://doi.org/10.1007/978-3-319-94229-2_21

27. Lee, J.H., et al.: A virtual reality system for the assessment and rehabilitation of the activities of daily living. CyberPsychol. Behav. **6**, 383–388 (2003)

28. Shibata, T., et al.: Mental commit robot and its application to therapy of children. In: 2001 IEEE/ASME International Conference on Advanced Intelligent Mechatronics. Proceedings (Cat. No. 01TH8556), pp. 1053–1058. IEEE (2001)

29. Charness, N., Boot, W.R.: Aging and information technology use: potential and barriers. Curr. Dir. Psychol. Sci. **18**, 253–258 (2009)

30. Sixsmith, A.: Technology and the challenge of aging. In: Sixsmith, A., Gutman, G. (eds.) Technologies for Active Aging, pp. 7–25. Springer, Boston (2013). https://doi.org/10.1007/978-1-4419-8348-0_2

31. Czaja, S.J., et al.: Designing for Older Adults: Principles and Creative Human Factors Approaches, 3rd edn. CRC Press (2019). https://doi.org/10.1201/b22189

32. Peek, S.T.M., Wouters, E.J.M., van Hoof, J., Luijkx, K.G., Boeije, H.R., Vrijhoef, H.J.M.: Factors influencing acceptance of technology for aging in place: a systematic review. Int. J. Med. Inform. **83**, 235–248 (2014). https://doi.org/10.1016/j.ijmedinf.2014.01.004

33. Gitlow, L.: Technology use by older adults and barriers to using technology. Phys. Occup. Therapy Geriatr. **32**, 271–280 (2014). https://doi.org/10.3109/02703181.2014.946640

34. Lee, C., Coughlin, J.F.: PERSPECTIVE: older adults' adoption of technology: an integrated approach to identifying determinants and barriers. J. Prod. Innov. Manag. **32**, 747–759 (2015). https://doi.org/10.1111/jpim.12176

35. Mitzner, T.L., et al.: Older adults talk technology: technology usage and attitudes. Comput. Hum. Behav. **26**, 1710–1721 (2010). https://doi.org/10.1016/j.chb.2010.06.020

36. Maher, M.L., Lee, L.: Designing for gesture and tangible interaction. Synth. Lect. Hum.-Center. Inform. **10**, i–111 (2017). https://doi.org/10.2200/S00758ED1V01Y201702HCI036

37. Dourish, P.: Where the Action is: The Foundations of Embodied Interaction. MIT Press (2004)

38. Clifton, P.: Designing embodied interfaces to support spatial ability. In: Proceedings of the 8th International Conference on Tangible, Embedded and Embodied Interaction, pp. 309–312. ACM, New York (2013). https://doi.org/10.1145/2540930.2558151

39. Gerling, K.M., Mandryk, R.L., Birk, M.V., Miller, M., Orji, R.: The effects of embodied persuasive games on player attitudes toward people using wheelchairs. In: Proceedings of the SIGCHI Conference on Human Factors in Computing Systems, pp. 3413–3422. ACM, New York (2014). https://doi.org/10.1145/2556288.2556962

40. Mitchell, R., Nishida, J., Encinas, E., Kasahara, S.: We-Coupling!: designing new forms of embodied interpersonal connection. In: Proceedings of the Eleventh International Conference on Tangible, Embedded, and Embodied Interaction, pp. 775–780. ACM, New York (2017). https://doi.org/10.1145/3024969.3025051

41. Shelley, T., Lyons, L., Zellner, M., Minor, E.: Evaluating the embodiment benefits of a paper-based TUI for educational simulations. In: CHI 2011 Extended Abstracts on Human Factors in Computing Systems, pp. 1375–1380. ACM, New York (2011). https://doi.org/10.1145/1979742.1979777

42. Ryokai, K., Misra, N., Hara, Y.: Artistic distance: body movements as launching points for art inquiry. In: Proceedings of the 33rd Annual ACM Conference Extended Abstracts on Human Factors in Computing Systems, pp. 679–686. ACM, New York (2015). https://doi.org/10.1145/2702613.2702958

43. Dael, N., Mortillaro, M., Scherer, K.R.: Emotion expression in body action and posture. Emotion **12**, 1085–1101 (2012). https://doi.org/10.1037/a0025737

44. de Rooij, A., Jones, S.: (E)Motion and creativity: hacking the function of motor expressions in emotion regulation to augment creativity. In: Proceedings of the Ninth International Conference on Tangible, Embedded, and Embodied Interaction, pp. 145–152. ACM, New York (2015). https://doi.org/10.1145/2677199.2680552

45. van Rheden, V., Hengeveld, B.: Engagement through embodiment: a case for mindful interaction. In: Proceedings of the TEI 2016: Tenth International Conference on Tangible, Embedded, and Embodied Interaction, pp. 349–356. ACM, New York (2016). https://doi.org/10.1145/2839462.2839498

46. Ramsey White, T., Rentschler, R.: Toward a new understanding of the social impact of the arts. In: AIMAC 2005: Proceedings of the 8th International Conference on Arts & Cultural Management (2005)

47. Moody, E., Phinney, A.: A community-engaged art program for older people: fostering social inclusion*. Can. J. Aging/La Revue canadienne du vieillissement 31, 55–64 (2012). https://doi.org/10.1017/S0714980811000596

48. Halpern, M.K., et al.: MoBoogie: creative expression through whole body musical interaction. In: Proceedings of the 2011 annual conference on Human factors in computing systems - CHI 2011, p. 557. ACM Press, Vancouver (2011). https://doi.org/10.1145/1978942.1979020

49. Schönböck, J., König, F., Kotsis, G., Gruber, D., Zaim, E., Schmidt, A.: MirrorBoard – an interactive billboard, vol. 11 (2018)

50. Russell, M., Vallade, L., Vallade, L.: Guided reflective journalling: assessing the international study and volunteering experience. https://doi.org/10.4324/9780203865309-17, https://www.taylorfrancis.com/. Accessed 09 Aug 2019

The Effect of Sensory Feedback on Time Perception of Interface Indicator from Age Difference

Shuo-Fang Liu, Yu-Wei Tseng[✉], and Ching-Fen Chang

Department of Industrial Design, National Cheng-Kung University, No.1, University Road, Tainan City 701, Taiwan, Republic of China
alex8184@gmail.com

Abstract. The aging of the population is an irreversible trend, and the physiological problems caused by aging make the use of mobile devices a challenge. This study started from the placebo theory of human-computer interaction and pointed out that tactile feedback could make users have a positive experience. Based on the attention door model, experiments were conducted to explore whether different types of feedback could reduce the waiting time perception of users. The experiment divided the experimental group and the control group by age, conducted three types of feedback and two tasks. Using the T-test to analyze significance, and then conducted interviews after the experiment to collect qualitative data. The results showed that in short-term tasks, there were significant differences in the types of feedback that include haptic feedback. For the elderly, the addition of haptic feedback might not reduce time perception. However, in terms of preference, the elderly generally liked the type which including haptic and visual feedback. According to the Qualitative result, haptic feedback could make the operation certainly for the elderly.

Keywords: Elderly · Haptic feedback · Placebo · Time perception · User interface

1 Background

Many interactive products found their way into our daily lives. State-of-the-art machinery (graphics, sound, networks, miniaturisation, etc.) allowed for more than mere functionality [1]. The advancement of science and technology constantly challenges five senses of people in interactive products. In addition to the development of HCI visualization, haptic sensation is also the continuous goal of modern research. Descartes had mentioned that it's hard to discard the evidence we got through touch. "Of all our senses, touch is the one considered least deceptive and the more secure." [2], written in his book

⌈The world and other writings⌋ . This also been used as "deceit" to achieve further user experience. After study, we realized there were three categories of benevolent deception in HCI, which including System Image Deceptions, Behavioral Deceptions and Mental

© Springer Nature Switzerland AG 2020
Q. Gao and J. Zhou (Eds.): HCII 2020, LNCS 12207, pp. 184–196, 2020.
https://doi.org/10.1007/978-3-030-50252-2_14

Model Deceptions [3]. And we would focus on the interaction of behavioral deceptions in the user interface.

Waiting is an unavoidable factor in the interaction process, so feedback plays an important role in it. Nielsen believed that the system should reasonably let users know what is happening [4], and Galitz said that feedback could assist and guide people's operations [5]. People were more and more concerned about the interaction on the mobile interface, and the "micro-interaction" research on visual feedback had also become a new research category [6]. We wanted to explore whether haptic feedback could be effectively applied to feedback. There were many studies supporting the discussion of older people with haptic feedback. For example, messages or better experience could be presented through different vibration modes [7, 8], or the feedback with vibration could significantly shorten the completion time of the pinch gesture [9]. These stimulated us to include the elderly in our experiments.

1.1 Placebo Effect and HCI

Placebo theory has been widely known in medical experiments. Although patients receive ineffective treatment, they "expect" or "believe" that the treatment is effective [10], which not only appears in the medical field but also in reality. The New York Times also revealed in 2004 that most of the walk buttons in New York did not work. With 3,250 pedestrian traffic lights In New York, only about 1,000 buttons had practical effect [11]. These "Placebo Buttons" felt relieved when pressed, but had no effect. However, like placebo, these buttons could still serve other indirect purposes. Ellen Langer put forward the concept of "control illusion". Taking some actions will make people feel that they have control over the situation and feel good, rather than just being passive bystanders [12]. In addition to the placebo button in the real environment, the placebo effect is also used in human-computer interaction. Eytan Adar [3] proposed three designs on HCI with benevolent deception. Among them, behavior deceptions were the one we mainly explore. The interface contains deceptive features that try to make the user feel more successful, where the slow-loading image was tiled, slowly appearing on screen, to provide the sensation of action and availability [13]. Such a design can often be seen in many APPs, a visual animation process is presented on many loading pages so that users can make the waiting process more confirmative after receiving such feedback.

1.2 Elderly and Haptic Feedback

As the physical condition of the elderly deteriorates, the sensitivity and stability of their hands decreases, which makes it more difficult for them to perform complex movements. With age, the body muscle fibers gradually reduced and shortened, which made the elderly more difficult to operate mobile devices. Besides, slower neural responses might affect the ability of the brain to receive and process information, which in turn affects its coordination and stability [14, 15]. Studies had found that technology can also cause negative emotional effects in some older people [16]. Although the touch accuracy and sensitivity of the elderly were lower than that of the young, touch operation was more effective than a mouse or other assistive device [17]. For the elderly, the direct operation of the mobile device was better than the operation performed by the auxiliary device, and the gesture operation could promote the interaction of the elderly and effectively reduce the error rate [18]. Studies had shown when haptic feedback is part of UI, speed and accuracy would be increased, and less frustration [19]. Many studies supported this result, using haptic feedback in different devices to convey information, such as navigation or warnings, without distracting users [20]. Or use the phone's vibration mode to let users know the right direction [21]. It also pointed out that when receiving haptic feedback, it is like being in a virtual environment [22]. Therefore, we wanted to know through experiments whether the addition of haptic feedback could improve the experience of the elderly, and whether the improvement of such experience was significant compared with the young group.

1.3 Time Perception and the Attentional-Gate Model Theory

The operation of many mobile devices must be waited for, and many studies were exploring the limits of their feedback time. In a report, the user's tolerance for page refresh was 2 s [23]. And 10 s is the user's waiting limit in usability, more than 10 s will make users want to leave the site [24].

Why people feel that time is passing fast when watching an interesting book or movie, but when listening to a boring lecture, feel that it will never end. In addition to emotions that affect time perception [25], Zakay [26] proposed the attention gate model (Fig. 1), which explaining how people allocate attention resources to external events or pay attention to the time of the event itself. Because attention resources are limited, when people pay more attention to time, the gate will widen, allowing more pulses to pass; if people's attention is diverted to other non-time-related events, the gate will narrow, the number of passing pulses will decrease, and the perception of time will decrease. In the

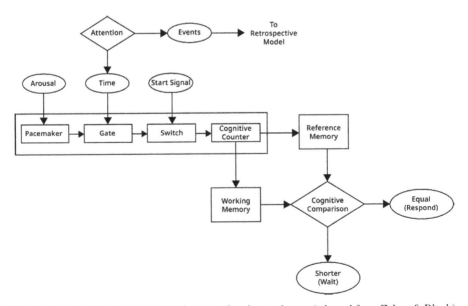

Fig. 1. The attentional-gate model of prospective time estimate. (adapted from Zakay & Block).

task of "expected time estimation", two factors that affected attention resources were temporal relevance and concurrent nontemporal activity. To summarized, when focusing on non-time-related information, users' judgments of waiting time will become shorter.

2 Research Purpose

In the research, the main purpose was to collect the user's perception of feedback time and evaluated various feedback types on the user interface of mobile applications. We wanted to explore the following things:

1. How do different waiting times affect users' time perception?
2. How do different types of feedback affect users' time perception?
3. Can the addition of haptic feedback improve users' preferences and reduce the perception of waiting time?

3 Method

In this study, a 3 × 2 mixed factor design was used. The two independent variables are "feedback type" and "task action". The types of feedback are visual feedback, haptic feedback, and visual + haptic feedback. Task operations are refresh and video play. Time perception and preference types are the variables of quantitative research, and then simple interviews and observations in the entire process are used to conduct qualitative research afterwards. The interface for the experiment was designed to help simulate a scenario, allowing participants to operate in a natural environment.

3.1 Experimental Setup

- Experimental tasks: Divided into 2 scenarios as experimental tasks, which were (1) Refresh. (2) Video play. The participants were required to experiment with three different feedbacks (VF = Visual feedback; HF = Haptic feedback; VHF = Visual + Haptic feedback) under the two experience modes. Perceived the time and conducted qualitative interviews at the end.
- Experimental sample: As shown in Table 1. Using the common social software Facebook as the experimental scenario simulation. There were two types of visual feedback.

(1) Refresh: After dragging down, a circle would appear at the top of the screen, and filled it with long-short-long-short lines. Each line segment was maintained for 0.5 s regardless of the length. The total time was 2 s.
(2) Video play: Tapped the video play icon, trapezoid would be arranged in a circle in the middle of the screen, one every 1 s, the total time is 10 s.

In order to obtain the fairness of the feedback form, the trigger gesture in the form of haptic feedback was the same as the visual feedback, designed with frequency and vibration time elements.

Table 1. The two task operation types presented on the mobile app user interface in this study.

Task	Feedback animation	Gesture
Refresh		Drag down
Video play		Tap

(1) Refresh: the two motors were high frequency (340 Hz): triggered at 0 s and 1 s, lasting 0.4 s, interval 0.6 s, and low frequency (240 Hz): 0.5 s delay, triggered at 0.5 s and 1.5 s, lasting 0.4 s, interval 0.6 s, total time 2 s.

(2) Video play: Two motors vibrated at the same time, with a frequency of 340 Hz, which was triggered once per second, lasting 0.9 s each time, with an interval of 0.1 s, and a total time of 10 s.

3.2 Apparatus and Prototype

The experimental design in this study used Adobe XD software, including the interface, animation design, and the final application prototype. This prototype was a mobile application developed to simulate social applications. In order to prevent the color from affecting the participants, the interface was presented in grayscale. It came with 5.15 in. Android smart phone (Xiaomi Mi 6), 1920 × 1080 pixels and 428 ppi. Two 10 mm × 3.4 mm shaftless vibration motor pasted onto the back of the prototypes.

3.3 Participants

Due to the decline of physiological functions, the tactile sensitivity of the elderly have decreased [27]. One study showed that the sensitivity of the sense of touch starts to deteriorate from the age of fifty [28].

There were 39 participants divided into experimental group and control group according to age in the experiment. All participants had experience of using smart phones and have normal behavior ability.

- Experimental Group: 24 people, aged over 55 years old.
- Control Group: 15 people, aged 20–30 years old.

3.4 Experimental Procedure

As shown in Fig. 2. The feedback sequence of the participants' operations was randomly assigned and experienced three types of feedback in a balanced manner. First, ask them to complete a personal survey, which includes some basic demographic issues (such as age, occupation, etc.). Second, they were provided with detailed instructions on how to operate the phone, perform experimental tasks, and perform time estimation. when completed a feedback-type operation, the participant would be instructed to answer the perceived feedback time. In order to ensure that the answer of the test participant is not disturbed, we would not inform the duration of the actual feedback. After getting the answer of the test subject, we would fill in the speed of the test participant's perception in three-level in the background (fast, same, slow). After completing the six tasks of the three types of feedback, the subjects were asked to choose their favorite feedback type and describe the reason. The duration of this experiment was about 10 min.

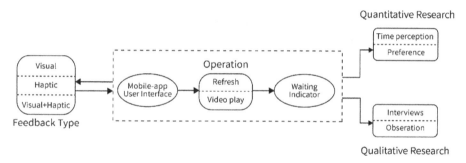

Fig. 2. Experiment model of this study.

4 Result

The results were analyzed using descriptive statistics and a T-test. Three types of feedback corresponding to two task operations ($2 \times 3 = 6$) plus preferences, a total of 7 groups were used for descriptive statistics. The age was divided into two independent samples, and the three feedback types in the two sets of operations were used as variables for the T-test.

4.1 Refresh

As shown in Fig. 3.

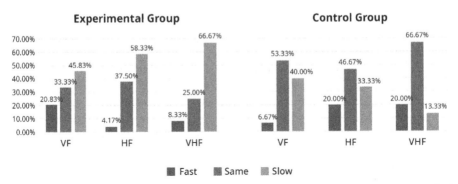

Fig. 3. The percentage of time perception choices of two groups for different feedback on refresh task.

- VF: In the experimental group, 20.83% thought that the feeling was rapid, 33.33% chose a consistent feeling, and 45.83% thought it was slow. In the control group, they were 20.83%, 33.33%, and 45.83% in order.
- HF: 4.17% of the experimental group thought that the feedback had reduced time feeling, 37.5% considered it the same, and 58.33% chose it more slowly; in the control group, there were 20%, 46.67%, 33.33% from fast, same, and slow, respectively.
- VHF: 8.33% of people in the experimental group felt fast, 25% thought they felt the same, and 66.67% thought it was slower; in the control group, fast, same, and slow accounted for 20%, 66.67%, and 13.33%.

4.2 Video Play

As shown in Fig. 4.

- VF: In order from fast, same, and slow, the experimental group received 33.33%, 62.5%, and 4.17%; the control group received 46.67%, 40%, and 13.33%, respectively.
- HF: The experimental group and the control group made 29.17%, 66.67%, 4.17% and 20%, 60%, and 20% of fast, same, and slow choices, respectively.
- VHF: It was 25%, 75%, and 0% in the experimental group; in the control group, it was 40%, 46.67%, and 13.33%, respectively.

4.3 T-Test

When performing independent sample t-test, know in advance whether the experimental group and the control group are homogeneity.

From Table 2, you can know that the significance value in the Refresh (VF), Refresh (HF), Refresh (VHF), Video play (VF), and Video play (HF), both experimental group

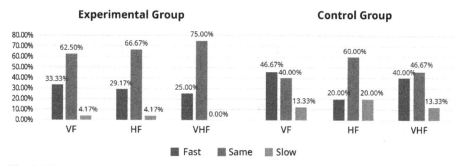

Fig. 4. The percentage of time perception choices of two groups for different feedback on video play task

and control group are >.05, which indicates that the two groups are homogeneity. Among them, Video play (VHF) is <0.05, indicating that the two groups are not homogeneity, so the value is taken with equal variances not assumed in t-test.

Table 2. The Levene's test for equality and Independent t-test of two groups.

Sample	Experimental group (Mean)	Control group (Mean)	F	Sig.	t	p-value	Significant difference (Yes/No)
Refresh (VF)	2.25	2.33	1.922	0.174	−0.346	0.731	No
Refresh (HF)	2.54	2.13	0.166	0.686	1.905	0.065	No
Refresh (VHF)	2.58	1.93	2.153	0.151	3.126	0.003	Yes
Video play (VF)	1.75	1.67	3.396	0.073	0.414	0.681	No
Video play (HF)	1.75	2.00	0.087	0.769	−1.307	0.199	No
Video play (VHF)	1.75	1.73	5.284	0.027	0.082	0.935	No

In Refresh (VHF), because P = 0.003 < 0.05, there is a significant difference between the experimental group and the control group. Compared with the control group, the time perception is generally considered to be slow for the experimental group (experimental group = 2.58, control group = 1.93).

4.4 Preference

After completing the task, participants were asked to choose which of the three feedbacks they liked best. In Fig. 5, 54% of the experimental group liked VHF. The preferences of VF and HP accounted for 25% and 21% respectively. In the control group in Fig. 6, 47% chose VF, the same number as VHF, while only 1 chose HF. In the results of all participants in Fig. 7, VHF received 51%, VF received 33%, and HF received 16%.

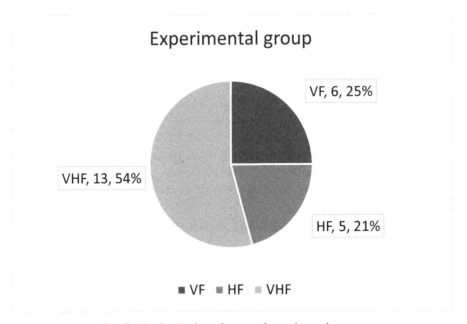

Fig. 5. The feedback preference of experimental group.

5 Discussion

From the refresh task, the experimental group generally perceived a slower speed on the three types of feedback, while the control group could almost perceive the correct time of operating on any types of feedback. Maybe we could find some clues from the perceived degradation of the elderly. In VHF, up to 66.67% of the experimental group thought that it was slower, which seemed to be inconsistent with our expected results, but in the analysis of preferences, they got the most choices.

From the video play task, the experimental group could almost perceive the correct operation seconds. This is very interesting. Compared with the 2 s feedback, the relatively long 10 s can be correctly sensed. On VF and HF, only one participant felt that it was slow, and on VHF, even no one felt that it was slow. In the control group, compared to the refresh task, the number of people who felt slower also decreased significantly.

In terms of preference, 54% of the experimental group liked VHF. From the previous time-perceived feedback on two different tasks, the feedback of the movie download task has positive results (the faster the time-perceived, the more participants will love). Although more than 60% of the participants considered the waiting time to be slow in the refresh task, it still received the highest support.

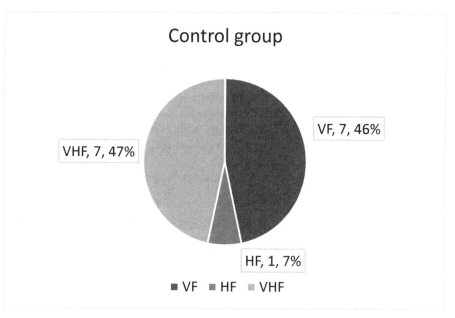

Fig. 6. The feedback preference of control group.

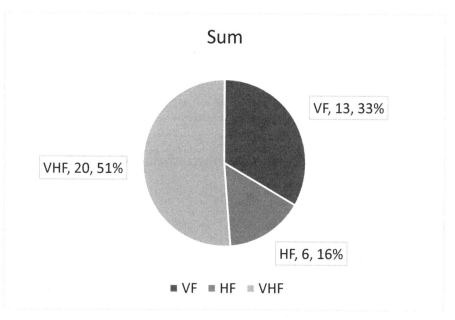

Fig. 7. The sum of the feedback preference.

6   Conclusion and Future Work

The purpose of this study is to explore whether the addition of haptic feedback on mobile interfaces can reduce the elderly's perception of time when using a smartphone, thereby improving the elderly's experience and reducing the frustration of the using process. The results of the study found that visual feedback had the best effect on the reduction of time perception, and the addition of haptic feedback did not reduce time perception significantly. Compared with the control group, it felt even longer in short-term tasks. But in terms of preference, more than half of the elderly still chose the type that contains haptic feedback.

From the qualitative interviews with participants, we reached the following conclusions:

- Most people who liked the type of visual + haptic feedback considered that haptic feedback made the operation feel more confirmative, which meant that the haptic feedback could achieve the effect of a placebo.
- Some participants thought that haptic feedback would make them feel irritable, known from their experimental results that this would indeed increase the perceived waiting time of the participant. Zacky's theory [26] also mentioned that when emotions are in a negative state, the time correlation will increase and the estimation of time will be overestimated.

The sense of operational confirmation may be the reason why users love haptic feedback, even if there is no decline in time perception. Related research can further explore the frequency of haptic feedback. Whether the vibration with different frequencies can increase the user experience or not. Or explore in what feedback operation should present haptic feedback. A study also mentioned that there is currently no real structure for haptic experience [29]. More and more researches are ongoing in this field, and it is hoped that this research can also contribute to related fields.

Acknowledgements. We are thankful for the financial support from The Ministry of Science and Technology (MOST), Taiwan. The grant MOST 107-2221-E-006-169 & MOST 108-2221-E-006-048.

References

1. Hassenzahl, M., Tractinsky, N.: User experience - a research agenda. Behav. Inform. Technol. **25**(2), 91–97 (2006). https://doi.org/10.1080/01449290500330331
2. René, D., Gaukroger, S.: The World and Other Writings. Cambridge University Press, Cambridge (1998). https://doi.org/10.1017/cbo9780511605727
3. Adar, E., Tan, D.S., Teevan, J.: Benevolent deception in human computer interaction. In: Proceedings of the SIGCHI Conference on Human Factors in Computing Systems (CHI 2013). Association for Computing Machinery, Paris, pp. 1863-1872 (2013) https://doi.org/10.1145/2470654.2466246
4. Nielsen, J.: 10 Usability heuristics for user interface design. Nielsen Norman Group **1**(1) (1995)

5. Galitz, W.O.: The Essential Guide to User Interface Design: An Introduction to GUI Design Principles and Techniques, 3rd edn. Wiley Publishing, Indiana (2007)
6. Saffer, D.: Microinteractions: Full Color Edition: Designing with Details, 1st edn. O'Reilly Media, Sebastopol (2013)
7. Liu, S.-F., Cheng, H.-S., Chang, C.-F., Lin, P.-Y.: A study of perception using mobile device for multi-haptic feedback. In: Yamamoto, S., Mori, H. (eds.) HIMI 2018. LNCS, vol. 10904, pp. 218–226. Springer, Cham (2018). https://doi.org/10.1007/978-3-319-92043-6_19
8. Banter, B.: Touch screens and touch surfaces are enriched by haptic force-feedback. Inf. Disp. **26**(3), 26–30 (2010). https://doi.org/10.1002/j.2637-496x.2010.tb00231.x
9. Liu, S.-F., Chueh, Y.-S., Chang, C.-F., Lin, P.-Y., Cheng, H.-S.: A study of performance on multi-touch gesture for multi-haptic feedback. In: Zhou, J., Salvendy, G. (eds.) HCII 2019. LNCS, vol. 11592, pp. 441–449. Springer, Cham (2019). https://doi.org/10.1007/978-3-030-22012-9_32
10. Beecher, H.K.: The powerful placebo. JAMA **159**(17), 1602–1606 (1955). https://doi.org/10.1001/jama.1955.02960340022006
11. Luo, M.: For exercise in New York futility, push button. New York Times (2004). https://www.nytimes.com/2004/02/27/nyregion/for-exercise-in-new-york-futility-push-button.html Accessed 27 Feb 2004
12. Langer, E.J.: The illusion of control. J. Pers. Soc. Psychol. **32**(2), 311–328 (1975)
13. Irani, K.B., Wallace, V.L., Jackson, J.H.: Conversational design of stochastic service systems from a graphical terminal. In: Parslow, R.D., Green, R.E. (eds.) Advanced Computer Graphics, pp. 91–101. Springer, Boston (1971) https://doi.org/10.1007/978-1-4613-4606-7_7
14. Seidler, R., Stelmach, G.: Motor Control, Encyclopedia of Gerontology: Age, Aging and the Aged. Academic Press, San Diego (1996)
15. Lee, C.-F., Kuo, C.-C.: Difficulties on small-touch-screens for various ages. In: Stephanidis, C. (ed.) UAHCI 2007. LNCS, vol. 4554, pp. 968–974. Springer, Heidelberg (2007). https://doi.org/10.1007/978-3-540-73279-2_108
16. Dickinson, A., Gregor, P.: Computer use has no demonstrated impact on the well-being of older adults. Int. J. Hum.-Comput. Stud. **64**(8), 744–753 (2006). https://doi.org/10.1016/j.ijhcs.2006.03.001
17. Findlater, L., Froehlich, J.E., Fattal, K., Wobbrock, J.O., Dastyar, T.: Age-related differences in performance with touchscreens compared to traditional mouse input. In: Proceedings of SIGCHI Conference on Human Factors in Computing Systems, pp. 343–346. ACM, New York (2013) https://doi.org/10.1145/2470654.2470703
18. Chaparro, A., Rogers, M., Fernandez, J., Bohan, M., Choi, S.D., Stumpfhauser, L.: Range of motion of the wrist: implications for designing computer input devices for the elderly. Disabil. Rehabil. **22**(13), 633–637 (2000). https://doi.org/10.1080/09638280050138313
19. Silfverberg, M.: Using mobile keypads with limited visual feedback: implications to handheld and wearable devices. In: Chittaro, L. (ed.) Mobile HCI 2003. LNCS, vol. 2795, pp. 76–90. Springer, Heidelberg (2003). https://doi.org/10.1007/978-3-540-45233-1_7
20. Elliott, L.R., van Erp, J.B.F., Redden, E.S., Duistermaat, M.: Field-based validation of a tactile navigation device. IEEE Trans. Haptics **3**(2), 78–87 (2010). https://doi.org/10.1109/toh.2010.3
21. Pielot, M., Poppinga, B., Heuten, W., Boll, S.: PocketNavigator: studying tactile navigation systems in-situ. In: Proceedings of the SIGCHI Conference on Human Factors in Computing Systems (CHI 2012). Association for Computing Machinery, New York, pp. 3131–3140 (2012). https://doi.org/10.1145/2207676.2208728
22. SalInas, E.L., Rassmus-Gruhn, K., Sjosstrom, C.: Supporting presence in collaborative environments by hap-tic force feedback. ACM Trans. Comput.-Hum. Interact. **7**(4), 461–467 (2000). https://doi.org/10.1145/365058.365086

23. Nah, F.-H.: A study on tolerable waiting time: how long are Web users willing to wait? Behav. Inf. Technol. **23**(3), 153–163 (2004). https://doi.org/10.1080/01449290410001669914

24. Nielsen, J.: Usability Engineering, 1st edn. AP Professional, Cambridge (1993)

25. Droit-Volet, S., Fayolle, S.L., Gil, S.: Emotion and time perception: effects of film-induced mood. Front. Integr. Neurosci., **5**(33) (2011) https://doi.org/10.3389/fnint.2011.00033

26. Zakay, D.: Experiencing time in daily life. Psychol. **25**(8), 578–581 (2012)

27. Liu, S.-F., Yang, Y.-T., Chang, C.-F., Lin, P.-Y., Cheng, H.-S.: A study on haptic feedback awareness of senior citizens. In: Zhou, J., Salvendy, G. (eds.) ITAP 2018. LNCS, vol. 10926, pp. 315–324. Springer, Cham (2018). https://doi.org/10.1007/978-3-319-92034-4_24

28. Fisk, A.D., Rogers, W.A., Charness, N., Czaja, S.J., Sharit, J.: Designing for Older Adults: Principles and Creative Human Factors Approaches, 2nd edn. Taylor & Francis Inc., Bosa Roca (2009)

29. Schneider, O., et al.: Haptic experience design: what hapticians do and where they need help. Int. J. Hum-Comput. Stud. **107**, 5-21 (2017) https://doi.org/10.1016/j.ijhcs.2017.04.004

Multimodal Coexistence Environment Design to Assist User Testing and Iterative Design of HiGame Emotional Interaction Design for Elderly

Ji-Rong Rachel Lu, Teng-Wen Chang(✉) , Yi-Sin Wu, and Chun-Yen Chen

National Yunlin University of Science and Technology, Yunlin, Taiwan
m10635004@gmail.yuntech.edu.tw, tengwen@yuntech.edu.tw,
rilla0918@gmail.com, m10635013@gmail.yuntech.edu.tw

Abstract. Usability testing is an important process in human-computer interaction and user experience design. It can help designers understand the difficult points of the user in the interaction process. Whether the interactive situation is correctly presented in the test process and whether the designer has correctly received the feedback from the subject will affect the accuracy of the test. With the rapid development of the IoT in recent years, more and more interactive designs are multimodal models. When performing traditional usability test, iterative design processes often take a lot of cost to fully present the interactive situation for the subject to experience. And because there are many kinds of adjustable elements, the subjects are also more complicated and time-consuming to communicate with the designer to describe the feelings. Therefore, this study takes the multi-object HiGame elderly interaction design as an example. Using MR technology combined with 3D printing in the coexistence environment to assist HiGame interactive design for user testing and iterative design. The virtual prototyping combined with some physical tactile methods gives the subject a more complete experience. With Hololens as the virtual body interactive medium, the subject can co-design with the designer in a dynamic feedback manner at the same time. To enable the elderly subject to achieve the highest efficiency, communicate with the designer in real time through dynamic feedback. At the same time, it helps designers reduce the time and cost required for the iterative design process of multi-object interactive testing.

Keywords: Multimodal interaction · Physical and virtual coexistence · Mixed reality · Usability test · Iterative design

1 Background

Usability testing is a very important process in human-computer interaction and user experience design. It can reduce errors in the interaction process and help you understand the behaviors, needs, and preferences of your target users. Nielsen [1] mentioned that a good interactive design, from conceptual design to actual development, it often requires

© Springer Nature Switzerland AG 2020
Q. Gao and J. Zhou (Eds.): HCII 2020, LNCS 12207, pp. 197–209, 2020.
https://doi.org/10.1007/978-3-030-50252-2_15

a large number of user tests through prototyping the interactive situations. Designer also communicates with users, and iterative design based on user's feedback to complete the user-friendly interaction design.

In an ongoing project, the multimodal interaction of the Internet of Things for elderly's emotional communication, called HiGame(Horticultural Interaction Game, Hi Game) studied by Wu, Chang and Datta [2] and HiGame 2.0 by Lu, Chang and Wu [3] is taken as an example. And we set interaction designers and elderly as the target audience. Then we discuss how to design an interactive mode through the integration of virtual and physical technologies, to use for scenario prototyping and physical object test of multi-modal interaction design. And we assist designers and test subjects in communication and test records to improve the accuracy of the assessment.

1.1   User Test Evaluation of IoT Multimodal Interactive Design

It is important that the interaction design process can realistically prototyping the inter-active situation during the user test phase. Because of designers cannot predict all the difficulties that users will encounter in the interaction process. Faulkner [4] believes that those users who have not participated in the development before can give the most valuable feedback, and they don't have too many stereotypes about the settings in the design. But it also because they don't know much about the interactive design they are experiencing. Whether the interactive situation presented by the test is complete and whether the test subject's experience is correct will seriously affect the accuracy of the test and evaluation.

As the rapid development of the IoT and a large number of IoT's applications, more interactive designs include multiple objects. Fauquex, Goyal, Evequoz and Bocchi [5] mentioned that due to the rise of smart homes, many interactive processes have combined multiple objects in the environment. In the user testing part, a single model cannot completely prototype the interactive situation to achieve user test fully. However, the iterative design process in the multimodal interaction mode usually requires iterative modification and re-prototype. Customized production of physical prototypes is costly and time consuming. Therefore, user test for interactive design with multimodal objects is a problem for carrying out multiple iterative designs.

1.2   Iterative Design Process Communication Between Designer and User

During the user testing process, the smooth communication between the designer and the user will affect the accuracy of the test evaluation. Moreland, Eyde, Robertson, Primoff and Most [6] point out that the increase and decrease and adjustment of each element and link in the interaction process come from the habits and needs of users. It's not just the designer's assumptions and feelings. Therefore, how the communication process helps interactive designers to correctly receive and understand the thoughts and opinions of users of different identities is very important.

Interaction design from requirements exploration, confirmation and conceptual pro-posal to the actual development stage, iterative design phase is indispensable. Adams and Atman [7] mentioned that designers must continuously iterate and correct based on test results in order to develop the suitable interaction model. Designers can use many tools to get user opinions. It is common for subjects to give static feedback through sketches or concept descriptions. Based on the collected feedback, designers can modify or adjust the design.

However, this process of communicating and confirming with users is time consuming process. Feedbacks on multimodal interaction's multiple functions and processes is more likely to cause confusion or misunderstanding in communication, that resulting in a gap in communication. Especially for the elderly test subjects who have limited expressive ability, it often takes time and energy during user test.

1.3 Modeling Multimodal Human-Computer Interaction

Regarding modeling multimodal human-computer interaction, Obrenovic and Starcevic [8] proposed Multimodal interaction is part of everyday human discourse. We speak, act and shift our sights in many effective ways of communication. Recent initiatives such as sensory and focused user interfaces put these natural human behaviors at the center of human-computer interaction. Because the multimodal interaction of multiple objects can make the user more clearly receive the correct instructions when they performing human-computer interaction. It was also suggested in research that the Meta model's main concept is that an HCI modality engages human capabilities to produce an effect on users. The human-computer interaction mode can be simple or complex. The simple human-computer interaction mode represents the original form of interaction. The complex HCI pattern integrates other patterns and uses them simultaneously, as shown in Fig. 1.

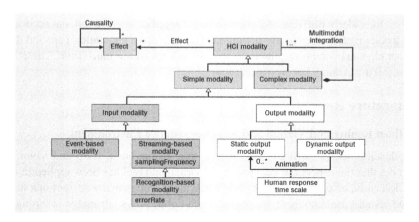

Fig. 1. Simplified HCI modality model [8]

They have proposed that when people modeling multimodal human-computer interaction, the output modalities present to the user either static or dynamic data. Some modes are dynamic in nature, but many dynamic presentations are just static animation modes. Human-computer interaction researchers agree that human-computer interaction has three important levels: perceptual processing, immediate response and unit task.

Perceptual processing time (about 0.1 s) is the time spent by the human perception system to integrate and process signals. During this time the stimuli merged and the response felt instantaneous. The immediate response time (about 1 s) is the shortest time a user needs to respond. The unit task time (about 10 s) represents the time range performance of the simplest task the user wants to perform. These multimodal human perception modes all are what designers need to consider in human-computer interaction design.

Each multimodal human-computer interaction method has human capabilities and has a certain impact on users. These impacts fall into four main categories' (1) Sensory effects describe the processing of stimuli by human sensory devices. (2) The perception effect comes from the analysis of sensor data by the human perception system. (3) Motion effects describe human mechanical actions, such as head movements or pressure. (4) Cognitive effects occur at higher levels of human information processing, including memory, attention, and curiosity processes.

1.4 The Problem

It is known from the literature that multimodal interaction design for human-computer interaction can increase the user's experience and help user more clearly to interact with the corresponding instructions. Therefore, in our research, the HiGame2.0 (Horticultural Interaction Game, Hi Game) it's user is the elderly that reaction are relatively slow to recognize and respond. We use a multimodal interaction to help elderly living alone receive more stimuli to interact with their family, and feel the care by their family.

However, in this case of multimodal interaction, there are multiple objects and complex interaction modes. These can make it difficult to complete usability tests and perform multiple iterative designs; it will take a lot of time and cost a lot of money. After the user test, when the elderly of HiGame 2.0 are to be surveyed or interviewed, the accuracy of the feedback given by the elderly is limited. There is also a generation gap, and due to their poor physical conditions, the test process can't spend too much time. These make HiGame 2.0 user testing become difficult.

2 Literature Review

2.1 Mixed Reality and Virtual and Real Coexistence Environment

As the development of virtual media technology, Billinghurst, Kato and Myojin [9] pointed out that the concept of coexistence of virtual and real has been applied in many places. Recently, mixed reality (MR) has been widely used in many designs that need to combine visual virtual bodies with physical solid objects. Its advantage is through the virtual interface, users can get the immersive experience. Additionally, the visual perception and physical feelings of objects during user testing including tactile sensations are also one of the items that must be evaluated and tested in interactive design. Billinghurst and Kato [10] said that MR virtual pictures can be combined with real environments and objects to present a comprehensive form. Break the boundary between real and virtual, and overlay virtual space in the real world.

MR is a virtual medium that is not a one-way experience. It provided a new interaction mode for the user test, helping users to interact with reality. It is a dynamic communication medium for designers and test subjects, and provides visualized feedback methods for test subjects.

2.2 Physical Integration of MR in User Test Evaluation

When an interactive design concept first came out, designers often felt that they didn't have enough information about user needs. Especially at the front end of the design process, the most important part of this process is testing and validating potentials. The research purpose of Choi [11] is to explore Augmented Reality (AR) and Tangible Augmented Reality (TAR) as tools to evaluate product availability. It evaluates the usability of the space heater product and its equivalent AR and TAR presentations. The results prove that TAR can be completely used to evaluate real products, especially for products with physical interface controls. TAR is a reliable method for usability testing. Relatively simple AR testers are not as reliable as TAR.

Ha, Chang and Woo [12] evaluated the usability of multimodal prototyping feedback in the immersion of an AR design environment. They investigate what happens if you provide users with multi-sensory feedback. For the usability test of visual feedback, in their research, the degree of visual immersion and the applicability between different users were tested. In the haptic feedback test, they presented AR virtual objects in a physical and tangible way, to assess the effect of physical contact on the test subject. Finally, the analysis results obtained from usability tests and reviews suggest that the usability test of multi-sensory feedback can help enhance the user's immersion in the design of augmented reality (AR) products.

It would be revolutionary to place 3D objects in a space and view it through an AR headset like HoloLens while adding some basic interaction. Hunsucker, Baumgartner and McClinton [13] mentioned that these user experiences are not just presented on the screen; they happen in the real world and need to be tested in real space. However, it should be noted that the smoothness of HoloLens in actual use depends on the quality of Wi-Fi, which is more uncontrollable in the environment. As a result, it becomes intermittent. At the same time, they using this evaluation method, whether users understand their surroundings are also a problem. In an environment where virtual and real overlap, the test subject is easily confused and may accidentally bump into things. This is also what must be considered in the design of AR interactive environment.

2.3 Our Approach

In this study, MR technology will be used in combination with 3D printing of physical objects to prototype the multimodal IoT interactive design usage scenario, and it will add virtual effects feedback. It used to help designers to perform user testing and iterative design for more complex multi-object interactions with lower interaction costs and higher efficiency. The interactive scenarios and technologies that previously took more time to prepare or that are not yet reachable can be quickly presented to the subject. It will enable users to feel the real experience of use before the actual development of the design. It makes the evaluation process faster and more accurate.

Aimed at the test subjects of HiGame interactive design, we use the immediate feedback method to optimize the user experience design of this communications channel. We also use MR for immediate interaction to embed user testing, so that the subject can give dynamic feedback immediately at the time of the test. And through the MR, the subject's visual feedback was specifically presented. It enables subjects and designers to co-design. Even elderly who do not understand the text can easily react and record their feedback, so as to improve the interaction process and speed up the communication between the designer and the elderly subject.

3   The Test: HiGame

3.1   Concept of HiGame

In this research, the multimodal interactive design of the HiGame 2.0 (HiGame from now on) is used as the test object. HiGame is a potted plant system that combines the emotional interaction of multiple objects and the environment. Internet of Things is used to connect the home environment of elderly people living alone with their families and children living in other places. Real plants and interactive potted plants of the Internet of Things set in the homes of the elderly are the medium mainly connected with the elderly. And around this potted plant that represents the elderly, an IoT environment with light and water will be formed by the IoT-related objects, as shown in Fig. 2.

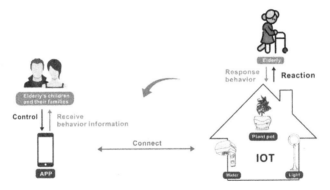

Fig. 2. HiGame IoT multimodal interactive design

The interactive mode is that family members of elderly people living in other places are notified through the APP. They must remotely control the plant care objects in the homes of the elderly according to the plant needs displayed on the app to perform remote automatic plant care, to enables family members in the field to connect with the environment of the elderly's home whenever and wherever possible. In this process of emotional interaction across space, the elderly need not personally take care of this interactive potted plant. Their interaction method only needs to observe and feel the growth of potted plants and the operation of IoT systems around potted plants, to feel this home is being taken care of, also feel that the children living outside care of them. This study conducts user testing and evaluation for the emotional interaction of elderly in HiGame.

3.2 Multimodal Interaction in HiGame

HiGame is a multimodal interaction design project for the elderly that uses multiple objects and effects to help elderly living alone and emotionally interactive with their children in other places. It uses the multimodal method to create an interactive situation by cascading multiple units and effects. Each object in the HiGame interactive mode has different interactive functions, and as shown in Fig. 3, it is the various Arduino objects required for HiGame interaction. In the user test process of HiGame interactive effect, if you want to present the interactive situation to the test subject, you must complete the potted sensor program and install the sensor. At the same time, the automatic watering and automatic lighting systems and mechanisms are completed, and prototypes are produced. This process takes a lot of time and cost, and the test process is prone to hardware technical issues that affect the test smoothness.

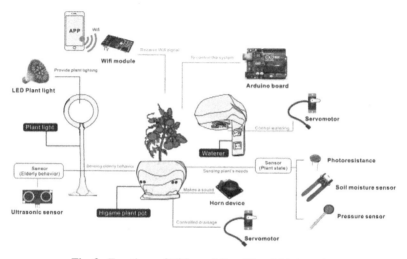

Fig. 3. Functions of HiGame 2.0 multimodal interaction

This research already performs virtual and real environment tests on the environment configuration and object types, and users are enables to give dynamic feedback on object types. Aiming at the technical effects, the sound and light visual interactions such as LED light emission and automatic water flow effect, if the user can also experience these through virtual body presentation, and allowing the subject to make real-time adjustments to the dynamic feedback of interactive effects in the virtual interface, it will be able to save the time and money of the designer before the test. And to avoid technical problems such as software and hardware during the test process from affecting the user's experience, it can also avoid damage to objects and equipment consumption during the test. The coexistence of false and real in the technical effect part is the next step of this research. In this study, we focus on multimodal space configuration and object type adjustment and iterative design.

3.3 Physical and Virtual Coexistence Usability Test of HiGame

The main user testing goal of HiGame interactive design for the elderly is to make the subjects feel the feeling of these planting related objects when they interact in the space. The interactive purpose of this design is to make the elderly feel companionship and concern through the overall situation. Therefore, it is very important for the designer to plan the multi-object type, location, and interaction mode for the environment, and whether the user's perception of the interactive situation can be truly experienced during the test.

To achieve the prototype of the HiGame multi-object scene, we increase the accuracy of the subject's interactive experience assessment and accelerate the interaction process and efficiency of the designer and the subject. Also we want to quickly record user testing and interaction process and reduce the cost of iterative design interaction process. This study uses MR technology in combination with 3D printing of solid objects, and we use HoloLens as the medium, we model the actual interactive script and environment in the MR system, and perform:

- It make subject to experience HiGame multi-object interactive scenarios through MR and 3D printing physical objects
- It make the subject to design with the designer through MR and dynamic feedback evaluation
- It enable designers to quickly modify and iterate designs through MR and 3D printing rapid prototyping technology

In the iterative design process of this interactive design, the interactive mode of feedback of the subjects is different from the static feedback of traditional user testing. Through MR, the subjects can give dynamic feedback in real time. And the subject's ideas are visualized and presented. During the testing process, the user and the designer jointly carry out the iterative design. HiGame test evaluation and iterative design with low cost and high efficiency, as shown in Fig. 4.

Fig. 4. Differences between user testing through dynamic feedback and traditional methods

4   Research Steps

4.1 Step 1: Building Prototype for Testing

For the prototyping of the environment required by HiGame, this study first designed the HiGame interactive script design based on the home environment of the elderly living alone in Taiwan. We design and plan according to the effect function settings and we required objects that the automatic care of plants will have. The IoT objects used in the interactive process are flower pots, watering equipment, and plant lighting equipment. The space connected by these objects assists the emotional interaction between elderly people living alone and their children.

In this research, each object model in HiGame interaction is modeled through Rhino and connected to Grasshopper. Since the potted objects in this HiGame interaction must be equipped with solid plants, in the interaction mode setting, the elderly will contact and actually move to feel it. Therefore, the potted objects are presented in 3D printing in the test process. The rest of the objects present the model in HoloLens to provide the subjects experience in virtual form. We design a virtual and real coexistence environment for users to test in HoloLens, combining physical potted plants and virtual multiple plant care objects. And we set up with Grasshopper, including interactive control User Interface design, and dynamic feedback interaction mode design of the subject. Enables users to adjust the parameters of the position, size, and proportion of each virtual object, provide immediate and visual feedback, and communicate with the designer for a common iterative design.

4.2 Step 2: Physical and Virtual Coexistence Usability Testing Design

The research uses HoloLens to design a HiGame interactive virtual-real coexistence environment. In this virtual-real environment, the two functions of object environment position setting and object size adjustment are adjusted. And two interactive communication modes and interfaces are designed for experiments.

In the HiGame interactive object environment location test, first we let the subject wear a HoloLens to watch the various plant care objects around the HiGame potted entity. And walk around to experience this environment setting scenario from different distance angles. After watching, the test subject can move the position angle of the object according to their own feelings. As long as the index finger and thumb are opened and closed, the virtual object can be taken for adjustment. After adjusting the position of the object, the subject can communicate with the designer about their ideas and why they made these adjustments. As shown in Fig. 5.

 (A) Before displacement   (B) Displacement   (C) After displacement

Fig. 5. HiGame interactive environment reset through HoloLens

After the adjustment of object environment is completed, the next step is to enter the individual size adjustment of the object. A menu icon will appear in HoloLens. The subject can click on the object that they want to adjust. The selected object will appear green for modification and adjusted. The subject can click different options in the menu icon to adjust the size and proportion of the object, as shown in Fig. 6. When each object reaches the most suitable state for the user, the feedback records of each subject can be stored for the designer to make subsequent iterative design references. During the test, HoloLens also recorded the dynamic feedback of each subject including the user's operation and interaction behavior, so that the designer has a better understanding of the user and their behaviors.

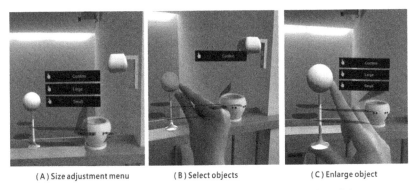

(A) Size adjustment menu   (B) Select objects   (C) Enlarge object

Fig. 6. HiGame interactive object type adjustment through HoloLens

Hololens system is incorporate-rated into user tests to record user preferences, such as selection of moving objects, preferences for environment settings, and adjusted object size ratios.

After a number of user test records, the parameterized records are organized by grasshopper to match the qualitative records of user perception. Conclude the environment that is most suitable for the intended user experience. To avoid the multimodal environment configuration with a lot of variable factors, the designer needs multiple iteration tests to find the most suitable environment plan. And through traditional user perception questionnaire interview methods to verify the conclusions, comparing dynamic feedback and static feedback, which one is more effective for the designer's record of user experience and the iterative process of multimodal environment settings.

4.3 Step 3: HiGame's Dynamic Feedback User Test Experiment

In this research experiment a target user, elderly person living alone was tested for this virtual and real coexistence environment user test, as shown in Fig. 7. The subject is quite smooth on the intuitive image operation. The prototyping of the virtual body in the physical and virtual coexistence environment indicates that the feeling will not be too different from the physical feeling. During the dynamic feedback process, the test subjects felt that, rather than filling out a static questionnaire and answering questions after the event, immediately adjusting the feedback through the visualized body under test immediately helped them express their feelings. And can make it easier to communicate with designers who have a large age gap with them.

Fig. 7. Elderly experiences on HiGame virtual reality coexistence environment for user test

4.4 Step 4: HiGame's 3D Prints Solid Objects for Iterative Design

In the iterative design after the first stage of testing, this study uses grasshopper to directly modify the interactive situation adjustment in the software based on the records of the results of the feedback from multiple subjects. For the testing of physical objects, based on the need to perform interaction requirements testing of physical contact such as touch feeling, In this study, FDM deposited 3D printing with low cost and short working hours was used as a preliminary prototyping tool for prototyping to reduce the resource consumption of the iterative design process.

After the first phase of user testing is completed, the 3D object model of the subject's feedback is printed for correction. Meanwhile the subjects' feedback on the prototype is recorded and carry out next iterative design, until it is confirmed that most of the subject agree with the model acceptance to a certain degree, as shown in Fig. 8.

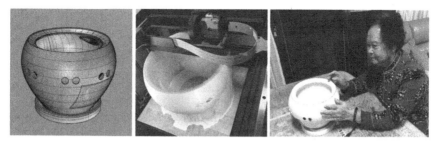

Fig. 8. Iteratively design the solid model that needs to be revised and 3D print out to retest

5 Discussion and Conclusions

According to the questionnaire analysis of the subject's feedback, dynamic feedback of interaction is indeed more convenient for subjects expressing their ideas than physical static usability test. And the user can more easily judge and think about what kind of setting is more suitable. One test can make subjects experience different environments. At the same time, the multi-object environment is completely presented and combined with the tactile sensation of the physical object, the experience is also relatively complete. But for the HoloLens experience process, it will be affected by the screen size that is easily disturb the subject and needs further investigation.

To the designer, letting the subject give dynamic feedback and record it in the system can quickly help the designer know the environment configuration suitable for the user through parameterization. With the help of MR and 3D printing, compared with the original iterative design process of HiGame interactive design relying on solid prototypes for user testing, the cost and time required have been greatly reduced. Accepting feedback from older subjects in a dynamic way is smoother than the original interaction with older subjects. It reduces communication problems, and also reduces the time and effort required to organize the subjects' feedback data and recall the test status.

This study conducted user test experiments on the type of test object and its environmental configuration. The effect did improve the interaction process between the iterative design designer and the subject. Subsequent research is expected to design different virtual and physical coexisting environments for HiGame's automatic plant care effects and HiGame's plant growth and change prototyping experience. And go deeper to explore how the testing method of combination of virtual and physical can be coordinated and improved to achieve the most realistic simulated product use situation. It enables designers and subject to conduct dynamic feedback interactive iterative design with the highest efficiency and lowest interaction cost.

References

1. Nielsen, J.: Iterative user-interface design. Computer **26**, 32–41 (1993)
2. Wu, Y.S., Chang, T.W., Datta, S.: HiGame: improving elderly well-being through horticultural interaction. Int. J. Architect. Comput. **14**, 263–276 (2016)
3. Lu, J.R., Chang, T.W., Wu, Y.S.: Higame2.0: planting as a medium to connect IoT objects in different environments to emotionally interact with elderly people living alone. In: CADDRIA (2020)
4. Faulkner, L.: Beyond the five-user assumption: benefits of increased sample sizes in usability testing. Behav. Res. Methods Instrum. Comput. **35**, 379–383 (2003)
5. Fauquex, M., Goyal, S., Evequoz, F., Bocchi, Y.: Creating people-aware IoT applications by combining design thinking and user-centered design methods. In: Proceedings of IEEE 2nd World Forum on Internet of Things (WF-IoT), pp. 57–62. IEEE (2015)
6. Moreland, K.L., Eyde, L.D., Robertson, G.J., Primoff, E.S.: Assessment of test user qualifications: a research-based measurement procedure. Am. Psychol. **50**(1), 14 (1995)
7. Adams, R.S., Atman, C.J.: Cognitive processes in iterative design behavior. In: Proceedings of FIE 1999 Frontiers in Education. 29th Annual Frontiers in Education Conference. Designing the Future of Science and Engineering Education, vol 1, pp. 11A16–13 (1999)
8. Obrenovic, Z., Starcevic, D.: Modeling multimodal human-computer interaction. Computer **37**, 65–72 (2004)
9. Billinghurst, M., Kato, H., Myojin, S.: Advanced interaction techniques for augmented reality applications. In: Shumaker, R. (ed.) VMR 2009. LNCS, vol. 5622, pp. 13–22. Springer, Heidelberg (2009). https://doi.org/10.1007/978-3-642-02771-0_2

10. Billinghurst, M., Kato, H.: Collaborative mixed reality. In: Proceedings of the First International Symposium on Mixed Reality, pp. 261–284 (1999)
11. Choi, Y.M.: Applying tangible augmented reality for product usability assessment. J. Usability Stud. **14** (2019)
12. Pan, Z., Zhang, X., El Rhalibi, A., Woo, W., Li, Y. (eds.): Edutainment 2008. LNCS, vol. 5093. Springer, Heidelberg (2008). https://doi.org/10.1007/978-3-540-69736-7
13. Hunsucker, A.J., Baumgartner, E., McClinton, K.: Evaluating an AR-based museum experience. Interactions **25**(4), 66–68 (2018)

Visual Attention of Young and Older Drivers in Takeover Tasks of Highly Automated Driving

Qijia Peng and Sunao Iwaki[✉]

Automotive Human Factors Research Center, National Institute of Advanced Industrial Science and Technology, 1-1-1 Umezono, Tsukuba, Ibaraki 305-8560, Japan
s.iwaki@aist.go.jp

Abstract. The objective of this study is to examine the differences of visual attention patterns between young and elder drivers affected by engagement of audio non-driving related task (NDRT) and traffic conditions. Previous research focus on influence of the interaction of NDRT in Highly Automated Vehicle (HAV) during take over tasks both in driving performance and visual attention, yet the research on aging effect on visual attention pattern with NDRT during take over tasks is still limited. Twenty-seven young and twenty-seven elder participants drove in a highly automated driving simulator in different traffic conditions and NDRT levels, and after the take-over request (TOR) they were required to change lanes to pass a stationary truck. The traffic conditions are set by numbers of cars on the right lane and NDRT is classic n-back task with audio stimuli. Results showed that elder drivers have higher collision rate and less stable lateral control than young drivers. For fixation transition number between different regions, both age group have fewer transitions when engaging NDRT, elder group have significantly fewer transitions than younger group and are more influenced by high traffic density. The analysis for fixation durations show similar results. For the change of distribution of fixation time, elder group focus more on the road ahead than young group which is more obvious in high-traffic condition. Around 4 s after the TOR, a decrease of attention on mirrors is observed in elder group. These results show a probable difference in visual attention patterns for young and elder drivers when facing TOR with engagement of NDRT and in high traffic density. Possible relevance between less attention on mirrors and worse driving behavior in elder group is also discussed. Further improvements of this study is illustrated according to the previous results and analysis.

Keywords: Automated driving · Non-driving task · Aging · Visual attention

1 Introduction

In recent years, most industrialized countries have encountered a great increase in elder population. Considering the increasing need for driving, it is likely that there will be increasing number of elder drivers in terms of both absolute number and proportion in the future. Meanwhile, the need for mobility is an important factor related to quality of life in old age [1, 2]. The implementation of the emerging technology Highly Automated

© Springer Nature Switzerland AG 2020
Q. Gao and J. Zhou (Eds.): HCII 2020, LNCS 12207, pp. 210–221, 2020.
https://doi.org/10.1007/978-3-030-50252-2_16

Vehicles (HAV) may benefit those old drivers to meet their mobility requirements [3]. Research also suggests that older drivers would like to perform a range of non-driving related tasks (NDRT) during the HAV [4], but older drivers may have differences in driving behavior pattern or take over quality compared with younger drivers because of age related changes in their cognitive performance [5–7].

However, researches have shown that elder drivers' are more involved in some kind of accidents, such as crashes in intersection, changing lanes, and multiple-vehicle crashes [8–10]. Previous researchers also found that the decline in cognitive abilities with aging were associated with unsafe driving behaviors [11], such as working memory [12], task switching [5] and visual attention [12, 13]. This study will focus on the measurement of visual attention to investigate the influence of aging in Highly Automated Driving.

Researchers also found that other external factors will influence on take-over quality, such as traffic conditions [14] or non-driving related tasks. The engagement of NDRT will change the visual attention distribution of the drivers [15–17], especially reduce their attention to the road [18]. The decline of visual attention abilities with aging may be relevant to the driving behavior and have even more significant influence on older drivers when NDRT is involved.

Previous studies have made efforts understanding the influence of the interaction of NDRT in HAV during take over tasks both in driving performance and visual attention, yet the research on *aging effect* on visual attention allocation during take over tasks is still limited.

1.1 Study Objectives

This study aims to fill the gap to examine the differences of visual attention patterns between younger and older drivers affected by some common factors (traffic and NDRTs) in a simulation of highly automated driving, and to investigate the relationship of glance behavior and driving performance influenced by NDRT of both age groups.

2 Methodology

2.1 Participants

54 participants in total were recruited for this study. 27 of them are elder drivers (13 males, 14 females, mean = 73.0 years, SD = 3.63 years) and 27 are younger drivers (19 males, 8 females, mean = 28.1 years, SD = 4.7 years). All of them are given informed consent complying the research protocol approved by institutional review board of National Institute of Advanced Industrial Science and Technology (AIST).

2.2 Driving Tasks and Non-Driving Related Tasks

The driving task (see Fig. 1) including take-over request (TOR) was set in a scenario in which a lane-blocking stationary truck is suddenly revealed by the lane changing of the front car.

The self-car (car 1) is always in automated driving, until the participant is warned by an audio warning message and asked to take over longitudinal and lateral control.

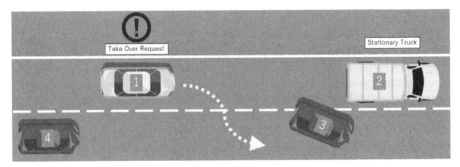

Fig. 1. Illustration of TOR and the scenario. Participant (vehicle 1) is driving in straight lane, when a stationary truck (vehicle 2) is suddenly revealed by the lane changing of the front car (vehicle 3). The participant is then asked to takeover and change lanes, but in some conditions there will be other cars (vehicle 4) on the other lane.

Participants are asked to change lanes in order to avoid collision and pass the stationary truck. Moreover, in some conditions there will be other moving cars on the other lane, so the participants would have to pay attention to them according to traffic conditions. The speed set for the vehicles is 90 km/h or 25 m/s. The TOR occurs 100 meters (or 4 s time to collision) in front of the stationary truck.

The NDRT was designed as n-back task. The cognitive n-back tasks can have similar effects on takeover behaviors as other visual NDRT such as a Surrogate Reference Task (SuRT) [14]. This design of the tasks aims to detect how cognitive NDRT may distract the drivers from their visual attention, and also to simulate some possible tasks that may cost drivers' attention resource during HAD.

In this study, we choose 1-back task as the NDRT, and the difficulty is just proper for most elder drivers to react during driving. For every 2 s, participants heard the voice (one of 4 different letters: A, B, O, and Y) and responded (press a button on the steering wheel) if the voice was the target letter. Before the take-over requests, the n-back tasks will continue for about 80 s or 40 trials.

2.3 Experiment Design

This study is a $2 \times 2 \times 3$ between- and within-subjects mixed factor design. The between-subjects factor is age (young and elder), and the within-subjects factors are NDRT involvement (no task, 1-back task) and traffic conditions (no car, one car every 50 m and one car every 100 m on the right lane).

2.4 Apparatus

This study was implemented on a set of desktop driving simulator in Automotive Human Factors Research Center (AHFRC) of AIST. The driving simulator apparatus includes a set of Logitech steering wheel and pedal, a Panasonic screen for display, and a set of Mitsubishi Driving Simulator software packs.

The eye tracking device is the Tobii Pro glass (See Fig. 2).

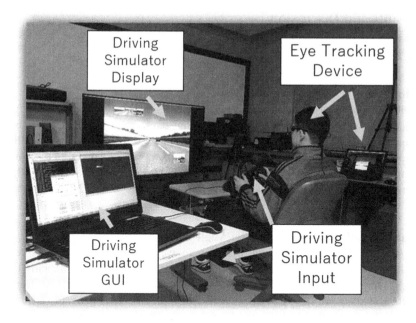

Fig. 2. Driving simulator and eye tracking devices.

2.5 Analysis

Data of driving performance and visual attention is recorded during each trial. We expect to find the influences of NDRT engagement and different traffic conditions on the driving behavior and the differences of visual attention distribution patterns between two age groups.

Driving Performance

As for measurements of take-over quality, we use collision rate and standard deviation of steering wheel to evaluate the drivers' performance. We watched the recorded video of each trial to find if the driver had a collision with other vehicles or/and with the road rail, and calculated the collision rate in each scenario. Standard deviation of steering wheel angle during take-over period is also calculated in each scenario from the raw data recorded.

Visual Attention

The eye tracking data during scenarios (5 s before TOR and 10 s after TOR) in 10 frames per second (10 Hz) were classified into different Area of Interest (AoI). 6 AoIs are defined: rearview/left/right mirror, front road, driver HMI, and others. The proportions of fixation time in each AoI, fixation duration on mirrors, and the number of transition between AoIs were counted or calculated separately. Other regions such as outside the display screen, and unknown glances are not counted in this study.

For statistical analysis, all possible measurements (SD of steering wheel angle, numbers of transitions between AoIs, and fixation duration on mirrors) were analyzed using a 2 (Age) × 2 (NDRT level) × 3 (Traffic condition) analysis of variance (ANOVA).

3 Results and Discussion

3.1 Driving Performance

Collision Rate

The collision rate (proportion of trails that have collision after TOR among all trails) for elder group is 27.2%, but only 8.2% for younger group. The collision number is significant greater in elder group than younger group, and the difference on collision rate shows evidently that take-over quality is much better in the young group than the elder group, judging by the final outcome (traffic accident happened or not). Collision proportions have no significant difference in different levels of both NDRT levels and traffic conditions.

Standard Deviation of Steering Wheel Angle

As for standard deviation of steering wheel angle, we also find significant main effect between age groups that young group (M = 20.70, SD = 8.31) are significantly lower than elder groups (M = 30.34, SD = 13.60; $F(1, 52) = 22.63$, $p = 0.031$). This difference on the measurements of steering wheel means that younger drivers generally have more stable lateral control than elder drivers, regardless of different traffic conditions and the engaging of NDRTs. This result may also confirm previous result about collision rate. The comparison of the results show, to some extent, the advantage of younger drivers over elderly drivers when dealing with TOR, and this is similar with previous findings by other researchers [5, 7].

In this study, we can only use collision rate and standard deviation of steering wheel angle, which were just general measurements of only lateral control. The collisions only happened on extreme situations, and the standard deviation of steering wheel angle is not good enough to measure lateral performance, or how "dangerous" the behavior was. The utility of other longitudinal measurements such as speed, TTC to stationary truck when lane changing, and more precise measurements like lateral lane position and steering wheel reverse rate may illustrate the take-over performance better in the further study.

3.2 Visual Attention

The eye tracking data during scenarios (5 s before TOR and 10 s after TOR) in 10 frames per second (10 Hz) in different AoIs were counted, and will be investigated from two aspects: the number of transition between AoIs and the patterns of fixation time in each AoI along time around TOR.

Number of Fixation Transition Between AoIs

The transition between AoIs were counted during the time 5 s before TOR and 10 s after TOR. The AoIs are defined as: rearview/left/right mirror, front road, driver HMI, and others. There are 14.5% of the trials in total when eye tracking data were not good enough and thus hard to distinguish the fixation point, and the number of transition in those trials are replaced by the average number in the same condition (age, traffic condition and NDRT level).

There are main effects of both age and NDRT, and a 3-way interaction according to the result of the 3-way ANOVA. The results are shown as Table 1. As for age groups, young group (M = 4.59, SD = 3.28) have significantly more transitions between AoIs than elder group (M = 1.88, SD = 2.20; $F(1,52) = 31.58$, p < 0.001). For conditions engaging with/without NDRT, transitions decrease significantly when engaging with NDRT (M = 2.75, SD = 2.84) compared with without 1-back tasks (M = 3.72, SD = 3.28; $F(1,52) = 9.43$, p = 0.003). This result is similar to previous researches that engaging with NDRT will influence drivers' visual attention distribution [18]. Considering that the NDRT used in this study is in auditory and more "mental" tasks, this result may imply that a non-visual related NDRT will also influence the drivers' glance behavior. Moreover, the less number of transitions in elder group may also reflect their relatively worse driving performance and higher collision rate found in previous analysis in this study.

Table 1. Results of ANOVA for number of fixation transition between AoIs

Effect	DFn	DFd	F	P
Age	1	52	31.58	<0.001 *
NDRT	1	52	9.43	0.003 *
Traffic	2	104	0.99	0.383
Age*NDRT	1	52	0.06	0.830
Age*Traffic	2	104	1.03	0.360
NDRT*Traffic	2	104	0.53	0.591
Age*NDRT*Traffic	2	104	5.05	0.008 *

Note: *p < 0.05

We will discuss in detail from the aspects of different levels of traffic conditions. The results are shown as Fig. 3.

For no-traffic condition (no car in the next lane), younger group (M = 4.20, SD = 2.98) has significantly more transition times than elderly group (M = 1.82, SD = 2.22; $F(1,52) = 17.45$, p < 0.001), and conditions when engaging with 1-back tasks (M = 2.45, SD = 2.85) has significantly less transitions than non-NDRT conditions (M = 3.56, SD = 2.82; $F(1,52) = 7.23$, p = 0.010). No interaction was found in no-traffic conditions, which may imply that the change of visual attention and eye-movement behavior caused by NDRT engagement may be similar for both age groups in this "easiest" traffic condition.

For medium-traffic condition (100 m/car in the next lane), main effect only showed between age groups, where younger group (M = 4.69, SD = 2.95) has significantly more transition times than elderly group (M = 2.11, SD = 2.35; $F(1,52) = 22.18$, p < 0.001), regardless of the NDRT. No main effect in NDRT and interaction were found in this traffic condition.

For high-traffic condition (50 m/car in the next lane), younger group (M = 4.90, SD = 3.86) has significantly more transition times than elderly group (M = 1.70, SD = 2.02; $F(1,52) = 23.86$, p < 0.001), and during 1-back task the transition times (M = 2.72, SD = 2.67) are significantly less than without NDRT (M = 3.88, SD = 4.04; $F(1,52)$

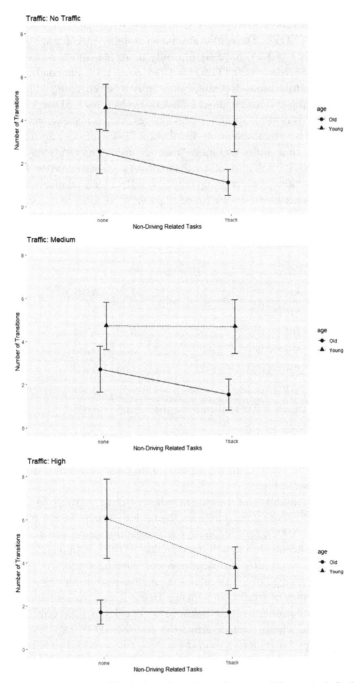

Fig. 3. The average and standard deviation of transitions between different AoIs for both young and elder group, with/without NDRT engaging, and in different traffic conditions.

= 5.53, p = 0.022). We also find significant interaction of age and NDRT engaging in high traffic density conditions (F(1,52) = 5.35, p = 0.025, see Fig. 3 Traffic: High). This means in high traffic conditions, number of transitions in young group decreased significantly more than elder group by the engaging of NDRT, and thus their visual attention patterns were influenced more by the engaging of NDRT than the elder group. In fact, we can find that the number of transitions of elder group is the lowest in high traffic density, regardless of whether engaging with NDRT. In high traffic condition, the elder group has a low number of fixation transitions even without NDRT engagement, and this may mean that the influence of traffic is more important in high traffic density conditions. Moreover, considering the similarity in the change of transition number by NDRT engaging in both age groups in no traffic conditions, we can infer that elder group may be affected more by the traffic conditions than young group, especially in high-traffic condition where the cars on the next lane should have caused more attention transitions. In no traffic conditions, the older drivers may not be so concerned about passing cars and thus focus more on the NDRT, thus the NDRT would influence their visual attention; however, driving in high traffic density may make the elder drivers more nervous and thus focus more on the controlling of the car, and less on NDRT or fixation transitions.

Patterns of Fixation Time in Each AoI Along Time Around TOR

In order to detect how drivers will allocate their visual attention around TOR tasks, fixation duration on mirrors in different conditions are analyzed in ANOVA, and line charts are generated by the proportion of fixation in different AoIs. In this study, time period was defined as from 5 s before TOR and 10 s after TOR.

Fixation Duration on Mirrors

We found significant main effects on age and engagement of NDRT. For age groups, fixation duration for younger group (M = 1.44 s, SD = 1.07 s) is significantly longer than elder group (M = 0.75 s, SD = 0.99 s; F(1,52) = 15.70, P < 0.001). For the engagement of NDRT, fixation duration on mirror decreased significantly when engaging with NDRT (M = 0.93 s, SD = 0.96 s) compared with no NDRT condition (M = 1.26 s, SD = 1.17 s; F(1,52) = 8.60, p = 0.005). No significant main effect on traffic and interaction were found. This result is similar with the previous analysis of fixation transitions. Elder group focus significant less time on the mirrors regardless of traffic conditions, and the engagement of NDRT will influence visual attention pattern in the fixation on mirrors.

Proportion of Fixation in Different AoIs

Figure 4 shows the proportion of different AoIs in different conditions. Fixations in the same AoI in each frame of all participants were counted together, and proportions of different AoIs in each frame is calculated.

Generally, both group's gazing is mainly focusing on the road, and the influence of NDRT levels is not significant. Among all AoIs of mirrors, right side mirror has the most proportion before 4 s after TOR, and left side mirror after 4 s. This may be caused by the take-over task (change to the lane on the right and back to the left) designed in this study. Also, we may find that the total proportion of fixations on mirror is not high (highest

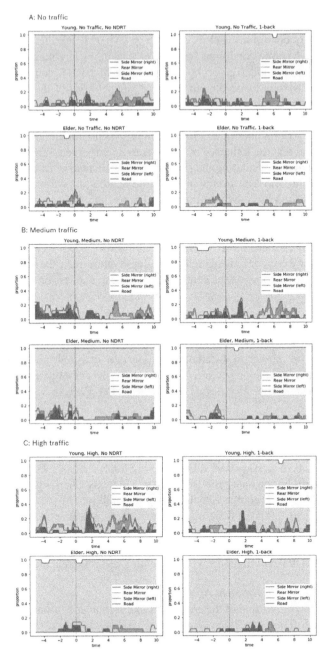

Fig. 4. Proportion of fixation in different AoIs over time in different conditions. A–C: No traffic, Medium traffic, High traffic. Different colors represent different AoIs. 0 point in x-axis is the time when TOR occurs. Proportions are already accumulated for each AoI.

is around 40%), and this may due to the none visual engagement of NDRT, compared with previous research [18].

From the chart, we can find that the elder group is obviously focusing more on the road ahead, and thus omitting checking side mirrors or rear mirror. This is consistent with the result of analysis in numbers of transitions among AoIs and fixation duration time in the previous part, where elder group has significantly fewer transitions in eye-gazing and less fixation time on the mirrors in almost all conditions.

Traffic conditions, especially in high traffic condition, affect elder group more than younger group (see Fig. 4 C). In high traffic condition, young drivers focus more on side mirrors after TOR than elder drivers. This result is consistent with previous analysis of fixation duration, where although not significant, elder group has relatively less fixation duration (M = 0.68 s, SD = 0.80 s) in high traffic condition. Compared with the previous analysis of transitions and driving behavior, it is probably because in high traffic condition, elder drivers need more attention on the road to maintain control of the car.

From the chart, we can find a probable pattern in young group for the distribution over time around TOR: around 2 s after TOR, fixation focus more on right side mirror; after 5 s, more fixation on left side mirror or rear mirror. Yet we can notice in the same time that during the period 2–4 s after the TOR, for the elder group, the proportion of eye fixation on road is nearly 100% in some conditions (especially in high-traffic), and also very high in other conditions, compared with young group. This shows that the elder drivers rarely pay attention to side mirror or rear mirror during that time. In that period, however, the driver had to perform certain move to change lane to avoid the stationary truck, yet with the low proportion on the mirror, in elder group there is a significant lack of visual attention on the right lane. Combined with less numbers of transitions and less fixation time on mirrors, this might be another part of explanation for the increased collision rate on the right lane and more unstable lateral control with vehicles in elder group. The results would be more convincing if other longitudinal measurements (such as minimum TTC to the truck before lane changing) can be analyzed in the further study.

4 Conclusions and Further Improvements

The objective of this study is to examine the differences of visual attention patterns between younger and elder drivers affected by engagement of audio NDRT (1-back task) and traffic conditions (no car, one car every 50 m and one car every 100 m on the other lane). The experiment was set in a simulation of highly automated driving with a $2 \times 2 \times 3$ between- and within-subjects mixed factor design.

From driving performance measurements, we find that elder drivers have higher collision rate than young drivers. For standard deviation of steering wheel angle, young group are significantly lower than elder group. The differences show the advantage of driving performance of younger drivers over elderly drivers when dealing with TOR, and this is similar with previous researchers.

As for visual attention, two aspects are considered: the number of transition between AoIs and the fixation time in each AoI along time around TOR.

For transition number, we find significant difference between age groups in all traffic conditions, showing that transition numbers of elder drivers are fewer than younger drivers, and fewer transitions when engaging in NDRT. We also find that elder drivers may be more influenced by heavy traffic density than young drivers.

For the fixation time in each AoI along time around TOR, we find fixation duration for younger group is significantly longer than elder group, and decreased significantly when engaging with NDRT compared with no NDRT condition. This result is consistent with the previous analysis of fixation transitions: elder group focus significant less on the mirrors, and NDRT engaging will significantly influence visual attention patterns. Charts are generated to illustrate the change of proportion of fixation time in each AoI, and in general elder group focus more on the road ahead than young group. This difference is more obvious in high traffic condition. However, comparing with transition number and fixation duration, in high traffic conditions the elder group focus relatively less on mirrors regardless of the NDRT engagement, showing that elder group may be more affected by high traffic density. We also find a difference in pattern of visual attention distribution between different age groups over time around TOR. This result shows evidently that the elder group pay less attention to mirrors around TOR occurs, and even worse in high traffic density. Combined with less numbers of transitions and less fixation time on mirrors, elder group have more unsafe visual attention patterns in those conditions, and this may account for the higher collision rate and more unstable lateral behavior found in previous analysis.

In our further improvement of this study, we plan to extend the participant to 35 for each group, and this may lower the influence of individual differences in the standard deviation in several quantitative analyses, and thus we can expect to find more significant differences or interactions in some measurement in different conditions, or a clearer trend or pattern of fixation distribution along time. Moreover, as for measurement method for driving performance, measurements in both lateral and longitudinal will be considered to evaluate the risk of take-over performance. We hope to find more explicit evidence for the relationship between the increase of unstable behavior and the decrease of attention on mirrors, especially in elder group.

References

1. Gabriel, Z., Bowling, A.: Quality of life from the perspectives of older people. Ageing Soc. **24**, 675–691 (2004). https://doi.org/10.1017/S0144686X03001582
2. Metz, D.H.: Mobility of older people and their quality of life. Transp. Policy **7**, 149–152 (2000). https://doi.org/10.1016/S0967-070X(00)00004-4
3. Reimer, B.: Driver assistance systems and the transition to automated vehicles: a path to increase older adult safety and mobility? Public Policy Aging Rep. **24**, 27–31 (2014). https://doi.org/10.1093/ppar/prt006
4. Li, S., Blythe, P., Guo, W., Namdeo, A.: Investigation of older drivers' requirements of the human-machine interaction in highly automated vehicles. Transp. Res. Part F: Traffic Psychol. Behav. **62**, 546–563 (2019). https://doi.org/10.1016/j.trf.2019.02.009
5. Körber, M., Gold, C., Lechner, D., Bengler, K.: The influence of age on the take-over of vehicle control in highly automated driving. Transp. Res. Part F: Traffic Psychol. Behav. **39**, 19–32 (2016). https://doi.org/10.1016/j.trf.2016.03.002
6. Clark, H., Feng, J.: Age differences in the takeover of vehicle control and engagement in non-driving-related activities in simulated driving with conditional automation. Accid. Anal. Prev. **106**, 468–479 (2017). https://doi.org/10.1016/j.aap.2016.08.027

7. Li, S., Blythe, P., Guo, W., Namdeo, A.: Investigating the effects of age and disengagement in driving on driver's takeover control performance in highly automated vehicles. Transp. Plan. Technol. **42**, 470–497 (2019). https://doi.org/10.1080/03081060.2019.1609221

8. Mayhew, D.R., Simpson, H.M., Ferguson, S.A.: Collisions involving senior drivers: high-risk conditions and locations. Traffic Injury Prevent. **7**, 117–124 (2006). https://doi.org/10.1080/15389580600636724

9. McGwin Jr., G., Brown, D.: Characteristics of traffic crashes among young, middle-aged, and older drivers. Acc. Anal. Prev. **31**, 181–198 (1999). https://doi.org/10.1016/S0001-4575(98)00061-X

10. Langford, J., Koppel, S.: Epidemiology of older driver crashes – identifying older driver risk factors and exposure patterns. Transp. Res. Part F: Traffic Psychol. Behav. **9**, 309–321 (2006). https://doi.org/10.1016/j.trf.2006.03.005

11. McGwin, G., Sims, R.V., Pulley, L., Roseman, J.M.: Relations among chronic medical conditions, medications, and automobile crashes in the elderly: a population-based case-control study. Am. J. Epidemiol. **152**, 424–431 (2000). https://doi.org/10.1093/aje/152.5.424

12. Horswill, M.S., et al.: The hazard perception ability of older drivers. J. Gerontol. B Psychol. Sci. Soc. Sci. **63**, P212–P218 (2008). https://doi.org/10.1093/geronb/63.4.P212

13. Anstey, K.J., Wood, J., Lord, S., Walker, J.G.: Cognitive, sensory and physical factors enabling driving safety in older adults. Clin. Psychol. Rev. **25**, 45–65 (2005). https://doi.org/10.1016/j.cpr.2004.07.008

14. Radlmayr, J., Gold, C., Lorenz, L., Farid, M., Bengler, K.: How traffic situations and non-driving related tasks affect the take-over quality in highly automated driving. In: Proceedings of the Human Factors and Ergonomics Society Annual Meeting, vol. 58, pp. 2063–2067 (2014). https://doi.org/10.1177/1541931214581434

15. Louw, T., Merat, N., Jamson, H.: Engaging with highly automated driving: to be or not to be in the loop? In: Driving Assessment Conference, pp. 190–196 (2015)

16. Zeeb, K., Buchner, A., Schrauf, M.: Is take-over time all that matters? The impact of visual-cognitive load on driver take-over quality after conditionally automated driving. Accid. Anal. Prev. **92**, 230–239 (2016). https://doi.org/10.1016/j.aap.2016.04.002

17. Louw, T., Madigan, R., Carsten, O., Merat, N.: Were they in the loop during automated driving? Links between visual attention and crash potential. Inj. Prevent. **23**, 281–286 (2017). https://doi.org/10.1136/injuryprev-2016-042155

18. Louw, T., Kuo, J., Romano, R., Radhakrishnan, V., Lenné, M.G., Merat, N.: Engaging in NDRTs affects drivers' responses and glance patterns after silent automation failures. Transp. Res. Part F: Traffic Psychol. Behav. **62**, 870–882 (2019). https://doi.org/10.1016/j.trf.2019.03.020

Practical Evaluation of the Emergency Usability Lab for Testing the Usability of Medical Devices in Emergency Situations

Peter Rasche[✉] [iD], Moritz Richter, Katharina Schäfer, Sabine Theis, Verena Nitsch, and Alexander Mertens

Institute of Industrial Engineering and Ergonomics, RWTH Aachen University, Bergdriesch 27, 52056 Aachen, Germany
{p.rasche,m.richter,k.schaefer,s.theis,v.nitsch,
a.mertens}@iaw.rwth-aachen.de

Abstract. In healthcare, clinical activities are increasingly being relocated to patients' home environment. Patients can thus continue their therapy in a self-determined manner at home. This trend challenges usability evaluations of medical devices, as patients represent a more heterogeneous user group in terms of experience and training than medical professionals and the use of medical devices by patients can also be influenced by their medical condition. The Emergency Usability Lab was developed as an approach for testing the usability of medical devices of home healthcare focusing on emergency situations. An emergency situation is determined as a situation the patient has to perform certain activities with a medical device while being limited in performance due to certain medical symptoms as dizziness, visual impairment or being short of breath.

This paper presents the results of the practical evaluation of the Emergency Usability Lab. Evaluation was carried out applying a between-group design. Within the study, two approved medical devices (blood glucose meter & emergency drug package) were subjected to a usability test. Each product was tested in two groups. In one group the Emergency Usability Lab was applied and the other served as control group. Both groups included 20 participants each. By using the Emergency Usability Lab, a blood glucose meter was tested under simulated conditions of hypoglycemia (lack of concentration and impaired vision) and an emergency drug package was tested under simulated conditions of pain-related shortness of breath (shortness of breath, dizziness and impaired vision). The results of both usability studies were compared with regard to the number of usability issues found and their risk in order to verify the applicability of the Emergency Usability Lab.

Keywords: Emergency · Usability · Simulation · Older adults · Digital health

© Springer Nature Switzerland AG 2020
Q. Gao and J. Zhou (Eds.): HCII 2020, LNCS 12207, pp. 222–230, 2020.
https://doi.org/10.1007/978-3-030-50252-2_17

1 Introduction

1.1 Motivation

Since the introduction of the Human Factors Guidelines of the Food and Drug Association in the USA in 2015 and the re-regulation of the Medical Device Directives in the European Union in 2017, usability of medical devices needs to be evaluated during official approval process of medical devices. As these directives are new and healthcare is changing fast due to digitization new methods are necessary to perform the usability evaluation. Additionally, clinical activities are increasingly being relocated to patients' home environment. Patients can thus continue their therapy in a self-determined manner at home. This trend challenges usability evaluations of medical devices, as patients represent a more heterogeneous user group in terms of experience and training than medical professionals and the use of medical devices by patients can also be influenced by their medical condition. The Emergency Usability Lab (EUL) was developed as an approach for testing the usability of medical devices of home healthcare focusing on emergency situations. An emergency situation is determined as a situation the patient has to perform certain activities with a medical device while being limited in performance due to certain medical symptoms as dizziness, visual impairment or being short of breath.

1.2 Aim of This Study

The aim of this study was to investigate in a between-group design what influence the use of the EUL has on the quality of results of two usability tests (EUL applied and control group). The first evaluated product is a blood glucose meter which can be connected to the iPhone (up to model 4S) and the second is a Bend-and-Peel tablet blister according to patent US8191711, which among other things is used for the distribution of fentanyl tablets. The aim is to determine whether the application of the EUL has an influence on the number of usability issues identified during a usability evaluation as well as the severity rating of these issues. Furthermore, it should be tested whether participants' subjective mental effort and workload differs between the two groups.

2 Method

A between-group design was chosen for this study. Accordingly, the usability test of both products was carried out in one group with and in a second (control group) without the application of the EUL. In accordance with the motivation described in the introduction, the two medical devices should be tested for their respective suitability for emergency situations. In the case of the blood glucose meter, the emergency situation was defined as an episode of severe hypoglycemia [1]. In such a situation, patients may show cognitive as well as visual impairment in extreme cases (lack of concentration and blurred vision) [1]. However, in order to react correctly, it is essential to determine the blood sugar level, and thus a blood glucose measurement needs to be performed by the patients. In the context of the Bend-and-Peel tablet blisters, emergency situation was defined as a situation in which patients suffer from extreme pain, which has led to shortness of breath, lack of concentration and visual impairment. Such pain is common in the context of cancer therapy or palliative care [2].

2.1 Questionnaire

For the evaluation of the usability of the products, a 16-sided questionnaire was developed, which was used in both groups in the same manner. The questionnaire initially collected demographic data of the study participants. Subsequently, the willingness to use technology according to Neyer and the health competence of the participants was surveyed using the EU-HLS-16 [3, 4]. A paper-based eye test for colour vision and visual acuity was then carried out. The Rating Scale of Mental Effort (RSME) was used to assess the mental stress of the participants during the individual usability tasks. In addition, the raw NASA TLX was recorded for each product to capture possible additional stress factors during product use.

Measuring Technology Readiness
Technology readiness was included as it might influence the use of modern information and communication technology, as well as the engagement with these products [3]. It is calculated based on 12 standardized items which are rated on a 5-point Likert scale (1 = not correct, 5 = fully correct). For positively formulated objects, the scale is converted so that a high point value corresponds with high technology readiness. Subsequently, the final score is calculated by mean value over all 12 items. The score therefore ranges between 1 point and 5 points [3].

Measuring Health Literacy
To gain further insight into the participants' knowledge and ability to manage potential diseases, a health literacy questionnaire was applied [4, 5]. This questionnaire assesses user's access, understanding, evaluation, and application of health-related information. The questionnaire contains 16 items rated on a 4-point Likert scale ranging from 'very difficult' to 'very easy'. Afterwards results are transformed into dichotomous answers and summed up. Thus, the score ranges between 0 point and 16 points [4].

Measuring Subjective mental Effort and Workload
All usability tasks were evaluated by the RSME to measure the subjective mental effort necessary for participants to accomplish the tasks [6, 7]. The participants rated mental effort on a 150-pointscale. All participants were familiarized with the RSME scale using five appropriate daily life examples.

Additionally, raw NASA TLX tool was used to analyse participants' workload. This tool divides a subjects' workload into six different factors. These factors are 'mental demand', 'physical demand', 'time pressure', 'expended effort', 'achieved performance level' and 'experienced frustration' [8].

Accessing Users' Experiences and Criticality of Identified Problems
Semi-structured interviews were performed to investigate whether participants identified any usability issues or misleading information or functions related to the two evaluated products.

2.2 Experimental Apparatus

Tested Products

Blood glucose meter

The blood glucose meter iBG-Star manufactured by AgaMatrix Inc., Salem, USA, was tested. Previous studies had shown the high accuracy of this device in measuring blood glucose [9]. Furthermore, the authors already used this device in a previous study including diabetes patients [10]. Thus, this product was chosen to enable a comparison between results of this study and the previous one.

Bend-and-Peel tablet blister

The second product to be tested was a Bend-and-Peel tablet blister. This blister is used in combination with fentanyl tablets, which can be used for breakthrough pain in cancer therapy and palliative care. It should be noted that the blister is opened in situations where the patient, and therefore the user, suffers extreme pain. It must be correspondingly easy to open. However, since it needs to be prohibited that children could take this medication, the blister must still be child-resistant. The structure of the blister is defined by patent US8191711.

Emergency Usability Lab

The Emergency Usability Lab is a modular system that can simulate breathing difficulties, cognitive impairment or visual impairment of performance by using stimulating stressors. Depending on the clinical picture under investigation, the stressors can be combined to provide a representation of the symptoms of the disease in an emergency situation [11]. In this study stroboscopic glasses and an interrupted white noise signal were used to simulate the symptoms of hypoglycemia. In combination with the tablet packaging, the two mentioned products and additionally a breathing mask and a weight vest were used, which simulate a respiratory distress under pain.

Cogstate Performance Testing Battery

Participant's cognitive performance was accessed using the CogState testing battery (www.cogstate.com). This battery was implemented on an iPad 3 (Apple, USA). This system was chosen as it provides a higher ecological validity of the results with regard to the performance with a mobile device than if a stationary computer-based system had been used. Results of this testing battery are comparable to pen and paper tests [12]. The testing battery itself consists of four different tasks. The task order was the same during all stressor exposures. The tasks were completed in the order shown below.

- Detection task (DET) - a reaction time test, measuring psychomotor function.
- Identification task (IDN) - a choice reaction time test, measuring visual attention.
- One Back task (ONB) - a task to measure working memory and attention.
- Groton Maze learning grid (GML) - a task to measure executive function by the total number of errors made.

2.3 Data Collection and Recruitment

The data collection was carried out at the Institute for Industrial Engineering and Ergonomics of RWTH Aachen University. For the participation in this study, an expense allowance of 15€ was paid. The participants were recruited online via social media channels, which are frequently used by students of RWTH Aachen University. Participants with experience in using one of the two evaluated products are excluded from participation to gain a realistic picture of product use by non-experts.

2.4 Procedure

Prior to the experiment, participants were informed about the purpose of the study and their right to withdraw at any time during the study without any adverse consequences. All sessions took place before lunch to avoid differences in performance due to the daytime. Participants answered a short questionnaire aiming to ascertain demographic information. Afterwards, participants' performance was accessed by performing the Cogstate testing battery. Execution of associated tasks was measured by RSME as well as NASA TLX as reference for following usability tasks. Next, the participants had five minutes to familiarize themselves with the blood glucose meter. They were provided with the original manufacturer's instructions. Afterwards the participants performed a simulated blood glucose measurement. Instead of pricking themselves with a real needle, the patients used a lancet without needle accordingly and had a drop of blood substitute (glucose test fluid) dripped onto their finger. Depending on which of the two groups (with/without Emergency Usability Lab) was tested, the mentioned stressors (stroboscopic glasses and interrupted white noise) were additionally applied during the simulated blood glucose measurement. After the simulated measurement, the participants filled out the raw NASA TLX and rated mental effort by RSME. Subsequently, a semi-structured interview was conducted in which the participants were asked about usability issues and challenges regarding the blood glucose measurement. At the end of the interview, the participants were asked to evaluate the identified usability issues on a 4-point Likert scale with regard to the need for a revision by the manufacturer. After a five-minute break, the procedure was repeated using the tablet-blister. Again, the participants had five minutes to familiarize themselves with the instructions for unpacking the tablet. They were then asked to unpack one tablet. If the blister was damaged during this attempt, the participants were free to start a second attempt in the same run by unpacking another tablet. Again, the raw NASA TLX and RSME scores were collected afterwards. Also, for this product, a semi-structured interview was performed to identify usability issues and challenges and their severity in terms of need for revision by manufacturer. Afterwards the participants were paid the expense allowance and were subsequently seen off.

3 Results

In this paper, the difference in subjective mental effort and workload (RSME and NASA TLX) and the number of identified usability issues and their severity were investigated in a between-group designed study.

3.1 Participants

In total 40 participants took part in this study, divided into two groups (EUL applied and control group). Each group was gender balanced. The average age of the participants was 25.55 years (standard deviation = 4.150). All participants showed normal average values regarding the measurements of the Cogstate performance testing battery and were enrolled at a university. None of the participants had experienced one of the two emergency situations or evaluated products before. Technical readiness and health literacy were also quite similar within both groups (Table 1).

Table 1. Participants demographics

	EUL applied	Control group
Age		
Minimum (years)	19	19
Maximum (years)	40	35
Mean (SD; years)	24.95 (4.477)	26.15 (3.815)
Technical readiness		
Mean (SD; points)	2.27 (0.493)	1.92 (0.492)
Health competence		
Mean (SD; points)	12.00 (2.772)	11.85 (2.942)

3.2 Usability Evaluation of the Blood Glucose Meter

The descriptive comparison of the results shows that based on the semi-structured interviews under the stress condition, participants named more usability issues than within the control group. Compared to this severity rating of the identified issues seems quite similar. RSME scores are also higher within the stressed group than within control group. It also applies to the NASA TLX scores.

The difference between the number of usability issues reported in stress and control group for the blood glucose meter is significant $(t(38) = 3.040, p = 0.004, r = 0.442)$. Severity rating of issues was not significantly different. Within the stressed group participants named more usability issues than within the control group. NASA TLX scores between the stressed and the control group are significantly different $(t(38) = 3.946, p < 0.001, r = 0.539)$. Within stressed group participants reported higher NASA TLX scores than within the control group. The difference between RSME scores for the blood glucose measurement is significant with a medium effect strength $(t(38) = 3.933, p < 0.001, r = 0.538)$ (Table 2).

Table 2. Usability evaluation results within EUL and control group for blood glucose meter

	EUL applied	Control group
Problems/Challenges mentioned		
Mean number (SD; points)	3.00 (1.486)	1.80 (0.951)
Mean severity (SD; points)	2.44 (0.832)	2.74 (0.890)
NASA TLX		
Mean (SD; points)	49.33 (14.827)	32.04 (12.817)
RSME		
Mean (SD; points)	59.50 (27.285)	30.75 (18.011)

3.3 Usability Evaluation of the Bend-and-Peel Tablet Blister

For the Bend-and-Peel blister participants within stressed and control group did not report a different number of problems regarding the product. Compared to this severity rating of the identified problems seems quite similar. Scores for RSME did not differ for the Bend-and-Peel tablet blister between stressed and control group. Same observations were made for NASA TLX evaluation.

Although reported NASA TLX scores are higher within the applied EUL group, no significant difference was revealed ($t(38) = 1.532$, $p = 0.134$, $r = 0.241$). The difference between RSME scores for the Bend-and-Peel tablet blister is not significant ($t(38) = 1.950$, $p = 0.059$, $r = 0.302$) (Table 3).

Table 3. Usability evaluation results within EUL and control group for bend-and-peel blister

	EUL applied	Control Group
Problems/Challenges mentioned		
Mean number (SD; points)	2.0 (0.973)	1.95 (1.234)
Mean severity (SD; points)	2.50 (0.892)	2.78 (0.820)
NASA TLX		
Mean (SD; points)	44.75 (17.619)	36.45 (16.585)
RSME		
Mean (SD; points)	43.60 (29.491)	26.20 (26.889)

4 Discussion

For the first time, results of this study show that the Emergency Usability Lab can be applied fundamentally within the framework of usability tests and represents a benefit. It was shown that the stressors applied in the laboratory do not restrict the participants to such an extent that they would not be able to solve the tasks assigned within the usability test. Results show that the application of stressors results in significantly higher number of usability problems in relation to more complex medical devices. In this study, a blood glucose meter was chosen as a complex medical device. As a representative of the group of "simpler" medical devices, a bend-and-peel blister packaging was chosen. While the usability task for the blood glucose meter took about one minute to complete, the usability task for the bend-and-peel blister packaging was completed in about 15-30 s. Possibly the differences mentioned are due to the respective exposure time to the stressors or the complexity of the product. Further studies focusing these aspects are necessary to investigate these circumstances in more detail. Moreover, the study showed that the application of the stressors leads to a higher subjective stress level for the same usability task measured by the RSME scale and the NASA TLX.

Due to the study design, various limitations have to be mentioned. The stressors used are products which are used for training purposes in competitive sports. Although it is known from previous studies by the authors that the stressors cause stress and a limitation of the performance of study participants, the use of these products to generate stress must nevertheless be questioned. Furthermore, only two medical devices were examined within the scope of this study. Therefore, it cannot be conclusively clarified whether the results regarding the identification of usability problems with complex medical devices can be attributed to the complexity of these devices, the application time of the stressors or to unknown reasons.

This fundamentally demonstrated that the Emergency Usability Lab provides a useful contribution to the evaluation of the usability of products for use in emergency situations. Future analysis of the collected data will yield further results regarding the practical use of the Emergency Usability Lab.

References

1. Carroll, M.F., Burge, M.R., Schade, D.S.: Severe hypoglycemia in adults. Rev. Endocr. Metabol. Disord. **4**(2), 149–157 (2003)
2. Bausewein, C., Simon, S.T.: Shortness of breath and cough in patients in palliative care. Deutsches Ärzteblatt Int. **110**(33–34), 563 (2013)
3. Neyer, F.J., Felber, J., Gebhardt, C.: Entwicklung und Validierung einer Kurzskala zur Erfassung von Technikbereitschaft. Diagnostica **58**(2), 87–99 (2012). https://doi.org/10.1026/0012-1924/a000067
4. RoÈ thlin, F., Pelikan, JM., Ganahl, K.: Die Gesundheitskompetenz der 15-jaÈhrigen Jugendlichen in Oesterreich. In: Abschlussbericht der oÈsterreichischen Gesundheitskompetenz Jugendstudie im Auftrag des Hauptverbands der oÈsterreichischen SozialversicherungstraÈger (HVSV). http://lbihpr.lbg.ac.at.w8.netz-werk.com/sites/files/lbihpr/attachments/hljugend_bericht.pdf. Accessed: 2017–09-19. (Archived by WebCite® at http://www.webcitation.org/6taVAKBVo). Accessed 19 Sep 2017

5. Hls-Eu Consortium. Comparative Report of Health Literacy in Eight EU Member States. In: The European Health Literacy Survey HLS-EU (2012)
6. Zijlstra, F.: Efficiency in work behaviour. In: A Design Approach for Modern Tools. In: Ph.D. thesis, TU Delft, Delft University of Technology. 1993. Available: http://repository.tudelft.nl/assets/uuid:d97a028b-c3dc-4930-b2ab-a7877993a17f/ide_zijlstra_19931123.PDF
7. Otto, T., Zijlstra, F.R.H., Goebel, R.: Neural correlates of mental effort evaluation-involvement of structures related to self-awareness. Soc. Cogn. Affect Neurosci. **9**(3), 307–315 (2014). https://doi.org/10.1093/scan/nss136
8. Hart, S.G., Staveland, L.E.: Development of NASA-TLX (Task Load Index). Results of empirical and theoretical research. Hum. Mental Workload **1**(3), 139–183 (1988)
9. Pfützner, A., Mitri, M., Musholt, P.B., Sachsenheimer, D., Borchert, M., Yap, A., et al.: Clinical assessment of the accuracy of blood glucose measurement devices. Curr. Med. Res. Opin. **28**(4), 525–531 (2012). https://doi.org/10.1185/03007995.2012.673479. PMID: 22435798
10. Rasche, P., Mertens, A., Miron-Shatz, T., Berzon, C., Schlick, C.M., Jahn, M., et al.: Seamless recording of glucometer measurements among older experienced diabetic patients ±A study of perception and usability. PLoS ONE **13**(5), e0197455 (2018). https://doi.org/10.1371/journal.pone.0197455
11. Rasche, P., Mertens, A., Schlick, Christopher M.: Emergency usability lab - concept to evaluate the usability of healthcare systems in emergencies. In: Duffy, Vincent G. (ed.) DHM 2017. LNCS, vol. 10287, pp. 354–364. Springer, Cham (2017). https://doi.org/10.1007/978-3-319-58466-9_32
12. Benoit, A., Malla, A.K., Iyer, S.N., Joober, R., Bherer, L., Lepage, M.: Cognitive deficits characterization using the CogState research battery in first-episode psychosis patients. Schizophr Res. Cogn. **2**(3), 140–145 (2015). https://doi.org/10.1016/j.scog.2015.03.006

"Just Because You're Older…": Seniors Respond to Telecom Sales Practices in Canada

Kim Sawchuk[✉] and Constance Lafontaine

Concordia University, Montreal, QC, Canada
kim.sawchuk@concordia.ca

Abstract. In 2018, the Canadian Minister of Innovation, Science and Industry, Navdeep Bains, commissioned the Canadian Radio-television and Telecommunications Commission (CRTC) to launch an inquiry into the "aggressive and misleading" sales practices of telecommunication service providers. This inquiry ensued after a series of news stories on the topic revealed the prevalence of such practices in Canada. Journalists, industry whistleblowers and consumer advocacy groups identified 'seniors' as one of the groups most likely to be targeted. This paper draws from interviews and focus groups to analyze the responses of 53 Canadians over the age of 64 on the topic of misleading and aggressive sales practices by the providers of Internet, mobile, phone and television services. While the industry suggests that these misleading and aggressive sales practices are infrequent, and the result of the antics of a 'few bad apples,' we found that most (75%) of our participants mentioned being misled or intimidated by sales personnel, or pressured into contracts that did not meet their needs or that contained unexpected charges on their monthly bills. We trace the experiences of older adults with misleading and aggressive sales practices, and explain some of the methods devised to mitigate their impacts. The comments from respondents demonstrate the ways older adults are put at a systemic disadvantage in the Canadian telecommunication sales landscape and shed light on the barriers that they face as consumers and citizens living in a rapidly changing digital world.

Keywords: Aging · Telecommunication · Media policy · Digital divide · Media use · Later life

1 Introduction

Since 2013, the Ageing + Communication + Technologies (ACT) team, an international network of researchers, has been studying the experience of ageing in a digital world. ACT often partners with community groups run by older adults or working with older adults in the Montreal, Québec area, including those living in situations of economic and social precarity [1–3]. This cohort of older adults is typically left out of the media studies agenda. Our digital workshops in Montreal social housing buildings for older adults often include "drop in" sessions, where seniors are invited to troubleshoot problems with their digital devices with our students and researchers [1, 2]. In 2017, several seniors living in these residences brought us their monthly bills for their landlines, Internet, mobiles and

© Springer Nature Switzerland AG 2020
Q. Gao and J. Zhou (Eds.): HCII 2020, LNCS 12207, pp. 231–244, 2020.
https://doi.org/10.1007/978-3-030-50252-2_18

television. Some had noticed charges for services for which they did not sign up, or for services that they did not use. Others were concerned with the price they were paying for services they needed, but which did not correspond to their original agreement. Many did not know who or where to turn for help.

At approximately the same time, reporting began to emerge in the Canadian media, most notably by the Canadian Broadcasting Corporation (CBC), our country's public broadcaster. Investigative journalists reported on the rise of aggressive door-to-door sales practices deployed to sell telecommunication services, and they relayed the stresses felt by employees working in the sales units of the industry [4]. Consumer advocacy groups requested a formal inquiry by the Canadian Radio and Telecommunications Commission, or CRTC, our government regulator of this industry [5]. The commission initially refused to take such steps, arguing that Canadians could "make use of well-established and effective mechanisms to resolve issues with their communications services providers" [6]. In the late spring of 2018, faced with increasing pressure from these groups and ongoing media coverage, the Minister of Innovation, Science and Industry, Navdeep Bains, mandated the CRTC to launch an inquiry into the misleading and aggressive sales practices of the telecommunication industry [7].

When quoted in the media accounts leading up to the inquiry, the telecommunications companies dismissed the scope of the problem, arguing that misleading and aggressive practices are infrequent and, when they occur, are most often due to the conduct of a handful of individual employees, or 'bad apples'. Consumers, including seniors, were told that they could reach out to the Commission for Complaints for Telecom-Television Services (CCTS) to complain. The telecommunication companies consistently tried to assure Canadians that industry regulations were sufficient. Our research data suggests otherwise.

This paper asks: (1) What are older adults' experiences with sales practices of telecommunication service providers in Canada, and (2) how do they respond to actions of telecommunication sales representatives? Further, (3) are older adults put at a systemic disadvantage in the current telecommunication landscape, and if so, how? To respond to these research questions, we describe the experiences of the older adults we interviewed and present the results of our intervention into this inquiry. We conducted qualitative interviews and focus groups with 53 Canadian adults aged 65 and over, a milestone often used in our Canadian context to identify the start of old age [8]. Seventy-five percent of our interviewees recounted some form of negative encounter with this industry. This high rate of encounters with aggressive or misleading sales practices in the senior population is supported by data from a private firm, IPSOS, which reported in a study mandated by the CRTC that 40% of all Canadians had disclosed experience misleading or aggressive tactics [9]. This paper details what these seniors have experienced, and what they tried to do to "protect themselves," in the words of one interviewee, when dealing with telecommunication service providers. These testimonies reveal the very human impacts of these practices on older adults, in particular those who are socially isolated, living in situations of precarity and who have lower levels of digital expertise. It documents some of the ways that our older interviewees try to deal with these disadvantages, proactively. Not only does this interview data indicate that experiences of misleading and aggressive sales practices may be alarmingly widespread in Canada among older adults, it suggests that this is a systemic issue.

2 Methods

2.1 Challenging the Government's Engagement Methods and Addressing Selection Biases

An analysis of systemic issues focuses not only on the behaviors of individuals, but on the social and structural conditions that enable and constrain agency and the potential for action, a theoretical point made by British sociologist Anthony Giddens [10]. To label a problem systemic problem may reveal the unintentional ways that relations of power may be exerted within a particular organization that is a part of the organizational culture. As researchers working with older adults from the perspective of communications, we had already encountered the ways that the reliance by governments on online surveys create a systemic "selection bias" that may exclude seniors in Montreal, because fewer older adults in Québec are regular users of the Internet. In fact, most Canadians over the age of 75 are not regular users of the Internet [11]. For these reasons we were immediately concerned when we noted that the CRTC opted for an online-only platform to solicit comments during the inquiry. Given this general situation of digital inequity, we were aware that this form of data collection was likely to miss many Canadians, especially older adults. A second systemic issue motivating us was the online survey itself. When we tested the online platform that the CRTC had created with some of our most tech-savvy seniors, it was clear that the website was extremely difficult to navigate and would be an additional barrier to civic participation [12]. There is also a third other systemic issue that motivated us to reach out to older adults to solicit their stories for this inquiry. We noticed that few media outlets were covering the inquiry in the press, on television, or on the radio. Many of the same companies who own the telecommunications services in Canada also own broadcasting stations and print media: one can surmise that it is not in their interest to solicit feedback.

In other words, right from the beginning of the inquiry process, three barriers to the participation of seniors were identified: a barrier for potential participants because of uneven digital access in Canada; a barrier based on the affordances within the media platform itself; and finally, an informational barrier, because of the converged media environment.

2.2 What We Did: Collecting Stories

Given the importance of the issue to the older adults we had encountered, ACT decided to launch a set of interviews and focus groups with older adults in a variety of settings—from shopping malls to legion halls—to solicit testimonies on the topic and to supplement the data-gathering mechanisms that had been established by the CRTC, which we believed could pose serious barriers to the participation of seniors. Between November 2017 and August 2018, we gathered and thematically analyzed conversations and testimonies with 53 seniors over the age of 64. We conducted five focus groups involving 25 older adults.

These focus groups took place in Montreal, Québec (two focus groups); Lanark, Ontario (one focus group); Maberly, Ontario (one focus group); and Kamloops, British Columbia (one focus group). Approximately 60% of the participants in these focus groups were from communities who would be considered in a heightened position of precarity in society because of their socio-economic status, ethno-cultural background or because their first language was neither French nor English.

Twenty one-on-one interviews were held over a period of two days in a mall located in downtown Montreal. This mall is notable for being heavily frequented by seniors during the day, and is in close proximity to several subsidized housing buildings for seniors in the Western part of the downtown area. Each interview lasted between 10 and 45 min. Approximately half of the respondents were over the age of 80, and most of the interviewees did not have access to the Internet from their homes. By going to the mall, we reached seniors who normally would not participate in the CRTC's inquiry. Another eight one-on-one interviews were conducted with seniors in Montreal, Québec; Gatineau, Québec; Ottawa, Ontario; Toronto, Ontario; Feversham, Ontario and Kamloops, British Columbia. Each of these interviews lasted between 20 to 60 min.

In the following sections, we present our findings, including excerpts from interviews and focus groups. As mentioned, some 75%, or three-quarters of the older adults whom we interviewed revealed disquieting stories of their experiences. Many interviewees only disclosed their stories towards the end of the formal interview. In conversation, many admitted to their frustration, but also to the sense that they were at fault, or that these practices had become "normal". Some felt embarrassed that they had been duped by sales representatives, and this contributed to their reluctance in disclosing this information or reporting the incidents. This observation is commensurate with Titus and Grover's point that victims of fraud or mistreatment often experience shame and embarrassment that stop them from reporting [13]. Burnes et al. similarly remind us that it is difficult to understand the prevalence and impact of fraud on older adults specifically because of these low reporting rates. They suggest that methodological choices like open-ended questions and one-on-one interviews may be key in better understanding the complexities of fraud and providing a more accurate representation of the scope of the issue [14]. Our research experience in the mall confirms these observations. It may be worth considering if this important methodological factor accounts for some of the disparities between the IPSOS survey and our own research findings in terms of the scope of misleading and aggressive practices in Canada. What did respondents tell us, specifically?

3 Experiences of Older Adults with Telecommunication Service Providers

3.1 Older Adults as Golden Opportunities

As we discuss in further details over the next sections, some older adults have characteristics that may put them, as a demographic group, in a position of increased vulnerability or perceived vulnerability in their dealings with telecommunication service providers. This includes lower use and expertise with digital technologies and a lack of awareness that telecommunication packages can be negotiated. In the context of Canada, sales representatives may take advantage of these traits, and may also see their dealings with older customers as opportunities to sell more extensive and expensive digital packages. Seniors subscribe to fewer telecommunications services than the average Canadian household. A recent CRTC report explains the Canadian context: "Households whose reference person [who typically handles financial matters in the home] is aged 40 to 54 spent the most on communications services ($257.75 per month), while those with reference persons aged 65 years or over spent the least ($182.33 per month)" [15]. In addition, Canadian seniors are more likely to still use landlines, providing another opportunity to bring them over into the wireless market. Canadian seniors, compared to their international counterparts, continue to rely heavily on traditional services like landlines and television and less so on data-heavy cell phone and Internet plans [16]. Research suggests that targeted sales tactics, which uses sales scripts and sets unrealistic quotas, are a commonly adopted marketing strategy [17, 18], and that age is the demographic variable most prominently used in consumer marketing [19]. Other research suggests that older adults may be specifically targeted because of their perceived vulnerability [20]. As such, older adults are thought of as providing a "golden" opportunity for sales representatives, including those whose livelihood depends on meeting sales quotas.

From the perspective of a sales agent needing to make a living, Canadian seniors are particularly good targets for a practice known as "upselling": pressuring people to purchase products and services that they did not initially intend to purchase, that they may not need, or which they cannot afford. Employees, particularly those working on commission or on a quota basis find that they are caught in a system that places intense pressures on them to upsell. This is corroborated by CBC reporting on the comments of former employees of telecommunication companies, who were instructed, specifically, to lie to seniors to sell them expensive telecommunication packages [21]. One employee candidly commented in response to the article and wrote:

I know all about Golden Lists and targeting seniors and the mentally challenged. You know exactly where you're calling and it's a celebration when you hit these demographics. Of course, now there is no need to pay for these lists as cold-calling the phone book you will automatically hit them, as they are just about the only people with landlines [21].

It is for this reason that consumer advocacy organizations, such as the Public Interest Advocacy Centre, have long argued for better working conditions, wages and an end to all commission-based sales for workers in this industry so that incentives to take advantage of consumers is minimized [22].

3.2 Upselling to Seniors

The older adults we interviewed shared stories that indicate the impact of these practices on their lives, and provide insight into how service providers may deliberately use language intended to scare, fear or shame the consumer into making a purchase. In one especially egregious case of upselling, an 86-year-old man from Montreal seeking a landline was told that landline technology was outdated. The sales representative then sold him a smartphone with an expensive data plan. The man had never owned a cellphone before and he was unable to turn the device on, navigate the interface, or make a call. This left him unable to communicate with his family or friends. Eventually, a social worker stepped in to call the service provider to resolve the issue. Not having access to a usable phone would have left this man extremely vulnerable in the event of an emergency.

One other form of upselling that we encountered involves selling inappropriate data packages. In this instance, seniors may not be aware, or fully informed, that they are being sold a service that they do not need or cannot use. One typical instance is paying large monthly sums for services, like high bandwidth and data limits, when the consumer does not need such advanced features. One low-income senior in his 80 s, for instance, was sold a telecommunication package that included unlimited Internet for his home. Yet he did not own a computer, a smartphone or any device that allowed him to access the Internet. This senior reported paying a monthly sum that was so high that it had required him to cut back on other life necessities. In these two cases, sales representatives recognized the opportunity to increase their individual sales and their company's profit without taking the time to understand and respond to the particular needs or skills of the older customers on the other end of the line.

3.3 Age, Disclosure and Deception

Interviewees discussed the dilemmas they faced in deciding whether or not to reveal their age on the phone. One woman from Montreal, Québec pointed to attempts by agents to make her feel powerless in the conversation specifically because of her age, but as well because of "ageist" conversational styles. As she stated:

> a lot of my friends have been pressured and they feel like, because of their age, they have not been treated as a full participant in the conversation. They're condescending, trying to explain this to you. And it's really demeaning for a lot of people. Just because you're older doesn't mean you're stupid.

Several interviewees spoke of the sense that they were being targeted *because* of their age. This awareness was sometimes triggered by their perception of a sales agent's tone and attitude. Yet as other participants noted, revealing one's age is rarely a question of individual choice, particularly if you have received a call. As one focus group participant warned, companies may know how old you are because of the data in their files. She cautioned that sales agents could use this information to take advantage of them.

Interviewees described other tactics deployed by sales agents, some of which were decidedly deceptive. Interviewees described being misled and lured into contracts under false pretenses. While being pressured into sales can be covert, in other instances interviewees described sales representatives blatantly lying to them and misrepresenting the terms of their contracts. These cases were recounted most often when sales representatives sought out potential consumers in person (at the door or in public), and when seniors were put in a position to decide or sign "on the spot".

In two harrowing examples, sales representatives surreptitiously signed seniors into agreements with companies without their knowledge. An older woman from Kamloops, British Columbia explained to us that she got "scammed" by a third-party sales representative hired by Telus, a major telecommunication service provider:

I got scammed this summer by Telus. Well, two young guys came around to the door. And they checked our account and they had their little tablets and they were checking on our account. And then they said, well, you're such good customers, we're going to give you a free phone: no obligation whatsoever. I said, "oh fine, I don't need a phone. I'm not upgrading or anything." And they said, "well, there's no obligation." So, I took this and it was an LG phone. I never did activate it or do anything with it. And then a couple months ago, my cell phone went up $200 extra! They were charging me a payout on this phone. So, that was a big fight to get rid of that.

In addition to revealing the use of deliberate deception, this story highlights how the sub-contracting of sales services to third-party providers may also be a factor in creating problems within the industry.

A similar story was told by an 82-year-old woman from Montreal, Québec, who explained what happened when she was approached by a young sales representative in an outdoor booth hosted by the company Bell. The man said that he was having a terrible day and needed "just one more signature" to end his shift and return home. He assured her that this was just a signature to confirm that he had spoken to her, and that it would not behold her to any obligation. She explained to us that she felt empathy for the sales representative and thought that she was helping him out by filling out the paperwork as she was instructed. Bell called her within a few days to secure payment. Only then did she realize that, unknowingly, she had signed a contract. She resolved the situation with Bell, but she felt deeply misled and explained that she lost a great deal of trust in Bell and, more broadly, in Canadian telecommunication companies.

While the above instance of deception into signing a contract may be infrequent, far more common are instances of difference between the price promised on the phone, and the amount that appears on the monthly invoice. In other cases, the promises made to the consumer were not upheld. In one instance, an interviewee explained that he was promised a cellphone for $138 by the Québec-based company Vidéotron, only to be given a substantially higher price when he went to the store in person to purchase the device. He came home empty-handed, still wanting the deal he was promised:

So, I go back home and I phone, and I actually was quite upset. I used some very bad words, so I won't repeat them here. So, I said, "Vidéotron lied to me, because if you check your records and I would wish you would check right now, what is the price that you gave me 4 days ago?". She answered that she could not give me that price. That's not very good for seniors.

These stories highlight the impact that misleading and aggressive practices have on individual lives, as well as some of specific the tactics being used to lure older adults into costly contracts or inappropriate services: from the use of condescending language to outright deception, to not providing full details on the final costs of a contract.

4 Confronting the Companies

In the previous section, we described some of the strategies used to pressure older adults into service contracts, into purchasing devices that they did not need, or into obtaining devices that could not be used. We recounted stories that point to instances of overt deception, to the age-related dilemmas that older adults face in the sales encounter, as well as their anger and disappointment in the industry.

Some of the seniors to whom we spoke explained how they try to mitigate the potential for harm in these encounters. However, as these interviews indicate, not all seniors have the resources, including time or the needed information, to make the right telecommunication choices. When things go wrong, finding satisfaction is not always evident. Most Canadians, for example, do not know where to turn if they have a complaint and have little recourse other than going to their service provider. Despite the fact that the CCTS found in 2018 that complaints against telecommunications providers had increased by 73% over a year [23], the seniors we interviewed were generally not aware of the CCTS and of its mandate. The seniors who had been misled had, by-and-large, not sought recourse with a third party.

4.1 Relying on Digitally-Savvy Family and Friends

Several seniors reported spending a significant amount of time on the phone with service providers in attempts to obtain reimbursements, or to adjust services to match the commitments that had been made. Many others reported asking loved ones to step in. Interviewees recounted the important role played by networks of friends or family in assisting them to mediate their dealings with service providers or to negotiate packages on their behalf. Several seniors reported that they rely on younger family members—children, grandchildren, nieces and nephews—or friends to help them deal with telecommunication service providers and to intervene in particular situations. One of them reported her experience purchasing a cell phone and described it as a 'need for protection':

> I actually had to go with somebody who wanted to protect me. You need somebody who knows how to speak to people and how much they're going to give you a discount, but now I just threaten to leave and it's terrible that we have to do that. A lot of people don't, and they just take a package.

The problem with this 'solution' is that not all seniors have the luxury of close family or friendship ties with tech-savvy individuals. In this context, those without close social networks are more susceptible to predatory practices or less able to contest bills or services that do not meet their needs.

Social workers and community group workers in Montreal have reported being asked to step in to deal directly with service providers on the behalf of their senior clients. Those to whom we have spoken recounted that this is not a viable solution, as telecommunication company representatives repeatedly refuse to let them help resolve the situation because they are not a family member. Other seniors with expertise in negotiation and with more digital experience reported that they often helped their friends get better deals. Not all seniors have this advantage, putting those who are the most socially isolated into greater jeopardy. One man explained that he spent "hours and hours" on the phone and dealt with at least five home visits so that his Internet speed would be increased to the level that he was promised, and the ordeal had brought about "a lot of stress".

Others reported having had to "cut their losses with bad deals," and just accepted to pay. As one of them explained: "It's just not worth it, for a few dollars, they make you jump through hoops and explain yourself, and they should be the ones explaining themselves. They know we don't have time to deal with all of this and they can get away with it." In other cases, seniors commented on the issue of their disadvantage as individual consumers, articulating that that it is their voice against that of the telecommunication provider and that they may not have access to written or recorded proof of the commitment that was made to them.

4.2 Expectations of Loyalty

A number of seniors cited the importance of trust in their dealings with telecommunication companies, twinned with a frustration that there are limited choices in their local market. A 72-year-old woman from Ottawa, Ontario told us: "You have to pick one, so sometimes you're better off with the devil you know!". Another senior pointed out how he had lost trust in Bell over time, which led him to transform his payment structure:

> Bell is the only company that I have taken off automatic payment from my bank account, I do not trust them. A year ago, I was paying between $50 and $70 dollars extra a month because they were making mistakes or overcharging me for whatever reason. I needed to scrutinize the billing every month and spend hours on the phone, and wait months for a credit. Now I only pay the amount that is actually due and I call and tell them to fix their own problems.

Research shows that seniors tend to display loyalty because of their affiliation with companies or brands earlier in life [24]. Many senior interviewees disclosed having been customers of the same telecommunication company for decades. Some stated that they dealt with hassles as they came because they believed their telecommunication service provider valued their years of loyalty. One interviewee, in his 60 s, expressed that he was upset that Bell had given his daughter a better price for similar telecommunication services. As he put it:

> My customer loyalty should have a value to them [Bell]. I've been a customer for years and I expect they will treat me well. You shouldn't have to pay more, or you shouldn't get a worse service than anybody else. And that is what I expect. It really annoys me when service providers offer these amazing promotional deals to newcomers.

Many interviewees described loyalty as a two-way street and expressed discontent when telecommunication companies did not reciprocate and, much worse, took advantage of them at the moment of sale. Other seniors reported that they were afraid to use their long-running loyalty as leverage in bargaining for rates. They reported fearing to reveal their years with a company because this would, in turn, reveal their age. One woman commented that this could make her more vulnerable to ruthless sales representatives. She said, "maybe we shouldn't tell them we've been with them for 40 years".

4.3 Negotiating Contracts

Nearly half of the seniors interviewed did not know that the prices of telecommunication packages in Canada might be negotiable, though this practice is considered common in Canada. Many of our interviewees, in particular those over the age of 75, told us that they accepted the first price and the first package that were suggested to them. As one participant explained: "that is just how it is, the price of the service, there is nothing to negotiate". During one focus group, half of the participants realized that the other half had been negotiating their telecommunication prices for years. Participants then began comparing the rates they pay, only to conclude amongst themselves that those who had been negotiating were paying lower prices.

There is a generational factor at play that impacts seniors' awareness of the ability to negotiate prices of telecommunication services. Many of the oldest seniors we interviewed first acquired communication services at a time when prices for telephone services in Canada were under federal regulation, and when prices were fixed and approved by regulatory bodies to ensure the affordability of communication services for all Canadians. Since the 1980s, the prices of vast majority of telecommunication services used by Canadians have become less regulated and more determined by free market forces, in a country where there is markedly little competition in the telecommunication industry. Younger adults, in contrast to older adults, have lived a larger proportion of their telecommunication consumer experience in an era of deregulated prices and have never had an expectation of 'fixed and fair' prices for telecommunication services.

There are several factors that help seniors negotiate a fair telecommunication package. Previous research we have conducted on seniors and cell phones shows that one's ability to negotiate contracts is often tied to one's professional experience [25]. This knowledge gives retired or pre-retirement white-collar workers, particularly those whose first language is English or French, an edge in dealing with sales or customer service representatives.

5 Discussion

While older adults over the age of 65 have never been so proficient in their use of digital technologies as they are at this moment in our national history. According to Statistics Canada, only 43% of Canadian seniors over the age of 75 use the Internet on a daily or weekly basis [11]. Yet data also indicates that the oldest Canadians, most notably those over the age of 75, who are much less connected and digitally experienced than the youngest seniors [26]. There are other intersectional elements to consider when discussing the systemic nature of digital divides, including gender [27], education [26, 28] and income [28]. Grimes, Hough, and Signorella, further suggest that older adults with lower levels of digital knowledge may be more exposed to risks and threats connected to telecommunication services like the Internet [29]. It is important to note that prices of telecommunication services in Canada are among the highest of the industrialized world. For some older adults, purchasing the telecommunication services they need is impossible, and for others paying for telecommunication services means cutting back on life necessities [30].

This multi-facetted digital divide creates systemic or structural inequities that sub-tend the conversations between older consumers and sales agents. In a society where knowledge of the ins and outs of the digital world is unevenly and unfairly distributed along lines of age, education, literacy and income, the industry and the regulator place the burden of digital expertise on individual consumers to resist the tactics of sales representatives, who are explicitly trained or incentivized to prey upon those with a prior lack of knowledge. This expectation normalizes predatory sales practices in the telecommunication industry.

Sales practices are facilitated and upheld by internal policies, directives, scripts and processes put into place by telecommunication companies. These may include undue pressures on employees to sell and retain customers, a commissions-based sale structure, a reliance on unaccountable third-party sales representatives, a lack of employee training and oversight, and implicit and explicit pressure on sales personnel to target vulnerable groups [21]. As Ramsey et al. point out, ethical sales practices need to be foregrounded by an organization otherwise employees, responding to sales quotas, may resort to unethical practices including practices that either do not take ageing into account [20], or precisely take age into account and thus target seniors as a potential 'golden' opportunity for the upselling of services.

This puts into focus the need for organizations to address the structures that fos-ter unethical sales practices, like employee training and taking measures to reprimand predatory behaviors. It is also the case that the industry puts Canadian telecommunication sales employees—many of them young adults—in positions where they are incentivized to take advantage of potential consumers who are systemically disadvantaged, including seniors. The normalization of abuse, the fear felt by customers, and the general lack of trust that Canadians have towards telecommunication service providers are all evi-dence of the systemic nature of the problem of misleading and aggressive sales and the impacts that this has on the lives of many. Indeed, when one story on the issue was published on the CBC website [31], it prompted hundreds of responses from the public in the comments section, the vast majority of them relaying tales of dismay at the high cost of telecommunications in Canada and testimonies of bad encounters with company representatives.

The interviews with older adults reveal the very real harms that can come to indi-viduals who are pressured into long-term contracts they cannot afford, or into buying devices that they do not know how to use. The presence of condescending attitudes and predatory practices that target older adults specifically because of their age attitudes, also point to the presence of what can only be described as ageism. This ageism is not only individual, but systemic. Sales agents are incentivized to target older adults; they may take advantage of generational differences in technological experience.

6 Conclusion

In this paper, we have sought answer three questions. First, we asked: (1) what are older adults' experiences with sales practices of telecommunication service providers in Canada and (2) what are their responses to misleading and aggressive practices? By drawing on interviews and focus groups with older adults, we explained the scope and impact of misleading and aggressive sales practices in Canada, by relaying accounts of blatant deception, upselling and overselling. Our interviews confirmed the widespread presence of misleading and aggressive sales practices in Canada, highlighting imbalances of power and demonstrating how these tactics impact older adults. They also make apparent, the on-going, recurrent obstacles and the "techno-stresses" [32] that older adults may face in their dealings with service providers. Many of the older adults we spoke to had devised strategies to mitigate the impact of these sales practice, such as negotiating or asking for help from people in their social circles. Yet these advantages are not afforded to all seniors. This creates a situation where older adults who are already most at risk of isolation and marginalization are placed at an even further disadvantage by the telecommunication industry.

Further, we asked (3) if older adults are put at a systemic disadvantage in the current telecommunication landscape, and how so? Through this paper, we pointed to different elements that can put certain older adults in a position of heightened vulnerability when faced with misleading and aggressive practices. Yet, it remains the case that many respondents felt targeted because of their age, something that is supported by the disclosures of telecommunication industry employees. Misleading and aggressive sales practices are facilitated and upheld by organizational features that have been put into place by telecommunication companies to prey on the actual and perceived vulnerabilities of consumers. The stories from older adults provide evidence of the presence of systemic age-related biases in the Canadian telecommunications industry; an industry that fails to acknowledge the power imbalances between different stakeholders when buying a service, negotiating a contract or making a complaint.

In Canada, telecommunication companies and the federal regulator tend to eschew the implementation of effective consumer safeguards and corporate responsibility. Instead, they place the onus on individual consumers, asking them to better inform themselves and to guard against unscrupulous sales agents. Likewise, blame is cast on individual employees without acknowledging the corporate structures that tolerate, encourage, incentivize and directly profit from misleading and aggressive practices. As the words of these interviewees makes clear, there is an urgent need for systemic change in Canada that must include a more robust regulatory environment for telecommunication service providers.

Acknowledgements. Ageing + Communication + Technologies (www.actproject.ca) is a research project funded by the Social Sciences and Humanities Research Council (SSHRC). We are thankful for the work of ACT research assistants and for the guidance of community organizations Groupe Harmonie and Respecting Elders: Communities Against Abuse (RECAA), as well as support from the Atwater Library and Computer Centre.

References

1. Lafontaine, C., Sawchuk, K.: Accessing InterACTion: ageing with technologies and the place of access. In: Zhou, J., Salvendy, G. (eds.) ITAP 2015. LNCS, vol. 9193, pp. 210–220. Springer, Cham (2015). https://doi.org/10.1007/978-3-319-20892-3_21

2. Lafontaine, C., Sawchuk, K.: Promising practices in collaborative digital literacy and digital media-making with older adults. In: Zhou, J., Salvendy, G. (eds.) Human Aspects of IT for the Aged Population. Acceptance, Communication and Participation, pp. 492–504 (2018). https://doi.org/10.1007/978-3-319-92034-4_37

3. Sawchuk, K., Lafontaine, C.: Activist aging: the tactical theatrics of RECAA. In: Chazan, M., Baldwin, M., Evans, P. (eds.) Unsettling Activisms: Critical Interventions on Aging, Gender and Social Change, pp. 50–65. Women's press, Toronto (2018)

4. Johnson, E., Denne, L., Cowley, J.: CBC Hidden Camera Investigation Captures Misleading Sales Tactics for Bell. CBC (2018). https://www.cbc.ca/news/business/hidden-camera-rev eals-misleading-sales-tactics-for-bell-1.4556536

5. Lawford, J.: Letter from the Executive Director and General Counsel of PIAC to the Chairperson and Chief Executive Officer of the CRTC (2018). https://www.piac.ca/wp-content/upl oads/2018/01/PIAC-Letter-CRTC-Sales-Practices-Inquiry-Request-FINAL.pdf

6. Scott, I.: Letter from the Chairperson and Chief Executive Officer of the CRTC to the Executive Director and General Counsel of PIAC Centre (2018). https://crtc.gc.ca/eng/archive/2018/lt1 80212.htm

7. Tunney, C.: Ottawa orders CRTC to investigate reports of 'aggressive' telecom sales practices (2018). https://www.cbc.ca/news/politics/crtc-telecom-sales-practices-investigation-1. 4706260

8. Government of Canada: Actions for seniors report (2014). https://www.canada.ca/en/employ ment-social-development/programs/seniors-action-report.html

9. Canadian Radio-television and Telecommunications Commission (CRTC): Inquiry on use of misleading or aggressive sales practices by large telecommunications service providers (2018). https://crtc.gc.ca/eng/phone/telsp.htm

10. Giddens, A.: The Constitution of Society: Outline of the Theory of Structuration. University of California Press, Berkeley (1984)

11. Statistics Canada: The Internet and digital technology (2017). https://www150.statcan.gc.ca/ n1/pub/11-627-m/11-627-m2017032-eng.htm

12. Besanger, K., Lafontaine, C.: Seniors participate in CRTC consultation (2018). https://www. youtube.com/watch?v=ip_N_fCRNAk

13. Titus, R., Gover, A.: Personal fraud: the victims and the scams. Crime Prev. Stud. 12, 133–151 (2001)

14. Burnes, D., Henderson, C.R., Sheppard, C., Zhao, R., Pillemer, K., Lachs, M.S.: Prevalence of financial fraud and scams among older adults in the United States: a systematic review and meta-analysis. Am. J. Publ. Health 107, e13–e21 (2017). https://doi.org/10.2105/AJPH. 2017.303821

15. Canadian Radio-television and Telecommunications Commission (CRTC): Communications Monitoring Report 2018. https://crtc.gc.ca/eng/publications/reports/policymonitoring/2018/ cmr1.htm

16. Loos, E., Nimrod, G., Fernández-Ardèvol, M.: Older audiences in the digital media environment: A cross-national longitudinal study (2018). http://spectrum.library.concordia.ca/983 866/

17. Fishman, A.A.: Understanding generational differences. Nat. Underwrit. 108, 4 (2004)

18. Meredith, G.E., Schewe, C.D., Karlovich, J.: Defining Markets, Defining Moments: Americas 7 Generational Cohorts, Their Shared Experiences, and Why Businesses Should Care. Hungry Minds, New York (2002)

19. Mitchell, S.: The Official Guide to the Generations: Who they are, How they Live, What they Think. New Strategist Publications, Ithaca (1995)

20. Ramsey, R.P., Marshall, G.W., Johnston, M.W., Deeter-Schmelz, D.R.: Ethical ideologies and older consumer perceptions of unethical sales tactics. J. Bus. Ethics 70, 191–207 (2007). https://doi.org/10.1007/s10551-006-9105-6

21. Johnson, E.: Former Bell and Rogers employees reveal sales secrets submitted to public inquiry (2018). https://www.cbc.ca/news/business/telecom-employees-submit-complaints-to-crtc-inquiry-1.4794953

22. Innovation, Science and Economic Development Canada: Government orders the CRTC to investigate high-pressure telecom sales practices (2018). https://www.newswire.ca/news-releases/government-orders-the-crtc-to-investigate-high-pressure-telecom-sales-practices-685582231.html

23. Public Interest Advocacy Centre (2020). https://www.piac.ca

24. Iyer, R., Reisenwitz, T.H., Eastman, J.K.: The Impact of cognitive age on senior's lifestyles. Market. Manage. J. **18**(2), 106–118 (2008)

25. Sawchuk, K., Crow, B.: I'm G-Mom on the phone. Feminist Med. Stud. **12**, 496–505 (2012)

26. Allen, M.K.: Insights on Canadian society: Consumption on culture by older Canadians on the internet (2013). https://www150.statcan.gc.ca/n1/en/pub/75-006-x/2013001/article/11768-eng.pdf?st=-cp_6rcV

27. CEFRIO: Les aînés connectés au Québec (2019). https://cefrio.qc.ca/media/2207/netendances-2019_a%C3%AEn%C3%A9s_vf.pdf

28. Fallows, D.: Women are catching up to men in most measures of online life. In: Men Like the Internet for the Experiences it Offers, While Women Like it for the Human Connections it Promotes, p. 54. PEW Research Centre (2005)

29. Grimes, G.A., Hough, M.G., Mazur, E., Signorella, M.L.: Older adults' knowledge of internet hazards. Educ. Gerontol. **36**, 173–192 (2010)

30. Middleton, C., Sawchuk, K., Lafontaine, C., DeJong, S., Henderson, J.: Meeting the needs of all Canadians: Older adults, affordability and mobile, wireless services (2019). https://actproject.ca/wp-content/uploads/2019/10/ACT-OCTOBER-2019-intervention-CRTC-2019-57-final.pdf

31. The Canadian Press: CRTC urged to hold inquiry into telecom sales tactics (2010). https://www.cbc.ca/news/business/bell-high-pressure-sales-reaction-1.4478586

32. Nimrod, G.: Technostress: measuring a new threat to wellbeing in later life. Aging Mental Health **22**, 1080–1087 (2018)

A Contextual Usability Exploration of Cash and Ticket Machines

Karolina Uggla(✉) and Yvonne Eriksson

Division of Information Design, Mälardalen University, 631 05 Eskilstuna, Sweden
{karolina.uggla,yvonne.eriksson}@mdh.se

Abstract. Today, many services, such as ticket purchase and cash withdrawal, are provided by stationary machines such as ATM and ticket machines placed in train stations and travel centers. Personalized service is not always available, and users are referred to machines and automats. Previous research on ATM and ticket machines mostly focus on user interface and do not take the contextual conditions into consideration. A well-designed interface may not work under conditions such as poor lighting and time limitations of the service which affects the usability. The focus of this paper is not the physical or digital design of ATM and ticket automats as such, but rather how they function in their environment, and how that will affect users; especially old people with some sensory limitations such as limited eyesight and partial motor skills. The empirical study indicates that the physical environment of these machines and automats is crucial for how the service works. Identified parameters that affect usability are light conditions, auditory conditions, the liveliness of the setting and time limitations of services. If the contextual conditions surrounding the automat or machine does not work, it will be inaccessible to many users, however deliberate the design of their physical and digital interface.

Keywords: Contextual design · Accessibility · Inclusive design · Task analysis · Automatic Teller Machine · ATM · Automatic Ticket Vending Machine · ATVM

1 Introduction

In the book *New Aging* the author stresses that old people should remember that they do have an extensive experience from societal transformations [1]. In the same book Hollwich calls upon the importance for old people to learn how to use smartphones and wearable devices since these are "becoming an extension of ourselves" [1]. This contradictory way of discussing old people and technology is common. It is easy to forget that, as mentioned by Hollwich, they have been involved in the development of and used various kinds of technical devices. Since machines for different purposes have been a part of people's lives in Western countries for a long time. Cash machines (ATM), ticket machines (ATVM) and parking meters all have a long history, for instance cash dispensers have been around since the 1960s [2]. Self-service as concept was initiated in the early 20th Century and was a part of modern society and the modernist ideal striving to make daily life more efficient, in line with ideas of scientific management

© Springer Nature Switzerland AG 2020
Q. Gao and J. Zhou (Eds.): HCII 2020, LNCS 12207, pp. 245–255, 2020.
https://doi.org/10.1007/978-3-030-50252-2_19

in the manufacturing industry [3]. Unmanned self-service was achieved by introducing various kinds of automats such as parking meters, vending machines for cigarettes, snacks and drinks. Early vending machines are generally said to have started to appear on a larger scale in the US in the 1880s [4]. Self-service with or without automats also became present in gas stations, grocery stores and restaurants. The idea of self-service was also a way to make people independent from personal service and cut costs of salaries and provide full service on hours when staff is off duty.

The following paper will discuss the usability of self-service machines – ATMs and ATVMs – from a design perspective which takes the context into consideration. It is not only the design of the machine as such that matters, it is also its location and context that affect the usability. The aim of the study is to explore how the context in which the machines are placed affect their design, use and functionality in order to reach the users' goal to withdraw money or buy a ticket. We have explored ATMs of the Swedish brand Bankomat AB, ticket machines of the Swedish national railway company SJ and ticket machines of local public transport company SL in Stockholm.

1.1 Background

There are records of coin-operated hydraulic automats in antiquity. The 17th Century saw some simple coin-operated boxes for selling tobacco wares in England. More advanced automats with single packets of tobacco appeared in England in the 1830s [4]. In the 1850s and 1860s automats for stamps and postcards were patented. Vending machines in America started to appear in public spaces in the 1880s. Generally, in the UK and US automatic vending machines from the late 1800s and early 1900s contained tobacco, drinks, sweets and newspapers and were a common sight at railways stations, ferry terminals and on street corners. Automats for all kinds of goods became popular in the 1920s and 30s in the US [4]. In Sweden, after the 1930s, strict regulations of opening hours created a demand for the availability of goods like groceries and drinks in evenings and weekends. Large arrays of automats could take the shape of a full-service around-the-clock grocery store. In the 1970s the rules for opening hours were lightened up and the demand for full-service grocery stores in an automated version declined [5].

Automatic Teller Machines (ATMs) for financial transactions, with some earlier exceptions, appeared in the UK and US in the 1950s [2, 6]. The early machines operated on single-use paper tokens with a magnetic strip. The idea of a PIN code stored on a card was patented in the mid 1960s [6]. In a Swedish context, the first offline ATMs were installed in the 1960s. Withdrawals were registered on punch paper tape that was sent back to the bank. There is records of one online ATM operating in Malmö as early as 1968, which was considered technologically advanced internationally. Concurrently, Swedish banks and association of banks were very interested in automation and a "cash-free society", cooperating for on-line services and networks. The two large brands of ATMs in Sweden were Minuten (first automat operational in 1976) and Bankomat (an association founded in 1972). These automats extended availability of financial services and cash withdrawal after bank opening hours [7]. The demand and expansion of ATMs in the 1960s and 70s in Sweden and the UK was not only driven by the aspiration to cut the costs of employees. It was also driven by long-term ideals of mechanization and automation and the development of computers and computer networks [2].

However, the earlier self-service machines could be considered as an additional service to banks and ticket offices. Today in Sweden we are facing a situation where the citizens hardly are provided with personal services such as withdrawals from a bank office or purchasing tickets from a ticket office. Many train and bus stations do not offer the opportunity of personalized ticket purchase. Neither is it possible to use cash to buy tickets on long-distance buses. Self-service of goods and services has accelerated and expanded further during the last decades and has taken on different and new forms. Self-service is increasingly moving into mobile apps, which is beyond the limitations of this paper. However, the generations that grew up with automats in public and semi-public places to buy different goods and services, are used to this and are reluctant to use mobile apps to access the same things. The European accessibility act is a directive that aims to improve the functioning of the internal market for accessible products and services. However, what it is not taken into consideration is the impact of the context and the situation that affect the usability. The European accessibility act focus on people with disabilities, but many old people experience hinders in daily life that could be defined as disabilities [8].

1.2 Previous Research

The growing number of old people that still are active, and economic conditions that allows them to spend money on travelling, clothes, interior design and ICT equipment has been recognized by many companies. Companies that address that target group has been growing during the last decade [9]. Some of the companies develop products for old people while others only advertise their products for people that has reached their retirement [9]. Many presumptions regarding old people do exist, especially when it comes to the use of technology [9, 10]. What is less discussed in relation to the ability to use ICT and other kinds of technical devices is the fact that old people go through different physiological and psychological changes, such as sensibility of hearing, sight, smell and touch [10]. Some people also get a weaker working memory that will affect the ability to perform in stressful situations that requires fast decisions [10]. As a consequence, old people often need more time to perform.

Previous research on usability has typically focused on artefacts, in order to get a deeper understanding of the meaning of usability it is necessary to combine several perspectives. In this case it is important to understand different aspects of the ATM and ticket machines, such as physiological and cognitive change caused by ageing, design of public space and the aim of a product from a cultural heritage perspective. The socio-cultural perspective of an artefact is important to take into consideration since it gives a better understanding of the original intention and how to evaluate if it has been incorporated. Research indicates that the products people found attractive also are experienced as easy to use. Norman refers to a study from early 1990s that was conducted in Japan and Israel on how people experience using different ATMs. The ATMs had identical functions, the same number of buttons, but some variations in how the buttons and screen where arranged. The version that the participants in the studies experienced as easiest to use, was the ones they found most attractive [11].

Chan, Wong, Lee and Chi have observed the use of existing ATMs and tested a prototype to enhance the use for older adults using universal design and participatory design perspectives [12]. A large number of users were involved in designing the tests and prototyping a few chosen tasks. The first part of the study, observing existing ATM user profiles for older adults was conducted in a laboratory environment, not on-site or in the context of ATMs in public places.

To understand and map where errors can occur in the process of money withdrawal, such as cards left and lost in ATMs, Lockton et al. perform a hierarchical task analysis [13]. This task analysis does not include any environmental or contextual factors for the use of the ATMs. Such an overview to addresses this common problem has led to a development towards card received before cash, also addressed in Zimmermann and Bridger [14]. In accessibility studies and universal design studies there are examples of ATMs as the prime example for usability testing with different digital methods in a lab environment. Li et al. [15] address problems with "seated reach" for users in wheelchairs, bringing users into a VR environment. Marshall et al. [16] are using data-driven tools for testing and designing, using anthropometrics models based on large sets of user data. There are of course benefits of using data-driven tools and virtual 3D or CAD environments at early stages in a design process. As we argue, such methods and models need to be supplemented with user studies in a real-life context with existing automats, since contextual factors, both indoors and outdoors, are hard to foresee in laboratory environments.

Contextual design is a user-centered approach to design processes, emerging in the 1980s, which takes into consideration design for everyday life, of both users and various ranges of products [17]. To understand users and avoid a design team detached from the users, making assumptions about users' needs, the design team in a first stage need to immerse in "the life of the user" [17]. Contextual design is in many ways addressing problems attached to engineering design in the 1980s and 1990s. Problems that are not as prevalent today when user centered design perspectives are more present in design practice. However, the lesson of immersion in the lives of the user, is something that has informed this study in the way that existing automats in their environment are studied.

According to Carmona [18] public space has become a key component of many regeneration and development schemes (both residential and commercial) worldwide, with far-reaching impacts on how the resulting places are perceived and used since 1980s [19, 20]. He continues to emphasize that it is important to design public spaces well since high quality public spaces offer huge economic, social and environmental benefits to their localities and communities [18]. A well-designed public space must include parts of the environment, its artefacts and various details that contribute to the space as whole. By well-designed artefacts we do not consider only the object itself but also how it is placed in an environment.

1.3 Theory

An ATM or ticket machine operates on a multitude of user interfaces regarding the hardware product and how it is designed with controls, screens, keypads and card slots. Also labels and signs can be included here. "An interface is the bridge between the world of the product or system and the world of the users. It is the means by which the users interact with the product to achieve their goals. It is the means by which the system reveals itself to the users and behaves in relation to the users' needs" [21]. However, if a product is perceived as complex it hinders users to fulfill their needs. Complexity is not the same as complicated, but some products are experienced as complicated even though they are not complex *per se*. If complexity is regarded as a system, it could be explained as multiple layers. Firstly, the complexity of the system, secondly the operational complexity which is what users have to deal with, and thirdly apparent complexity. This third level consists of cognitive complexity, perceived complexity and task complexity [22].

Cognitive complexity refers to the complexity of the logic of a system [22]. It has also been described as the ease or difficulty of understanding and using a product or services [22]. Factors that contribute to cognitive complexity are such as the numbers of objects, symbols and properties of components in a system; and the number of linkages or relationship between them [22]. The cognitive complexity is driven by the characteristic of the system while perceptual complexity refers to how the system is presented for the user. The perceptual complexity affects the task complexity and increases the mental load among users that struggle to act in an intended way. Cognitive, perceptual and task complexity are interlinked and how complex a task is perceived by a user is also depending on her/his mental model, which is expectation. Cognitive complexity can be perceived by a customer even in more or less simple devices. If one is expecting a touch screen because of the design of the machine and facing a screen with buttons beside the screen, which are intended to be pressed instead of the screen, the user is experiencing a high degree of cognitive load if he/she is in a stressful situation. Stressors have different impact on the cognitive processes, and people tend to become less efficient [22]. The environment could easily be a stressor for old people and effect the experienced usability of an ATM or a ticket machine, as well as the placement of the machine – if it is placed in an environment that could be considered as secure or not. Stress is the cause of factors such as lack of influence over what happens, lack of decision space, lack of self-control and lack of authority [23]. In a stressful situation the brain sends signals to the sympathetic nervous system that is activated, which affects the entire body. Among other things, substances in the blood are secreted, for example sugar, and stress hormones such as adrenaline, norepinephrine and cortisol. The capability to decompose cortisol decrease because of age, and this could explain why old people experience stress more easily [22].

1.4 Method

Qualitative ethnographic methods have been used at randomly selected ATMs of the brand Bankomat AB. The ticket machines of the national railway company SJ have been observed in different locations in the Mälardalen area and Stockholm. In addition, the ticket automats of the Stockholm public transport company SL have been observed at various metro stations in Stockholm. The ATM and ticket machines have been analyzed from a usability perspective. The machines have been observed according to certain criteria, and how the chosen automats work in different times of the day. Factors observed are lighting conditions, indoors, outdoors, sound and noise conditions, considering usability and principles of good design, for instance inconsistency of combinations of touchscreens and keypads, and how easy they are to find.

In this paper we are interested in the usability of ATM and ticket machines in their actual context with focus on people with limited cognitive and physical abilities caused by age. Thereby, the digital interface and software used as such is not in focus, other than the process that leads to fulfilling the user goal of buying a ticket or withdrawing cash. This can be divided into tasks which facilitates observation of when and where problems occur, if there are discernible patterns or similarities between the use of different types of automats. Norman defined a "seven stages of action" sequence of human action which comprises of goals, execution and analysis, starting with goal, plan and specification of the action, the performing the sequence of actions, followed by perceiving, interpreting and comparing [11]. This model sequence holds more of user's emotions and feelings about a task with proceeding and subsequent thought.

We translated the use of the automats into a basic task list, in order to explore when and where difficulties and delays can occur when using them. The tasks differ in order between different machines and machine types. Factors that are considered here are time spent with each task, how difficult each task is, how critical they are in the process. The process outcome of obtaining a ticket or make a withdrawal includes choices, there is a simple, yet distinct *procedural analysis*, one task can lead to different paths dependent on the choice made. Since the order of the tasks differ slightly between the two types of machines (ATM and ticket machines), they have different *task sequences*. The task list with the goal to make a withdrawal or to obtain a ticket consists of four general steps: 1. Finding machine, 2. Primary choices, 3. Action requests, and 4. Completion.

Limitation of Study and Further Research. The result from this empirical study will be discussed from a usability perspective that takes the context of the various self-service machines into consideration. The analyses have been made from theories regarding task performance and cognitive complexity and not by involving users. Further research would be to make an extended user study.

2 Empirical Data and Result

We have explored ATMs in Eskilstuna and Stockholm under various weather conditions that affect the usability and of different times of the day (daylight and darkness). We have studied various SJ ticket machines indoors and machines outdoors by the tracks or in the train station building. The SL ticket machines are always placed indoors at metro stations. In the following part the ATMs and the ticket machines are described from their distinctive features. The national railway companies SJ, and Stockholm public transportations, SL, ticket machines are almost like a hybrid between a touchscreen interface and a card slot and keypad module, like an ATM, incorporated into it.

A general observation is that the screens of the ATM and SJ ticket machines are highly affected by the lighting and weather conditions. The use of an outdoor ATM causes problems when the sun is reflected on the screen, it is almost impossible to read the information. When it is dark in late afternoons and evenings, the shield aimed to protect unauthorized from getting access to the pin code shadows the upper part of the keypad causing problems for the user to see it. However, SL ticket machines do have shields they do not really protect the PIN code, since the keypads are exposed for people that pass by.

ATM. The ATM type that has been studied is made by Bankomat AB which is a chain based on a collaboration between several banks in Sweden. Depending on what bank a customer is connected to it is possible not only to withdraw money, but also make cash deposits, bank statements, transfer between accounts and change PIN. All Bankomats in Sweden have the same interface. The ATMs are typically placed inside shopping centers, at railway stations, outside banks and in strategical places in cities, close to shops, cafés and restaurants. However, in small towns there is a tendency that the ATMs are removed because of the frequent use of cards for payment in Swedish shops and in addition many shops do not accept cash any longer.

1. Finding Machine. Most ATMs can be found by means of a blue sign with white letters with the name Bankomat on. The sign is illuminated, to be visible in the dark. The ATMs are all intercalated in the wall, either with light from above or only by light from the screen. The sign is not always visible from all directions. Not all of them protrude from the wall.

2. Primary Choices. The welcome screen switches between "Welcome to Bankomat" and "Insert your card". When the card has been inserted the instruction reads "Enter your PIN code and 'Done'". There is also a reminder to protect the code. The PIN code has to be entered on a keyboard that is partly covered by a shield for protection. The shield not only protects from unauthorized people to see the code, it also shadows the upper part of the keypad.

3. Action Requests. Once the correct PIN code has been entered the user is asked to choose or enter the amount of money to withdraw. This can be done by quick choices on the screen. Bankomats do not have touch screens so choices are made by pressing buttons on the sides of the screen. The amount can also be typed in by using the keypad under the screen. The user can choose to get a receipt or not.

4. Completion. First the card is given back, then the cash is presented to the user, and finally the receipt if this option was chosen.

Ticket Machines. SJ is a state-owned train operator in Sweden. Several of the large train stations in Sweden are included in what is called *Resecentrum* (travel centre). The travel center is the coordination of traffic and service in and around a railway station. The concept includes trains, buses, taxis and car parking and takes place in collaboration between train operators, property owners, county transport companies and municipalities. The purpose of the travel center is to facilitate passenger transitions between different types of traffic. A travel center usually contains a railway station and a bus station for long-distance buses and local buses and is often located slightly on the outskirts of the city center. The hub for local buses may be located elsewhere, at the city's central square. During the 19th century, railway stations were built on the outskirts of the city of that time to avoid demolishing buildings. SJ ticket machines have been observed at various Resecentrum in Mälardalen and in Stockholm on several occasions.

1. Finding Machine. Typically, there are ticket machines placed indoors, in the main station building waiting area, and outdoors on the platform. This space is often narrow, especially if there is a line or if there are people waiting for a train. The machines indoors are not that hard to find. They are centrally located in the waiting area, which on the other hand is quite narrow and can be crowded at times. However, the SJ automats do not have any signs to guide the user. The only signal is their design and colors, to which one has to be familiar. The outdoor automats are thereby harder to find and reach, since they can be partly hidden and placed close to the train tracks.

2. Primary Choices. The machine is dominated by a touch screen. On the right from the screen is the keypad, and below the keypad is the card reader and a card slot. Under the screen is the slot where printed tickets come out. The start screen normally just shows a welcome sign for SJ, but sometimes represents both SJ (national trains) on the left and Movingo (tickets for regional travel and commuting, also valid on the SJ trains) on the right. This double start screen can be very confusing for those not travelling and using these machines regularly. Under the touch screen there is a sign with a phone number to a help desk, also in braille. Choosing "SJ" on the start screen the user is presented with the SJ welcome screen, which says "Hi, where do you want to go?". The two top choices are "buy tickets" and "collect tickets". Below are two text boxes: "from" on the left and "to" on the right, and the green button says "continue". Destination is typed in on a digital keyboard appearing on the same screen, and there are preselected destinations. Having chosen the destination (the default starting point is the station where the automat is located), the user is presented with a screen reading "Buy the next departure with SJ regional". "Adult" is the default, followed by discount tickets like Student and Senior. On the right the next departure is presented and there is also a choice between first and second class. If one would like to make other choices, such as buying more than one ticket at a different departure time, one would have to find the blue box in the top right corner of the screen.

3. Action Requests. Having chosen the destination, one has to check the box "I accept SJ's Purchasing Conditions" to be able to continue to payment. This is a step that can easily be missed. The there is a request to insert payment card and to follow the instructions on the card terminal on the right where a green lamp blinks for attention and guidance.

4. Completion. When PIN code is typed correctly, paper ticket and receipt are printed and provided in a plastic covered slot below the screen.

Ticket Machine Public Transport in Stockholm, SL. The SL public transport consists of bus, metro, regional and suburban rail, light rail, tram and archipelago boats. It is possible to buy tickets at the ticket center located at the Central station in Stockholm, some of the commuter train stations and the metro stations in the inner city of Stockholm offers the ability to buy tickets a manned ticket counter. Since 2010, SL Access has been the main ticket system for the region of Stockholm. The system uses electronic tickets that are loaded on contactless cards, but it is also possible to buy single paper tickets.

Finding Machine. The machines are placed closed to the latches of the metro stations. There are no machines at bus stops. The machines are grey and typically placed at the wall. The machines are recognized from the blue oval sign with an icon showing a hand holding a card. The machines are placed in an area that are often busy.

Primary Choices. The screen is inserted in the machine which reduce the mirroring from outside. On the right hand-side is the keypad and below is the card reader and the card slot. There is a welcoming text on the screen, and a description of the two offers, to buy a paper ticket or to use the Access card.

Action Request. You can either hold the card at the blue card reader or press on the text "Press here" to buy a paper ticket. The information is available in Swedish and English. After choosing the paper ticket, it is possible to choose from different categories of tickets. The five categories are presented on grey rectangular fields with white text, which make it hard to read. After selecting one category the costumer will gain information about the prize before the confirmation of the purchase. While using the Access card, it should be held against the blue card reader below the screen. The menu that is shown on the display after the card has been read, gives information of the status of the card such as balance. The other part of the screen, with the same layout as the paper tickets alternative, display five alternatives of amounts to load onto the card.

Completion. The last step is to insert the credit card in the card slot and enter the PIN code. The keypad is exposed, and it is hard to protect the PIN code from unauthorized people if there is a queue to the machine. If the alternative was to load money onto the Access card one has to hold it against the blue card reader after the payment with the credit card is finished.

3   Discussion

The Swedish ATM Bankomat AB is part of a complex banking system where it is possible to withdraw many from several bank companies in identical ATMs. The ATMs could be considered as easy to use, but the context and the situation effect the task performance in several ways. The lighting conditions are often bad, and the shield that protect the customers PIN code shadow the keyboards upper line of keys. That hinders the customer to fulfill their task performance since they might experience cognitive complexity that results in cognitive load, because they need to remember the figures that are on the upper line of the keyboard since they are invisible. Since most of the Bankomats are placed outdoors on busy roads in Stockholm where people pass by and at the same time people are queuing for withdrawal of money. This creates a stressful situation for people that need more time than the expected average for individuals to withdraw money. From the Bankomats explored with focus on the placement and the time that is offered in the system to withdraw money before the service is interrupt and requires a restart, the ATM is a stressor by itself. Since stressors leads to perceptual complexity [22], stressors such as bad lighting, busy environment and time pressure could affect customers´ ability to fulfill their task, to withdraw money. In addition, the Bankomats are not very well maintained, the keyboard shields are broken, the ATMs are full of graffiti and the keys are well worn. This contradicts the fact the studies indicating that people found attractive ATMS easy to use.

The train ticket machines are often placed on the tracks or close to the tracks. This seems convenient by a first glance, but in many cases, it is the opposite. The lighting conditions over 24 h and in various weathers affect the ability to read what is on the screen. If the ticket machine lacks some kind of cover the screen is exposed for sun during daytime and for surrounding lights in evenings, both conditions causes mirroring on the screen that creates problems for the customer. Taking into consideration people with partly lost eyesight because of age, they will have severe difficulties reading the text on the screen since it does not support reading disabilities.

SLs Access card machine has several limitations when it comes to usability in practice. Firstly, they are not easy to find since they lack a clear visible sign. Secondly, the alternative presented for the customer on the screen has a very poor layout, the inverted text on the grey rectangular surface is hard to read, the letters are far too small. A stressor for the user of the SL machine is the requirement to end the procedure of loading money on the Access card by holding it to the blue card reader. An old person with weak working memory could easily forget this last step, and by that losing the money drawn from their credit card.

The placement of ATM and ticket machines and lack of clear signs that are visible from long distance makes it hard for old people to find them which requires a lot of physical effort.

4 Conclusions

The findings of this study indicate that there is need for a follow-up of how the automats work in different environments and contexts, with different users. The automats have been tested, for instance in usability testing, with methods such as customer journeys. But it is not likely that they have been tested in different kinds of contexts and environments, considering different lightning conditions and stress.

Only focusing on the digital interface and security will lead to risks of missing out on contextual factors. With all respect to the importance of usable interfaces for withdrawal of money and buying tickets, the paper aims to stress the impact of the context on users perceived cognitive stress in various situations. The goal for the customer is to withdraw money or to obtain a ticket. The first task is to find the machine. There does not exist a common system for placement of signs for the Swedish ATM Bankomat. Recognizing the place for the Bankomat might be problematic for old people, especially if a person has limited eyesight.

The SJ ticket machines can be hard to find when they are placed in narrow passages close to train tracks. They do not have any guiding signs. The SJ ticket machine start screen is sometimes informing about regional travel as well as about national trains, which can be confusing for a non-regular traveler. The SL ticket machines with their grey color are nearly invisible from distance. The second step where the user makes his or her primary choices, the instructions can be unclear since the start screen changes between three different variants. Most ATM keypads have a protecting shield for unauthorized people to see the code being typed. This shield is a problem since it tends to shadow the upper half of the keypad, especially in an outdoor setting. The SJ ticket machines have many choices on destination and different reduced fares. One crucial step to be able to purchase a ticket is to cross the box of accepting terms and conditions. This is a step easily missed. The SJ and SL automats have a multitude of different components: touch screen, keypad and card slot with a small, separate screen, and the slot for tickets and receipts. However, the Bankomat ATMs have a very clear order for completion of the goal where the card is presented first, then the money and lastly, the receipt.

References

1. Hollwich, M.: New Aging: Live Smarter Now to Live Better Forever. Penguin Books, London (2016)
2. Bátiz-Lazo, B.: Emergence and evolution of ATM networks in the UK, 1967–2000. Bus. Hist. **51**(1), 1–27 (2009)
3. Wren, D.: The Evolution of Management Thought. Wiley, New York (1994)
4. Segrave, K.: Vending Machines: An American Social History. McFarland & Company, Jefferson (2002)
5. Handelns historia, Centre for Business History. http://www.handelnshistoria.se/historien/olika-sorters-handel/varuautomaterna. Accessed 21 Feb 2020
6. Sagar, B., Singh, G., Saket, R.: Design concept and network reliability evaluation of ATM system. Int. J. Comput. Aided Eng. Technol. **3**(1), 53–76 (2011)
7. Thodenius, B. (ed.): Uttagsautomater: Transkript av ett vittnesseminarium vid Tekniska museet i Stockholm den 16 januari 2007. Tekniska museet, Stockholm (2008)
8. Directive (EU) 2019/882 of the European Parliament and of the Council of 17 April 2019 on the accessibility requirements for products and services. https://eur-lex.europa.eu/eli/dir/2019/882/oj. Accessed 24 Feb 2020
9. Eriksson, Y., Sjölinder, M.: The role of designers in the development and communication of new technology. In: Sayago, S. (ed.) Perspectives on Human-Computer Interaction Research with Older People. HIS, pp. 37–48. Springer, Cham (2019). https://doi.org/10.1007/978-3-030-06076-3_3
10. Eriksson, Y.: Technologically mature but with limited capabilities. In: Zhou, J., Salvendy, G. (eds.) ITAP 2016. LNCS, vol. 9754, pp. 3–12. Springer, Cham (2016). https://doi.org/10.1007/978-3-319-39943-0_1
11. Norman, D.: The Design of Everyday Things. Basic Books, New York (2013)
12. Chan, C., Wong, A., Lee, T., Chi, I.: Modified automatic teller machine prototype for older adults: a case study of participative approach to inclusive design. Appl. Ergon. **40**(2), 151–160 (2009)
13. Lockton, D., Harrison, D., Stanton, N.: The design with intent method: a design tool for influencing user behaviour. Appl. Ergon. **41**(3), 382–392 (2010)
14. Zimmermann, C., Bridger, R.: Effects of dialogue design on Automatic Teller Machine (ATM) usability: transaction times and card loss. Behav. Inf. Technol. **19**(6), 441–449 (2000)
15. Li, K., Duffy, V., Zheng, L.: Universal accessibility assessments through virtual interactive design. Int. J. Hum. Factors Model. Simul. **1**(1), 52–68 (2006)
16. Marshall, R., et al.: HADRIAN: a virtual approach to design for all. J. Eng. Des. **21**(2–3), 253–273 (2010)
17. Beyer, H., Holtzblatt, K.: Contextual Design: Design for Life, 2nd edn. Elsevier, Cambridge (2016)
18. Carmona, M.: Principles for public space design, planning to do better. Urban Des. Int. **24**, 47–59 (2018)
19. Crowhurst Lennard, S.: Livable Cities Observed. Gondolier Press, Carmel, CA (1995)
20. Corbett, N.: Transforming Cities, Revival in the Square. RIBA, London (2004)
21. Hackos, J., Redish, J.: User and Task Analysis for Interface Design. Wiley, New York (1998)
22. Endsley, M., Jones, D.: Designing for Situation Awareness: An Approach to User-Centered Design, 2nd edn. CRC Press, Boca Raton (2012)
23. Levi, L.: Society, stress and disease. Br. J. Psychiatry **154**(1), 133–134 (1989)

Aging and Mobile and Wearable Devices

Assessing Alternative Text Presentation and Tablet Device Usage for Low Vision Leisure Reading

Erin Gannon[1,2P(✉)], Laura Walker[3,4P], Alex Chaparro[5], and Barbara S. Chaparro[5]

[1] Wichita State University, Wichita, USA
ErinRGannon@gmail.com
[2] Google Inc., Seattle, WA, USA
[3] Envision, Inc., Wichita, USA
[4] Apple, Inc., Cupertino, USA
[5] Embry-Riddle Aeronautical University, Daytona Beach, USA

Abstract. We conducted 3 studies to learn about elements of satisfaction for leisure reading in low vision. Study 1 focused on alternative reading formats such as scrolling text and rapid serial visual presentation (RSVP). Study 2 explored use and satisfaction with alternative formats over time using a tablet device. Study 3 meant to assess prevalence and perceptions of tablet devices as low vision aids for sustained reading. Nine low vision participants used a tablet to read with three presentation types (Page, Scroll, Modified RSVP) over a three-week period. Study 3 involved surveys administered to 73 participants 1–3 months after a vision consultation with a low vision professional in which multiple options for reading devices were demonstrated.

Studies 1 and 2 point to the need to emphasize personal preferences and satisfaction with reading devices, in addition to reading performance. Alternative presentations may be beneficial to certain people with low vision, especially those with difficulties navigating lines of text and controlling eye movements. Study 3 showed that participants were generally satisfied with their reading aids and used them frequently at a 1–3 month follow up. Participants appeared interested in tablets as a reading method, despite many having little to no experience with them prior to the study. Barriers to using a tablet were primarily cost and lack of familiarity.

Keywords: Low vision · Tablets · Reading · Devices

1 Introduction

1.1 What is Low Vision?

The term *low vision* can be defined as chronic form of vision impairment that cannot be corrected with eyeglasses and affects everyday function characterizes low vision (Elliott et al. 1997; Legge 2016). As a heuristic, people with low vision often have trouble

© Springer Nature Switzerland AG 2020
Q. Gao and J. Zhou (Eds.): HCII 2020, LNCS 12207, pp. 259–279, 2020.
https://doi.org/10.1007/978-3-030-50252-2_20

reading newspaper text from 40 cm viewing distance. From a clinical perspective, low vision a best corrected (e.g., eyeglasses or contact lenses) visual acuity worse than 20/60 in the better seeing eye (Legge et al. 1997).

Low vision is a widespread experience. In 2010, low vision affected 246 million people worldwide. The National Eye Institute (2014) estimates between 3.5 and 5 million Americans have some sort of visual impairment, and cases appear to be growing as life expectancy increases (Pascolini and Mariotti 2012). One of the most common causes of visual impairment is age-related macular degeneration (AMD), in which damage to the macula, area of the eye that includes the high-acuity fovea, causes central vision loss. A blind spot, or scotoma, appears that can affect central and/or peripheral vision and make common daily tasks difficult or impossible. The reduced independence that can coincide with central vision loss has been suggested to reduce mental health and quality of life (Casten et al. 2004; Slakter and Stur 2005).

1.2 Central Vision Loss and Reading

Considerable work has been dedicated to the topic of reading with vision loss; loss of central vision, as in the case with common eye diseases like AMD, has been the subject of growing research as the disease increases in prevalence (Smith 2010; Velez-Montoya 2014). Individuals with central vision loss can take advantage of peripheral vision or a preferred retinal locus (PRL) for tasks like reading (Legge et al. 1992; Watson et al. 2006), but it is often significantly slowed and cumbersome.

Because our eyes achieve the highest acuity within $2°$ of central fixation, reading becomes increasingly difficult as acuity drops in the parafovea and periphery. Research involving artificial scotomas have shown the importance of the fovea in reading. By masking the fovea in normally sighted readers, studies have shown that obscuring even one character potentially reduced reading speeds (i.e., increased reading time) by 50%. As a greater number of characters are masked around central fixation, reading speeds continued to suffer (Rayner et al. 1981).

By taking advantage of any residual vision in the parafovea and periphery, even individuals with acuities as low as 20/2000 can read (Legge 2016). As a visual impairment progresses, magnification is rendered ineffective (Chung et al. 1998; Cummings and Rubin 1992). These effects are pronounced in those with AMD and similar pathologies where scotomas prevent readers from seeing parts of words, and can cause them erroneously skip lines of text following regressive eye sweeps (Fletcher et al. 1999; Watson et al. 1990).

Previous work has suggested that people affected by central vision loss make more saccades (rapid eye movements from one fixation point to the next) while reading, and may make multiple saccades in one word (Fig. 1), as opposed to one fixation per word in typically sighted readers (Rubin 2001; Crossland and Rubin 2006). Studies also shown that those with central vision loss demonstrate increased fixations during regressive eye movements (Rubin and Feely 2009), which account for 10–15% of saccades for normally sighted readers, and are usually accomplished in a single saccade (Rayner 1975).

While many studies have focused on the performances differences between typically sighted and low vision readers, work has also been dedicated to the psychological affects of losing reading ability as a result of vision loss. Johnson et al. (2014) found that while

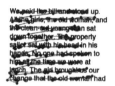 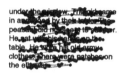 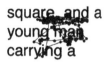

Fig. 1. From left to right: eye movements while reading with a full visual field, reading with a 3.5° scotoma one character to the right of fixation, and a 3.5° scotoma directly over the fixation point.

96% of visually impaired participants enjoyed reading prior to losing their vision, only 36% reported enjoying it after the onset of vision loss. Morrice et al. (2017) replicated these findings.

Reading performance has been suggested as a reliable indicator of vision-related quality of life by Hazel et al. (2000), and reading is often the number one reason low vision patients seek rehabilitation (Rubin 2013). In addition to impacting functional daily activities, reduced reading ability also inhibits many individuals from taking advantage of once-loved hobbies and leisure activities, which has been linked to reduced mental health (Rovner and Casten 2002).

A questionnaire that assesses the effect of macular disease on quality of life implied that leisure activities is one of the most negatively affected domains for people with AMD (Mitchell and Bradley 2004). Mitchell et al. (2002) found that nearly 60% of AMD patients experienced a reduction in the number of leisure activities due to visual impairment since the onset of their vision loss. Prior to their diagnosis, 59% of patients reported enjoying reading. At the time of the study, this number had reduced to 20%. Compared to all other hobbies, reading was the most negatively affected.

1.3 Low Vision Aids

The most common low vision aids (LVAs) for readers with pathologies like AMD are optical magnifiers, which can be handheld or mounted on spectacles or a stand, and may include a light to add more contrast and clarity reading material (Rohrschneider 2013; Watson et al. 1997). Manual, handheld magnifiers allow patients to read a variety of materials such as books, mail, and medicine labels. Stand magnifiers can reduce strain on hands and wrists by allowing users to glide the device as it sits above text (Virgili et al. 2013).

Electronic magnifiers are also beneficial for some, as they offer customizable features and adjustments in lighting and positioning all in one device. For example, electronic magnifiers allow users to change degree of magnification, text and background color, and contrast polarity (Rohrschneider 2013). Research has suggested optical magnifiers are the more common LVAs (Casten et al. 2016), but electronic devices may lead to increased reading speed (Peterson et al. 2003) than optical magnifiers.

1.4 Digital Reading

Modern devices like tablets and e-readers have shown recent promise as reading devices for those with visual impairments. The portability, convenience, and reduced stigma associated with these common devices can be considered advantages over more traditional reading aids. Similar to electronic magnifiers discussed above, tablets and e-readers also afford the user a more customized experience, which is essential for the high variability of reading difficulties observed in low vision populations (Southall and Wittich 2012; Watson et al. 2005).

Since only 1.5% of print books are converted to large print formats that enable those with low vision to read (Lockyer et al. 2005), electronic books offer a virtually endless supply of content compared to print alternatives. Another significant advantage of modern devices is affordability. Many patients are forced to choose between paying out of pocket for their reading aids or simply going without. Kindles are often offered for under $100 compared to $500–$3,000 for many electronic magnifiers. E-books are also often more affordable than print books (Bunkell and Dyas-Correia 2009; Wischenbart et al. 2013).

Research has begun to address the intuitive practical benefits of modern devices for low vision reading. In particular, studies have shown improved reading speeds with iPads compared to print (Gill et al. 2013; Roth et al. 2012) and maintained or improved reading speeds when compared to CCTVs and patients' typical reading aid (Johnson et al. 2014; Feng et al. 2017; Morrice et al. 2017). Another study demonstrated that 94% of patients could read standard newspaper print using a browser zoom feature on an iPad compared to 22% reading with only eyeglasses (Haji et al. 2015).

While work has been done to assess reading performance between digital methods and traditional devices, less is known about the prevalence of using devices like tablets and e-readers. While studies show that older adults (Pew Research Center 2014) and those with low vision (Crossland et al. 2014; Watanabe et al. 2015) are using tablets and e-readers, not many visually impaired older adults are using them as their primary device for reading (Casten et al. 2016). Crossland et al. (2014) found that 48% of survey respondents ($n = 132$) used a tablet device. Of tablet users, 60% used them to read e-books.

One reason for this discrepancy could be awareness; Crossland et al. (2014) found that people with low vision are largely unaware that they can use tablets and e-readers. In fact, lack of awareness was one of the major reasons for not using a tablet or e-reader, alongside cost, perception of difficulty (Fisher and Easton 2019) and lack of interest. Also interesting is that, of those that knew about tablets and e-readers, few participants learned about the efficacy of those devices in clinical or rehabilitation settings. Rather, evidence suggest family and friends may play a greater role in modern device adoption.

More recent research suggests attitudes may be shifting toward a preference for mainstream devices. A recent study (Martiniello et al. 2019) also showed that about half of survey respondents ($n = 466$) used a tablet device, and more severe impairments were more likely to use tablets. Roughly 66% reported using tablets or smartphones specifically for reading e-books, and 87% of the total sample indicated that modern devices are replacing more traditional devices. Interesting to note is the relatively small differences between Crossland et al. (2014)'s study and Martiniello et al. (2019)'s study;

results may indicate that the number of people with low vision using tablets, and using modern digital devices for reading, has not greatly increased since 2014.

Variations in text presentations on electronic devices have also been explored. Given the difficulties in reading and eye movements for people with central vision loss, researchers have evaluated methods like rapid serial visual presentation (RSVP), where individual words are presented serially and flashed in a fixed position on the screen (Potter 1984) and scrolling. These methods allow for maximum text size to take advantage of small screens and reduced need for eye movements to navigate lines of text.

Research has shown modest improvements in reading speed for RSVP compared to traditional static text, if any (Rubin and Turano 1994; Benedetto et al. 2015). Some studies have compared RSVP reading speed with a scrolling text presentation, in which text moves in one line continuously right side of the screen to the left (Legge et al. 1985). Results have shown mixed results, with low vision participants benefitting little from dynamic methods (Fine and Peli 1998; Bowers et al. 2004). However, some research suggests novelty could play a role in reduced performance with these methods (Aquilante et al. 2001), and a modified approach to RSVP that gave users more control over reading speed could be beneficial, elicited sequal presentation (ESP) (Arditi 1999). Also interesting is that dynamic methods have been chosen as the preferred method in reading studies, even when reading performance was less than traditional methods (Bowers et al. 2004; Harvey and Walker 2014; Walker et al. 2016).

The present research is largely anchored on the interest findings from prevalence studies on reading devices usage, as well as studies of performance and preference of low vision reading with traditional vs. modern electronic devices. Given the criticality of reading, hobbies, and their impact on vision-related quality of life, this research aims to emphasize leisure reading rather than strictly functional reading. This work employed multiple methods to understand contributing factors to reading satisfaction, as well as usage and perceptions of devices like tablets and e-readers as reading aids for low vision.

2 Study 1: Alternative Text Presentations in Typical and Low Vision

2.1 Purpose

Study 1 aimed to evaluate five text presentation methods on a tablet to assess performance and satisfaction between typically sighted and low vision readers. Our specific research questions were:

1) How does reading on a tablet compare to participants' current reading method in terms of satisfaction with reading?
2) Do low vision readers benefit from alternative text presentations in terms of satisfaction with reading?
3) What factors contribute to satisfaction and preference between reading methods?

2.2 Method

Participants. 10 typically sighted (TS) participants via email using a subscription database provided by Wichita State University. All participants met the following inclusion criteria: age 50 or older (*Range* = 59–80, *M* = 68.30, *SD* = 7.33), native English speaker, and no history of ocular disease with the exception of removed cataracts.

Nine low vision (LV) participants were recruited via referrals from Envision Research Institute in Wichita, Kansas. LV patients met the same age (*Range* = 59–101, *M* = 73.89, *SD* = 12.56) and language criteria as the TS group, but were diagnosed with a visual impairment.

Text Presentation. A 10.1" Lenovo Yoga Tab 3 was used for text presentation. This tablet was chosen for its screen size and flexible kickstand that allows the tablet to be propped up on a surface for hands-free use. Android applications were developed to display each text presentation method using Java and the Android SDK.

Five text presentations were compared: A traditional Page presentation (static paragraph text that would be found on a typical e-reader), Scroll, RSVP, Modified RSVP (RSVP where longer words appeared on the screen for longer than shorter words), and ESP (participants tapped the screen to elicit each individual word).

Reading Material. Fifteen text passages and comprehension questions were adapted from *501 Comprehension Questions* (Learning Express, LLC 2006) and modified to fit 150–200 words in length (*M* = 174.90, *SD* = 21.12) and under a 12th grade reading level (*M* = 10.62, *SD* = 0.61) according to the Flesch-Kinkaid Grade Level Formula (Flesch 1994). The order of experimental passages was counterbalanced, while practice passages remained consistent between participants.

Text Size and Reading Speed. Participants were allowed to adjust text size and speed to their comfort during a practice passage prior to beginning each presentation method. The preferred size and speed were used for the remaining experimental passages. Initial text size was set to 32 pt font. Scroll speed began at 160 WPM, while RSVP and Modified RSVP began at 250 WPM. Reading speed was automatically recorded on a text file saved to the tablet.

Measures. Clinical features were assessed with the MNRead Acuity Chart. Comprehension was measured with one multiple choice question following each passage. Reading satisfaction and overall preference were assessed with questionnaires.

Procedure. Participants were able to choose whether to hold the tablet or rest it on the table while reading. One practice passage was performed to let participants get used the presentation method and customize their settings for speed. When necessary, the experimenter read comprehension questions aloud to low vision participants. Each participant read using all five presentation methods and order effects were reduced using partial counterbalancing as suggested by Goodwin and Goodwin (2013). Participants completed the satisfaction questionnaire following each presentation type. After reading with all methods, participants were interviewed about their experience with each method, overall preference, and comfort reading with a tablet.

2.3 Results

Performance. A 2 × 5 mixed-model ANOVA was conducted to assess the effects of vision type (LV or TS) and text presentation type on reading speed. Results showed a significant main effect for vision type, in which LV readers ($M = 87.63$, $SD = 40.62$) read more slowly than TS ($M = 172.09$, $SD = 77.70$), $F(1, 81) = 35.27$, $p < .001$, p2 $= 0.32$. We also found a significant main effect for presentation type, $F(4, 81) = 3.73$, $p < .001$, p2 $= 0.17$. Tukey's HSD revealed that Page ($M = 188.49$, $SD = 94.08$) was read significantly faster than all other presentations: ESP ($M = 111.83$, $SD = 64.52$), RSVP ($M = 127.07$, $SD = 71.77$), Scroll ($M = 96.29$, $SD = 47.48$), and Modified RSVP ($M = 134.28$, $SD = 68.15$). The vision type × presentation type interaction was not significant, $F(4, 81) = 2.08$, $p > .05$. See Fig. 2.

Reading Speed

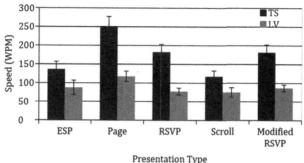

Fig. 2. The Page method was read significantly faster than the alternatives by both LV and TS groups. Error bars represent standard error of the mean.

A 2 × 5 mixed-model ANOVA was conducted to assess the effect of vision type and presentation type on comprehension scores. No significant main effect was found for vision type, $F(1,123) = 1.69$, $p = .20$ or presentation type, $F(4,123) = 0.22$, $p = .93$. The interaction between vision type and presentation type was also not significant, $F(1,123) = 1.58$. $p = .18$.

Satisfaction. Wilcoxon-Mann-Whitney tests were done to assess differences in reading satisfaction between LV and TS groups. Participants rated each presentation type with respect to overall satisfaction compared to their current reading method on a 5-point scale (1 = Significantly worse, 5 = Significantly better). LV participants reported higher satisfaction than TS with Scroll ($Z = 2.03$, $p = .04$, $r = 0.47$), Modified RSVP ($Z = 2.14$, $p = .03$, $r = 0.49$), and Page ($Z = 2.76$, $p = .01$, $r = 0.63$), but these differences were not significant after a Bonferroni correction. No significant differences were found between LV and TS in ratings for RSVP ($Z = 1.30$, $p = .23$) or ESP ($Z = 1.97$, $p = .06$).

Ratings of overall preference indicated similar patterns for each group; Page (84% of all participants ranked Page first: 90% of TS, 78% of LV), Scroll (63% overall: 70% of TS, 56% of LV), Modified RSVP (42% overall: 30% of TS, 56% of LV), RSVP (63% overall: 50% of TS, 78% of LV), ESP (58% overall: 40% of TS, 78% of LV). See Fig. 3.

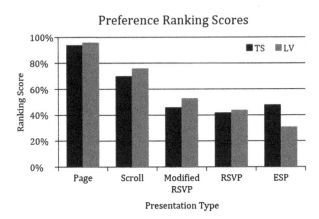

Fig. 3. Most participants preferred Page over all over methods.

2.4 Discussion

Results imply similar performance and satisfaction ratings for TS and LV groups with this small sample. It is worth noting that LV participants reported higher satisfaction with the alternative methods than the TS group, implying there may be value in these methods overall for certain LV readers. Qualitatively, LV participants responded positively to reading with a tablet. This is a promising finding for the potential of tablet devices as reading aids. Further research is need to determine what clinical features may be consistent with higher perceptions of mainstream digital reading aids.

3   Study 2: Prolonged Use of Electronic Text Presentations

3.1   Purpose

To understand the effect of novelty on satisfaction ratings with various text presentation methods, we conducted a longer-term study using a diary methodology with three of the five formats tested in Study 1: Page, Scroll, and modified RSVP. With this applied design, we learned how satisfaction changes over time with an electronic reading method and with using alternative text presentations. Our specific research questions were: 1) Will prolonged use of a tablet and alternative text presentations affect attitudes toward reading with those methods over time? 2) In terms of typical reading behaviors and satisfaction, how will using the tablet and the various text presentations compare to participants' current reading method? 3) What factors contribute to satisfaction and preference between reading methods? 4) Will participants develop any strategies to or adaptive behaviors to adjust to the new reading methods?

3.2 Method

Participants. Nine participants (6 female, 3 male) with low vision were recruited through referrals from Envision Research Institute in Wichita, Kansas. Participants were over age 50 ($M = 66.44$, $SD = 8.80$, *Range* $= 24$), fluent English speakers, and had a diagnosed visual impairment.

Text Presentation. Stimuli and tablet used were the same as those used in Study 1.

Reading Materials. Participants selected books upon being invited to the study. Each chosen book was downloaded onto the tablet and formatted for the app.

Measures. Satisfaction questionnaires were administered to understand enjoyment, likelihood of using that method, and satisfaction compared to their current reading method. Participants reported on satisfaction before and after using each text presentation method. Overall preference rankings between the three presentations were collected at the end of the study.

Procedure. The diary design was arranged into a total of four in-person meetings with each participant over the course of three weeks, and two interviews by phone each week. Each participant experienced each format for one week. The order of formats was counterbalanced using the same method as Study 1. Table 1 outlines the study timeline and procedures.

Table 1. Diary design structure.

Week 1		Week 2		Week 3	
Meeting 1	2 Phone interviews	Meeting 2	2 Phone interviews	Meeting 3	2 Phone interviews
Informed consent MNRead Demographics First impressions of text format 1	Estimated reading time per day Feature use Likes/dislikes about text format 1	End of week impressions of text format 1 First impressions of text format 2	Estimated reading time per day Feature use Likes/dislikes about text format 2	End of week impressions of text format 2 First impressions of text format 3	Estimated reading time per day Feature use Likes/dislikes about text format 3

3.3 Results

Inductive thematic analysis was done on qualitative data (Braun and Clarke 2006). Analysis was performed using the Reframer tool from Optimal Workshop (Optimal Workshop 2018). Two researchers conducted qualitative coding prior to analysis. Data

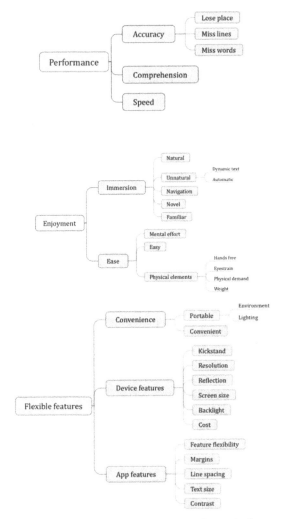

Fig. 4. Themes from Study 2 qualitative analysis.

analysis resulted in 40 unique codes. These codes were categorized into four broad themes: Performance, Enjoyment, Flexible Features, and Personal Factors. Figure 4 breaks down each theme and corresponding codes.

Performance referred to the functional, objectively measurable features of reading such as accuracy, comprehension, and speed. Enjoyment describes the pleasure associated with the reading experience, including how immersed the reader felt in the book and how easy reading felt. Flexible features referred to the physical device as well as the subjective assessment of customizability of features offered by the tablet. Three sub-themes emerged from Flexible Features: Convenience (how portable and convenient the tablet was), Device Features (e.g., kickstand, resolution), and App Features (e.g., feature flexibility, text size, margins). The final theme, Personal Factors, involved two subthemes: Determination and Awareness. These were intrinsic characteristics that varied from participant to participant but affected their respective reading experience. Determination describes the perseverance and desire to continue reading despite visual difficulty, and Awareness describes the degree to which participants knew about possible reading techniques for low vision.

Themes were consolidated into a model that describes drivers to reading satisfaction with this sample. See Fig. 5.

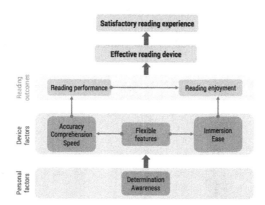

Fig. 5. Qualitative model for reading satisfaction.

The two personal factors, Determination and Awareness, were the first fundamental elements that contributed to the model. Participants were most successful when they were intrinsically determined to continue reading, but they also need to have access to a technique that met their unique needs.

Once the foundation was laid for successful reading by personal factors, the characteristics of the device came into play. A key feature was flexibility of features, as each participant had individual needs based on their vision difficulties, which allows for more accurate and efficient reading. Feature flexibility also led to more immersive, easy reading by allowing readers to concentrate on the book and reduce cumbersome distraction from visual deficiencies. These benefits contributed to two key outcomes for satisfactory reading: reading performance and reading enjoyment.

Reading performance resulted from accuracy, comprehension, and efficiency, the more functional and objectively measurable aspects of reading. If reading was too difficult or slow, readers could not enjoy the text given the frustrating lack of performance; therefore, successful perceived performance leads to greater enjoyment of reading. A satisfactory reading experience could be reached when readers reported both high reading performance and enjoyment.

Data collected via closed-ended survey questions were analyzed using R (R Core Team 2013). Due to the small sample size, ordinal scales, and violations of normality observed in the distributions, nonparametric tests were applied. The Aligned Rank Transform (ART) procedure (Wobbrock et al. 2011) was used in R (Kay and Wobbrock 2016) to format the data as aligned ranks to examine the effect of time and presentation type on participant satisfaction ratings. A 2 × 3 repeated-measures ANOVA was then performed on the ranked scores.

To assess how presentation type and time affect comparisons to their typical method, participants were asked to rate each method on a 5-point scale before and after using each method. A main effect of presentation type was found, $F(2, 40) = 8.30, p < .001$, p2 = 0.29. Tukey's post hoc tests revealed that page (*Median* = 4.0, *IQR* = 3–5) was rated significantly higher than both modified RSVP (*Median* = 1.5, *IQR* = 1–4) and scroll (*Median* = 3.5, *IQR* = 2.5–5). There was no significant main effect for time, $F(1, 40) = 0.12, p = .773$, nor a significant interaction between presentation type and time, $F(2, 40) = 1.08, p = .350$. See Fig. 6. Violin plots show box plots within mirrored kernel density estimates, depicting a smoothed histogram to detail the underlying distribution.

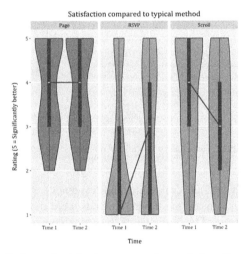

Fig. 6. Ratings of satisfaction compared to typical reading method.

Enjoyment was measured on a 7-point scale at the beginning and end of each week. A main effect of presentation type was found, $F(2, 40) = 26.12, p < .001$ p2 = 0.57. Tukey's post hoc tests revealed that page (*Median* = 7.0, *IQR* = 7–7) was rated higher in enjoyment than both modified RSVP (*Median* = 4, *IQR* = 1–6) and scroll (*Median* = 5.0, *IQR* = 4.25–6). There was not a significant main effect for time, $F(1, 40) = 0.02$, $p = .882$, nor a significant interaction between presentation type and time, $F(2, 40) = 1.73, p = .190$.

We also asked participants to rate their likelihood to continue using each presentation type as a long term reading method before and after reading with each presentation. A main effect of presentation type was found, $F(2, 40) = 52.65, p < .001$, p2 = 0.72. Tukey's post hoc tests revealed that page (*Median* = 7.0, *IQR* = 7–7) was rated higher than both modified RSVP (*Median* = 1.0, *IQR* = 1–5) and scroll (*Median* = 4.5, *IQR* = 2–5.75). There was not a significant main effect for time, $F(1, 40) = 0.02, p .392$. A significant interaction between presentation type and time was also found, $F(2, 40) = 4.10, p = .024$, p2 = 0.17. Contrast tests (Kay 2016) were done to determine differences between comparisons. Results showed that the difference between modified RSVP and scroll at time 1 differed significantly from the difference between modified RSVP and scroll at time 2.

Median ratings for page and modified RSVP indicate these methods would encourage them to read more often, though no significant differences were found with a Nemenyi test (Demšar 2006).

Participants ranked each method in terms of preference after completing all three methods. A Friedman test found a significant effect, $\chi^2(2) = 15.2, p < .001$. The Nemenyi test showed that page (*Median* = 1.0, *IQR* = 1–1) was ranked significantly higher than modified RSVP (*Median* = 3.0, *IQR* = 2–3). No other comparisons were significant. Rankings followed the same pattern as Study 1, wherein Page was ranked as first (best) preference, Scroll second, and modified RSVP third. To represent these results, scores were calculated with the same reverse-scale method as Study 1.

Results from a Wilcoxon signed-rank test showed that ratings of tablet comfort improved from the beginning (*Median* = 5.0, *IQR* = 4–6) to the end (*Median* = 7.0, *IQR* = 6–7) of the study, $Z = 3.74, p < .001, r = 1.25$.

3.4 Discussion

One of the primary findings from the qualitative data is the importance of intrinsic factors in determining reading satisfaction. In particular, awareness may be a key reason why many people low vision are dissatisfied with their reading experience. Four of the nine participants were not aware tablets could be used for reading before participating in the study. Despite tablets being a novel method for some, most participants preferred the tablet to their original method.

Another consistent finding was the common comparison to "natural" reading. RSVP and Scroll were most often criticized for feeling too "unnatural" or "robotic." These results suggest emulating natural reading and giving participants control of pace and display characteristics could be critical to satisfaction. The ability to pause and move backwards in text was also important.

Similar to Study 1, we found that alternative text presentations may benefit a subset of low vision readers. Page was still the preferred method overall, which can be explained by our qualitative model: Page retained a sense of natural reading and allowed flexibility to improve reading performance by allowing them to easily re-read text, thus preserving both reading enjoyment and performance.

Quantitatively, we saw that Page was the consistently preferred method and that ratings for modified RSVP increased slightly with time. Studies with larger sample sizes may be able to better determine whether a statistically significant difference exists. Scroll was consistently rated in second place, likely due to its retention of some 'natural' features reminiscent of Page. Results also suggested that a tablet method is a promising alternative to traditional devices and satisfaction with use may increase with exposure.

4 Study 3: Awareness, Usage, and Satisfaction with of Low Vision Reading Aids

4.1 Purpose

Studies 1 and 2 showed the potential benefit of tablets as low vision reading aids. Study 3 acted in part to generalize the findings of the small-sample previous studies, and to further explore why tablets may be under-utilized as a reading method by those with low vision. We surveyed low vision patients to understand the devices offered by their practitioners, their usage of them, and satisfaction after at least one month of use. Research questions included:

1) Which reading devices are low vision patients exposed to at an initial consultation?
2) Which devices are being used as reading aids for those with low vision?
3) What factors contribute to choice of device for leisure reading following an initial consultation?
4) What is the state of satisfaction and use of the selected device one month after the consultation?
5) What is the nature of the training patients receive with their selected device?
6) What are patients' perceptions of tablets as leisure reading devices for low vision?

4.2 Method

Participants. Participants were 73 (38 female, 35 male) patient referrals from five agencies: Envision (Wichita, Kansas), Lighthouse Louisiana, New View Oklahoma, Ensight Skills Center (Fort Collins, Colorado), and Vista Center for the Blind and Visually Impaired (Palo Alto, California). Patients were all over age 50 ($M = 76.67$, $SD = 11.76$, $Range = 47$), had a diagnosed visual impairment, and were native English speakers. Data were collected from patients who did ($n = 37$) and did not ($n = 36$) begin using a new device for leisure reading following their consultation appointment.

Materials. Participants were contacted by phone and offered the survey by paper or an online survey developed with Qualtrics. Online surveys were dispersed via email. Surveys were also conducted by phone at the participant's request upon receiving the phone by paper or email.

Procedure. The survey was administered 1–3 months after participants' consultation with a low vision rehabilitation professional or clinician in which they selected a new device for the specific purpose of leisure reading. If participants did not select a new device for leisure reading, they were given a condensed version of the full survey that asked about their last appointment and their attitudes about tablets as reading aids.

4.3 Results

Results regarding devices demonstrated at the consultation appointment suggested hand-held magnifiers as the most commonly suggested device, followed by audio books and reading glasses. Fifteen people (21.4%) reported seeing a tablet, and only 5 (7.1%) reported being offered an e-reader as a reading option.

Participants that began using a new device after their consultation were asked which device they selected at their appointment. Patients who did not select a new device were asked which device they currently use for leisure reading, if any. Results showed that handheld magnifiers were the most common, followed by eyeglasses and audio books. Four people (5.8%) reported using a tablet as their primary reading aid, and only one (1.4%) reported using an e-reader (Fig. 7). This pattern was similar when looking at data only for those that selected a new reading device at the last consultation.

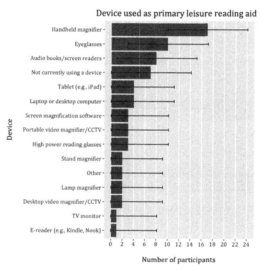

Fig. 7. Primary device used for leisure reading. These data include both participants who did and did not select a new device at their last consultation. Error bars represent 95% confidence intervals $n = 69$.

Participants who did not select a new device did so mostly due to giving up reading due to visual decline (16, 44.4%), followed by lack of confidence in the proposed devices' effectiveness (13, 36.1%).

Patients who selected a new device reported which factors most contributed to their decision. Median ratings suggested that ease of use, portability, and recommendations by the low vision/rehabilitation professional were important factors (Fig. 8). Satisfaction ratings for new leisure reading devices revealed that participants were generally satisfied with aspects besides speed. See Fig. 9.

Most participants (30, 88.2%) indicated they were still using the same device they initially selected multiple times per day (19, 65.5%), and 28.6% were using the device for more than 60 min in one sitting.

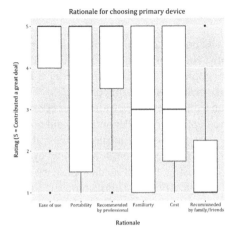

Fig. 8. Rationale for selecting the primary leisure reading aid $n = 24$–31.

Fig. 9. Satisfaction with primary leisure reading aid $n = 29$–31.

Most participants felt they received adequate training with their device, despite most patients receiving no additional training (16, 55.2%).

Participants generally had little familiarity with tablets prior to the study (33, 57.9%). Of those with knowledge of tablets, most learned through friends and family (27, 55.1%). About half of participants were aware that tablets could be used for low vision reading.

After seeing a description and photo of a tablet as a reading aid, participants were asked about their perceptions of the device as a reading option for them. Results indicated relatively high interest, with over 50% of participants reporting a response of at least "Somewhat agree".

4.4 Discussion

Results about devices provisioned confirmed expectations that handheld magnifiers would be the most common suggestions. It's clear there is still a preference for more traditional devices in consultation appointments compared to modern electronic devices. The findings regarding rationale for not selecting a new reading device suggest that participants may not be finding adequate solutions that suit their needs, resulting in ceasing leisure reading altogether. This lack of suitable solutions could be the result of many factors, including visual diagnosis, personal factors like determination, or lack of awareness/options demonstrated at the consultation. Further research should examine the potential causes for deciding against a reading device during rehabilitation.

Satisfaction with selected devices was generally high, with the exception of speed. This dissatisfaction with speed is consistent with qualitative findings from Studies 1 and 2. Patients reported using their devices frequently and for long periods of time in one sitting; this suggests more work is warranted to ensuring devices will work well for prolonged use. Handheld magnifiers, for example, may not be the best solution for extended reading due to the physical demands.

Tablets and e-readers were evaluated positively, even when participants weren't previously ware of the option. Given past research, it is not surprising tablets and e-readers were not often recommended as reading devices. Given the promising work demonstrating higher reading performance and satisfaction, these results suggest more time should be dedicated to modern electronic devices during rehabilitation appointments.

5 General Discussion

In contrast to much of the previous work on low vision reading, this series of studies focused primarily on subjective aspects of reading and satisfaction with leisure reading. In conjunction with past studies implying the importance of leisure activities and sustained desire to continue reading despite visual impairment, our results suggest leisure reading should be more seriously considered as a use case. In particular, results suggest clinicians and low vision professionals can help increase awareness about modern electronic devices as reading aids. As noted in prior research (Longenecker Rust and Smith 2004), more work is necessary to develop a comprehensive, well-defined metric for LVA satisfaction. More rigorously defining satisfaction and developing a reliable measurement tool would aid in the standardization called for in rehabilitation programs (Adelsberger et al. 2014; Smallfield et al. 2013).

Studies 1 and 2 suggested that a traditional e-reader format will likely outperform alternative text presentations for most low vision readers, though experience may help with satisfaction. Study 3 confirmed the viability of tablets and e-readers as reading aids, showing that many patients expressed interest in a tablet or e-reader. Despite interest, these devices were under-utilized by low vision professionals in practice.

LVAs are often used for more than just one task (Watson et al. 1997). One possible reason for this under-utilization is that clients are selecting a more general-purpose device rather than using one device for all reading needs. If patients think they must choose either functional or leisure reading, function could be more important. Some experts do recommend patients select multiple devices to serve distinct purposes (Switliski 2007; Watson et al. 1997).

Given that work in this tablet/e-reader space is also relatively new, it could also be that more time is needed to make practical change with respect to device provision. More research demonstrating the need for leisure reading as a use case and the advantages of mainstream devices would be beneficial in moving this work forward.

References

Adelsberger, J., Bertolet, A., Humphreys, E., Kreydin, I., Woodward, H., Zebrowski, J.: Bridging the Gap: Improving the Efficacy of Referrals from Primary Care Optometrists to Low Vision Specialists. NECO Public Health Poster Repository (2014). http://necopublichealthposters.omeka.net/items/show/533

Aquilante, K., Yager, D., Morris, R.A., Khmelnitsky, F.: Low-vision patients with age-related maculopathy read RSVP faster when word duration varies according to word length. Optom. Vis. Sci. **78**(5), 290–296 (2001)

Arditi, A.: Elicited sequential presentation for low vision reading. Vis. Res. **39**(26), 4412–4418 (1999)

Benedetto, S., Carbone, A., Pedrotti, M., Le Fevre, K., Bey, L.A.Y., Baccino, T.: Rapid serial visual presentation in reading: the case of Spritz. Comput. Hum. Behav. **45**, 352–358 (2015)

Bowers, A.R., Woods, R.L., Peli, E.: Preferred retinal locus and reading rate with four dynamic text presentation formats. Optom. Vis. Sci. **81**(3), 205–213 (2004)

Braun, V., Clarke, V.: Using thematic analysis in psychology. Qual. Res. Psychol. **3**(2), 77–101 (2006)

Bunkell, J., Dyas-Correia, S.: E-books vs. print: which is the better value? Serials Libr. **56**(1–4), 215–219 (2009)

Casten, R.J., Rovner, R.C.W., Fontenot, J.L.: Targeted vision function goals and use of vision resources in ophthalmology patients with age-related macular degeneration and comorbid depressive symptoms. J. Vis. Impair. Blind. **110**(6), 413–424 (2016)

Casten, R.J., Rovner, B.W., Tasman, W.: Age-related macular degeneration and depression: a review of recent research. Curr. Opin. Ophthalmol. **15**(3), 181–183 (2004)

Chung, S.T., Mansfield, J.S., Legge, G.E.: Psychophysics of reading XVIII: the effect of print size on reading speed in normal peripheral vision. Vis. Res. **38**(19), 2949–2962 (1998)

Crossland, M.D., Rubin, G.S.: Eye movements and reading in macular disease: further support for the shrinking perceptual span hypothesis. Vis. Res. **46**(4), 590–597 (2006)

Crossland, M.D., Silva, R., Macedo, A.F.: Smartphone, tablet computer and e-reader use by people with vision impairment. Ophthalmic Physiol. Opt. **34**(5), 552–557 (2014)

Cummings, R.W., Rubin, G.S.: Reading speed and saccadic eye movements with an artificial paracentral scotoma. Invest. Ophthalmol. Vis. Sci. **33**, 1418 (1992)

Demšar, J.: Statistical comparisons of classifiers over multiple data sets. J. Mach. Learn. Res. **7**, 1–30 (2006)

Elliott, D.B., Trukolo-Ilic, M., Strong, J.G., Pace, R., Plotkin, A., Bevers, P.: Demographic characteristics of the vision-disabled elderly. Invest. Ophthalmol. Vis. Sci. **38**(12), 2566–2575 (1997)

Feng, H.L., Roth, D.B., Fine, H.F., Prenner, J.L., Modi, K.K., Feuer, W.J.: The impact of electronic reading devices on reading speed and comfort in patients with decreased vision. J. Ophthalmol. (2017)

Fine, E.M., Peli, E.: Benefits of rapid serial visual presentation (RSVP) over scrolled text vary with letter size. Optom. Vis. Sci. **75**(3), 191–196 (1998)

Fisher, K., Easton, K.: The meaning and value of digital technology adoption for older adults with sight loss: a mixed methods study. Technol. Disabil. **30**(4), 177–184 (2019)

Flesch, R.: The Art of Readable Writing. John Wiley, Hoboken (1994)

Fletcher, D.C., Schuchard, R.A., Watson, G.: Relative locations of macular scotomas near the PRL: effect on low vision reading. J. Rehabil. Res. Dev. **36**(4), 356–364 (1999)

Gill, K., Mao, A., Powell, A.M., Sheidow, T.: Digital reader vs print media: the role of digital technology in reading accuracy in age-related macular degeneration. Eye **27**(5), 639–643 (2013)

Goodwin, C.J., Goodwin, K.A.: Research Methods in Psychology, 7th edn. John Wiley, Hoboken (2013)

Haji, S.A., Sambhav, K., Grover, S., Chalam, K.V.: Evaluation of the iPad as a low vision aid for improving reading ability. Clin. Ophthalmol. **9**, 17–20 (2015)

Harvey, H., Walker, R.: Reading with peripheral vision: a comparison of reading dynamic scrolling and static text with a simulated central scotoma. Vis. Sci. **98**, 54–60 (2014)

Hazel, C.A., Latham, P.K., Armstrong, R.A., Benson, M.T., Frost, N.A.: Visual function and subjective quality of life compared in subjects with acquired macular disease. Invest. Ophthalmol. Vis. Sci. **41**, 1309–1315 (2000)

Johnson, A., Nadon, C., Morrice, E., Marinier, J., Overbury, O., Wittich, W.: The effectiveness of the Apple iPad as a reading tool for individuals with low vision. Visibility **9**, 12–13 (2014)

Kay, M.: Contrast tests with ART, 24 October 2016. https://cran.r-project.org/web/packages/ARTool/vignettes/art-contrasts.html

Kay, M., Wobbrock, J.: ARTool: aligned rank transform for nonparametric factorial ANOVAs. R package version 0.10.4. (2016)

Learning Express, LLC: 501 Comprehension Questions, 3rd edn. LearningExpress, LLC, New York (2006)

Legge, G.E.: Reading digital with low vision. Vis. Lang. **50**(2), 103–124 (2016)

Legge, G.E., Ahn, S.J., Klitz, T.S., Luebker, A.: Psychophysics of reading XVI: the visual span in normal and low vision. Vis. Res. **37**(14), 1999–2010 (1997)

Legge, G.E., Ross, J.A., Isenberg, L.M., Lamay, J.M.: Psychophysics of reading: clinical predictors of low-vision reading speed. Invest. Ophthalmol. Vis. Sci. **33**, 677–687 (1992)

Legge, G.E., Rubin, G.S., Pelli, D.G., Schleske, M.M.: Psychophysics of reading II: low vision. Vis. Res. **25**, 253–266 (1985)

Lockyer, S., Creaser, C., Davies, J.E.: Availability of accessible publications: designing a methodology to provide reliable estimates for the Right to Read Alliance. Health Inf. Libr. J. **22**(4), 243–252 (2005)

Longenecker Rust, K., Smith, R.O.: Satisfaction with assistive technology: what are we measuring? In: Conference Proceedings from the 27th International Conference on Technology & Disability. Paper Presented at the RESNA 27th International Annual Conference, Orlando, FL (2004)

Martiniello, N., Eisenbarth, W., Lehane, C., Johnson, A., Wittich, W.: Exploring the use of smartphones and tablets among people with visual impairments: are mainstream devices replacing the use of traditional visual aids? Assist. Technol. (2019). https://doi.org/10.1080/10400435.2019.1682084

Mitchell, J., Bradley, C.: Design of an individualised measure of the impact of macular disease on quality of life (the MacDQoL). Qual. Life Res. **13**(6), 1163–1175 (2004)

Mitchell, J., Bradley, P., Anderson, S.J., Ffytche, T., Bradley, C.: Perceived quality of health care in macular disease: a survey of members of the macular disease society. Br. J. Ophthalmol. **86**(7), 777–781 (2002)

Morrice, E., Johnson, A.P., Marinier, J.A., Wittich, W.: Assessment of the Apple iPad as a low-vision reading aid. Eye **31**(6), 1–7 (2017)

National Eye Institute: National Plan for Eye and Vision Research (2014). https://nei.nih.gov/sites/default/files/nei-pdfs/nationalplan1.pdf. Accessed 1 April 2018

Optimal Workshop (2018). https://www.optimalworkshop.com/reframer

Pascolini, D., Mariotti, S.P.: Global estimates of visual impairment: 2010. Br. J. Ophthalmol. **96**(5), 614–618 (2012)

Peterson, R.C., Wolffsohn, J.S., Rubinstein, M., Lowe, J.: Benefits of electronic vision enhancement systems (EVES) for the visually impaired. Am. J. Ophthal. **136**(6), 1129–1135 (2003)

Potter, M.C.: Rapid serial visual presentation (RSVP): a method for studying language processing. In: Kieras, D., Just, M. (eds.) New Methods in Reading Comprehension Research, pp. 91–118. Erlbaum, Hillsdale (1984)

R Core Team: a language and environment for statistical computing [Computer software]. R Foundation for Statistical Computing, Vienna, Austria (2013). http://www.R-project.org/

Rayner, K.: The perceptual span and peripheral cues in reading. Cognit. Psychol. **7**(1), 65–81 (1975)

Rayner, K., Inhoff, A.W., Morrison, R.E., Slowiaczek, M.L., Bertera, J.H.: Masking of foveal and parafoveal vision during eye fixations in reading. J. Exp. Psychol. Hum. Percept. Perform. **7**(1), 167 (1981)

Rohrschneider, K.: Low vision aids in AMD. In: Holtz, F.G., Pauleikhoff, D., Spaide, R.F., Bird, A.C. (eds.) Age-Related Macular Degeneration, pp. 295–307. Springer-Verlag, Berlin Heidelberg (2013). https://doi.org/10.1007/978-3-642-22107-1_20

Roth, D.B., Feng, H.L., Fernandes, A., Feuer, W., Fine, H. F., Prenner, J.L.: Electronic reading devices increase reading speed and comfort in patients with moderate vision loss. In: Poster Session Presented at 116th Annual Meeting of the American Academy of Ophthalmology, Chicago, IL, November 2012

Rovner, B.W., Casten, R.J.: Activity loss and depression in age-related macular degeneration. Am. J. Geriatr. Psychiatry **10**(3), 305–310 (2002)

Rubin, G.S.: Vision rehabilitation for patients with age related macular degeneration. Eye **15**, 430–435 (2001)

Rubin, G.S.: Measuring reading performance. Vis. Res. **90**, 43–51 (2013)

Rubin, G.S., Feely, M.: The role of eye movements during reading in patients with age-related macular degeneration (AMD). Neuro-Ophthalmology **33**(3), 120–126 (2009)

Rubin, G.S., Turano, K.: Low vision reading with sequential word presentation. Vis. Res. **34**, 1723–1733 (1994)

Slakter, J.S., Stur, M.: Quality of life in patients with age-related macular degeneration: impact of the condition and benefits of treatment. Surv. Ophthalmol. **50**(3), 263–273 (2005)

Smallfield, S., Clem, K., Myers, A.: Occupational therapy interventions to improve the reading ability of older adults with low vision: a systematic review. Am. J. Occup. Therapy **67**(3), 288–295 (2013)

Smith, A.F.: The growing importance of pharmacoeconomics: the case of age-related macular degeneration. Br. J. Ophthalmol. **94**(9), 1116–1117 (2010)

Southall, K., Wittich, W.: Barriers to low vision rehabilitation: a qualitative approach. J. Vis. Impairment Blind. **106**(5), 261–274 (2012)

Switliski, M.: Lack of awareness stymies aid to low-vision patients. Review of Ophthalmology (2007). https://www.reviewofophthalmology.com/article/lack-of-awareness-stymies-aid-to-low-vision-patients

Velez-Montoya, R., Oliver, S.C., Olson, J.L., Fine, S.L., Quiroz-Mercado, H., Mandava, N.: Current knowledge and trends in age-related macular degeneration: genetics, epidemiology, and prevention. Retina **34**(3), 423–441 (2014)

Virgili, G., Acosta, R., Grover, L.L., Bentley, S.A., Giacomelli, G.: Reading aids for adults with low vision. Cochrane Libr. (2013)

Walker, R., Bryan, L., Harvey, H., Riazi, A., Anderson, S.: The value of tablets as reading aids for individuals with central visual field loss: an evaluation of eccentric reading with static and scrolling text. Ophthalmic Physiol. Opt. **36**, 459–464 (2016)

Watanabe, T., Yamaguchi, T., Minatani, K.: Advantages and drawbacks of smartphones and tablets for visually impaired people: analysis of ICT user survey results. IEICE Trans. Inf. Syst. **98**(4), 922–929 (2015)

Watson, G.R., Baldasare, J., Whittaker, S.: The validity and clinical uses of the pepper visual skills for reading test. J. Vis. Impairment Blind. **84**(3), 119–123 (1990)

Watson, G.R., Maino, J., De l'Aune, W.: Comparison of low-vision reading with spectacle-mounted magnifiers. J. Rehabil. Res. Dev. **42**(4), 459 (2005)

Watson, G.R., Schuchard, R.A., De l'Aune, W.R., Watkins, E.: Effects of preferred retinal locus placement on text navigation and development of advantageous trained retinal locus. J. Rehabil. Res. Dev. **43**(6), 761 (2006)

Watson, G.R., Stelmack, J., Maino, J., Long, S.: National survey of the impact of low vision device use among veterans. Optom. Vis. Sci.: Official Publ. Am. Acad. Optom. **74**(5), 249–259 (1997)

Wischenbart, R., Kovač, M., Carrenho, C., Licher, V., Mallya, V.: The Global eBook Report: Current Conditions & Future Projections. Rüdiger Wischenbart Content and Consulting (2013)

Wobbrock, J.O., Findlater, L., Gergle, D., Higgins, J.J.: The aligned rank transform for nonparametric factorial analyses using only ANOVA procedures. In: Conference on Human Factors in Computing Systems – Proceedings. Paper Presented at the 29th Annual CHI Conference on Human Factors in Computing Systems, Vancouver, BC, Canada, pp. 143–146. ACM, May 2011

Understanding Continuous Wearable Technology Use Behavior for Fitness and Self–health Management Among Middle-Aged and Elderly People

Wen-Tsung Ku[1], Hui-Min Lai[2], and Pi-Jung Hsieh[3（✉）]

[1] Department of Physical Medicine and Rehabilitation, St. Martin De Porres Hospital, Chia-Yi, Taiwan, R.O.C.
kib56265@gmail.com
[2] Department of Business Administration, National Taichung University of Science and Technology, Taichung, Taiwan, R.O.C.
hmin.mis@msa.hinet.net
[3] Department of Hospital and Health Care Administration, Chia Nan University of Pharmacy and Science, Tainan, Taiwan, R.O.C.
beerun@seed.net.tw

Abstract. With the increasingly aging population and smart wearable technology advances, fitness exercise and self–health management have become important research topics. Middle-aged and elderly people are considered to be at higher risk of contracting multiple chronic diseases, thus increasing the need for self–health management. Many people have started using wearable devices to monitor their physical activities and improve their health. However, although several studies have examined the factors affecting the adoption of wearable technology, the literature directly related to middle-aged and elderly people's continuous use behavior is scant. Thus, the purpose of this study was to combine the theory of planned behavior and flow theory to explain middle-aged and elderly people's continuous use behavior of wearable technology. A field survey was conducted in Taiwan to collect data from middle-aged and elderly people. A total of 150 valid responses were obtained, constituting a response rate of 75%. The results indicate that attitude, subjective norm, perceived enjoyment, and concentration have positive effects on continuous use behavior, whereas perceived control does not significantly affect it. The results also indicated that perceived enjoyment and concentration have positive effects on attitude. The study has implications for the development of strategies aimed at increasing wearable technology adoption.

Keywords: Aging and technology acceptance · Wearable technology · Flow theory · Theory of planned behavior

1 Introduction

Due to falling birth rates and longer average life expectancy, Taiwan officially became an aged society in 2018, with people aged 65 or older surpassing 14% of the population,

© Springer Nature Switzerland AG 2020
Q. Gao and J. Zhou (Eds.): HCII 2020, LNCS 12207, pp. 280–288, 2020.
https://doi.org/10.1007/978-3-030-50252-2_21

and is estimated to enter the stage of a super-aged society by 2026 [1]. With Taiwan now officially an aged society, as middle-aged and elderly people are considered to be at higher risk of contracting chronic diseases, the need for fitness activities is increasing. Advances in wearable technology and the growing demand on the part of users who wish to take control of their own health has affected the healthcare and technology industries. Wearable technology refers to smart electronic devices that can be worn by a user and often track physical activity [2]. Examples include the Xiaomi Mi Band, the Apple Watch, the Fossil Gen, the Fitbit Inspire/Inspire HR, the Samsung Galaxy Watch, and the TicWatch. Wearable technologies monitor a number of activities, such as running, climbing, bike riding, pool swimming, and golf. They also help users keep track of set daily goals to ensure that they stay active and healthy. Beside tracking user times and pace, they also offer cadence, heart rate, sleep tracking, and aerobic and anaerobic outputs. They provide convenient, smart all-in-one health management tools for maintaining a healthy lifestyle. Thus, it has become possible for middle-aged and elderly people to use wearable technologies that provide accurate health tracking information and foster behaviors that result in significantly improving their health, which in turn reduces medical costs. However, although several prior studies investigated the factors that affect the adoption of wearable technologies [2–4], the literature directly related to middle-aged and elderly people's behavior is scant. However, in the case of middle-aged and elderly people, self–health management is not a leisure activity, but an interactive social and economic process. The existing variables of technology adoption models do not fully reflect the motives of use. Previous research has suggested the need for incorporating additional behavior factors to improve the predictive capacity and explanatory power of these dimensions. The purpose of this study was to fill this research gap by specifically investigating the relationship between continuous use behavior and its antecedents.

A variety of behavior theories can be used to explain health technology adoption. Among them, two theoretical models that have been extensively used to explain individual technology adoption behaviors are the theory of planned behavior (TPB) [5] and flow theory [6]. The theory of planned behavior has been proven successful in explaining individuals' adoption and continuance behavior across various innovative health technologies [7, 8]. Flow theory allows us to capture the elements of motivation related to enjoyment [9]. This study aimed to expand the TPB model by including the variables used in flow theory to explore middle-aged and elderly people's continuous use behavior and explain their intrinsic motivations. From a practical standpoint, this study contributes to the sports, healthcare, and wearable technology industries by offering new insights for promoting wearable technologies, which will in turn motivate individuals to engage more actively in fitness and self–health management activities.

2   Literature Review

2.1   The Theory of Planned Behavior

The theory of reasoned action (TRA) [10] proposes that an individual's behavior is determined by his or her intention to engage in that behavior, and consequently, this intention is a function of the individual's attitude and his or her subjective norm regarding the behavior. Although the TRA has been tested in numerous research contexts, it provides a weak explanation of the essence of individual behavior. Ajzen [5] proposed the TPB to overcome the TRA's limitations regarding behavior over which people have incomplete volitional control. The TPB posits that both attitude and subjective norm (SN) influence behavioral intention, which in turn affects the actual behavior. Perceived behavioral control (PBC) influences both behavioral intention and actual behavior. Behavioral intention refers to the strength of a person's willingness to expend effort when performing certain behavioral activities. Attitude refers to a person's feeling of favorable or unfavorable assessment of a certain behavior. Subjective norm refers to the perceived of important people's opinions about performing or not performing the behavior. Perceived behavioral control is composed of a person's beliefs concerning capability and the controllability of engaging in a certain behavior; it explains the perception of ease or difficulty of performing the behavior. Prior studies found that these three variables can predict and explain an individual's intention to use various innovative health technologies [7, 8].

2.2 Flow Theory

Flow occurs when a person can achieve a task with a purpose, the outcome of which is called an optimal experience. This theory has been used to explain a state in which a person is so involved in a certain activity that nothing else seems to matter [6]. When middle-aged and elderly people use wearable technologies, they can experience flow, as most wearable devices provide experience sports and leisure activity functions (e.g., running, climbing, bike riding, pool swimming, and golf), all of which may offer enjoyment and lead to increased concentration and engagement. Therefore, this study applied flow theory to examine users' continued use of wearable technology. Flow is a complex concept, and prior studies have often measured it through multiple constructs, such as perceived enjoyment, concentration, perceived control, and curiosity [9, 11, 12]. Perceived enjoyment refers to conditions of playfulness under which a person finds an action intrinsically interesting and thus performs it for enjoyment rather than for extrinsic rewards [12]. Concentration refers to a state in which a person loses self-consciousness and becomes absorbed in an activity, and is more intensely aware of his or her mental processes when in a playful condition [12, 13]. Perceived control is similar to PBC in the TPB [11, 13]. Curiosity refers to cases where a person remains curious and tries to achieve technological competence while engaging in an action [12].

3 Research Model

In this study, we used two TPB constructs—attitude and SN—and three flow theory constructs—perceived enjoyment, concentration, and perceived control—to investigate attitude and continuous use intentions of middle-aged and elderly people. Perceived behavioral control of the TPB was not used because, as previously noted, it is similar to flow theory's perceived control. Curiosity was also excluded, as it less relevant to fitness and self–health management experiences. Figure 1 presents the proposed research model.

Attitude is a person's general feeling about the desirability or undesirability of a certain behavior. Prior studies have demonstrated that attitude affects behavioral intentions [14]. Individuals who form positive attitudes toward wearable technology have a

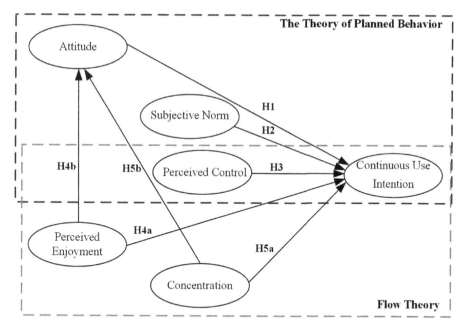

Fig. 1. Research framework.

stronger continuance intention and are thus more likely to use it. Prior studies on individuals' adoption of health technology have also found a correlation between attitude and behavioral intention [11, 14, 15]. Thus, we proposed the following hypothesis:

H1. Attitude is positively related to the intention of continued wearable technology use.

Subjective norm is the extent to which a person feels that people who are important to him or her want him or her to engage in a certain behavior [14]. The more people perceive that others believe that they should perform a certain behavior, the greater their motivation to perform it. Prior studies have shown that the perceived SN has a substantial effect on a person's behavioral intention [11, 14]. Therefore, we proposed the following hypothesis:

H2. Subjective norm is positively related to the intention of continued wearable technology use.

Perceived control describes an individual's perception of ease or difficulty in performing a certain behavior [14]. A person has a higher level of perceived control if he or she has adequate access to resources that facilitate the behavior; thus, perceived control has a positive influence on his or her behavioral intention. Accordingly, a person has a stronger intention to use wearable technology if he or she possesses adequate resources. Perceived control has been found to have positive influence on users' behavioral intention [11, 14, 15]. Thus, we proposed the following hypothesis:

H3. Perceived control is positively related to the intention of continued wearable technology use.

Perceived enjoyment is the extent to which using a specific technology is perceived as enjoyable in its own right, regardless of any system performance consequences arising from its use [16]. Perceived enjoyment has been found to have a positive influence on users' behavioral intention [9] and attitude [14]. Users are intrinsically motivated to use innovative technologies that can offer them fun and pleasure. Wearable technology often has rich leisure and fitness functions from which users can derive great enjoyment. Thus, perceived enjoyment improves their positive attitude toward wearable technology and promotes their intention to continue using it. Therefore, we proposed the following hypotheses:

H4a. Perceived enjoyment is positively related to the intention of continued wearable technology use.

H4b. Perceived enjoyment is positively related to the attitude toward wearable technology.

Concentration is described as a state in which a person loses self-consciousness and becomes absorbed in an activity, and is more acutely aware of his or her mental processes when in a playful condition [13]. If a person carries out many tasks simultaneously, he or she is unable to have a flow experience. Further, wearable technology users who focus their attention on leisure and fitness activities find it easier to be in a state of flow, which in turn positively affects their attitude toward it and encourages its use. Concentration has been found to have a positive influence on users' behavioral intention [11, 14] and attitude. Thus, we proposed the following hypotheses:

H5a. Concentration is positively related to the intention of continued wearable technology use.

H5b. Concentration is positively related to the attitude toward wearable technology.

4   Research Methodology

4.1   Questionnaire Development

The survey questionnaire consisted of two parts. The first part included nominal scales and five-point Likert scales ranging from *strongly agree* to *strongly disagree*. It was used to collect basic information about the respondents' characteristics, including age, gender, education, and wearable technology use experience. The second part was based on the constructs of attitude, SN, perceived control, concentration, perceived enjoyment, and continuous use intention. The scale items for attitude, SN, and perceived control were adapted from Hsieh [15], while those for continuance intention were adapted from Lee [14]. The items measuring perceived enjoyment and concentration were adapted from Moon and Kim [12]. We conducted structural equation modeling (SEM) using partial least squares (PLS) estimations for the data analysis and tested the reliability and validity of the proposed research model. The model was deemed reliable if the Cronbach's alpha was greater than 0.6 [17]. Convergent validity was assessed according to the following criteria: 1) statistically significant item loading greater than 0.7 [18];

2) composite reliability (CR) greater than 0.6; and 3) average variance extracted (AVE) greater than 0.5 [19]. The discriminant validity of the constructs was assessed based on the criterion that the square root of the AVE for each construct should be greater than the corresponding correlations with all the other constructs [19].

4.2 Sample and Data Collection

The target participants were middle-aged and elderly people in Taiwan who had experience using wearable technology. The study employed an online survey for data collection. Online surveys provide researchers with various benefits such as saving time and reducing expenses by eliminating geographical distances [20]. A total of 200 questionnaires were distributed and 150 questionnaires were returned. We assessed nonresponse bias by comparing early and late respondents (e.g., those who replied during the first three days and those who responded in the last three days). We found no significant difference between the two respondent groups based on the sample attributes (e.g., gender and age).

5 Results and Analysis

The 150 valid responses obtained represent a response rate of 75%. Slightly more than half (55%) of the respondents were male. The majority (61%) were aged between 45 and 49. The education level of 44% of the respondents was university education. Seventy-five percent of the respondents had more than two years of wearable device use experience. All Cronbach's alphas were greater than 0.8. For the convergent validity, all item loadings and CR were greater than 0.8, and the AVEs ranged from 0.77 to 0.94. For the discriminant validity, the square root of the AVE for each construct was greater than its corresponding correlations with the other constructs. Table 1 presents the descriptive statistics of the principal constructs and the correlation matrix, respectively. These results indicate acceptable reliability, convergent validity, and discriminant validity.

Table 1. Reliability and validity of the scale.

Construct	Item loading	CR	AVE	Correlation					
				AT	SN	PC	PE	CO	US
AT	0.85–0.95	0.92	0.86	**0.93**					
SN	0.88–0.93	0.95	0.94	0.32	**0.97**				
PC	0.88–0.92	0.93	0.80	0.45	0.36	**0.90**			
PE	0.89–0.92	0.93	0.81	0.53	0.42	0.57	**0.90**		
CO	0.82–0.92	0.88	0.77	0.54	0.48	0.47	0.33	**0.88**	
US	0.80–0.95	0.92	0.80	0.21	0.36	0.13	0.56	0.46	**0.90**

Note: The leading diagonal shows the square root of the average variance extracted (AVE) of each construct. AT: Attitude; SN: Subjective norm; PC: Perceived control; PE: Perceived enjoyment; CO: Concentration; US: Continuous use intention

Figure 2 presents the structural model test results. The results indicate that attitude ($\beta = 0.63$, standardized path coefficient, $p < 0.001$), SN ($\beta = 0.18$, $p < 0.05$), perceived enjoyment ($\beta = 0.38$, $p < 0.01$), and concentration ($\beta = 0.36$, $p < 0.01$) had positive effects on continuous use behavior and taken together explained 60% of its variance.

Consequently, hypotheses 1, 2, 4a, and 5a were confirmed. Perceived enjoyment (β = 0.49, p < 0.001) and concentration (β = 0.35, p < 0.01) significantly influenced attitude and explained 62% of the total variance. Accordingly, hypothesis 4b and 5b were confirmed. On the other hand, perceived control (β = 0.10, p > 0.05) did not significantly influence continuous use intention. Thus, hypothesis 3 was not supported.

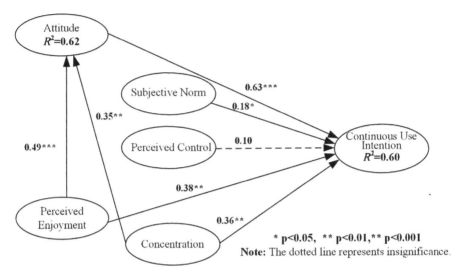

Fig. 2. Structural model results.

6   Discussion

The results show that of the two main determinants, attitude has the stronger effect on behavioral intention. This is in line with the findings of prior studies on health technology adoption [15, 21] and highlights the critical role of attitude in wearable technology use. It indicates that a positive attitude toward wearable devices can be fostered by focusing on their compatibility with the values and needs of middle-aged and elderly people, as well as design simplicity. Furthermore, the results suggest that SN is an influential element on the users' continuous intention to use a wearable device, although its effect was found to be smaller than that of attitude. Thus, when middle-aged or elderly people have a strong perception that most people who are important to them believe that they should continue to use wearable technology, they are more likely to give in to this perceived pressure. On the other hand, contrary to our expectation, perceived control was found to have no effect on continuance intention. This is inconsistent with findings of previous studies on health technology adoption [14, 15]. A plausible explanation is that wearable device operation may not be particularly complex, and thus the level of ability to use such devices has no influence on continuance intention.

Regarding flow experience, our findings suggest that perceived enjoyment strongly affects attitude and behavioral intention, which is consistent with the findings of Koufaris

[9]. Users adopt wearable devices not only for sport and leisure but also for fun and for a flow experience. Therefore, perceived enjoyment as a user's intrinsic motivation is an important driver of positive attitude and continuance intention. The results also suggest that concentration strongly affects attitude and behavioral intention. This is consistent with the findings of previous studies on health technology adoption [11, 14]. If users can concentrate on using wearable technology, it is easier to have a flow experience, which makes them more willing to continue using it. Moreover, when concentrating on using wearable technology, a user may realize it, which may positively affect his or her attitude.

7 Limitations and Conclusion

This study has two main limitations. A key limitation is the sample size. Future research could duplicate this research model using a larger sample size. It would also be useful to compare the results of our study with survey results from other population groups, as the antecedents of wearable technology–related behavior may differ across population groups. Second, our study concerned short-term user behavior. Longitudinal studies could provide a clearer picture of how user behaviors and the relationships between variables change over time.

Compared with other theories, the flow theory approach employed for the research model provides a more complete set of determinates that better explain the continued use of wearable technology. The main contribution of this study is that it is the first to explore middle-aged and elderly people's continued use behavior by combining TPB and flow theory.

Several practical implications can be derived from the study. First, as attitude has a significant impact on continued use intention, sports managers and healthcare providers should develop health management strategies that promote fitness activities among middle-aged and elderly people and ensure that they have a positive attitude toward the wearable technology. Second, since SN can positively affect users' continued use intention, healthcare and wearable technology providers should implement promotion strategies to attract middle-aged and elderly people and increase the number of users through social pressure. Third, perceived enjoyment is an important factor in attitude and continued use intention; thus, sports managers, healthcare providers, and wearable device manufacturers should make efforts to improve their functions. This will increase middle-aged and elderly people's motivation to adopt self–health management, which can reduce or prevent the severity of diseases and their consequences. Fourth, concentration is an important factor affecting users' attitude and continuance intention. Therefore, healthcare providers and wearable device manufacturers should employ user-friendly designs to ensure that the devices can be learned and used easily. Finally, we hope that this study will stimulate further interest in the important wearable technology use phenomena and motivate other studies to examine in greater depth this unexplored yet potentially fertile area of research.

References

1. The National Development Council.: Population Projections for the R.O.C. (Taiwan): 2018–2065. https://www.ndc.gov.tw/en/cp.aspx?n=2E5DCB04C64512CC. Accessed 8 Nov 2019
2. Cheung, M.L., et al.: Examining consumers' adoption of wearable healthcare technology: the role of health attributes. Int. J. Environ. Res. Publ. Health **16**(13), 2257 (2019)
3. Chen, C.C., Shih, H.S.: A study of the acceptance of wearable technology for consumers - an analytical network process perspective. Int. J. Anal. Hierarchy Process **29**, 1–5 (2014)
4. Jain, K., Sharma, I., Singh, G.: An empirical study of factors determining wearable fitness tracker continuance among actual users. Int. J. Technol. Mark. **13**(1), 83–109 (2019)
5. Ajzen, I.: From intentions to actions: a theory of planned behavior. In: Kuhl, J., Beckmann, J. (eds.) Action Control. SSSSP, pp. 11–39. Springer, Heidelberg (1985). https://doi.org/10.1007/978-3-642-69746-3_2
6. Csikszentmihalyi, M.: Beyond Boredom and Anxiety: The Experience of Play in Work and Games. Jossey-Bass, San Francisco (1977)
7. Chapman, K.M., Ham, J.O., Liesen, P., Winter, L.: Applying behavioral models to dietary education of elderly diabetic patients. J. Nutr. Educ. **27**(2), 75–79 (1995)
8. Gupchup, G.V., Abhyankar, U.L., Worley, M.M., Raisch, D.W., Marfatia, A.A., Namdar, R.: Relationships between hispanic ethnicity and attitudes and beliefs toward herbal medicine use among older adults. Res. Soc. Adm. Pharm. **2**(2), 266–279 (2006)
9. Koufaris, M.: Applying the technology acceptance model and flow theory to online consumer behavior. Inf. Syst. Res. **13**(2), 205–223 (2002)
10. Fishbein, M., Ajzen, I.: Belief, Attitude, Intention, and Behavior: An Introduction to Theory and Research. Addison-Wesley, Reading (1975)
11. Lu, Y., Zhou, T., Wang, B.: Exploring Chinese users' acceptance of instant messaging using the theory of planned behavior, the technology acceptance model, and the flow theory. Comput. Hum. Behav. **25**(1), 29–39 (2009)
12. Moon, J.W., Kim, Y.G.: Extending the TAM for a world-wide-web context. Inf. Manage. **38**(2), 217–230 (2001)
13. Chen, C., Chen, W.: Speeding for fun? Exploring the speeding behavior of riders of heavy motorcycles using the theory of planned behavior and psychological flow theory. Accid. Anal. Prev. **43**, 983–990 (2011)
14. Lee, M.C.: Explaining and predicting users' continuance intention toward e-learning: An extension of the expectation–confirmation model. Comput. Educ. **54**, 506–516 (2010)
15. Hsieh, P.J.: Physicians' acceptance of electronic medical records exchange: an extension of the decomposed TPB model with institutional trust and perceived risk. Int. J. Med. Inform. **84**(1), 1–14 (2015)
16. Venkatesh, V., Davis, F.D.: A theoretical extension of the technology acceptance model: four longitudinal field studies. Manage. Sci. **46**(2), 186–204 (2000)
17. Hair, J., Black, W.C., Babin, B.J., Anderson, R.E., Tatham, R.L.: Multivariate Data Analysis, 6th edn. Pearson Education, London (2006)
18. Chin, W.W., Gopal, A., Salisbury, W.D.: Advancing the theory of adaptive structuration: the development of a scale to measure faithfulness of appropriation. Inf. Syst. Res. **8**(44), 342–367 (1997)
19. Fornell, C., Larcker, D.: Structural equation models with unobservable variables and measurement error: algebra and statistics. J. Mark. Res. **18**(3), 382–388 (1981)
20. Alharbi, S., Drew, S.: Using the technology acceptance model in understanding academics' behavioural intention to use learning management systems. Int. J. Adv. Comput. Sci. Appl. **5**(1), 143–155 (2014)
21. Deng, Z., Mo, X., Liu, S.: Comparison of the middle-aged and older users' adoption of mobile health services in China. Int. J. Med. Inform. **83**(3), 210–224 (2014)

Digital Mobile Technology Enhancing Social Connectedness Among Older Adults in Sweden

Sanna Kuoppamäki[(✉)] and Britt Östlund

Department of Biomedical Engineering and Health Systems, Division of Technology in Health Care, KTH Royal Institute of Technology, Stockholm, Sweden
{sannaku,brittost}@kth.se

Abstract. Older adults are an active but a heterogeneous group of digital technology users. Their digital inclusion and active engagement with digital technologies are influenced by social inclusion and connectedness with other people. This paper discusses the connection between digital and social inclusion by focusing on digital mobile practices and social connectedness among older adults in Sweden. The study reports findings from a Swedish data set from the cross-national survey 'Being connected at home – Making use of digital devices in later life', collected among 55–79 year-old smartphone users in 2019 in Sweden (N = 121). The study analyses the usage of smartphone for digital mobile practices and their association with social connectedness. Results show that older smartphone users in Sweden use the smartphone for versatile mobile practices. Nearly all respondents use the smartphone for text messages, but receiving or sending voice or video calls is relatively rare. The differences between the three age groups (55–59; 60–69; 70–79) are relatively small. Using the smartphone for gaming is a more frequent activity among younger age groups. Furthermore, the results demonstrate that the usage of the smartphone for digital mobile practices is positively associated with connectedness with community, and less associated with connectedness with personal relationships and society. Older adults who use their smartphone in a more versatile way report more social activities with community than respondents with less versatile digital activity. Age did not remain a significant predictor to any form of social connectedness.

Keywords: Digital inclusion · Digital mobile technology · Smartphone · Older adults · Social connectedness

1 Introduction

Most older adults in contemporary Western societies nowadays have access to the internet, mobile phones or tablet computers, but differences between older adults' digital skills seem to persist [12, 18, 23]. Besides socioeconomic status, such as higher education and income level [11, 21], older adults' digital inclusion, i.e. active engagement with digital technologies, is influenced by social inclusion. Social inclusion indicates the involvement in and attachment to networks that give a person access to the knowledge and support of others [6, 13]. Older adults who have access to a more profound social

© Springer Nature Switzerland AG 2020
Q. Gao and J. Zhou (Eds.): HCII 2020, LNCS 12207, pp. 289–302, 2020.
https://doi.org/10.1007/978-3-030-50252-2_22

support are more likely to benefit from digital technology use in terms of improved social connectedness [19].

This paper discusses the connection between digital and social inclusion by addressing the role of digital mobile practices in social connectedness among older adults in Sweden. Digital inclusion, defined as an access to digital technologies in daily life contexts [10, 13] is expected to enhance social inclusion, such as older adults' experiences of social connectedness [2, 27]. Social connectedness, indicating the perceived engagement and belonging to one's social networks [8], can be defined as "the feeling of connectedness to others and to a community of neighbourhood" [4, 27]. It relates the quality of social networks in terms of embedded social ties [1]. Additionally, it can be considered as an indicator of social support that benefits older adults' digital inclusion. Social support, received through social relationships, networks and social structures, can strengthen older adults' digital inclusion [20, 25]. Social support enhances digital technology use by providing access to information, assisting in interpreting the meaning of technologies, and providing practical support in digital technology use [6]. Similarly, the connection between digital and social inclusion also operates another way round. Advanced digital mobile practices may contribute to increased social connectedness [1, 8, 27].

This paper contributes to existing research by investigating the connection between digital mobile practices and social connectedness among older smartphone users in Sweden. In this context, the paper asks RQ1) To what extent older smartphone users have adopted digital mobile practices in Sweden? RQ2) Are digital mobile practices associated with social connectedness? RQ3) Does this effect remain when other socio-demographic variables (age and education) are taken into consideration?

The study analyses a Swedish data set from the cross-national survey 'Being connected at home – Making use of digital devices in later life' [8]. The survey data was collected among 55–79 year-old smartphone users in 2019 in Sweden (N = 121). The study first describes the differences in the adoption and use of digital mobile practices among older smartphone users from three age groups. This is followed by an exploratory factor analysis of the dimensions of social connectedness. Using the Generalized linear model (GLM), the study investigates the effect of digital mobile practices to connectedness with personal relationships, connectedness with community and connectedness with society. Finally, the study tests whether or not this effect remains when age and education are taken into consideration.

2   Digital Inclusion and Social Connectedness

Digital inclusion can be defined as a level to which a person has access to and engages with digital technologies in daily life contexts to reconcile subjectively experienced digital divides [10, 13]. Sweden, among other Nordic countries, can be considered a digitally advanced society where most older people nowadays have access to digital technologies such as smartphones and tablet computers. According to Internetstiftelsen (The Swedish Internet Foundation) [16], the amount of older people using the internet has increased significantly during the past 10 years, and nowadays 93% of people aged 66–75 use the internet in Sweden. Of the oldest age group (aged over 75), 69% are now online.

Among internet users aged 66 to 75, the internet is used most often via mobile phone (73%), computer (58%) and tablet computer (44%). The oldest age group (aged over 75) prefers using the internet via computer relatively more often than younger age groups. Digital exclusion in Sweden has therefore diminished, but not entirely vanished, and has concentrated to vulnerable groups, i.e. those with lower education, the unemployed and the socially isolated [14].

Additionally, a report from Internetstiftelsen [16] shows that internet users in Sweden have become more concerned about personal privacy online, and only a quarter of people consider the time spent on social media as meaningful to them anymore. Sharing other people's posts on social media, and the use of social media overall, seems to have begun to level off, particularly among younger Facebook users. Older internet users, aged 66 and over, have started to use Facebook, but they still engage with social media applications (Instagram, Snapchat or Twitter) less actively than internet users from younger age groups. About a half of internet users aged 66 to 75 in Sweden used Facebook in 2019. Social media applications such as LinkedIn or Flashback, on the other hand, are relatively actively used by older groups (46–55, 56–65 and over 66) too.

Digital inclusion, implicating the access and skills to use digital technologies in a beneficial way, is therefore dependent on several socio-demographic and socio-economic factors, age, education and income level perhaps being the most significant [11, 21]. Individuals in socially advantageous positions are more likely to be digitally included, while individuals in socially disadvantageous positions may be at risk for digital exclusion [13, 14]. Therefore digital inclusion is closely connected to social inclusion, defined by the involvement in and attachment to networks that provide a person with access to the knowledge and support of others [6]. Social inclusion can be regarded a significant determinant of digital technology use particularly among vulnerable groups, who may benefit from social, emotional or technical support in digital technology use.

Although the connection between social and digital inclusion is well documented [6, 11, 13], much less is known about the reciprocal connection between digital and social inclusion among older adults. Once older adults have been digitally included, does digital inclusion enhance their social inclusion? *Social inclusion* involves experiences of connectivity and social connectedness that can be understood in relation to (lack of) isolation and loneliness [1, 27]. Social isolation describes the circumstances in which people have less advanced possibilities to engage with other people [27]. It can be measured as a lack of contact with family members, friends, acquaintances or neighbours [2]. On the one hand, socially included older adults may experience a lower level of isolation and loneliness, as they have access to support from others [6]. On the other hand, older adults may personally experience isolation and loneliness despite being socially included [2]. Therefore, social inclusion does not necessarily result in a lack of subjective experience of isolation and connectivity [2, 27].

One form of social inclusion is *social connectedness* that can be described through three interrelated dimensions. At the individual level, social connectedness is shaped by the quality and quantity of personal relationships and contacts with friends, family members and neighbours [8]. Having access to various personal relationships increases the opportunities of getting personal support [6] as well as enhances the sense of being valued in reciprocal relationships [27]. At the community level, connections and activities that take place outside the home connect individuals across associations, neighbour-hoods and communities, and enhance social connectedness through collective feelings of group belongings [8]. Interactions that occur in local neighbourhood settings can help older adults to affirm their identity as a member of social community [22], and a famil-iar neighbourhood provides a context for social lives and a foundation for routines and relationships [9]. At the societal level, social connectedness describes the engagement with the wider society, in tefams of having access to information and resources, as well as an ability to contribute to society [8, 27]. For instance, television may be viewed to maintain connection to the society and the outside world [26]. In this context, Way-cott et al. [27] present technological interventions that can support each dimension of social connectedness. These interventions can, for instance, provide a sense of connec-tion with significant others, facilitate reciprocal communication, emulate neighbourhood connections and facilitate access to the sharing of information.

Digital Technologies and Social Connectedness among Older Adults

The importance of social connectedness to older adults' health and wellbeing is well recognized and documented in previous research [2, 4, 27]. Much less research has been conducted on how digital technology can support this social connectedness; which technologies facilitate these connections in a beneficial manner, and which user groups among older people benefit from digital technology use in terms of increased social connectedness. Research findings, based on different data samples, are slightly contro-versial [1, 8, 27]. Previous research shows that internet usage among older adults supports social connectedness due to social affordances that offer synchronous and asynchronous communication possibilities [7]. Using the internet can reduce feelings of loneliness among older adults [5], if the internet is used to communication with family members and not with strangers [1, 25]. In a study by Neves et al. [1], the implementation and feasibility of communication technology to enhance social connectedness was tested among frail older adults in residential care. The usage of iPad-based communication apps increased perceived social interaction, but increased social connectedness was pro-nounced only with participants with geographically distant relatives. Acceptability and efficacy of the communication app, active involvement of one social tie, and perceived usefulness and functionality influenced the perceived increased social connectedness. Therefore, the characteristics of technological innovations and applications influenc-ing the acceptability of technology, as well as individual differences between users and their social networks, are likely to influence whether or not technologies enhance social connectedness among older adults.

3   Data and Methods

3.1   Data and Participants

The study reports findings from a Swedish data set of a cross-national survey 'Being connected at home – Making use of digital devices in later life' [8]. The survey data covers responses from 55–79 year-old smartphone users in Sweden in 2019. The survey was administrated by Norstat between 7th and 26th June, gathering 121 responses. The sample was designed to be representative of the Swedish population from the age group

55–79. The sample was drawn from the Norstat web panel including 55–79 year-old smartphone users. Of the 13,721 participants invited to the study, 121 were selected as valid responses through several stages. The socio-demographic characteristics of the participants are presented in Table 1.

Table 1. Sample characteristics (N = 121)

	Frequency	Percentage
Age		
55–59	24	19.8
60–69	57	47.1
70–79	40	33.1
Gender		
Male	81	66.9
Education		
Primary	9	7.4
Secondary	37	30.6
Post-secondary	66	54.5
Post-graduate	9	7.4
Employment status		
Full-time worker	26	21.5
Part-time worker	7	5.8
Unemployed	2	1.7
Retired	81	66.9
Unpaid occupation in the home	1	0.8
Volunteering or unpaid occupation	1	0.8
Other	3	2.5
Household status (number of persons living in the same household)		
0 people (living alone)	35	28.9
1 person (2 at home)	79	65.3
2 or more persons	7	5.7
Residential area		
Big city	65	53.7
Medium-size city	13	10.7
Small city, town, country village	20	16.5
Farm or countryside	23	19.0

The survey questionnaire was composed of 34 questions, measuring self-reported social connectedness (14 questions), digital mobile practices (7 questions), perceived essentiality (1 question), media ecology (1 question), socio-economic background and household typology (10 questions). Social connectedness was measured with the frequency and quality of social contacts with friends, family members, neighbours and other social networks. Digital mobile practices were measured with the usage of smartphone to various activities, evaluation of the benefits of using a mobile internet, the location of usage of smartphone and users involved in using the smartphone.

3.2 Variables

Dependent variables consist of 14 statements measuring the perceived social connectedness with personal relationships, community and society. Respondents were asked to evaluate their social and personal connections and engagement with social activities using a 7-point Likert-scale (1 = Never or almost never, 4 = Sometimes, 7 = Always or almost always). These statements covered access to social activities home and outside home, volunteering activities, attending and engaging in social events, having contacts with friends, family and neighbours, sharing personal matters, ideas and information, feelings associated with being a part of society and being happy with social contacts.

Independent variables consist of digital mobile practices, with age and education as control variables. Regarding digital mobile practices, respondents were asked to report their usage of smartphones for text messaging, images, videos or audios, receiving and making voice or video calls, watching TV, videos or listening to audio books/recordings, finding out about current events, checking tutorials, shopping, gaming, managing safety. In each statement, respondents were asked 'What do you use your smartphone for' and to select as many options as necessary. Respondents were asked to specify their age in years along with their level of education with four options: primary, secondary, post-secondary and post-graduate.

3.3 Statistical Procedures

To investigate the frequency of digital mobile practices among older internet users in Sweden, a contingency table was conducted together with statistical tests. In the contingency table, the frequency of each statement regarding the usage of smartphones for various activities was tested among three age groups (55–59; 60–69; 70–79). Pearson's chi-squared test was used to evaluate the statistical significance of the differences between age groups.

Exploratory factor analysis (EFA) was carried out for variables measuring the respondents' evaluations of their social connectedness. Exploratory factor analysis was conducted with the principal axis factoring method and promax rotation to reveal the latent dimensions of social connectedness. Cronbach's alfas were used to evaluate the reliability of factor dimensions.

Three aggregate variables were constituted based on the loadings of factor scores of each dimension. The Generalized Linear Model (GLM) was then executed to examine the effects of the usage of smartphones to three dimensions of social connectedness when other socio-demographic variables (age and education) were looked at. The continuous variables were aggregate variables of social connectedness, based on factor scores for each dimension, singular statements of usage of smartphones as categorical variables. The GLM model was conducted separately for each dependent variable, taking age and education into consideration in each case.

4 Results

4.1 Digital Mobile Practices Among Older Internet Users in Sweden

Results from descriptive statistics show that older smartphone users in Sweden have adopted and use their internet connection and smartphone for versatile mobile practices. The differences between the three age groups (55–59; 60–69 and 70–79) are relatively small. Age categories, based on classification used in developmental studies [15], therefore describe digital mobile practices in various life stages. Along with smartphones, laptops are the most common digital device among older smartphone users in Sweden. Nearly all respondents use smartphones for text messaging, but receiving or sending voice or video calls is relatively rare (29% of respondents aged 55-59; 55% of respondents aged 70–79). Regarding age differences, gaming with smartphones is a more frequent digital practice among younger age groups (63% of respondents aged 55–59) than older age groups (15% of respondents aged 70–79) (Table 2).

Table 2. Digital mobile practices among older smartphone users in Sweden (N = 121) (%)

Age	55–59	60–69	70–79
Apart from my current phone, I usually use…			
Desktop computer (yes)	50.0	57.9	65.0
Laptop	83.3	82.5	80.0
Tablet	62.5	54.4	60.0
Smart TV	37.5	61.4	55.0
Smart watch	29.2	22.8	25.0
I use my smartphone for…			
Text messages (SMS, WhatsApp, Messenger)	100.0	98.2	100.0
Images, videos or audios (MMS, WhatsApp, Facebook)	87.5	91.2	87.5
Receive and make voice or video calls (Phone, Whatsapp, Facetime, Skype …)	29.2	45.6	55.0
Watching TV, videos or listening to audios (YouTube, Radio, Spotify)	62.5	70.2	55.0
Find out about current events (newspapers, Twitter, Facebook)	83.3	78.9	72.5
Looking up for practical information (timetables, maps)	95.8	98.2	95.0

(*continued*)

Table 2. (*continued*)

Age	55–59	60–69	70–79
Checking tutorials (recipes, home improvements, house keeping, hobbies)	54.2	70.2	47.5
Shopping (looking for information or paying)	62.5	56.1	60.0
Gaming (Candy Crush…)	62.5	38.6	15.0***
Managing safety and emergency-care issues (monitor activity and mobility; alerting and reporting in the event of emergencies, falls)	20.8	24.6	42.5
With regard to the internet connection on my smartphone			
At home, I mainly use Wi-Fi	95.8	93.0	92.5
In places that I visit often I use Wi-Fi if it is available (at relatives', friends', my workplace…)	75.0	68.4	67.5
Outside home, I mainly use mobile data	75.0	86.0	85.0
If available, I use a public Wi-Fi	66.7	70.2	62.5

***$p < 0.001$; **$p < 0.01$; *$p < 0.00$

4.2 The Association Between Digital Mobile Practices and Social Connectedness Among Older Internet Users in Sweden

Table 3 shows the results from exploratory factor analysis. Factor analysis confirmed the latent dimensions of social connectedness. The Kaiser-Meyer-Olkin measure of sampling adequacy was 0.693 and Bartlett's test of sphericity was significant at the level of $p = 0.000$. In each of the three factors, the rotation sums of squared loadings varied from 3.44 to 3.97 based on the factor loadings of the statements. The Cronbach's alphas in each factor indicated the reliability of each factorial dimension and thus verified their suitability to use as dependent variables in the GLM model.

To investigate the association between digital mobile practices and social connectedness, the GLM model was executed with age and education as control variables. Table 4 displays the results from the main effect tests of the GLM for different dimensions of social connectedness. The overall statistical significances of the independent variables were indicated by the F value. The unstandardized parameter estimates (β) describe how much the means of the different categories of independent variables deviate from the reference category. The R-square value indicated the goodness-of-fit of measures, where the higher value predicts the better model fit for the data.

The results from the GLM model demonstrate that digital mobile practices are strongly associated with connectedness with community, and less associated with other forms of social connectedness. A versatile use of smartphone for digital mobile practices predicts social connectedness with community, but does not predict connectedness with personal relationships or with society to the same extent. In the GLM model, age did not remain a significant predictor to any form of social connectedness. Higher education was

Table 3. Social connectedness among older adults, exploratory factor analysis (EFA)

Thinking about my life in general…	Dimension of social connectedness		
	Factor 1. Personal relationships	Factor 2. Community	Factor 3. Society
I meet or talk with my neighbours	.533		
I have contact with friends or family	.595		
I have somebody with whom to discuss intimate and personal matters	.634		
I am happy with the contact I have with friends and/or family	.824		
I am happy with the people with whom I can discuss intimate and personal matters	.871		
I am happy with the social activities I do	.572		
I have social activities in the place where I live		.544	
I have social activities outside the place where I live		.453	
I attend events where people gather		.643	
I engage in other social activities		.849	
I share ideas or information beyond my family, friends and immediate networks		.509	
I engage in voluntary activities			.720
I believe I contribute to society in other non-digital ways			.610
Eigenvalue, % (cumulative %)	34.7 (34.7)	15.4 (50.1)	8.0 (58.1)
Cronbach's alfa	.784	.760	.653

associated with connectedness with community. The effect of digital mobile practices to social connectedness remained when age and education were taken into consideration.

Connectedness with Personal Relationships. Table 4 shows that the usage of smartphones for text messages, images, videos or audio or watching TV or videos was not associated with connectedness with personal relationships. Instead, using smartphones for finding out about current events and looking up practical information was positively associated with connectedness with personal relationships. The smartphone users active in information seeking therefore reported a higher level of connectedness with personal relationships. Furthermore, connectedness with personal relationships was not predicted by age or education.

Table 4. The association between digital media practices and social connectedness

I use my smartphone for…	Dimension of social connectedness		
	Factor 1. Personal relationships	Factor 2. Community	Factor 3. Society
	Parameter estimates (β)		
Text messages (SMS, WhatsApp, Messenger) (ref. no)	n.s.	F = 3.992*	n.s.
Yes		1.846*	
R-squared (Adjusted R2)		.037(.013)	
Images, videos or audios (MMS, WhatsApp, Facebook) (ref. no)		F = 4.972*	
Yes	n.s.	2.230*	n.s.
R-squared (Adjusted R2)		.045(.021)	
Watching TV, videos or listening to audios (YouTube, Radio, Spotify) (ref. no)		F = 8.007**	
Yes	n.s.	.486**	n.s.
R-squared (Adjusted R2)		.068(.044)	
Find out about current events (newspapers, Twitter, Facebook) (ref.no)	F = 5.247*	F = 8.314**	n.s
Yes	.464*	.569**	n.s.
R-squared (Adjusted R2)	.060(.036)	.071(.047)	
Looking up practical information (timetables, maps) (ref.no)	F = 5.903*	F = 7.492**	F = 6.578*
Yes	1.143*	1.261**	1.100*
R-squared (Adjusted R2)	.065(.041)	.065(.041)	.56(.032)

***P < 0.001; **p < 0.01; *p < 0.00

Connectedness with Community. The usage of smartphones for all digital mobile practices was positively associated with connectedness with community. The smartphone users who used their device for text messages, images, videos or audio, watching TV or videos, finding out about current events and looking up practical information, reported a higher level of connectedness with community. The effect of smartphone use to connectedness with community remained even though age and education were taken into consideration.

Connectedness with Society. Among the different factors, the usage of smartphones for digital mobile practices was least associated with connectedness with society. The usage of smartphones to look up practical information was the only digital mobile practice that was positively associated with connectedness with society. Age or education did not have any effect on connectedness with society.

5   Discussion and Conclusions

In this paper we have reported findings from the Swedish data set of the cross-national survey 'Being connected at home – Making use of digital devices in later life', with a focus on the association between digital mobile practices and social connectedness among older internet users in Sweden [8]. The study asked, RQ1) To what extent older smartphone users have adopted digital mobile practices in Sweden? RQ2) Are digital mobile practices associated with social connectedness? RQ3) Does this effect remain when other socio-demographic variables (age and education) are taken into consideration?

In response to RQ1, the results show that older smartphone users in Sweden have widely adopted digital mobile practices to their daily lives. Differences between age groups are relatively small; instead, differences are pronounced between digital mobile practices. The study contributes to a discussion of aged heterogeneity [18, 23] by showing that older smartphone users in Sweden are surprisingly homogeneous in their smartphone use, when focus in one the frequency of digital mobile activities, the device and location of use. Digital mobile practices where heterogeneity between age groups was pronounced included using smartphone for receiving and making video or phone calls, watching TV, videos or listening to audio, finding out about current events, gaming and managing safety. Interestingly, in some mobile practices such as receiving or making voice calls, the oldest age group (70–79) reported the most frequent activity. These findings suggest that the chronological age of the smartphone user has perhaps become a less significant predictor of digital activity [17]. The oldest age group is involved in the mobile practices that represent their life stage, such as managing safety.

In response to RQ2, the study demonstrates that the connection between digital mobile practices and social connectedness is pronounced in relation to a respondent's sense of social connectedness with community. The usage of smartphones is positively associated with a sense of social connectedness with community, and less associated with connectedness with personal relationships and society. Older smartphone users who use their device in a more versatile way report more social activities with community than those who use their smartphones in a less versatile way. These social activities include, for example, attending events where many people gather, engaging in cultural activities and sharing ideas or information beyond family. Regarding RQ3, the study confirms that the effect of digital mobile practices to social connectedness remained when age and education were taken into consideration.

The study therefore shows that digital mobile technology has a different role in one's perceived engagement with social networks depending on the dimension of social connectedness. Even though the most frequent mobile activity among older adults is sending text messages, this activity does not contribute to an increased sense of connectedness with personal relationships. Instead, the connectedness with personal relationships is predicted by using smartphones to search for information, such as finding out about current events or searching for information. This can be interpreted in relation to changing personal relationships in later life [3], as well as the characteristics of these digital mobile practices. As many digital mobile practices investigated in this study are well-established in everyday life among older adults, their actual purpose of use may extend beyond their original purpose of use (e.g. using smartphones for text messages).

6   Limitations and Implications for Future Research

Our study investigated older internet users in Sweden who have access to and use smartphones regularly for various practices. Due to the small sample size of the survey, the findings should be interpreted as representing quite average smartphone users in Sweden, without ethnic or sexual minorities. Further research could deepen the understanding of digital mobile practices and social connectedness by shedding light on the meanings and interpretations of social connectedness in relation to changing personal relationships, increasing diversity and decreasing normativity of social connections and family situations [3]. Despite the limitations, our study has shown empirical evidence of the connection between smartphone activity and social connectedness, by proposing that only some practices of digital inclusion contribute to social inclusion, and this connection is mostly pronounced in social inclusion with the community.

Acknowledgements. The research project BConnect@Home – Making use of digital devices in later life (https://www.jp-demographic.eu/wp-content/uploads/2017/01/BCONNECT_2017_conf 2018_brochure.pdf) is funded by the JTP 2017 - JPI More Years, Better Lives (Grant Agreement 363850), FORTE (ref. 2017-02301).

References

1. Barbosa Neves, B., Franz, R., Judges, R., Beermann, C., Baecker, R.: Can digital technology enhance social connectedness among older adults? A feasibility study. J. Appl. Gerontol. **38**(1), 49–72 (2017)
2. Beneito-Montagut, R., Cassián-Yde, N., Begueria, A.: What do we know about the relationship between internet-mediated interaction and social isolation and loneliness in later life? Qual. Ageing Older Adults **19**(1), 14–30 (2018)
3. Bildtgård, T., Öberg, P.: Intimacy and Ageing: New Relationships in Later Life. Policy Press, Bristol (2017)
4. Bruggencate, T.T., Luijkx, K.G., Sturm, J.: Social needs of older people: a systematic literature review. Ageing Soc. **38**(9), 1745–1770 (2017)
5. Choi, M., Kong, S., Jung, D.: Computer and internet interventions for loneliness and depression in older adults: a meta-analysis. Health Inf. Res. **18**(3), 191–198 (2012)

6. Courtois, C., Verdegem, P.: With the little help from my friends: an analysis of the role of social support in digital inequalities. New Media Soc. **18**(8), 1508–1527 (2016)
7. Delello, J., McWhorter, R.: Reducing the digital divide: connecting older adults to iPad technology. J. Appl. Gerontol. **36**(1), 3–28 (2015)
8. Fernández-Ardèvol, M., et al.: Methodological strategies to understand smartphone practices for social connectedness in later life. In: Zhou, J., Salvendy, G. (eds.) HCII 2019. LNCS, vol. 11593, pp. 46–64. Springer, Cham (2019). https://doi.org/10.1007/978-3-030-22015-0_4
9. Forsman, A.K., Herberts, C., Nyqvust, F., Wahlbeck, K., Schierenbeck, I.: Understanding the role of social capital for mental wellbeing among older adults. Ageing Soc. **33**(5), 804–825 (2013). https://doi.org/10.1017/S0144686X12000256
10. Gingrich, L.G., Lichman, N.: The empirical measurement of a theoretical concept: tracing social exclusion among racial minority and migrant groups in Canada. Soc. Incl. **3**(4), 98–111 (2015)
11. Haight, M., Quan-Haase, A., Corbett, B.A.: Revisiting the digital divide in Canada: the impact of demographic factors on access to the Internet, level of online activity, and social networking site usage. Inf. Commun. Soc. **17**(4), 503–519 (2014)
12. Hargittai, E., Piper, A.M., Morris, M.R.: From internet access to internet skills: digital inequality among older adults. Univ. Access Inf. Soc. **18**(4), 881–890 (2018). https://doi.org/10.1007/s10209-018-0617-5
13. Helsper, E.J.: The social relativity of digital exclusion: applying relative deprivation theory to digital inequalities. Commun. Theory **27**(3), 223–242 (2017). https://doi.org/10.1111/comt.12110
14. Helsper, E.J., Reisdorf, B.C.: The emergence of a "digital underclass" in Great Britain and Sweden: changing reasons for digital exclusion. New Media Soc. **19**(8), 1253–1270 (2017)
15. Hutteman, R., Hennecke, M., Orth, U., Reitz, A.K., Specht, J.: Developmental tasks as a framework to study personality development in adulthood and old age. Eur. J. Pers. **28**(3), 267–278 (2014)
16. Internetstiftelsen: Svenskarna och Internet (2019). https://svenskarnaochinternet.se/app/uploads/2019/10/svenskarna-och-internet-2019-a4.pdf
17. Kuoppamäki, S.: Digital home: life transitions and digital domestic practices in later life. In: Zhou, J., Salvendy, G. (eds.) HCII 2019. LNCS, vol. 11593, pp. 393–404. Springer, Cham (2019). https://doi.org/10.1007/978-3-030-22015-0_31
18. Loos, E.F.: Senior citizens: digital immigrants in their own country? Observatorio (OBS*) J. **6**(1), 1–23 (2012)
19. Lüders, M., Gjevjon, E.R.: Being old in an always-on culture: older people's perceptions and experiences of online communication. Inf. Soc. **33**(2), 64–75 (2017)
20. Piper, A.M., Garcia, R.C., Brewer, R.N.: Understanding the challenges and opportunities of smart mobile devices among the oldest old. Int. J. Mob. Hum. Comput. Interact. **8**(2), 83–98 (2016)
21. Robinson, L., et al.: Digital inequalities and why they matter. Inf. Commun. & Soc. **18**(5), 569–582 (2015)
22. Steward, J., Browning, C., Sims, J.: Civic socialising: a revealing new theory about older people's social relationships. Ageing Soc. **35**(4), 750–764 (2015)
23. Stone, M.E., Lin, J., Dannefer, D., Kelley-Moore, J.A.: The continued eclipse of heterogeneity in gerontological research. J. Gerontol. Ser. B **72**(1), 162–167 (2017)
24. Sum, S., Mathews, R.M., Hughes, I., Campbell, A.: Internet use and loneliness in older adults. Cyberpsychol. Behav. **11**(2), 208–211 (2008)
25. Quan-Haase, A., Mo, G.Y., Wellman, B.: Connected seniors: how older adults in East York exchange social support online and offline. Inf. Commun. Soc. **20**(7), 967–983 (2017)

26. van der Goot, M., Beenties, J.W.J., van Selm, M.: Meanings of television in older adults' lives: an analysis of change and continuity in television viewing. Ageing Soc. **32**, 147–168 (2012)

27. Waycott, J., Vetere, F., Ozanne, E.: Building social connections: a framework for enriching older adults' social connectedness through information and communication technologies. In: Neves, B.B., Vetere, F. (eds.) Ageing and Digital Technology, pp. 65–82. Springer, Singapore (2019). https://doi.org/10.1007/978-981-13-3693-5_5

Wearable Technologies: Acceptance Model for Smartwatch Adoption Among Older Adults

May Jorella S. Lazaro[1]($\boxtimes$), Jaeseo Lim[1], Sung Ho Kim[2], and Myung Hwan Yun[2]

[1] Interdisciplinary Program in Cognitive Science, Seoul National University, Seoul, South Korea
ellalazaro@snu.ac.kr
[2] Department of Industrial Engineering, Seoul National University, Seoul, South Korea

Abstract. Wrist-worn wearable technologies such as smartwatches are seen to be one of the breakthrough devices that would help older adults age successfully. However, to date, there is still a lack of systematic evaluation of smartwatch adoption for older adults. Thus, in order to gain a better understanding of older adults' attitude towards the acceptance of wearable technologies, a user acceptance model was proposed by extending the previously validated Technology Acceptance Model (TAM). A 26-item Likert-type questionnaire was administered to 76 older adults, aged 50 to 74, following the actual demonstration of the usage and features of two smartwatches (Samsung Galaxy Watch 42 mm and MiBand 4). Results reveal that prior experience, affective quality and technology-related anxiety affected older adults' perception of ease of use. While social support impacted their attitude, accessibility had an effect on their intention to use the smartwatch. These results provide a good insight with regards to the acceptability factors for smartwatch adoption among older adults.

Keywords: Smartwatch · Older adults · Technology Acceptance Model · Wearable technology

1 Introduction

Over the years, the population of older adults is significantly increasing leading to a dramatic demographic shift that raises concerns across different sectors. According to the recent demographic research, the global population of older adults aged 60 years and above reached 962 million in 2017, which is more than twice as large as in the record in 1980 (World Population Ageing 2017). It is predicted that by 2050, the number of older persons will be doubled and would reach nearly 2.1 billion which will eventually outnumber the population of adolescents and youth aged 10–24 (World Population Aging 2017). These changes in demographic ratio present both opportunities and challenges for existing health care systems, mental health services, psychological research, government sectors and many more.

One of the solutions being proposed to address the increasing needs of the older population is through the use of technology and information systems. To date, there are a lot of different types of technology being developed in order to aid the needs

© Springer Nature Switzerland AG 2020
Q. Gao and J. Zhou (Eds.): HCII 2020, LNCS 12207, pp. 303–315, 2020.
https://doi.org/10.1007/978-3-030-50252-2_23

of older adults in the most efficient way possible. One of which is the development of wrist-worn wearable technology, which people often refer to as 'smartwatch', for health care assistance, monitoring and communication (Muchna et al. 2018; Piwek et al. 2016). Despite the fact that some studies have already proved the potential benefits of smartwatches for older adults, the evaluation of this type of technology in the perspective of user acceptance is seemingly neglected in research (Kim and Shin 2015; Peek et al. 2014). There are existing user acceptance researches but only a few of them focused on the older population, and among those few, only a couple of researches focused on wrist-worn wearable technologies. Additionally, most of the studies in this area are exploratory in nature, thus further studies are considered essential. Therefore, this study aims to examine different key factors (i.e. affective quality, tech-related anxiety, prior experience, perceived usefulness, perceived ease of use, accessibility, and social support) that are closely associated with older adults' perception and attitude towards wrist-worn technologies. This study aims to bridge the gap in the literature by developing a user acceptance model for smartwatch adoption among older adults through extending the previously established Technology Acceptance Model (TAM).

2   Background & Related Work

2.1   Older Adults and Smartwatch Adoption

Older Adults. The increase in population trend of the elderly has led a lot of researchers, designers and scholars to shift their attention to this specific population in order to address their increasing needs (Schulz et al. 2014). Nowadays, interest in technology for older adults have been gaining notable attention in the research field due to several reasons (see Schulz et al. 2014). Despite the growing attention, the elderly are still under-considered in the field of technological advancement and there is still a persisting stereotype that older people are viewed as "non-technological", "non-adapters" or "technology laggers" (Lee and Coughlin 2015; Conci et al. 2009). Although it is expected that older people may have a different approach towards technology in comparison to the younger generation because of the differences in sensory, motor, and cognitive ability mostly due to the effects of aging, this does not equate to older people fully rejecting the use of technology (Conci et al. 2009). In fact, there are several studies that proved that older adults may be open and accepting of different technologies under several conditions (Lee and Coughlin 2015; Peek et al. 2014; Lewis and Neider 2017). According to the findings of Czaja and his colleagues (2006), older adults' relationship with technology is much more complex than the preexisting stereotype that older adults are just generally afraid and unwilling to use any technology (as cited in Mitzner et al. 2010). In order to shed light upon this complexity, further investigation is considered to be essential.

Smartwatch Adoption. With the rapid development of technology, miniaturization, and the mass production of cheaper, smaller and faster electronic parts, digital watches have evolved from a simple machine that tells the time and date to a small but complex machine with smart and computer-like features (Kim and Shin 2015). For the past few years, wrist-worn wearable technologies or smartwatches have been considered to possess great potential for the future of technological advancements (Lewis and Neider

2017). A small percentage of the available smartwatches in the market today are geared towards the older population. Most of the smartwatches for older adults possess some common features such as GPS location tracking system, physical condition monitoring system (e.g. ECG, body temperature etc.), activity. monitor, fall-risk alert, emergency alert and motion sensor (Saner 2018; The Best Senior Wearables and Trackers 2018; Piwek et al. 2016) These features offer great potential for older adults to help them in their day-to-day living and increase their feelings of independence and quality of life (Saner 2018; Piwek et al. 2016). For example, in a review conducted by Cooper and her colleagues (2018), it was concluded that wearable fitness trackers with accelerometer increased physical activity among older adults. However, despite its promising features studies regarding smartwatches in older adults are more focused on enhancing its features and designing it according to their needs and capacities rather than focusing on the consumers' perspective. One of the few studies that taken user acceptance into account, is a study by Mercer and colleagues (2016) which concluded that following the TAM, smartwatches are perceived to be useful and acceptable by older adults with chronic illness. However, the researchers also suggested that more research needs to be carried out in order to fully explain smartwatch acceptance among older adults.

2.2 Technology Acceptance Model (TAM)

As different kinds of technology continue to develop throughout the years, various theoretical models were proposed in order to explain technology adoption. One of the most prominent and extensively utilized models for technology adoption is the Technology Acceptance Model (TAM). Originally, the model suggests that perceived ease of use (PEOU) and perceived usefulness (PU) are the key determinants to predict user's attitude towards the product (AT) and the user's behavioral intention to use the product (BI) (Davis et al. 1989, 1993). According to this model, when a product is perceived to be easy to use by users in general, the product may be seen to be more useful and the users may have a more positive attitude towards it. In which increased PU and AT leads to an increase in BI.

The TAM has been extensively studied and utilized by many researchers in studying adoption of different types of technologies such as mobile phone (Conci et al. Conci et al. 2009; Joo and Sang 2013; Kim and Sundar 2014), e-learning (Masrom 2007), ICT (Edmunds et al. 2012) and smartwatch (Kim and Shin 2015). This model has also been utilized in studies for technology adoption for older adults (Conci et al. 2009; Lee and Coughlin 2015). The model's variables and its predictive power have been validated multiple times across different studies. Therefore, this study aims to adopt this model as the foundation of the theoretical framework for investigating the user-acceptance of wrist-worn wearable technology among older adults. Following the original model, the researcher proposes that:

H1. AT will be positively correlated with BI
H2. PU will be positively correlated with AT
H3. PEOU will be positively correlated with AT
H4. PEOU will be positively correlated with PU

2.3   Factors Affecting Smartwatch Adoption in Older Adults

Prior Experience (PE). In general, the perception of technology is affected by prior experiences (Walsh and Callan 2010). In order to understand the use and value of new technology, people tend to rely on the familiarity of the technology based on their previous experiences (Brown and Venkatesh 2005; as cited in Lee and Coughlin 2015). As noted in the review of literature conducted by Lee and Coughlin (2015) previous exposures play a bigger role among older adults than their younger counterparts. Moreover, the causal relationship between past experience is said to be stronger for older adults as well (Niemelä-Nyrhinen 2007; Quinn, 2010; as cited in Lee and Coughlin 2015). Extending this assumption to wearable technology, one study found that wearable activity trackers may be less useful for individuals who are less familiar with mobile technology (Mercer et al. 2016). Thus, PE is seen as an important factor that shapes individuals', especially older adults', perception towards the use of new technology. In a previous study, PE was found to affect PEOU and is considered to be a key factor in determining future usage of a product (Bajaj and Nidomolu 1998; as cited in Saade and Kira 2007). Therefore, it is hypothesized that:

H5. PE will be positively correlated with PEOU

Affective Quality (AQ). AQ is seen to be a very important aspect of product design. The affective quality is the ability of a product to evoke specific impression, feelings and emotions from the users, which affects how the users perceive a certain product (Yanagisawa 2011). There are several studies that assert that AQ has a positive effect on technology-related user acceptance. For example, in a study conducted by Zhang and Li (2005), it was concluded that perceived AQ significantly affects how university students perceived the ease of use of a newly created website. Additionally, one study revealed that the user's perception and rating of usability were heavily influenced by their judgment of its perceived hedonic or affective quality (Harbich and Auer 2005). Furthermore, AQ is also said to be an important factor for older adults in determining their acceptance attitude towards technology (Lee and Coughlin 2015). Extending these findings into smartwatches, this study predicts that AQ will play a significant role in older adults' perception towards smartwatches. Thus, predicting the following hypotheses:

H6. AQ will be positively correlated with PEOU

Technology-Related Anxiety (TRA). TRA, or sometimes called as more specifically computer anxiety, is concept-specific anxiety that is associated with a person's interaction with technology or computers (Oetting 1983; as cited in Saade and Kira 2007). It is basically the tendency of a person to experience a level of uneasiness over his or her impending use of a technological product. Technology-related anxiety is not only experienced by older adults but the younger generation as well (see Saade and Kira 2007). However, it was found that older adults generally have lower self-confidence and are more anxious in interacting with high-tech devices than younger people (Lee and Coughlin 2015). In an in-depth study regarding older adults' experience with interactive technology conducted by Turner and his colleagues (2007), it was found that older adults think that they are "too old" for technology and they feel anxious and alienated towards it (as cited in Barnard et al. 2013). Comparatively, according to the study conducted by Czaja and his fellow researchers (2006), it was found that low self-efficacy regarding computer use and high anxiety for computer use are the two most significant personal barriers to technology adoption for older adults (as cited in Mitzner et al. 2010). Thus, TRA is an important factor in technology adoption for older adults. Several studies have related TRA with PEOU (Saade and Kira 2007; Phang, et al. 2006; Venkatesh 2000), and PU (Heerink et al. 2012). Therefore, it is hypothesized that:

H7. TRA will be negatively correlated with PEOU

H8. TRA will be negatively correlated with PU

Social Support (SS). SS is seen as an essential factor for older adults to overcome barriers to technology adoption (Lee and Coughlin 2015). Much like for younger people, older adults also seem to rely on their peers and family with regards to the validation of behaviors, which includes the purchase and use of technology. People who are within older adults' social groups play an important role in the technology adoption process (Wang et al. 2010; as cited in Lee and Coughlin). In a study conducted by Conci and colleagues (2009) it was found that social factors such as social pressure and social support are considered to be an important factor towards older adults' adoption of mobile phones. Similarly, in a more recent study, it was found that pre-implementation acceptance of technology of older people also depends on social factors since family, friends, professional caregivers, and peers are all described as having an influence (Peek et al. 2014). With this notion, the researcher predicts that:

H9. SS will be positively correlated with AT

Accessibility (ACC). ACC refers to whether technology is perceived as easy to obtain (Kothgassner et al. 2012; as cited in Disztinger et al. 2017). In general, ACC is considered to be an important factor in technology adoption. Basically, adoption is less likely to happen if the product is not effectively delivered into the market. This notion is important to consider especially in the case of older adults because according to research older adults are generally less aware of new technologies, even the ones which are specially designed for them (Heinz et al. 2013). This lack of awareness and knowledge can act as a barrier to adoption (Tanriverdi and Iacono 1999; as cited in Lee and Coughlin 2015). In a study regarding assistive technologies, ACC was found to be a mediating factor between older adults and technology use (McCreadie and Tinker 2005). In addition to this, there are also a lot of studies that relate ACC to technology adoption (Kim and Shin 2015; Wixom and Todd 2005) and behavioral intention to use VR technology (Disztinger et al. 2017). Thus, extending this literature to smartwatches for older adults, it is proposed that:

H10. ACC will be positively correlated with BI

2.4 Summary

After an extensive review of related journals and articles, the research assumptions of this study and its proposed acceptance model for smartwatch adoption among older adults are summarized by the illustration below (Fig. 1):

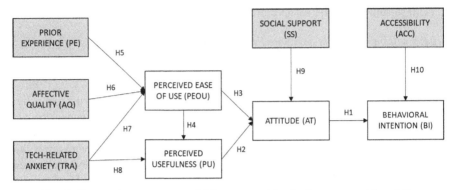

Fig. 1. Proposed acceptance model for smartwatch adoption among older adults

3 Methodology

3.1 Participants and Procedure

A total of 76 older adults (40 male, 36 female) participated in an experiment which involves an actual demonstration of the usage and features of a smartwatch (Samsung Galaxy Watch 42 mm and MiBand 4). The average age of the participants was 57.6 (Min = 50, Max = 74, SD = 5.83). Before the experiment, 37% of the participants declared that they do not have any knowledge about smartwatches while 63% said they did. Moreover, 87% declared that they haven't had any experience of using smartwatches and only 13% had actual experience.

The actual demonstration includes informing the participants about some basic information with regards to the usage, procurement and features of the smartwatch which includes personalization, communication features, health-related features and etc. After the actual demonstration, the participants were given some time to experience and test the smartwatch by themselves and then followed by an administration of a 26-item, 5-point Likert-type survey designed to test the proposed model.

3.2 Questionnaire

The administered survey was a combination of items from previously validated questionnaires and researcher-made questions. Questionnaire items for PEOU, PU, AT and BI were adopted from the questionnaire used from previous TAM studies (Davis 1989, 1993; Venkatesh et al., 2003; Kim and Sundar 2014). Items for AQ was adopted from

Table 1. Questionnaire for the proposed acceptance model

Construct	Item
Prior experience	
PE1	I have used several technological devices (e.g., smartphone, tablet PC) before
PE2	I know how to use smartwatch pretty well
Affective quality	
AQ1	I feel excited when using this smartwatch
AQ2	This smartwatch is attractive and pleasing
Tech-related anxiety	
TRA1	I feel uncomfortable when using high-tech products
TRA2	I feel that I will be more uncomfortable if I use a smartwatch
TRA3	I am anxious about adopting new technologies
Social support	
SS1	I can get help from my family or acquaintance when using a smartwatch
SS2	I have technological or economic support to use this smartwatch
Accessibility	
ACC1	I have seen people use smartwatch frequently
ACC2	I know where to purchase a smartwatch
Perceived usefulness	
PU1	Using this smartwatch helps me productively complete my tasks
PU2	Using the smartwatch helps me effectively do my job
PU3	This smartwatch is useful in doing my job
PU4	Using this smartwatch improves my ability to complete my tasks
PU5	Using this smartwatch makes it easier to complete my tasks
Perceived ease of use	
PEOU1	Operating this smartwatch is easy for me
PEOU2	I find this smartwatch easy to use
PEOU3	Using this smartwatch does not require a lot of my mental effort
Attitude	
AT1	Using this smartwatch is a good idea
AT2	I have a generally favorable attitude toward using this smartwatch
AT3	I like the idea of using this smartwatch
AT4	Overall, using this smartwatch is beneficial
Behavioral intention	
BI1	I predict I will use this smartwatch in the future
BI2	I plan to use this smartwatch in the future
BI3	I expect my use of this smartwatch to continue in the future

the measures developed by Kim and Sundar (2014). Lastly, items for TRA, PE, SS and ACC were constructed by the researchers for this study (Table 1).

The survey items were randomized to create three unique versions (set A, B and C) for counterbalancing and eliminating the order effects.

3.3 Data Analysis

The data was analyzed through confirmatory factor analysis (CFA) and structural equation modelling (SEM) using AMOS 26 statistical software, with a maximum likelihood estimation method. CFA was used for both the reliability and validity measurements of the proposed factor structure, while SEM was used in order to analyze the strength and direction of the hypothesized causal paths among the constructs.

4 Results

This study employed confirmatory factor analysis (CFA) and structural equation modelling (SEM) to test the proposed model and corresponding hypotheses.

The structural equation model results showed that some of the measurement model's fit indices are found to be acceptable considering the small sample size: ratio of χ^2 to the degrees of freedom (χ^2/df) = 1.788, goodness-to-fit index (GFI) = 0.832, and root mean square error of approximation (RMSEA) = 0.078. Furthermore, as depicted in Fig. 2, it was revealed that the standardized coefficients of all proposed paths were significant at p = 0.05, PU and AT path was significant at p = 0.10, except for the PEOU and AT path (H3, $\beta = -0.797$, p = 0.189).

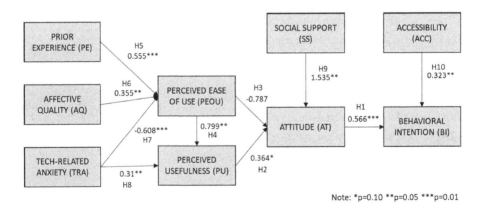

Note: *p=0.10 **p=0.05 ***p=0.01

Fig. 2. Structural equation modelling results

The structural equation modeling results are shown in Fig. 2. The summary of the path coefficients and results of the hypotheses testing are shown in Table 2. From the results, it is found that attitude was a significant factor influencing behavioral intention to use (BI) ($\beta = 0.566$, p < 0.01), supporting the first hypothesis. Moreover, perceived usefulness

(PU) appeared to have a significant causal relationship with AT ($\beta = 0.364$, p < 0.05). However, even though perceived ease-of-use (PEOU) significantly influenced PU ($\beta = 0.799$, p < 0.001), it did not have a direct influence on AT as expected ($\beta = -0.787$, p > 0.10). Prior technology-related experience (PE) significantly had an effect on PEOU ($\beta = 0.555$, p < 0.001.). Similarly, affective quality significantly impacted PEOU ($\beta = 0.355$, p < 0.05.). As expected, technology-related anxiety was negatively correlated with PEOU ($\beta = -0.608$, p < 0.001.). Initially, it was expected that TRA would also have a negative correlation with PU as well, however, the relationship appeared to be positive ($\beta = 0.310$, p < 0.05.). On the other hand, social support (SS) significantly affected AT ($\beta = 1.535$, p < 0.05.) and accessibility (ACC) directly affected BI ($\beta = 0.323$, p < 0.05.). In summary, eight of the initial hypotheses were accepted and two were rejected.

Table 2. Summary of hypothesis tests

Hypotheses	Standardized coefficient	SE	CR	P-value	H_1
H1: AT → BI	0.566	0.553	2.81	0.01	Accepted
H2: PU → AT	0.364	0.094	1.94	0.05	Accepted
H3: PEOU → AT	−0.787	0.310	−1.31	0.19	Rejected
H4: PEOU → PU	0.799	0.206	4.03	***	Accepted
H5: PE → PEOU	0.555	0.108	3.43	***	Accepted
H6: AQ → PEOU	0.355	0.186	2.27	0.02	Accepted
H7: TRA → PEOU	−0.608	0.115	−3.78	***	Accepted
H8: TRA → PU	0.310	0.105	2.19	0.02	Rejected
H9: SS → AT	1.535	0.309	2.23	0.03	Accepted
H10: ACC → BI	0.323	0.125	2.37	0.02	Accepted

Note: ***p < 0.001

5 Discussion

With the rise of aging societies and the rapid growth of technology, increasing attention has been paid to the research and development of wearable technologies that address the needs of the older population. Wrist-worn wearable technologies such as smartwatches may be one of the breakthrough devices that would help older adults age successfully by keeping their health on track and by being socially connected. With its growing potential, an evaluation of how older adults perceive such technology is essential. In this study, the proposed model was found to have a potential in representing older adults' attitude towards smartwatch adoption. Through this study, it was revealed that older adults have a fairly positive attitude towards the use of smartwatches. During the actual demonstration and trial period, most of the participants displayed interest and reacted enthusiastically.

Previous studies showed that prior technology experience influences older adults' likelihood of adopting emerging technology (e.g., Quan-Hasse et al. 2018). Similarly, based on the results of the analysis, it was revealed that having prior experience in using similar technologies positively affects how they think about smartwatches. More specifically, older adults who had more technology-related experience thought that smartwatches are easy to use. This may be due to the fact that increased technology experience can enhance familiarity and increase the likelihood of acquiring an adequate mental model which allow them to understand the mechanism of the smartwatch with less effort. Thus, making them perceive that it is easier to use.

In addition, similar to the findings of previous studies, products with high affective quality tend to be perceived as more usable than those with low affective quality (Harbich and Auer 2005). The impact of affective quality, in this case, may be explained as a result of a psychological phenomenon called 'halo effect'. This phenomenon occurs when one aspect of a certain object affects how a person perceives the quality of an object overall. Thus, the perception of high affective quality might have led to an overall positive impression, in which it affected the judgment on its usability. However, further research is needed to confirm this claim.

Moreover, it was hypothesized that technology-related anxiety would negatively influence older adults' perception of the usefulness and ease of use of smartwatches. However, despite that both assumptions showed significant results, only the relationship between technology-related anxiety and perceived ease-of-use appeared to be negative. Results show that older adults who experience anxiety towards the use of technology-related products tend to perceive the smartwatch to be complex and hard to use. This result confirms the findings of the previous studies regarding technology adoption (Czaja et al. 2006, Saadé and Kira 2007; Phang, et al. 2006; Venkatesh 2000). Furthermore, this is in line with the recent findings of Tsai and colleagues (2020) whereby it was found that older adults who experience anxiety towards the general use of technology also feel that the use of smart clothing is difficult. Although this finding focused on a different type of technology, this similar finding could signify the crucial role of technology-related anxiety in technology adoption for older adults in general. On the other hand, surprisingly, technology-related anxiety was found to be positively related to the perceived usefulness of the smartwatch. This result could mean that anxiety only affects their perception of the complexity of the device but not its actual value. That even though they experience some sort of anxiety they are still able to find the smartwatch useful. However, information from the questionnaire is not enough to explain that actual cause of the positive relationship, thus, this finding accounts for further investigation.

As hypothesized, social support was seen to have a positive effect on older adults' overall attitude towards the use of smartwatches. However, this finding is not only limited to the adoption of smartwatches. As can be seen from previous findings, the impact of social support is rather general and has been applied to various technologies (e.g. Wang et al. 2010; Conci et al. 2009). Similarly, it was mentioned by Lee and Coughlin (2015) that social support plays an important role in technology adoption for older adults. Thus, it is important to note that, in order for older adults to adopt wearable technology successfully, people inside their social circle such as family and friends should also have a positive attitude towards smartwatch as well.

By the same token, accessibility was positively related to older adults' intention to actually use the smartwatch. This confirms previous findings whereby accessibility impacted older adults' technology use (McCreadie and Tinker 2005).

Lastly, the original TAM showed good relationship values except for the PEOU and AT path. This could indicate that for older adults, their attitude towards wearable technologies is not dependent on the usability of the product. This could mean that even though some older adults think that smartwatches are difficult or complicated, it does not mean that they think that it is not useful. This interesting result accounts for further investigation. This could mean that some aspects of the original TAM is not applicable to certain population, such as older adults.

6 Conclusion

Overall, the proposed model displays a huge potential in identifying key factors that affect older adults' adoption to technology, specifically in smartwatches. Findings from this study are not only limited to smartwatches but with continuous investigation, it can also be applied to different wearable technologies as well. However, this study is not without its limitations. First and foremost, the number of participants is relatively low to conduct structural equation modeling. Testing the model to a larger number of participants would verify and further confirm the results of this study. Moreover, the participants were only given a limited amount of time to test and learn about the smartwatches. It might be better for future researchers to consider extending the trial period to have a better grasp of older adults' attitude and perception of such devices. Additionally, participants in the present study included older adults aged 50 and above. Although the age-range of this particular population differs across studies, to some, this range may be a little broad to determine the older adult population. Thus, future studies could consider narrowing down the range to have a better focus on the target population. In conclusion, despite some certain limitations, the present study provides a good insight with regards to the acceptability factors for smartwatch adoption among older adults.

References

Barnard, Y., Bradley, M.D., Hodgson, F., Lloyd, A.D.: Learning to use new technologies by older adults: perceived difficulties, experimentation behaviour and usability. Comput. Hum. Behav. **29**(4), 1715–1724 (2013)

Bajaj, A., Nidumolu, S.R.: A feedback model to understand information system usage. Inf. Manag. **33**(4), 213–224 (1998)

Brown, S.A., Venkatesh, V.: Model of adoption of technology in households: a baseline model test and extension incorporating household life cycle. MIS Q. 399–426 (2005)

Conci, M., Pianesi, F., Zancanaro, M.: Useful, social and enjoyable: mobile phone adoption by older people. In: Gross, T., et al. (eds.) INTERACT 2009. LNCS, vol. 5726, pp. 63–76. Springer, Heidelberg (2009). https://doi.org/10.1007/978-3-642-03655-2_7

Cooper, C., et al.: The impact of wearable motion sensing technology on physical activity in older adults. Exp. Gerontol. **112**, 9–19 (2018)

Czaja, S.J., et al.: Factors predicting the use of technology: findings from the center for research and education on aging and technology enhancement (CREATE). Psychol. Aging **21**(2), 333 (2006)

Davis, F.D.: User acceptance of information technology: system characteristics, user perceptions and behavioral impacts. Int. J. Man Mach. Stud. **38**(3), 475–487 (1993)

Davis, F.D., Bagozzi, R.P., Warshaw, P.R.: User acceptance of computer technology: a comparison of two theoretical models. Manag. Sci. **35**(8), 982–1003 (1989)

Disztinger, P., Schlögl, S., Groth, A.: Technology acceptance of virtual reality for travel planning. In: Schegg, R., Stangl, B. (eds.) Information and Communication Technologies in Tourism 2017, pp. 255–268. Springer, Cham (2017). https://doi.org/10.1007/978-3-319-51168-9_19

Edmunds, R., Thorpe, M., Conole, G.: Student attitudes towards and use of ICT in course study, work and social activity: a technology acceptance model approach. Br. J. Edu. Technol. **43**(1), 71–78 (2012)

Harbich, S., Auer, S.: Rater bias: the influence of hedonic quality on usability questionnaires. In: Costabile, M.F., Paternò, F. (eds.) INTERACT 2005. LNCS, vol. 3585, pp. 1129–1133. Springer, Heidelberg (2005). https://doi.org/10.1007/11555261_121

Heinz, M., et al.: Perceptions of technology among older adults. J. Gerontol. Nurs. **39**(1), 42–51 (2013)

Joo, J., Sang, Y.: Exploring Koreans' smartphone usage: an integrated model of the technology acceptance model and uses and gratifications theory. Comput. Hum. Behav. **29**(6), 2512–2518 (2013)

Kim, K.J., Shin, D.H.: An acceptance model for smart watches: Implications for the adoption of future wearable technology. Internet Research **25**(4), 527–541 (2015)

Kim, K.J., Sundar, S.S.: Does screen size matter for smartphones? Utilitarian and hedonic effects of screen size on smartphone adoption. Cyberpsychol. Behav. Soc. Networking **17**(7), 466–473 (2014)

Lee, C., Coughlin, J.F.: PERSPECTIVE: older adults' adoption of technology: an integrated approach to identifying determinants and barriers. J. Prod. Innov. Manag. **32**(5), 747–759 (2015)

Lewis, J.E., Neider, M.B.: Designing wearable technology for an aging population. Ergon. Des. **25**(3), 4–10 (2017)

Masrom, M.: Technology acceptance model and e-learning. Technology **21**(24), 81 (2007)

McCreadie, C., Tinker, A.: The acceptability of assistive technology to older people. Ageing Soc. **25**(1), 91–110 (2005)

Mercer, K., Giangregorio, L., Schneider, E., Chilana, P., Li, M., Grindrod, K.: Acceptance of commercially available wearable activity trackers among adults aged over 50 and with chronic illness: a mixed-methods evaluation. JMIR mHealth and uHealth **4**(1), e7 (2016). https://doi.org/10.2196/mhealth.4225

Mitzner, T.L., Boron, J.B., Fausset, C.B., et al.: Older adults talk technology: technology usage and attitudes. Comput Human Behav. **26**(6), 1710–1721 (2010)

Muchna, A., Najafi, B., Wendel, C.S., Schwenk, M., Armstrong, D.G., Mohler, J.: Foot problems in older adults: associations with incident falls, frailty syndrome, and sensor-derived gait, balance, and physical activity measures. J. Am. Podiatr. Med. Assoc. **108**(2), 126–139 (2018)

Niemelä-Nyrhinen, J.: Baby boom consumers and technology: shooting down stereotypes. J. Consum. Mark. (2007)

Oetting, E.R.: Manual for Oetting's Computer Anxiety Scale (COMPAS). Rocky Mountain Behavioral Science Institute (1983)

Peek, S.T., Wouters, E.J., van Hoof, J., Luijkx, K.G., Boeije, H.R., Vrijhoef, H.J.: Factors influencing acceptance of technology for aging in place: a systematic review. Int. J. Med. Inform. **83**(4), 235–248 (2014)

Phang, C.W.J., Sutano, A., Kankanhalli, L., Yan, B.C.Y., Teo, H.H.: Senior citizens' acceptance of informations systems: a study in the context of e-Government services. IEEE Trans. Eng. Manage. **53**, 555–569 (2006)

Piwek, L., Ellis, D.A., Andrews, S., Joinson, A.: The rise of consumer health wearables: promises and barriers. PLoS Med. **13**(2), e1001953 (2016)

Quan-Hasse, A., Williams, C., Kicevski, M., Elueze, I., Wellman, B.: Dividing the grey divide: Deconsructing myths about older adults' online activities, skills, and attitudes. American Behavioral Scientist **62**(9), 1207–1228 (2018)

Saadé, R.G., Kira, D.: Mediating the impact of technology usage on perceived ease of use by anxiety. Comput. Educ. **49**(4), 1189–1204 (2007)

Saner, H.: Wearable sensors for assisted living in elderly people. Front. ICT **5**, 1 (2018)

Schulz, R., Wahl, H.W., Matthews, J.T., De Vito Dabbs, A., Beach, S.R., Czaja, S.J.: Advancing the aging and technology agenda in gerontology. Gerontologist **55**(5), 724–734 (2014)

Tanriverdi, H., Iacono, C.S.: Toy or useful technology?: the challenge of diffusing telemedicine in three boston hospitals. In: Success and Pitfalls of Information Technology Management, pp. 1–13. IGI Global (1999)

The Best Senior Wearables and Trackers (2018). https://smartwatches.org/learn/best-senior-wearables-gps-trackers/. Accessed 10 Nov 2018

Tsai, T.H., Lin, W.Y., Chang, Y.S., Chang, P.C., Lee, M.Y.: Technology anxiety and resistance to change behavioral study of a wearable cardiac warming system using an extended TAM for older adults. PLoS ONE **15**(1), e0227270 (2020)

United Nations, Department of Economic and Social Affairs, Population Division. World Population Ageing 2017 - Highlights (ST/ESA/SER.A/397) (2017)

Venkatesh, V.: Determinants of perceived ease of use: Integrating control, intrinsic motivation, and emotion into the technology acceptance model. Inf. Syst. Res. **11**(4), 342–365 (2000)

Wixom, B.H., Todd, P.A.: A theoretical integration of user satisfaction and technology acceptance. Inf. Syst. Res. **16**(1), 85–102 (2005)

Yanagisawa, H.: Kansei quality in product design. In: Fukuda, S. (ed.) Emotional engineering, pp. 289–310. Springer, London (2011). https://doi.org/10.1007/978-1-84996-423-4_16

Zhang, P., Li, N.: The importance of affective quality. Commun. ACM **48**(9), 105–108 (2005)

Exploring the Feasibility of the Elderly in the Space Guidance of Tactile Feedback Technology

Shuo-Fang Liu, Shi-Yu Wang(✉), and Ching-Fen Chang

Department of Industrial Design, National Cheng-Kung University, No. 1, University Road, Tainan City 701, Taiwan, Republic of China
wangshiyu638@gmail.com

Abstract. With the development of mobile devices, vibration feedback technology is also developing to help the deaf and the elderly. At present, mobile devices still use motor technology to provide vibration feedback. Therefore, the purpose of this study is to explore the feasibility of tactile feedback technology for the elderly in spatial guidance, and to provide a foundation for the development of mobile device manufacturers, so that the elderly can have good tactile feedback experience and improve the use quality. In this study, the elderly and the young were divided into the experimental group and the control group. The tactile feedback experiment of vibration was conducted in human hands, and the subjects were asked to draw direction graphs for the vibration samples. The results showed that the accuracy of the control group was 22.26% higher than that of the experimental group. The experimental group and the control group were tested by t test, and most of the samples were significant (P < 0.05). There were indeed differences in recognition ability among people of different age groups. The tactile feedback technique is feasible in space guidance.

Keywords: Touch · Tactile feedback · The elderly · Aging · Space navigation

1 Introduction

The world's population is getting older. In 2018, the number of people over the age of 65 exceeded the number of children under the age of 5 for the first time in the world, and the population of almost all countries and regions in the world is developing towards the aging trend [1]. As the aging of society becomes more and more serious, people pay more and more attention to the quality of life and happiness index of the elderly. Therefore, addressing the physiological and spiritual needs of the elderly has become the current design direction.

Nowadays, people are in the era of abundant science and technology and intelligent products, and more attention has been paid to the vibration and tactile feedback technology. Human perception system is the main channel for human body to obtain external information [2], including vision, hearing, smell, taste and touch. Touch is the most complex and widely distributed sense [3]. Compared with vision and hearing, touch shows

© Springer Nature Switzerland AG 2020
Q. Gao and J. Zhou (Eds.): HCII 2020, LNCS 12207, pp. 316–324, 2020.
https://doi.org/10.1007/978-3-030-50252-2_24

significant advantages in human body, for example, touch is all over the body, continuous information can be generated without special attention, and the contour orientation of objects can be effectively perceived through tactile stimulation [4, 5]. Vibratory touch is the most common form of tactile feedback, which can assist in information acquisition, orientation, motor training, and medical treatment .1 Vibratory touch has good bandwidth and is easy to realize in practical work (such as using blunt needles, voice coils or piezoelectric crystals to generate vibration) [6], which is an effective way to assist other senses such as visual hearing [7]. In the haptic system, the hand is a sensitive and complex sensory system, and the touch of the hand is crucial [8].

In the preliminary experiment of this group, we know that touch and gesture show good performance for increasing product interaction experience [9]. The sensory functions of the elderly will obviously decline with age, and the visual, hearing and spatial perception abilities will gradually decrease with age [10–13], resulting in inconvenience for the elderly when they use navigation tools to identify paths and directions. Tactile vibrations are used in different devices to convey information, such as navigation or warnings, without distracting the user [16]. Some uses of vibratory touch include vibratory vests [17], vibratory arm-type wristbands [18], or vibratory modes of mobile phones to let the user know the correct direction [19]. Although many haptic feedback techniques have not yet widely used, research has shown that haptic feedback can be applied to various parts of the body and can be developed in different functions, especially in noisy environments, to provide different information.

According to the results of previous experiments related to tactile feedback in our laboratory, there are differences between the elderly and the young in tactile feedback perception, which can also appropriately improve the usability of the elderly, as detailed below:

In terms of the perception of vibration size, the accuracy rate was 77.7% for people aged 20 to 50. For people over 50, the accuracy was 65.7%. From these data, we can clearly compare the deterioration of the sense of touch in the elderly. Their accuracy was 12% lower than that of people under 50. 14.

An experiment was carried out to explore the possible application of vibration feedback of motor. Four electric motors were used and they are mounted at four corners of the 5.5-in. and 9.7-in. prototypes. Test subjects are asked to touch the center of the device with their index finger and identify the vibrating motor. The results showed that there were significant differences in the perception of vibration position among different age groups, but no significant differences between the two sizes of the devices. The experiment used a 5.5-in. device to compare the sensation of vibrating positions in a handheld device. The results showed that there was little difference in the use of prototypes among different age groups. However, there is a big difference between single-finger use and handheld use in determining the vibration position [15].

In addition, kneading open/close and clockwise/counterclockwise rotation gestures were combined with four different types of vibration modes, and task completion time and idle rate for each task were compared. The aim is to increase the diversity of haptic feedback and to explore the applicability of haptic feedback technology in the future. The results showed that, comparing with the non-vibration mode, the vibration mode can shorten average running time, and the permanent vibration mode can significantly shorten the running time. In terms of the ratio of idling time, there is a significant difference between the non-vibrating continuous vibration (p value = 0.04) and non-vibrating and reminder vibration (p value = 0.039) in the pinch open gesture [9].

According to the above experimental data, we can know the feasibility of haptic feedback application. Therefore, the purpose of this experiment is to apply physical haptic feedback technology (drive motor) to assist middle-aged and elderly people to haptic feedback on mobile devices. The purpose of this paper is to investigate the feasibility of direction identification by receiving vibration feedback data.

Up to now, the research on tactile navigation assistance for the elderly is incomplete. Therefore, this study aims to explore the identification ability of elderly people for the orientation guidance generated by vibration and touch, which may be used in the future to remind elderly people of their behaviors or to improve their use experience.

2   Method

The purpose of this study was to investigate the ability of elderly people to recognize tactile sense of vibration and orientation guidance. The participants were all people without haptic and cognitive impairments. The samples were drawn based on a grid of 3*3. According to the directions of part of the navigation system as the basis of the experimental samples, the final data obtained were statistically analyzed by T test. The experimental instructions are as follows:

- This experiment is to explore the feedback of the recognition ability of the elderly and the young for the same vibration samples. It is known from previous experiments that there are differences in the perception of vibration and touch between elderly people and young people [14], so the participants are divided into two groups, 15 each: the experimental group is over 65 years old; The control group was young people aged 20 to 35. The participants responded based on the sensory representation of the vibration sample.
- Experiment objective: Exploring the feedback of elderly and young people's ability to identify the same vibration samples and explore whether the vibration combination samples can achieve the purpose of guiding the square. Participants gave feedback based on their perception of the vibration samples to see if they could provide orientation guidance.
- Measuring position: left palm. At present, due to the lack of human size data of the elderly over 65 in China, and the atrophy and decline of muscle and strength of the elderly hand, the data of their hand size will not exceed the corresponding adult hand size. According to relevant literature on human hand size, the width of an adult's palm is 6.2 cm.The length is 6.1 cm; Describe your diagram in order, as shown in Fig. 1.

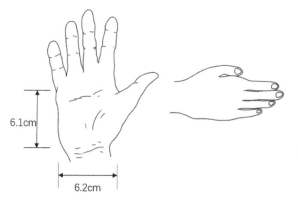

Fig. 1. Definition of human hand size (redrawn in this study)

Considering the future application of the technology and the fact that the direction information is mainly provided by vibration, it should be assisted without affecting the user to perform other operations, so the non-dominant hand will be used as the experimental stimulus site in the final experiment.

- Experimental equipment: motor/12 mm, motor and specification (Fig. 2).

Specification	Value
Voltage [V]	3
Voltage Range [V]	2.5~3.8
Rated Speed [rpm]	12000
Rated Current [mA]	75
Start Voltage [V]	2.3
Start Current [mA]	85
Terminal Resistance [Ohm]	75
Vibration Amplitude [G]	0.8

Fig. 2. Motors and specifications

- Experimental samples: the grid of 3*3 was used as the benchmark (Fig. 3), and the interval between each point was 2 cm. The numerical sequence was used to represent the vibration sequence of the motor, and the experimental samples were used (Table 1). Sample legend (Fig. 4).
- Statistical analysis: The experimental group (over 65 years old) and the control group (20–35 years old) were analyzed (using SPSS statistical software for t test). Whether there are differences among different ethnic groups.

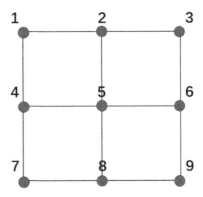

Fig. 3. Motor distribution diagram

Table 1. Experimental samples

Vibration direction	Project
	Experimental sample
Horizontal direction	P1/4-5-6
	P2/6-5-4
Vertical direction	P3/2-5-8
	P4/8-5-2
Turning direction	P5/1-2-3-6-9; P6/3-6-9-8-7; P7/9-8-7-4-1; P8/7-4-1-2-3
	P9/9-6-3-2-1; P10/7-8-9-6-3; P11/1-4-7-8-9; P12/3-2-1-4-7

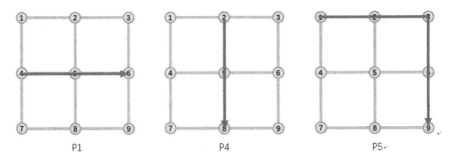

Fig. 4. Sample legend

3   Result

The mean response rate of the control group samples was 86.68%, the mean response rate of the experimental group samples was 64.42%, and the response rate of the control group samples was 22.26% higher than that of the experimental group samples (Fig. 5).Thus, young people have a higher degree of recognition of the directivity generated by vibration, while older people have a lower degree of recognition. Among the 12 samples, the response rate of samples in the control group was basically higher than that in the experimental group, with particularly obvious performance of samples P1/P2/P3 (Fig. 6). In samples P4~P12, the difference between the two groups was small. It can be seen from this that the experimental group performed poorly in recognizing the straight direction, and well in recognizing the turning direction.

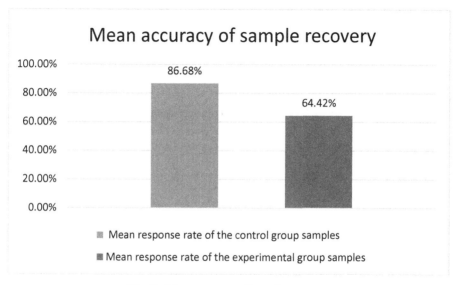

Fig. 5. Mean accuracy of sample recovery

As shown in Table 2, t test of samples of the experimental group and control group showed that all samples were significant except P4/P6/P12 ($P < 0.05$), indicating that there were indeed differences between the experimental group and control group in spatial orientation guidance.

It can be concluded from the experimental results that in the identification of the vertical and horizontal samples (p1–p4), sample P4 is not significant ($P > 0.05$), and the accuracy is low ($\leq 60\%$).After observing the response samples, we found that most of the error responses were similar, and the test subjects were susceptible to the influence of adjacent motors, resulting in the perception error. Therefore, errors occurred during the sample response stage. In the identification of the turning direction samples (p5–p12), samples 6 and 12 were not significant ($P > .05$).We observed that the commonality between the two samples was that the end point was point 7, and point 7 was at the

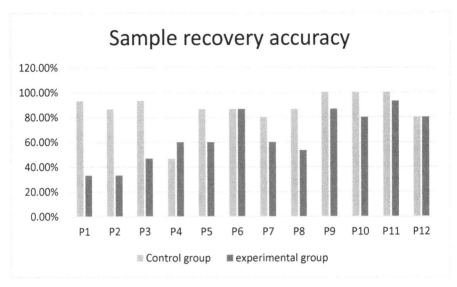

Fig. 6. Sample recovery accuracy

Table 2. T-test of experimental samples

The sample	The experimental group (mean)	The control group (mean)	t	P - value
P1	1.67	1.07	4.209	0.000
The P2	1.67	1.13	3.434	0.011
P3	1.53	1.07	3.130	0.000
P4	1.40	1.53	7.140	0.526
P5	1.40	1.13	1.673	0.002
P6	1.13	1.13	0.000	1.000
P7	1.40	1.20	1.183	0.029
P8	1.47	1.13	2.066	0.000
P9	1.13	1.00	1.468	0.002
P10	1.20	1.00	1.871	0.000
P11	1.07	1.00	1.000	0.040
P12	1.20	1.20	0.000	1.000

projection of the human palm. Therefore, it can be speculated that the protruding part of the human palm has a low sensitivity, and the vibration is easy to spread out, which is not easy to be recognized by the test subjects. As a result, the accuracy of the subjects' response to the samples decreased.

4 Conclusion

According to the latest literature, it is known that user satisfaction can be improved by providing different kinds of tactile feedback. The elderly has visual and auditory problems and reduced use of cognitive and motor functions. These problems may cause the elderly to have difficulty using mobile devices. But current feedback technology in mobile devices can help older users cope with these physical changes.

Through the tactile vibration experiment on human hands, this study concludes that vibratory tactile sense is indeed effective in assisting the elderly to identify spatial guidance, and the elderly can identify the directivity generated by vibratory tactile sense. However, due to the equipment limitations of this study, some of the results may have errors. During the experiment, we found that the electric motor should fit the human hand as closely as possible on the experimental equipment. Secondly, the spacing between motors should be larger in consideration of the diffusion of motor vibration. In addition, since the physiological characteristics of prominent depression in the palm will affect the accuracy of directional expression, experiments can be conducted on the relatively flat back of the hand or other parts in the later stage.

In the future, in order to make the product meet the use needs of the elderly, more experiments need to be conducted to verify the effectiveness, so as to improve the tactile feedback experience of the elderly and help them learn and use smart devices. This experiment provides relevant tactile feedback reference for mobile device developers, so as to provide assistance and support for the product experience of the elderly in the future.

Acknowledgements. We are thankful for the financial support from the Ministry of Science and Technology (MOST), Taiwan. The grant MOST 107-2221-e-006-169 & MOST 108-2221-e-006-048.

References

1. United Nations, Department of Economic and Social Affairs, Population Division. World Population Prospects 2019: Highlights (ST/ESA/SER.A/423) (2019)
2. Wickens, C.D.: Multiple resources and mental workload. Hum. Factors **50**(3), 449–455 (2008). https://doi.org/10.1518/001872008x288394
3. Lei, C.X., Ding, J.Z., Si, G.C., et al.: Research status and applications of tactile vibration. J. Navy Med. **31**(4), 373–375 (2010)
4. Maeno, T., Kobayashi, K., Yamazaki, N.: Relationship between the structure of human finger tissue and the location of tactile receptors. Bull. JSME Int. **41**(1), 94–100 (1998)
5. Liu, S.Q., Huang, W.Y., Wang, A.M., et al.: Overview and prospect of research and development on robot tactile sensory technology. Robot **24**(4), 362–374 (2002)
6. Gunther, E., O'Modhrain, S.: Cutaneous grooves: composing for the sense of touch. J. New Music Res. **32**(4), 369–381 (2003). https://doi.org/10.1076/jnmr.32.4.369.18856
7. Diamond, D.D., Kass, S.J., Andrasik, F., Raj, A.K., Rupert, A.H.: Vibrotactile cueing as a master caution system for visual monitoring. Hum. Factors Aerosp. Saf. **2**, 339–354 (2002)

8. Bensmaia, S., Tillery, S.I.H.: Tactile Feedback from the Hand. In: Balasubramanian, R., Santos, Veronica J. (eds.) The human hand as an inspiration for robot hand development. STAR, vol. 95, pp. 143–157. Springer, Cham (2014). https://doi.org/10.1007/978-3-319-030 17-3_7

9. Liu, S.-F., Chueh, Y.-S., Chang, C.-F., Lin, P.-Y., Cheng, H.-S.: A study of performance on multi-touch gesture for multi-haptic feedback. In: Zhou, J., Salvendy, G. (eds.) HCII 2019. LNCS, vol. 11592, pp. 441–449. Springer, Cham (2019). https://doi.org/10.1007/978-3-030-22012-9_32

10. Head, D., Isom, M.: Age effects on wayfinding and route learning skills. Behav. Brain Res. **209**(1), 49–58 (2010). https://doi.org/10.1016/j.bbr.2010.01.012

11. Iaria, G., Palermo, L., Committeri, G., Barton, J.J.S.: Age differences in the formation and use of cognitive maps. Behav. Brain Res. **196**(2), 187–191 (2009). https://doi.org/10.1016/j.bbr.2008.08.040

12. León, I., Tascón, L., Cimadevilla, J.M.: Age and gender-related differences in a spatial memory task in humans. Behav. Brain Res. **306**, 8–12 (2016). https://doi.org/10.1016/j.bbr.2016.03.008

13. Tascón, L., Castillo, J., Cimadevilla, J.M.: Age-related differences in the elderly in a spatial recognition task. Memory (2019). https://doi.org/10.1080/09658211.2019.1663216

14. Liu, S.-F., Yang, Y.-T., Chang, C.-F., Lin, P.-Y., Cheng, H.-S.: A study on haptic feedback awareness of senior citizens. In: Zhou, J., Salvendy, G. (eds.) ITAP 2018. LNCS, vol. 10926, pp. 315–324. Springer, Cham (2018). https://doi.org/10.1007/978-3-319-92034-4_24

15. Liu, S.-F., Cheng, H.-S., Chang, C.-F., Lin, P.-Y.: A study of perception using mobile device for multi-haptic feedback. In: Yamamoto, S., Mori, H. (eds.) HIMI 2018. LNCS, vol. 10904, pp. 218–226. Springer, Cham (2018). https://doi.org/10.1007/978-3-319-92043-6_19

16. Elliott, L.R., van Erp, J.B.F., Redden, E.S., Duistermaat, M.: Field-based validation of a tactile navigation device (2010)

17. Hung, C.-T., Croft, E.A., Van der Loos, H.F.M.: A wearable vibrotactile device for upper-limb bilateral motion training in stroke rehabilitation: a case study (2015)

18. Kandel, E.R., Schwartz, J.H., Jessell, T.M.: Principles of Neural Science (1991)

19. Pielot, M., Poppinga, B., Heuten, W., Boll, S.: PocketNavigator: studying tactile navigation systems in-situ (2012)

Attitudinal and Behavioral Differences Between Older and Younger Adults Using Mobile Devices

Elizabeth Nichols[(⊠)], Erica Olmsted-Hawala[(⊠)], Andrew Raim[(⊠)], and Lin Wang[(⊠)]

U.S. Census Bureau, Washington D.C., USA
{elizabeth.may.nichols,erica.l.olmsted.hawala,andrew.raim,
lin.wang}@census.gov

Abstract. Research has shown that older adults take more time to perform tasks and have higher satisfaction than younger adults for a variety of activities. Through a series of controlled experiments at the U.S. Census Bureau, we confirm that older adults do take longer to complete surveys on smartphones, but the increase in satisfaction compared to younger adults is only marginally significant. In these experiments, we also found that the age effects do not vary by the smartphone survey designs tested, suggesting that designers could focus on improving designs for older adults and younger adults would benefit from those changes.

Keywords: Mobile survey design · Older adults · Time-on-task · Positivity effect

1 Introduction

A significant body of research has documented age-related decline in cognitive and motor abilities among adults over 60 [1–7]. These declines manifest themselves in a variety of ways. Slower reaction time for older adults has been documented for a number of tasks, for example: naming items [8], wayfinding [9], and simple and complex auditory tasks [10].

Age-related differences have also been found in accomplishing tasks with technology devices. Some studies have focused on measuring behavioral differences when using a computer mouse or when touching the screen. Older users took longer to select targets using a PC mouse than younger or middle-aged adults but there was no time difference by age when the task was to touch the target on the PC screen [11]. When using touch on smaller devices, age related differences appear. For example, one study found that older adults took longer to touch targets, and made more selection errors in terms of misses and slip rate (where the person originally hits the target but slips off the target before lifting the finger) compared to younger adults on smaller devices [12]. Other researchers found that while older adults were slower in touch target tasks than younger adults, the gap between the two groups was smaller with iPad touch screens than with a mouse on desktop screens [13]. Similarly, another study found that the computer mouse increased both cognitive- and motor-demands compared to touch pad and touch screen for tasks involving static image selection [14]. Touch screens, especially with large touch buttons,

This is a U.S. government work and not under copyright protection
in the U.S.; foreign copyright protection may apply 2020
Q. Gao and J. Zhou (Eds.): HCII 2020, LNCS 12207, pp. 325–337, 2020.
https://doi.org/10.1007/978-3-030-50252-2_25

more easily accommodate older adults compared to a mouse or keyboard for input [15]. In addition to reaction time, website research has found differences in eye movement between older and younger adults [16, 17]. These data suggest smaller devices lead to more performance issues for older adults.

In general these findings suggest that devices activated by touch might be easier for older adults to use than desktop or laptop computers, which require an external navigation device such as a mouse or keyboard. These studies also suggest that device size influences performance, with larger touch devices leading to fewer differences between older and younger users. This is especially the case for novice users as research also shows the amount of time spent using and interacting with devices affects older adult performance [14, 18]. The direction of the relationship is as expected with more experience with a device type leading to more positive usability outcomes such as higher accuracy and increased speed accomplishing tasks.

Some studies have focused on improving the usability of smartphones by designing inputs on smartphones for older adults. For touch entry, Murata & Iwase (2005) found 16.5 mm (about .6 in.) button size and gaps between buttons resulted in the fastest reaction time for older users [11]. In order to reduce performance error rates for older users, the optimal amount of spacing between buttons was found to be between 3.17 mm and 12.7 mm (about .12 to .5 in.) [15]. One study warns against using small buttons and placing frequently used buttons on the right side, especially the lower right side, of the screen because of thumb mobility issues in older adults, given the assumption of right-single handed phone operation [19].

While tasks on mobile devices still might take longer for older adults to accomplish, that does not necessarily mean that older adults will be less satisfied with accomplishing those tasks. Older adults have been associated with what has been called a "positivity effect" [20]. That is, researchers have observed a shift in behavior and attitude from a negativity bias early in life to a positivity bias in middle and late adulthood [21]. One study concludes that older adults rate experiences more positively not because they forget or suppress negative experiences or have fewer negative experiences compared to younger adults, but rather they simply assess those experiences more favorably than younger adults [26]. This was true for both real and hypothetical life experiences. In that study, older adults could recall negative experiences (both real and hypothetical) as well as younger adults. However their appraisal of those real and hypothetical experiences were more positive than their younger counterparts. While there is some contradictory evidence, the effect has been documented in over 100 studies [22]. Examples of this positivity effect include but are not limited to visual attention (older adults remembered and focused on pictures of positive social interactions more so than younger adults) [23], working memory (responded better to positive images) [24], and short-term memory (remembered the positive words and pictures more) [25].

The mission of the U.S. Census Bureau is to produce accurate statistics of the American people, households and economy. Determining the best questions and designs to use to collect the information is essential to producing accurate data. During development of surveys, we measure reaction time and user satisfaction with different survey designs with the goal of developing surveys that collect accurate data in the least burdensome manner. In this present study we use data from three experiments on smartphones to explore whether optimal survey designs for older users are also optimal for younger users as measured by time-on-task; whether older adults take more time to complete survey questions (regardless of design) compared to younger adults; and whether the positivity effect holds when older adults complete surveys on smartphones.

The original data collection was focused on optimal designs for mobile web surveys [27–29]. The data were generated from a series of experiments where older adults completed different survey tasks on mobile phones using different screen designs. Based on their performance, satisfaction, and preference, mobile web survey design guidelines were proposed. The assumption was that if older adults performed optimally with a specific design, then younger adults would do at least as well because of their superior perceptual and motor capabilities. To validate this underlying assumption, younger adults were also recruited for this work. This paper has a two-fold purpose. First, it explores whether survey designs that take less time for older adults to complete also reduce the time younger adults need to complete the survey. Hypothesis 1 is that given the same device size and touch feature size, the effect of age on question completion time will not vary by survey design. That is, if one design takes older adults more time to complete, then it also will take younger adults more time to complete. Second, the paper compares the behavioral and attitudinal differences of older adults and younger adults by examining the reaction time and satisfaction data collected for these experiments to determine if reaction time increases for older adults using mobile survey designs than younger adults and whether there is a positivity effect for a common usability metric of satisfaction in use of the online mobile survey. Hypotheses 2 and 3 are that older adults will take more time to answer questions on mobile web surveys than younger adults regardless of design and they will have higher satisfaction answering those surveys than younger adults.

2 Methods

Below are highlights of methods relevant to the three experiments described in this paper. In the analyses, we consider significance to be at $p = 0.05$ or less.

2.1 Participants

The participants were a convenience sample recruited from senior centers, community centers, and community colleges in a major metropolitan area in the U.S. between late 2016 and the summer of 2018. We prescreened participants to make sure they owned a smartphone and had at least 12 months of experience using a smartphone. Additionally, we prescreened participants to include only individuals who had an 8th grade education or higher, who were fluent in English, and who had normal (or corrected to normal) vision.

Participant characteristics are provided in Table 1. Experiments 1, 2 and 3 were conducted with a pool of 122, 71, and 40 participants respectively. The mean, median and range of participant ages are provided in Table 1 to show that the data skewed older for some experiments and younger for others. Some participants participated in more than one experiment.

Table 1. Participant demographics for 3 experiments.

Experiment	Average age (St. Deviation)	Median age	Age range	Male/Female
Experiment 1 Field labels (n = 122)	48.3 (23.0)	60	17–77	73/49
Experiment 2 Dropdowns (n = 71)	54.2 (22.0)	64	18–80	26/45
Experiment 3 State dropdown (n = 40)	31.6 (16.9)	21	17–64	25/15

2.2 Data Collection Methods

One-on-one sessions were conducted at senior centers, community centers, and community colleges. Participants were walk-ups that day or were pre-scheduled. At the appointment time, they were screened by Census Bureau staff and signed a consent form. Then, each participant worked with a test administrator (TA) and completed between 4 to 6 experiments, only a subset of which are the subject of this paper. In this paper, we draw upon the experiments that collected data from older and younger adults. The experiments were implemented as mobile apps which were loaded on a Census-owned iPhone 5s or 6s. Test administrators provided participants with one of these devices for purposes of the experiment, and gave instructions to the participants. This included instructing participants *not* to talk aloud during the session, and to complete the survey to the best of their ability as though they were answering the survey at home without anyone's assistance. The participants performed the task independently, taking 10–20 min for each experiment, depending upon the experimental design. At the end of the session, each participant was given a $40 honorarium.

2.3 Stimuli

Each experiment consisted of a series of survey questions, with one question per screen and distinct design conditions. While the same questions were asked within each experiment, the design of the screens differed depending on the condition. The questions also differed across experiments. The following description is provided for each experiment so the reader has a sense of the stimuli participants encountered.

Using a between-subjects experimental design, Experiment 1 tested five different label location conditions for text input fields as shown in Figs. 1, 2, 3, 4 and 5. Participants were randomly assigned to one condition. Each condition had the same 14 open-ended questions on a range of topics. All the questions required the participant to interact with the keyboard or keypad on the phone. Participants were instructed to answer the questions as they would if they were at home and with no researcher present.

Using a between-subjects experimental design, Experiment 2 tested three different select-one conditions as shown in Figs. 6, 7 and 8. Two of the conditions (Figs. 6 and 7) were dropdowns. When focus was placed on the dropdown, the answer choices appear in the default manner of either an iOS display (with the answer choices at the bottom

Fig. 1. Label above box.

Fig. 2. Inline labels that move.

Fig. 3. Label to the left of the box and left aligned.

Fig. 4. Label to left and right align.

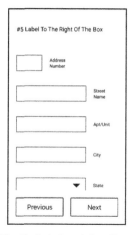

Fig. 5. Label to right of box.

in a spinner wheel – Fig. 6) or an Android display where the answer choices appear as a pop-up window (Fig. 7). Participants were randomly assigned to one condition. Each condition had the same 12 questions. All the questions required only a single answer, but some questions had a long list of possible response choices and other questions had fewer response options. Again, participants were instructed to answer the questions as they would if they were at home and with no researcher present.

Using a between-subjects experimental design, Experiment 3 tested three different ways to display the states in an Android spinner design as shown in Figs. 9, 10 and 11. Participants were randomly assigned to one condition. There was only one question "What state shall I select?" The participant was instructed to read that question aloud and the TA replied by reading a state name from a randomized list. The participant recorded the state, selected next and the sequence repeated 50 more times with the TA responding

Fig. 6. iOS picker.

Fig. 7. Android spinner.

Fig. 8. Radio button/keypad.

with a new state so that all 50 states and the District of Columbia were entered. In this experiment, participants answered the questions based on data provided to them orally by the TA.

Fig. 9. Full state name.

Fig. 10. State abbreviation.

Fig. 11. State abbr. & name.

2.4 Analytic Strategy

The original goal of the experiments was to determine which mobile survey designs worked the best for users. To answer that question, we compared behavioral measures captured within the app between the conditions within an experiment. Two behavioral measures captured across all experiments were time-on-screen and a self-reported satisfaction rating as measured by the participant rating the task on a scale of easy to difficult. The latter was captured once for each participant after he or she had finished the survey. The participant was asked to rate how easy or difficult it was to complete the task on a 5-point scale with the endpoints labeled 1 = Very Easy and 5 = Very Difficult. In this paper, we use these data to answer age-related questions.

To answer the first research question, whether the effect of age on question completion time varies by survey design, we used a mixed model (PROC MIXED in SAS) for each experiment. The outcome measure was the log of time to complete a screen at the question level. Modeling at the question level increases the number of observations and allows us to account for different question characteristics. We controlled for the condition, the age of the participant, and the interaction between condition and age. Because participants contribute a response for each question in the survey, we included a random effect for each participant. If the interaction between condition and age was significant, then the effect of age on completion time varies by survey design; if the interaction was not significant, then there is insufficient evidence that a design that is optimal for older adults (with regard to time-on-task) would differ from that for younger adults. We ran three separate models instead of collapsing the data together because some experiments produced significant differences by design.

To answer the second research question, whether older adults take longer to answer survey questions on a mobile phone than younger adults regardless of design, we ran the same models but without the interaction term. If the fixed effect of age is significant in the model, then the sign of the coefficient indicates whether the association between age and response time is positive or negative: i.e., a positive association indicates that increased age corresponds to increased response time.

To answer the third research question, whether older adults are more satisfied with the mobile web survey than younger adults, we combined the satisfaction data across the experiments and ran a proportional odds model (PROC LOGISTIC in SAS) with the satisfaction score (1 through 5) as the dependent variable and the age as the predictor variable. If age is significant in the model, then the sign of the coefficient indicates whether the association between age and satisfaction is positive or negative: i.e., a positive association indicates that increased age corresponds to increased satisfaction. We collapsed the data across the three experiments together for this analysis because there were so few dissatisfied participants based on the scores.

3 Results

3.1 Hypothesis 1: The Effect of Age on Question Completion Time Will not Vary by Survey Design

Table 2 contains the model results predicting time with the interaction term, the condition (design) and age for each of the experiments. Examining the p value for the interaction terms in these models, across all three experiments, we do not find sufficient evidence that time to complete different survey designs varies by the age of the participant, meaning that designs that take older adults longer to complete also take younger adults longer to complete, when compared to other designs. Therefore we do not reject Hypothesis 1.

3.2 Hypothesis 2: Older Adults Will Take More Time to Answer Questions on Mobile Web Surveys Than Younger Adults Regardless of Design

Table 3 displays results for models of log response time, without the interaction term, for each of the experiments. Examining the p value for the fixed effect of age in these

Table 2. Type 3 Test of fixed effects for models with interaction term. Each column displays three (individual) F-tests for the specified experiment. Each entry shows the p value of the test, along with the numerator and denominator degrees of freedom in parentheses.

Fixed effects	Experiment 1	Experiment 2	Experiment 3
Condition	0.3 (4, 1560)	0.1 (2, 755)	0.5 (2, 2000)
Age	<0.01 (1, 1560)	<0.01 (1, 755)	<0.01 (1, 2000)
Condition*age	0.4 (4, 1560)	0.9 (2, 755)	0.9 (2, 2000)

models, we find that age significantly predicts time-on task in each of the experiments. The β coefficient in each of the models for age was positive. The positive coefficient means that as age increases, so does the time to answer the survey questions. Therefore we do not reject Hypothesis 2. We conclude that older adults take longer than younger adults to complete questions on mobile web surveys for questions that require the user to answer a question by touching an answer choice after reading a question (Experiment 2 and 3) and for questions that require the user to type an answer (Experiment 1). The coefficient was larger for Experiment 1 than the other experiments, which implies that the reaction time gap between older and younger users is wider for touch typing than for simply selecting touch buttons.

Table 3. Solution for Fixed Effects for main effect models only. Note these values come from individual tests and not a joint experiment. Estimated coefficient values are displayed with associated p-values in parentheses.

Fixed effects	Experiment 1	Experiment 2	Experiment 3
Intercept	2.8 (<0.01)	2.3 (<0.01)	1.6 (<0.01)
Condition	2 = −0.1 (0.3) 3 = −0.1 (0.5) 4 = −0.1 (0.5) 5 = −0.1 (0.3) 1 = reference cell	2 = −0.3 (<0.01) 3 = −0.6 (<0.01) 1 = reference cell	2 = −0.3 (<0.01) 3 = −0.1 (0.4) 1 = reference cell
Age	0.01 (<0.01)	0.006 (<0.01)	0.008 (<0.01)

Figures 12, 13 and 14 show the estimated line for the effect of age on time for each of the experiments. The dotted lines represent pointwise 95% confidence bounds, which become wider as age increases, suggesting that there is more variability in reaction time for older adults than for younger adults. While it could also mean that there are fewer older adults, in Experiment 1 and 2, this is not the case, as the median age is 60 or older.

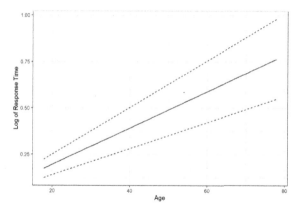

Fig. 12. Estimated line for the effect of age on log of time for Experiment 1.

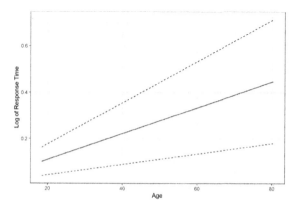

Fig. 13. Estimated line for the effect of age on log of time for Experiment 2.

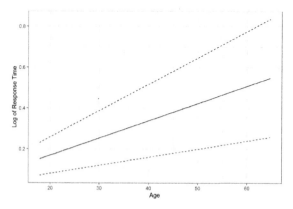

Fig. 14. Estimated line for the effect of age on log of time for Experiment 3.

3.3   Hypothesis 3: Older Adults are More Satisfied with the Mobile Web Survey Than Younger Adults

Figure 15 contains the distribution of satisfaction scores combined across all three experiments for older (n = 109) and younger adults (n = 118). Older adults were defined as individuals 60 years old or older. The scores indicate that most participants regardless of age found the tasks and interfaces easy to use.

Fig. 15. Distribution of satisfaction scores combined across the three experiments by participant age.

The proportional odds model found age to be marginally associated with satisfaction (*p* value 0.079) with coefficient $\hat{\beta} = 0.0104$. Here, a positive coefficient represents a *negative* association between age and survey difficulty, so that older participants are more likely to report lower difficulty with the survey. This provides marginal evidence in favor of Hypothesis 3.

4   Discussion

The purpose of this research was to add to the literature on age-related differences on mobile survey completion and satisfaction with mobile web surveys.

Our first hypothesis was that there would not be a significant interaction between age and different mobile web designs when predicting time to complete a survey question. We could not reject the hypothesis for any of the experiments, meaning that designs that worked well for older users also worked well for younger users or the designs work equally poorly regardless of participant age. This research provides some evidence that for mobile web survey design, testing with older users could be sufficient for testing different touch and keyboard designs to come up with design guidelines that are based on time-on-task metrics.

In all three experiments, the time needed to complete the experiments increased as the age of the participant increased which supports Hypothesis 2. This finding was in-line with other research which found older adults taking longer to complete tasks on mobile phones [12]. This increase in time was found for subtasks that required on-screen keyboard/keypad use, and for surveys that required touching buttons. Based on the model coefficients, the gap between older and younger users is wider for tasks that involve touching and interacting with the keyboard and keypad compared to simply touching buttons. Based on the confidence bounds, there is more variability in time-on-task as participants age. As an overall measure of time needed with designs, testing only with older users will lead to a bias of longer time; while testing only with younger users will lead to the opposite conclusion. This highlights the importance of recruiting participants of different ages for any human-computer design testing.

This research also suggests that surveys are generally easy to complete and generate high satisfaction scores. We found a marginally significant increase in positive scores for older adults over those of younger adults to support our third hypothesis. This finding was also in line with other research which finds a positivity effect at work in older adults [22].

5 Limitations

Much of the cognitive aging literature is based on relatively small samples of college students and older adult volunteers brought into university labs, whereas middle-aged adults or those without some college education are included less often [30]. Our research also used a convenience sample of young adults from community colleges and older adults who traveled to community centers. Additionally, our sample lived in one major metropolitan area. While we are unaware of any regional differences in smartphone use, it could be that older adults who cannot travel outside of their homes would behave differently. It also could be that non college-educated younger individuals and middle-aged individuals would behave differently. While we did not have a random sample, the statistical methodology used assumes a random sample. Future research should aim to recruit these other user groups to determine if results differ. Additionally, future studies could include other survey tasks besides typing answers and selecting buttons, such as navigating between pages, dragging and dropping actions, and reading text. Besides time-on-task, future studies could look at accuracy of responses.

Disclaimer. This report is released to inform interested parties of research and to encourage discussion. The views expressed are those of the authors and not necessarily those of the U.S. Census Bureau. The disclosure review number for this paper: CBDRB-FY20-143.

Acknowledgements. The study was supported by the U.S. Census Bureau's Innovation and Operational Efficiency Program. We thank Russell Sanders, Christopher Antoun, Brian Falcone, Ivonne Figueroa, Alda Rivas, Joanna Lineback, Sabin Lakhe, Kevin Younes, and the MetroStar team. We also thank Eugene Loos, Jenny Childs, Thomas Mathew, Shaun Genter, Paul Beatty, and Joanne Pascale for reviews of the paper.

References

1. Craik, F.I.M., Salthouse, T.A.: The Handbook of Aging and Cognition, 3rd edn. Psychology Press, NewYork (2008)
2. Hofer, S.M., Alwin, D.F.: Handbook of Cognitive Aging: Interdisciplinary Perspectives. SAGE Publications Inc., Thousand Oaks (2008). https://doi.org/10.4135/9781412976589
3. Karlamangla, A.S., Miller-Martinez, D., Aneshensel, C.S., Seeman, T.E., Wight, R.G., Chodosh, J.: Trajectories of cognitive function in late life in the United States: demographic and socioeconomic predictors. Am. J. Epidemiol. **170**, 331–342 (2009). https://doi.org/10.1093/aje/kwp154
4. Bashore, T.R., Osman, A., Heffley III, E.F.: Mental slowing in elderly persons: a cognitive psychophysiological analysis. Psychol. Aging **4**(2), 235–244 (1989). https://doi.org/10.1037//0882-7974.4.2.235
5. Salthouse, T.: When does age-related cognitive decline begin? Neurobiol. Aging **30**(4), 507–514 (2009)
6. Hultsch, D.F., Hertzog, C., Dixon, R.A.: Ability correlates of memory performance in adulthood and aging. Psychol. Aging **5**(3), 356–368 (1990). https://doi.org/10.1037/0882-7974.5.3.356
7. Kester, J.D., Benjamin, A.S., Castel, A.D., Craik, F.I.M.: Memory in elderly people. In: Baddeley, A.D., Kopelman, M.D., Wilson, B.A. (eds.) The Handbook of Memory Disorders, pp. 543–568. Wiley (2002)
8. Zhang, H., Eppes, A., Diaz, M.T.: Task difficulty modulates age-related differences in the behavioral and neural bases of language production. Neuropsychologia **124**, 254–273 (2019)
9. Head, D., Isom, M.: Age effects on wayfinding and route learning skills. Behav. Brain Res. **209**(1), 49–58 (2010)
10. Tun, P.A., Lachman, M.E.: Age differences in reaction time and attention in a national telephone sample of adults: education, sex, and task complexity matter. Dev. Psychol. **44**(5), 1421–1429 (2008)
11. Murata, A., Iwase, M.: Usability of touch-panel interfaces for older adults. Hum. Fact. **47**(4), 767–776 (2005)
12. Sultana, A., Moffatt, K.: Effects of aging on small target selection with touch input. ACM Trans. Access. Comput. **12**(1), 1–35 (2019)
13. Findlater, L., Froehlich, J.E., Fattal, K., Wobbrock, J.O., Tanya Dastyar, T.: Age-related differences in performance with touchscreens compared to traditional mouse input. In: Proceedings of the SIGCHI Conference on Human Factors in Computing Systems (CHI 2013), pp. 343–346. ACM, New York (2013)
14. Wood, E., Willoughby, T., Rushing, A., Bechtel, L., Gilbert, J.: Use of computer input devices by older adults. J. Appl. Gerontol. **24**(5), 419–438 (2005)
15. Jin, Z.X., Plocher, T., Kiff, L.: Touch screen user interfaces for older adults: button size and spacing. In: UAHCI 2007 Proceedings of the 4th International Conference on Universal Access in Human Computer Interaction: Coping with Diversity, pp. 933–941 (2007)
16. Loos, E.F., Romano Bergstrom, J.: Older adults. In: Romano Bergstrom, J., Schall, A.J. (eds.) Eye Tracking in User Experience Design, Elsevier, Amsterdam, pp. 313–329 (2014)
17. Al-Showarah, S., AL-Jawad, N., Sellahewa, H.: Effects of user age on smartphone and tablet use, measured with an eye-tracker via fixation duration, scan-path duration, and saccades proportion. In: Stephanidis, C., Antona, M. (eds.) UAHCI 2014. LNCS, vol. 8514, pp. 3–14. Springer, Cham (2014). https://doi.org/10.1007/978-3-319-07440-5_1

18. Grewal, S., Sahni, R.K.: Effect of smartphone addiction on reaction time in geriatric population. J. Novel Physiotherapy Phys. Rehabil. **6**(1), 005–009 (2019)
19. Xiong, J., Muraki, S.: Thumb performance of elderly users on smartphone touchscreen. SpringerPlus **5**(1), 1218 (2016)
20. Kennedy, Q., Mather, M., Carstensen, L.L.: The role of motivation in the age-related positivety effect in autobiographical memory. Psychol. Sci. **15**, 208–214 (2004)
21. Carstensen, L.L.: Integrating cognitive and emotion paradigms to address the paradox of aging. Cogn. Emot. **33**(1), 119–125 (2018)
22. Reed, A.E., Chan, L., Mikels, J.A.: Meta-analysis of the age-related positivity effect: age differences in preferences for positive over negative information. Psychol. Aging **29**(1), 1–15 (2014)
23. Sasse, L.K., Gamer, M., Büchel, C., Brassen, S.: Selective control of attention supports the positivity effect in aging. PLoS One **9**(8) (2014)
24. Mikels, J.A., Larkin, G.R., Reuter-Lorenz, P.A., Carstensen, L.L.: Divergent trajectories in the aging mind: changes in working memory for affective versus visual information with age. Psychol. Aging **20**(4), 542–553 (2005)
25. Mammarella, N., Di Domenico, A., Palumbo, R., Fairfield, B.: When green is positive and red is negative: aging and the influence of color on emotional memories. Psychol. Aging **31**(8), 914–926 (2016)
26. Schryer, E., Ross, M.: Does the age-related positivity effect in autobiographical recall reflect differences in appraisal or memory? J. Gerontol. Ser. B: Psychol. Sci. Soc. Sci. **69**(4), 548–556 (2014)
27. Nichols, E., Olmsted-Hawala, E., Wang, L.: Optimal designs of text input fields in mobile web surveys for older adults. In: Zhou, J., Salvendy, G. (eds.) HCII 2019. LNCS, vol. 11592, pp. 463–481. Springer, Cham (2019). https://doi.org/10.1007/978-3-030-22012-9_34
28. Olmsted-Hawala, E., Nichols, E., Falcone, B., Figueroa, I.J., Antoun, C., Wang, L.: Optimal data entry designs in mobile web surveys for older adults. In: Zhou, J., Salvendy, G. (eds.) ITAP 2018. LNCS, vol. 10926, pp. 335–354. Springer, Cham (2018). https://doi.org/10.1007/978-3-319-92034-4_26
29. Wang, L., et al.: Experimentation for developing evidence-based UI standards of mobile survey questionnaires. In: Proceedings of the 2017 CHI Conference Extended Abstracts on Human Factors in Computing Systems, pp. 2998–3004, Colorado. ACM Press (2017)
30. Hughes, M., Agrigoroaei, S., Jeon, M., Bruzzese, M., Lachman, M.: Change in cognitive performance from midlife into old age: findings from the midlife in the United States (MIDUS) study – erratum. J. Int. Neuropsychol. Soc. **24**(8), 891 (2018)

Identification Issues Associated with the Use of Wearable Accelerometers in Lifelogging

Angelica Poli⊙, Annachiara Strazza, Stefania Cecchi⊙,
and Susanna Spinsante$^{(\boxtimes)}$⊙

Dipartimento di Ingegneria dell'Informazione,
Università Politecnica delle Marche, 60131 Ancona, Italy
`s.spinsante@staff.univpm.it`

Abstract. Personal lifelogging builds upon the pervasive and continuous acquisition of sensor measurements and signals in time, and this may expose the subject, and eventually bystanders, to privacy violations. While the issue is easy to understand for image and video data, the risks associated to the use of wearable accelerometers is less clear and may be underestimated. This work addresses the problem of understanding if acceleration measurements collected from the wrist, by subjects performing different types of Activities of Daily Living (ADLs), may release personal details, for example about their gender or age. A positive outcome would motivate the need for de-identification algorithms to be applied to acceleration signals, embedded into wearable devices, in order to limit the unintentional release of personal details and ensure the necessary privacy by design and by default requirements.

Keywords: Lifelogging · Wrist accelerometer · Classification · Privacy

1 Introduction

In lifelogging applications [12], the pervasive and continuous acquisition of sensor measurements and signals along time may expose the subject at risks associated to privacy violations. This holds not only for the *lifelogger* but also for bystanders [11]. Considering the different sensors that can be adopted in lifelogging applications, it is quite easy to understand that information-rich sensors, such as video- and image-based ones, are particularly prone to the risk of privacy violations [5], and suitable techniques are consequently studied and applied to ensure privacy by default and privacy by design [9]. For other types of sensors, like wearable

Authors gratefully acknowledge the support of the *More Years Better Lives JPI* and the Italian Ministero dell'Istruzione, Università e Ricerca (CUP: I36G17000380001), for this research activity carried out within the project PAAL - Privacy-Aware and Acceptable Lifelogging services for older and frail people (JPI MYBL award number: PAAL_JTC2017).

Q. Gao and J. Zhou (Eds.): HCII 2020, LNCS 12207, pp. 338–351, 2020.
https://doi.org/10.1007/978-3-030-50252-2_26

accelerometers or non-video ambient sensors (i.e. presence sensors or magnetic sensors applied on windows and doors), the risk of privacy violations associated to the type of signals collected is not immediately clear or understandable. This often leads to underestimate the privacy-related issues, when such types of sensors are used and the related measurements collected for the aim of lifelogging or activity recognition [21].

Focusing our attention on acceleration signals collected by means of wearable devices, it is shown in the literature that authentication mechanisms may be implemented by exploiting personal gait characteristics of a subject, extracted from accelerometer signals. In fact, every individual has a distinctive way of walking and for this reason gait can be a key element of biometric techniques aimed at authenticating and/or identifying the user of a wearable device. Such identification becomes more challenging when considering elderly users, due to the intra-subject gait fluctuation [25]. However, the user's typical gait pattern may be learned by suitable algorithms or multiple matching, that process acceleration measurements collected from wearable devices, such as wrist-worn ones [6]. Similarly, methods to recognize users by exploiting data from a phone's embedded accelerometer sensors are presented as well in the literature. Based on such findings, it is possible to state that acceleration signals generated by a subject's gait embed specific individual features, that enable identification and authentication. Looking at this result from a different perspective, it means that the acceleration signal associated to a subject's gait may release details about the subject, for example about his/her sex or individual features, potentially leading to his/her identification.

The research question we aim to address within our research is to understand if the same risk of exposure of personal information exists when the collected acceleration measurements are not related to gait, but associated to different types of Activities of Daily Living (ADLs). For example, would it be possible to classify the sex of subjects by analyzing the acceleration measurements collected on their wrist, when performing house cleaning or when brushing teeth? A positive outcome would motivate the need for approaches to privacy by design and by default in wearable devices, and for designing de-identification algorithms to be applied onto acceleration signals collected by wrist-worn devices, in order to limit the unintentional release of personal details.

The paper is organized as follows: Sect. 2 provides a short review of the scientific literature addressing the problem of user's authentication based on gait-related acceleration signals. The same section also highlights a few works targeting the problem, but exploiting acceleration signals not associated to gait. Section 3 describes the materials and methods used in the study herein presented, to perform experiments that are presented in Sect. 4. The attained results are discussed in Sect. 5, where the main conclusions are provided as well.

2   Background

Several works in the scientific literature have addressed the issue of evaluating how many personal details may be disclosed from the analysis of gait-related acceleration signals. In fact, gait is one of many physical and behavioral traits of an individual, and it can be used to recognize a person, i.e. as a biometric measure. Gait refers to a person's specific manner of walking, which can be impacted by age, gender, body shape and mass, diseases, and several studies have proven that gait information is usable to distinguish between individuals. Most of the research studies aimed at identifying subjects according to their gait-related information exploit video data to capture personal traits that are specific and unique to each subject. Other studies exploit underfoot-pressure-based modalities, which, however, usually require quite complex and not-so-comfortable to use sensors and equipments, like pressure-sensitive mats or platforms. Besides the aforementioned modalities, gait-related recordings from accelerometers, gyroscopes, microphones, and radar have also been shown to discriminate between individuals.

Acceleration is a direct function of the forces and masses involved in gait generation, so it is considered as a strong candidate signal to provide features from which the subject's authentication may be enabled [7]. Using the acceleration signal, a possible challenge must be accounted for, i.e. the orientation of the device (like the smartphone) may shift in transit, or the device can be carried differently on the person, due to a change in clothing, habits, situation. In some studies this is partly compensated by the use of the acceleration magnitude (square root of the sum of each acceleration component squared) as the primary signal. Accelerometer and gyroscope data from smartphones was exploited in [18] to attain gender classification of the user. Again, gait-related data was collected, and the histogram of gradient method was used to extract features from the gait data. The proposed approach is robust against walking speed variations and the gender recognition performance is consistent across different smartphones used, equipped with the same type of sensors. Back in 1984, Gabell and Nayak already reported about the influence of age on the variability of both temporal and spatial parameters related to gait [13]. Based on such findings, later studies correlated the gait variations determined by age to, for example, the risk of falling, as in [27], observing that most of the typical gait features of older age do not result from a slow evolution over the life course, but gait instability likely begins to increase at an accelerated rate as early as age 40–50. In [28], the elicitation of age and gender information from gait traces generated by IMU (Inertial Measurement Unit) sensors is investigated, being those sensors frequently used in advanced consumer electronics, such as wearable devices and smartphones. By performing a state-of-the-art review, authors of this work highlight how it is feasible to elicit gender, age and height features from a single inertial sensor attached at four locations (chest, lower back, right wrist and left ankle) [23]. In [2], authors propose to extend classical Human Activity Recognition (HAR) exploiting inertial sensors (INS) onboard smartphones, to identify specific subjects as well. As the individual *inertial signature* of a person is expected to be more distinguishable while walking than in quasi-static conditions (such as laying, sitting, standing), authors limit their objective to the personal identification of walkers. Through properly combined machine learning (ML) techniques, a classification accuracy higher than 90% is attained, for 86.7% of the users.

A novel deep learning approach on gender and age recognition using a single inertial sensor is proposed in [26], and tested using the largest available inertial sensor-based gait database, with data collected from more than 700 subjects. An averaged accuracy of $86.6\% \pm 2.4\%$ is reported, for distinguishing teen and adult age groups. The performance of the approach in recognizing gender provides averaged accuracies of $88.6\% \pm 2.5\%$ and $73.9\% \pm 2.8\%$, for adults and teens, respectively. Similarly, a method to recognize users by exploiting data from a phone's embedded accelerometer sensors is presented in [24]. In all the cases mentioned above, acceleration signals related to gait have been considered. In this work, the focus is on acceleration signals collected from the wrist, which are not associated to gait but to the way a subject performs ADLs in real life conditions.

3   Materials and Methods

3.1   Measurement Tools

In our experiments, acceleration signals were measured using an Empatica E4 device [17], a multi-sensor system designed to be worn on the wrist, which integrates different types of sensors and provides the capability to simultaneously collect different biosignals. The smart wristband is classified as a class IIa Medical Device in the EU, according to CE Cert. No. 1876/MDD (93/42/EEC Directive). The E4 device embeds four different sensors:

- Photoplethysmographic sensor (PPG): it measures blood volume pulse, from which heart rate (HR) and inter-beat-interval (IBI) signals may be derived, with a sampling frequency $f_s = 64\,\text{Hz}$;
- Electrodermal Activity (EDA) sensor: it measures the activity of the sympathetic nervous system thus providing features related to stress or anxiety condition. The EDA circuit drives a small amount of ionic current through the skin to operate, $100\,\mu\text{A}$ as a maximum, as mandated by IEC 60601-1:2005 (range: 0.01–$100\,\mu\text{S}$; resolution: approximately $900\,p\text{S}$). The EDA sensor operates at $f_s = 4\,\text{Hz}$;
- 3-axis MEMS accelerometer: it measures motion-related activity (range $\pm 2g$; resolution: $0.015g$) with $f_s = 32\,\text{Hz}$;
- Optical infrared thermometer: it measures skin temperature (accuracy: $\pm 0.2\,^{\circ}\text{C}$, in the range $[36, 39]\,^{\circ}\text{C}$), with $f_s = 4\,\text{Hz}$.

The E4 may operate in two different modalities: *streaming mode*, in which data is visualized in real-time, by means of a mobile app (called E4 realtime) running on a smartphone connected to E4 via Bluetooth Low Energy (BLE); and *recording mode*, that stores the measured data in the device internal memory. In the former modality, the battery lifetime declared by the manufacturer amounts to 24 h, while it increases to 48 h in the latter case. By using the device in the *streaming mode*, measurement data is locally transmitted to the smartphone via BLE, and then relayed to a remote server platform, named Empatica

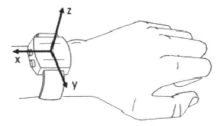

Fig. 1. Position of the wrist-worn Empatica E4 with the coordinate system on the device.

Connect, where it is necessary to setup an account before starting to use the device. Each E4 device and its account are uniquely associated through the serial number, that allows to identify the device itself. Once a measurement session is over, the collected data are available on the remote server in the form of a .zip archive containing separated .csv files for each sensor. The .csv file relative to the accelerometer is organized in as many rows as the amount of data samples collected, and three columns corresponding to the acceleration sample values along the three different axes X, Y and Z relative to the sensor, according to Fig. 1.

The 3-axis accelerometer onboard the E4 features 8 bits resolution of the selected range, and accelerometer data are expressed in m/s^2: considering what is reported in the E4 manual [10], a sample value equal to 64 corresponds to $1g$ (where g is equal to $9{,}81\,m/s^2$). So, for each acceleration sample acquired by Empatica E4 with the three components (A_x, A_y, A_z), the true acceleration value is obtained dividing each component by 64 and multiplying it by g: $(A_x/64, A_y/64, A_z/64)g\ m/s^2$.

3.2 Measurement Protocol

A total amount of 36 subjects (18 men and 18 women) were involved in our study and participated in the data collection phase, with a mean age and standard deviation of (29.5 ± 3.4) years. Among this cohort, 11 subjects were left-handed, and the remaining ones were right-handed. The participants were in good health status and no current physical conditions could affect the performed ADLs. In particular, each subject was asked to perform six different ADLs, pertaining to *personal hygiene* and *housekeeping* domains:

- Washing Hands (WH)
- Brushing Teeth (BT)
- Grooming Hair (GH)
- Dusting (D)
- Ironing (I)
- Washing Dishes (WD).

Each ADL was performed in a 5 min-long session and repeated three times by each subject, in free-living conditions. Recordings were acquired in a home environment, using real tools as recommended in [22], in the true daily moments when subjects had to perform the activities, in order to collect as much realistic signals as possible, except for their duration that was longer than in real life. In fact, usually, in normal daily life some activities last less than 5 min, such as washing hands and brushing teeth. Accelerometer data was recorded by wearing the Empatica E4 on the dominant wrist as, according to the literature, it is an appropriate place for analysing and recognising some of the ADLs performed in our experiments, such as GH, BT and WH [3,14,16]. Before data collection, the device was coupled with the Empatica smartphone app: after pressing the button to start the recording, the device takes around 15 s to calibrate the system, thus improving the accuracy of the sensor reading. The files recorded on the remote platform were later downloaded and renamed with labels corresponding to the scenario and the activity performed.

3.3 Measurement Data Pre-processing

The raw acceleration measurement data needs to be cleaned and validated. To this aim, a 4th low-pass Butterworth filter with cut-off frequency set at 15 Hz, and a 3rd order median filter were used to remove the signal noise [15,20]. Additionally, considering the automatic calibration performed by the device, the measurement samples collected during the initial 15 s of each session were discarded from each acquisition. Following the filtering step, each accelerometer signal was divided into fixed-size and non-overlapping windows of 3 s duration (corresponding to 96 samples) [1], thus resulting in 92 windows. This window duration has been used because it includes a significant number of samples and it allows to rapidly extract representative features for each activity [15]. Meaningful metrics about each activity were extracted from each segment, reducing the errors and inaccuracy in the classification phase.

3.4 Features and Classification Algorithms

Each performed activity can be discriminated by looking for certain motion properties. This way, the corresponding features might be used to classify and distinguish the different activities. From this idea, a set of 17 common features expressed in time domain were extracted from the collected signals, and computed according to the equations and definitions provided in [8]. As specified in Table 1, some features were computed from the acceleration values along the three X, Y and Z axes, others were obtained from the acceleration Signal Magnitude Vector (SMV $= \sqrt{a_x^2 + a_y^2 + a_z^2}$). In fact, the latter ones exhibit a reduced sensitivity to changes in the orientation of the device [4]. The sample plot shown in Fig. 2 illustrates the single acceleration components (a_x, a_y, a_z) and the resulting SMV computed as detailed above. Three additional features in the frequency domain were considered as well, as detailed in Table 2.

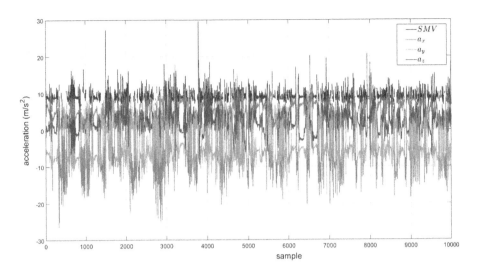

Fig. 2. Sample plot showing the behavior of the single acceleration components (a_x, a_y, a_z) and the corresponding SMV.

Table 1. List of features in time domain.

Features	Description	Computation
Mean	Average of values	X, Y, Z axes, SMV
Median	Median value	X, Y, Z axes, SMV
Standard Deviation	Amount of deviation	X, Y, Z axes, SMV
Maximum	Highest value	X, Y, Z axes, SMV
Minimum	Lowest value	X, Y, Z axes, SMV
Range	Difference between max and min value	X, Y, Z axes, SMV
Axis Correlation	Correlation between the three directions	XY, YZ, ZX axes
Signal Magnitude Area	The trapezoidal area calculated	SMV
Coefficient of Variation	Relationship of the standard deviation to the mean	X, Y, Z axes, SMV
Median Absolute Deviation	Variability of the sample	X, Y, Z axes, SMV
Skewness	Measurement of symmetry in the distribution of values	X, Y, Z axes, SMV
Kurtosis	Sharpness of the feature value distribution	X, Y, Z axes, SMV
Zero Crossing	Number of times the signal crosses its median	X, Y, Z axes, SMV
Autocorrelation	Comparison between a value at time t_i and the value at t_{i+1}	X, Y, Z axes, SMV
Percentiles (20th-50th-80th)	Distribution of values across the sequences	SMV
N. of Peaks	Number of peaks	SMV
Peak - Peak Amplitude	Distance between two consecutive peaks	SMV

Table 2. List of features in frequency domain.

Feature	Description
Spectral Energy	Energy of the signal in frequency domain, calculated for the SMV
Spectral Entropy	Entropy of the signal in frequency domain, calculated for the SMV
Spectral Centroid	The center of mass of the spectral power distribution, calculated for the SMV

About the activity classification based on the computed features, in supervised learning approaches the algorithm learns from a set of training examples, with pre-classified features, as labeled classes are provided. In unsupervised learning approaches, instead, the basic idea is to find patterns in the data using only the input variables. Finally, in so-called reinforcement learning approaches, the algorithm learns from feedback received back after the decision was made. This way the classifier learns which decisions were correct and which, instead, were not. Most of the HAR systems work with a supervised learning approach, because of its capability to learn the relationship between the input attributes, the features extracted, the target attributes and the labeled classes. The model defined by such a relationship can be used for predicting the target attribute, knowing only the values of the input data.

In our study, using the WEKA learning tool [19] we assessed the performance of six machine learning algorithms: Decision Tree (J48), Random Forest (RF), Naïve Bayes (NB), Neural Networks (NNs), k-Nearest Neighbor (kNN), and Support Vector Machines (SVM). They were selected based on the analysis of the scientific literature mentioned in the previous sections. The 10-fold cross validation testing strategy was used, in which all the sessions are divided into training (90% of data) and testing (10% of data) set, and the overall accuracy is computed as an average of the 10 iterations.

4   Experimental Results

The main experiment performed in our study, for evaluating the disclosure of personal details from accelerometer traces collected from the wrist, aims to train the classifiers using a dataset composed only by acceleration data collected from a young population, and then to test the classifiers with a completely new dataset created by collecting the signals acquired from an elderly subject. Basically, this way, we aim to check if it is possible to gather features discriminating the age of the subject, from the acceleration signals collected on the wrist.

An 86 years old elderly woman participated in the study performing all the previously described six different ADLs for 5 min. The activities were repeated twice, and recordings were acquired in a home environment using real tools, when needed, as shown in Fig. 3.

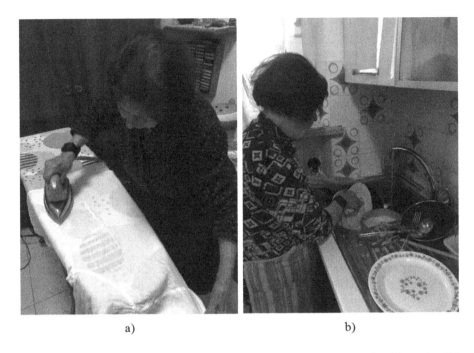

a)   b)

Fig. 3. Example of a) Ironing and b) Washing Dishes activity, wearing Empatica E4.

The acceleration measurement data was processed in the same manner in both the datasets, according to the filtering method mentioned previously, and computing the time and frequency domain features detailed above. By differently arranging the data, five subsets were prepared:

- Subset S1: dataset containing features in time domain, extracted from the SMV signal
- Subset S2: dataset composed by features in frequency domain, calculated from the SMV signal
- Subset S3: dataset including features in time and frequency domain, extracted from the SMV signal
- Subset S4: dataset containing features in time domain, calculated from X, Y, Z components and the SMV signal
- Subset S5: dataset with features in time and frequency domain, extracted from X, Y, Z components and SMV signal.

With the aim of looking for the best classifier operating with the minimum amount of features, first the three best classifiers are selected after testing over Subset 1, 2 and 3. Then, the best classifier out of the three ones is tested again over Subset 4 and 5, including more features, in order to look for improved results. Given the fact that J48, RF and NNs algorithms are those providing the best accuracy performance in correctly classifying the six different ADLs, the same classifiers are evaluated with respect to the capability of discriminating

Table 3. Accuracy of different algorithms for S1.

Classifier	Accuracy
J48	32.1%
RF	**53.4%**
NNs	50.9%

Table 4. Accuracy of different algorithms for S2.

Classifier	Accuracy
J48	26.7%
RF	**28.9%**
NNs	26.8%

among different age ranges, by training on the features collected from young subjects, and testing on the data relative to the elderly woman.

The results reported by Tables 3, 4, and 5 show that the three algorithms, when testing on the data from the elderly woman, provide very low accuracy values. This first evaluation addresses Subset 1 (features in time from SMV), Subset 2 (features in frequency from SMV) and Subset 3 (features in time and frequency from SMV), respectively. Even with a quite low accuracy value, the RF classifier performs best over all the three subsets. However, since the obtained accuracy outcomes are not satisfactory, Subset 4 and 5, containing also the features extracted from the single 3-axis acceleration components, are examined, in order to improve the performances of the classification in the elderly subject dataset. The results of this experiment are reported in Table 6.

As it can be noticed from Fig. 4 as well, by adding the X, Y and Z acceleration components the accuracy provided by the RF classifier increases: the highest value is attained in Subset 4, so it means that those features are significant for the *collateral* aim of age discrimination, and are more informative than those computed on the acceleration SMV.

Table 5. Accuracy of different algorithms for S3.

Classifier	Accuracy
J48	31.5%
RF	**53.1%**
NNs	43.9%

Table 6. Accuracy of RF classifier on S4 and S5.

Subset	Accuracy
S4	**66.1%**
S5	59.8%

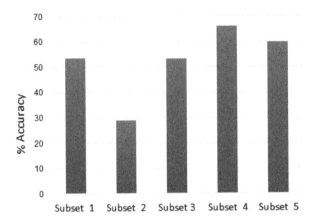

Fig. 4. Accuracy values for all the five different Subsets, evaluated using Random Forest classifier.

5   Discussion and Conclusion

The experiment described in this work addresses the training of classifiers on a dataset of signals collected from young subjects, and their testing on a subset of signals collected from an elderly volunteer. The training on the young population set is performed in order to create a model, which is then evaluated to test the performances of the three selected best classifiers on a completely different dataset. In fact, the accelerometer signals acquired by the elderly subject feature evident differences with respect to the signals collected by young volunteers, at a parity of the ADL performed, as qualitatively shown in Fig. 5.

Physical limitations may appear or increase with increasing age: movements become slower, the intensity and the energy involved to perform ADLs decrease. The results of the experiment proposed in this work show that accuracy values obtained on the testing model are very low, and this confirms the idea that acceleration signals from the wrist feature quite different characteristics in young and elderly subjects. This could lead to a disclosure of the observed subject's age range, somehow releasing a personal information that is not actually relevant for the aim of ADLs classification and automatic recognition.

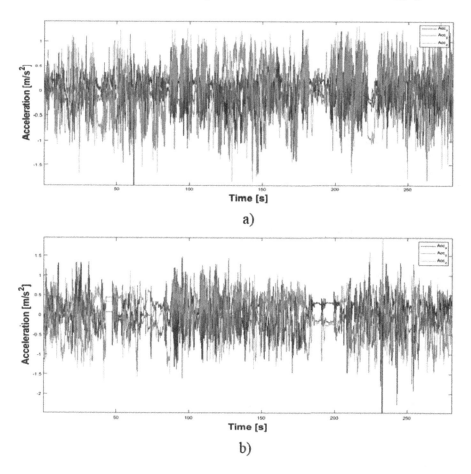

Fig. 5. Wrist acceleration signal components (a_x, a_y, a_z) collected for the Washing Dishes ADL from a) a young subject, and b) the elderly one.

References

1. Attal, F., Mohammed, S., Dedabrishvili, M., Chamroukhi, F., Oukhellou, L., Amirat, Y.: Physical human activity recognition using wearable sensors. Sensors **15**, 31314–31338 (2015)
2. Campos, R.S., Lovisolo, L.: Person identification based on smartphones inertial sensors. In: 2018 International Joint Conference on Neural Networks (IJCNN), pp. 1–7, July 2018
3. Chin, Z.H., Ng, H., Yap, T.T.V., Tong, H.L., Ho, C.C., Goh, V.T.: Daily activities classification on human motion primitives detection dataset. In: Alfred, R., Lim, Y., Ibrahim, A., Anthony, P. (eds.) Computational Science and Technology. LNEE, vol. 481, pp. 117–125. Springer, Singapore (2019). https://doi.org/10.1007/978-981-13-2622-6_12

4. Cleland, I., Donnelly, M.P., Nugent, C.D., Hallberg, J., Espinilla, M., Garcia-Constantino, M.: Collection of a diverse, realistic and annotated dataset for wearable activity recognition. In: 2018 IEEE International Conference on Pervasive Computing and Communications Workshops (PerCom Workshops), pp. 555–560. IEEE (2018). https://doi.org/10.1109/PERCOMW.2018.8480322

5. Climent-Pérez, P., Spinsante, S., Mihailidis, A., Flórez-Revuelta, F.: A review on video-based active and assisted living technologies for automated lifelogging. Expert Syst. Appl. **139**, 112847 (2020)

6. Cola, G., Avvenuti, M., Musso, F., Vecchio, A.: Gait-based authentication using a wrist-worn device. In: Proceedings of the 13th International Conference on Mobile and Ubiquitous Systems: Computing, Networking and Services, MOBIQUITOUS 2016, pp. 208–217. Association for Computing Machinery, New York (2016)

7. Connor, P., Ross, A.: Biometric recognition by gait: a survey of modalities and features. Comput. Vis. Image Underst. **167**, 1–27 (2018)

8. Cook, D.J., Krishnan, N.C.: Activity Learning: Discovering, Recognizing, and Predicting Human Behavior from Sensor Data. Wiley, Hoboken (2015). https://doi.org/10.1002/9781119010258.ch3

9. EC: Complete guide to GDPR compliance. https://gdpr.eu/. Accessed Feb 2020

10. Empatica: E4 Wrist Band from Empatica User's Manual (2018)

11. Ferdous, M.S., Chowdhury, S., Jose, J.M.: Analysing privacy in visual lifelogging. Pervasive Mob. Comput. **40**, 430–449 (2017)

12. Flórez-Revuelta, F., Mihailidis, A., Ziefle, M., Colonna, L., Spinsante, S.: Privacy-aware and acceptable lifelogging services for older and frail people: the PAAL project. In: 2018 IEEE 8th International Conference on Consumer Electronics - Berlin (ICCE-Berlin), pp. 1–4, September 2018

13. Gabell, A., Nayak, U.: The effect of age on variability in gait. J. Gerontol. **39**(6), 662–666 (1984). https://doi.org/10.1093/geronj/39.6.662

14. Galluzzi, V., Herman, T., Polgreen, P.: Hand hygiene duration and technique recognition using wrist-worn sensors. In: Proceedings of the 14th International Conference on Information Processing in Sensor Networks, pp. 106–117. ACM (2015). https://doi.org/10.1145/2737095.2737106

15. Hassan, M.M., Huda, M.S., Uddin, M.Z., Almogren, A., AlRubaian, M.A.: Human activity recognition from body sensor data using deep learning. J. Med. Syst. **42**, 1–8 (2018)

16. Huang, H., Lin, S.: Toothbrushing monitoring using wrist watch. In: Proceedings of the 14th ACM Conference on Embedded Network Sensor Systems CD-ROM, pp. 202–215. ACM (2016). https://doi.org/10.1145/2994551.2994563

17. Empatica Inc.: Empatica e4. http://support.empatica.com/hc/en-us/categories/200023126-E4-wristband. Accessed 4 Nov 2019

18. Jain, A., Kanhangad, V.: Gender classification in smartphones using gait information. Expert Syst. Appl. **93**, 257–266 (2018)

19. Kaufmann, M.: Data mining: practical machine learning tools and techniques. https://www.cs.waikato.ac.nz/ml/weka. Accessed 27 Dec 2019

20. Ni, Q., Cleland, I., Nugent, C., Hernando, A.B.G., de la Cruz, I.P.: Design and assessment of the data analysis process for a wrist-worn smart object to detect atomic activities in the smart home. Pervasive Mob. Comput. **56**, 57–70 (2019)

21. Pires, I.M., Garcia, N.M., Pombo, N., Flórez-Revuelta, F., Spinsante, S., Teixeira, M.C.: Identification of activities of daily living through data fusion on motion and magnetic sensors embedded on mobile devices. Pervasive Mob. Comput. **47**, 78–93 (2018)

22. Poli, A., Spinsante, S., Nugent, C., Cleland, I.: Improving the collection and under-standing the quality of datasets for the aim of human activity recognition. In: Chen, F., García-Betances, R.I., Chen, L., Cabrera-Umpiérrez, M.F., Nugent, C. (eds.) Smart Assisted Living. CCN, pp. 147–165. Springer, Cham (2020). https://doi.org/10.1007/978-3-030-25590-9_7

23. Riaz, Q., Vögele, A., Krüger, B., Weber, A.: One small step for a man: estimation of gender, age and height from recordings of one step by a single inertial sensor. Sensors **15**(12), 31999–32019 (2015). https://doi.org/10.3390/s151229907

24. Singha, T.B., Nath, R.K., Narsimhadhan, A.V.: Person recognition using smart-phones' accelerometer data. arXiv.abs/1711.04689 (2017)

25. Sun, F., Zang, W., Gravina, R., Fortino, G., Li, Y.: Gait-based identification for elderly users in wearable healthcare systems. Inf. Fusion **53**, 134–144 (2020)

26. Sun, Y., Lo, F.P., Lo, B.: A deep learning approach on gender and age recognition using a single inertial sensor. In: 2019 IEEE 16th International Conference on Wearable and Implantable Body Sensor Networks (BSN), pp. 1–4, May 2019

27. Terrier, P., Reynard, F.: Effect of age on the variability and stability of gait: a cross-sectional treadmill study in healthy individuals between 20 and 69 years of age. Gait Posture **41**(1), 170–174 (2015)

28. Van hamme, T., Garofalo, G., Argones Rúa, E., Preuveneers, D., Joosen, W.: A systematic comparison of age and gender prediction on IMU sensor-based gait traces. Sensors **19**(13) (2019). https://doi.org/10.3390/s19132945. https://www.mdpi.com/1424-8220/19/13/2945

Older Women Living in Unfavorable Contexts and Tablets in Uruguay: A Design for Access and Use of Inclusive Information

Martha Sabelli[✉]

Universidad de la República Uruguay, Montevideo, Uruguay
martha.sabelli@fic.edu.uy

Abstract. The paper focuses on theoretical reflections and the results obtained by research with poor international experience in the areas of *gender, ageism and digital media*, focused on the project "Perspective of old age and gender in disadvantaged environments: towards inclusive strategies of information and communication, The Ibirapita Plan and the Attention System" (April 2017 to April 2019). The objective of the project has been to contribute to the studies of information behavior and information practices of older women living in unfavorable contexts and the use of tablets, in the context of a National Plan that distributes tablets to all older adults in disadvantaged situations. Two specific aspects are raised from a constructionist perspective: 1) the approach based on the understanding of the social construction of information and communication by older women and their tablets; 2) the design, creation, implementation and evaluation of new content of quality information for tablets (digital products) in a participatory approach of the users and the interdisciplinary team (Information Sciences, Communication, Sociology and Computer Engineering).

During the first year (2017) four methodological tools were applied to collect data: a survey, in-depth interviews with qualified informants and trainers of the Plan courses and several focus groups in two departmental capital cities and two small cities in two departments of Uruguay (Paysandú and Rocha). The second stage (2018 and early 2019) focused on the design of the digital solution on tablets in order to incorporate and promote the search and use of inclusive local information.

Keywords: Older women · Inclusive information · Tablets · Digital design · Information behavior · Plan Ibirapitá (Uruguay)

1 Introduction

This paper seeks to reflect on the purposes and results of the project "Perspective of old age and gender in disadvantaged environments: towards inclusive information and communication strategies, the Ibirapita Plan and the Care System" (April 2017–April 2019), in the light of a gender, old age and ICT perspective. It was selected and funded by the Sectorial Commission for Scientific Research (CSIC) of the University of the

© Springer Nature Switzerland AG 2020
Q. Gao and J. Zhou (Eds.): HCII 2020, LNCS 12207, pp. 352–371, 2020.
https://doi.org/10.1007/978-3-030-50252-2_27

Republic, Uruguay. The objective of the project is to contribute to the studies of Information Behavior and Information Practices of older women with their tablets, in the context of a National Plan that distributes tablets to all older persons in disadvantaged situations, a unique case without international precedents.

The research is inserted in a research line focused on informative human behaviors, and the appropriation of inclusive information that seeks to bring academia closer to problems related to the complex phenomenon of information and communication of the elderly. In spite of being an important part of the country's present and future citizenship, they are very limited in the access and real *meaningful* use of the informative contents necessary and essential for their individual and collective development. In interdisciplinary teams with an inquiring look, not only the phenomena of informative behaviors are analyzed, interpreted and understood, but also the creation of creative and innovative digital information resources is explored in a participatory manner with the subject-objects of investigation and the social mediators, based on the theoretical and epistemological foundations these disciplines provide.

In general, demographic and sociological studies prioritize several dimensions that condition the situation of older women, but the dimensions related to access and use of information are absent. These should be incorporated into the research and guide the inquiry about information needs and informational behaviors. Disinformation appears as a barrier to their inclusion and social integration. The analysis and interpretation of the actual use and content appropriation contribute to the public social policies of the country and to the design of information and reading systems and services referred to this social sector.

In this sense, the Political Declaration and Madrid International Plan of Action on Ageing [1] includes the access and use of information for the elderly: 21.Objective 1.(d) Provide information and access to facilitate the participation of older persons in mutual self-help, intergenerational community groups and opportunities for realizing their full potential; 40.Objective 1.(d) Ensure that the benefits of new technologies, especially information and communication technologies, are available to all, taking into account the needs of older women. It focuses on two specific aspects from a constructionist perspective: 1). the approach based on the understanding of the social construction of information and communication by older women in their social and community environment; 2). the universal nature of the Ibirapita Plan in Uruguay, which provides one tablet for each low-income retired woman and the need to create a participatory design of a digital tablet solution with the aim of providing inclusive information.

Some common dimensions are noted among the diversity of the older women studied, despite their different contexts of life, socio-cultural environments, personalities, attitudes and personal skills. In addition, a long lifespan led to long life stories, which resulted in various influences on their behaviors and information practices.

At the end of the first year of the project (2017), free tablets for people over 65 distributed reached 170.000 and currently 230.000 (late 2019), a considerable figure for a small country of approximately 3.5 million inhabitants.

Before presenting the main results of the project according to the proposal of this communication, in the next sections, we provide some statistical data and theoretical approaches on the subject in relation to the phenomenon of aging, gender and ICT in a small country in the South, Uruguay, with some modern characteristics and social public policies that highlight it in the Latin American context.

2 Aging, Gender and ICT

2.1 Aging in Uruguay in the Global Context: Present and Prediction

As a recent report of the United Nations [2] indicates, the world's population is growing older, with the age group of 65 and over growing the fastest. By 2050, one in six people in the world will be over age 65 (16%), up from one in 11 in 2019 (9%). In 2018, for the first time in history, persons aged 65 or above outnumbered children under five years of age globally. The number of persons aged 80 or over is projected to triple from 143 million in 2019 to 426 million in 2050.

Uruguay's population, placed in the high-income countries [3], in the year 2019 is of 3,462,000, and predictions until 2100 show approximately the same number from 0.31 in 2015, it decreases to −0,32 and −0,39 in the last decades of the century.

2.2 ICTs in Uruguay

In the context addressed in the abovementioned substantiation, the development of inclusion projects, particularly digital, for the elderly is crucial. These initiatives include those that also strengthen family and intergenerational ties and allow to attack the stereotypes generated on older people [4]. Evaluations made on inclusion programs based on the intergenerational relationship have shown that they have a positive and improving impact on attitudes towards the elderly [5]. These programs allow older people to develop new types of activities in a way integrated to society, reducing the risk of isolation. Likewise, in the younger generations their feeling of utility and support for society increases [6].

The privileged situation of Uruguay with respect to ICT according to the different national and international indicators, enable and engage the country in the development and tools for the elderly. Uruguay has the highest percentage of households with computers in the region and, in a study of the population aged 14 years or above who have access to the Internet, 96% are believed to use it at least weekly and 84% daily.

The ICT Development Index 2017 [7, 8] placed Uruguay in the 42nd place on the list of 176 countries, with an IDI of 7.16, in the highest place in Latin America and well above the countries in process of development (4.12).

Uruguay's high Internet penetration rate in recent years has led the country to the first places in Latin America. The recent report of The profile of the Uruguayan Internet user [9], shows there is at least some type of computer in 97% of Uruguayan homes, and smartphones would be 45% of the total number of devices with internet access in homes; 73% of homes have WiFi (more than 700,000) As in previous years, people over 50, and especially over 65 years old is the segment where Internet penetration has grown the most. 89% of Uruguayans of all ages are already internet users.

2.3 Aging and Gender: Perspectives

The aforementioned progressive growth of the population of elderly people in Uruguay is accompanied by an unequal distribution by sex; women represent 60.28%, increasing as people get older to 67.57% for the population older than 79 [10]. Regarding the activity condition, 13.07% of the elderly are employed or looking for a job; when introducing the sex variable, the percentage of active men doubles that of women, of which less than 10% are inserted in the labor market [10].

As for unpaid work, the 2011 census data show that almost 86% of elderly women do chores at home. As the sociologist Carina Batthyány points out, gender injustices in the distribution of the care burden, the analyzes of the social organization of care, and demographic and family changes were visualized, as well as the most comprehensive views of social protection systems [11]. The construction of the care system has been a demand also evidenced in different activities organized by the national government, academia, civil society and international cooperation [12]. Recent literature from specialists in Uruguay emphasizes this issue [13–15].

From this scenario, the need to address old age from a gender perspective is evident, taking into account the specificity of female aging, characterized by a double risk of social exclusion. Social policies have responded from the perspectives of different aging models, from a traditional paradigm oriented to deterioration and dependence and based on protection and assistance measures, to others based on the conception of "active aging" referred to the possibility of a continuous participation in the socioeconomic, cultural and political level, throughout the whole life cycle, not limiting the notion of active life to participation in the labor market. On the other hand, "active aging" has also given rise to debates by being constructed, according to critics, on the basis of public policies that do not seem to recognize the contribution of older people to social welfare.

On the perspectives to which we adhere, we highlight the contributions in the Latin American field of a collective work product of a research project in Spain by Ezquerra, Pérez Salanova, Pla y Subirats [15] and the recent book by Rosario Aguirre and Sol Scavino [16].

Among the main ideas raised that guided us in our research are: the integral vision of old age, conceived as a non-uniform construction with social meanings, which consider chronological, physiological and social age; the existence of different facets of old age contributed by critical gerontology and different ways of aging; the analysis of old age from a gender perspective, as a "variable that highlights the vulnerability of many women, who face the last stage of their life course with fewer resources than men, measured in terms of family support, economic income and available assets [16]. Also, the diversity existing in the ways of aging and the determination of *thresholds in old age,* and the necessary dialogue between old age and gender and new perspectives of participation and empowerment of older people that can complement and deepen aspects that in the initial paradigm of active aging were barely raised [15].

3   InfoCoMayores Research Project

3.1   Background and Objectives

The flow of information and communication in the society of older common citizens with fewer socio-economic resources has been little investigated from the perspective of access, use, and appropriation of meaningful information, and is still absent in the specific case of older women.

The research team of the InfoCoMayores Project, formed by information science researchers, sociologists, communication scientists and computer engineers, has 10 years of experience on information behaviors in disadvantaged backgrounds research. It has carried out two previous research projects aimed at information behaviors of teenage and young women who do not study or work. In fact, those previous experiences were the ones that made older women and their problems visible to the team.

InfoCoMayores project worked in two sub-teams. The first one will be called the FIC Team, responsible for the presentation and coordination of the project, formed by one Information Science senior researcher, four Information Science junior researchers, a Sociologist, a Communication researcher and Information Science students, who carried out the study of informative behavior. The *INCO* (School of Engineering's Institute of Computing) research was formed by three students with their graduation thesis of Computer Engineering, and their tutors, incorporated in the second year of the project.

As previously said, this academic research independent from the plan is targeted to the users (2017–2018) of the *Ibirapitá plan, digital inclusion of retirees* (www.ibirap ita.org.uy). Created in 2015, it aims to promote equal access to knowledge and social inclusion to retirees by providing tablets with Internet connectivity.

Objectives. The objectives for the first year of the project were: evaluating the state of the art in information behaviors and information practices of older women with respect to ICT; identifying the information needs of the older women of the Ibirpitá plan in their family and community contexts; describing the relationship that older women of the Ibirapitá plan have with sources and resources of electronic information in two different regions of the country and selecting and collecting local information in the two regions chosen, according to the results of the information behavior study.

The objectives for the second year of the project were: provide the tablets with quality local informational content that motivate the search for inclusive information by users in the selected regions; participatory design and construction of a digital information product for tablets; develop interdisciplinary research between two teams made up of different disciplines and university services and evaluate the results in the light of theoretical references.

3.2   Theoretical References

The theoretical and methodological references come from the field of information behavior and information practices of the Information Science and the field of gender, older women and ICT.

The concept of information poverty and the role of mediators by Chatman [17–19], the ELIS model (everyday life information seeking) of Savolainen and colleagues [20–24], the notion of information ground by Fisher and co-authors [25–28] and the contributions of constructionist perspectives are central to this exploration of the subjects-objects' information behaviors and information practices in their daily life.

The bibliography recovered on older adults and ICT is broad and interdisciplinary. Between the main referents on third-agers as users of tablets are authors from the United States, Australia, the United Kingdom and the Nordic countries. The pioneer works of Williamson and colleagues [29–33] and most recent works from diverse disciplines, like those by Vroman et al. [34], Barnard et al. [35], Wright [36], Magsamen-Conrad et al. [37], Alvseike et al. [38] are also relevant to this research.

Finally, a substantial contribution is the constructionism of Talja and his colleagues [39–41] to which we have adhered in previous researches.

The literature review reveals a few works studying the information behaviors and information practices of older adults from a holistic point of view. There are just a few studies which consider in their approaches factors related to personality, attitudes and the integration of third-agers to their family environment, neighborhood and friendships. No references were found to works that specifically focus on the study of older adult's experiences with tablets distributed universally and free of charge at a country level.

First, we focus on some research concepts and results in the access and use of ICT by the elderly that are relevant to the inquiry of our research questions. The most prominent are the findings on the main variables associated with the elderly. There is coincidence in some referents from the area of aging and the use of ICTs, in the lower use of ICTs with related variables, among others, with increased age, a lower degree of education and lower income [42]. These variables influence the perception of themselves and their chronological age, especially self-esteem; social and cultural stereotypes of the social reality in which they live acts on it. Hence the emerging concept of cognitive age [43]. The differences between cognitive and chronological ages are recently emerging by some authors; Hong et al. [44] consider their influence on the acceptance and use of the use of social networks, based on previous studies.

Based on some references, these authors identify the state of anxiety as a characteristic of the personality of an individual, who predispose in their behavior to perceive a set of objectively non-dangerous circumstances as a threat and that induces negative impacts in the individual's cognitive responses. But, they affirm that this variable can be modified mainly through training and experience with computers.

In line with constructionist theorists of Information Science, especially with ELIS, they consider the psychological characteristics of people, in this case the elderly, which provide a better explanation of the digital divide than traditional sociodemographic variables.

3.3 Methods

In the first year (April 2017–April 2018), the activities of the FIC team went from retrieving documents about empirical researches on information behaviors and information practices of older adults and ICT, and doing a systematic review of the documentation, to the identification and analysis of the information needs of older adults in their family and community contexts. 14 in-depth interviews were conducted with qualified informants from the main public and private organizations, which work with older adults. A questionnaire was designed and applied to 184 older adults beneficiaries of the plan. 10 trainers of the courses dictated by the plan were interviewed. Observations in 15 courses and 3 focus groups. In the last months of the first year, work began with the INCO team; in several meetings, they exchanged on the proposal for the design of the technological solution for tablets. In the second year (May 2018–April 2019), the activities of the FIC team focused on working with older women in focus groups to deepen the identification of their local information needs, interviews with trainers in order to collect their perceptions about the informative behavior of women with their tablets, and organization and observation of the verification workshops of the INCO team; selection and elaboration of the informative contents of Paysandú and Rocha; and loading of data on tablets. The INCO Team developed the product and carried out the validation process, supported by the FIC team.

3.4 Results Analysis

In-depth Interviews to Qualified Informants. Interviews with qualified informants, recorded and transcribed, can be divided into three groups selected and executed at the beginning of the project (April–May 2017): a) three referents of the Ibirapitá plan, general coordinator and territorial coordinators of the selected departments, Paysandú and Rocha; b) four referents in Paysandú and seven in Rocha; and c) referent related to the Care System. The coordinators of the Ibirapitá plan expressed in their responses a great harmony between the approach and guiding perspectives of the plan and the theoretical-methodological referents of the project.

The interviewees of the first group, considered the value of the mandatory three-hour workshops when delivering the tablet, *"which have a motivational tone, it is not something in which we think that a retiree can end up knowing how to use the device"*. [R1]. The fundamental thing for the plan *"is that there is a cheerful, relaxed atmosphere, an atmosphere of celebration in which they progressively explore, turning on the tablet for example is success or […] our main objective there is motivational. We know that in those three hours we will not get experts in computer science and technology because for many of them it is the first time they face a digital device […] what we try is that the person in that workshop can find the meaning of the tablet"* [R3].

When asking about the relationship in the territory with social institutions, ER2 clarifies: *"Whenever we arrive at a town, the first thing we do in the deployment is to make contact with the social institutions […] we establish the link with them. In the association of retirees, it is where we give priority for delivery."* The trainers that dictate the workshops were a center of interest of the project from the beginning, as they are considered potential mediators for overcoming the information gap, for that reason their profile was asked. ER2 said: *"It is a profile focused on education, an educational profile, but that does not mean that we only hire teachers, because we need a facilitator"*. The eleven qualified informants of Paysandú and Rocha stated about the local reality, the distribution of tablets and workshops, as well as their perceptions about the users and non-users in the city where they reside. A dichotomy is expressed in the relationship of the users and the tablet after receiving the tablet and attending the workshop: *"some leave with visible joy, and others leave with bitterness and anger because they forget, and now not anymore, but at the beginning there are those who came back irritated because the tablet did not work*" (ER4). On the difficulties of the elderly and the ICT, numerous interviewees expressed, like ER5: "*... sometimes it is very difficult even to use the cell phone; as a basic 3-h workshop is really very basic, the workshop was very short and the person could not get all that information and process it*". When asked about the role of family members, several interviewees answered, by way of example: "*In the family of the elderly, each one has their occupation. Children at work and grandchildren with their studies, and of course, they go, put the finger and ... The older adult needs more time, more repetition of the same thing.*" ER5.

Undoubtedly, the analysis of these interviews deserve upcoming dissemination work as they are 200 pages of transcription, with rich concepts in the speeches about older women and their tablets, but also about their place not chosen. We refer to those that live in homes granted free of charge by the State, just as the delivered tablets, and do not feel them as the place chosen and adopted by their own decision: "*... In the cooperative there is a life option, here there is no option, here it is out of necessity, because I cannot pay the rent or because I have no place in my children's home, and I am not an owner, I need to go and ask the State for a house.*"

We confirm the ideas of Barnard *et al.* [35] and its assertions about the differentiation between adoption and acceptance (an attitude), the relevance that the factor acceptance-adoption takes place whether or not you adopt both your place and tablets.

The Questionnaire and the Analysis of its Main Results. The application of a questionnaire to a sample of elderly users and non-users of the Ibirapitá plan allowed the collection of initial data that would guide the other qualitative methodological techniques. The questionnaire was carried out over a sample of 163 users and 21 non-users of the tablets in three age cohorts: 55–60 (the reason why people between 55 and 64 years old is included in the sample is due to the retirement system legislation), 61–70 and 71–80 years old. The places chosen to apply the questionnaire were social organizations, homes and public spaces of two urban centers in Paysandú region (capital city Paysandú and in a small town: Quebracho) and Rocha region (capital city Rocha and a small Town: La Paloma). The questionnaire form has 56 questions, mostly closed (only 6 open), grouped in the following sections: Demographic data (age, sex, education, place of residence); Home; Access and use of the tablet; Social networks; Cell phone use; Internet search on the tablet (critical incident); Social and family environment; Issues of interest; Leisure (radio, television, music, reading); Description of the respondent's environment.

The questionnaire covered users and non-users, men and women, because they wanted to have data on the percentage of non-users and visualize the results of women in relation to men. Below, we present basic data of old men and women to provide some comparative percentages of users and non-users according to sex and age, and then, we focus on the gender approach that this the topic of this communication. The main demographic data of users and non-users are expressed in the following Tables 1, 2, 3 and 4.

With respect to the variable access and use of tablets, 48% use the tablet every day, 38% sometime in the week and 13.5% sometime in the month; 44% needed help to use it

Table 1. Use of the tablet (users and non-users), by region.

	Quantity		Percentage	
Region	User	Non-User	User	Non-User
Paysandú	105	14	64.4	66.7
Rocha	58	7	35.6	33.3
Total	163	21	100	100

Table 2. Use of the tablet, users and non-users by sex and age groups.

Age group	Male	Female
55–60 years old	1.9	5.3
61–70 years old	37.7	44.3
71–80 years old	60.4	50.4
Total	100	100

Table 3. Use of the tablet by sex.

	Quantity		Percentage	
Users/Non-Users	Male	Female	Male	Female
Users	46	117	86.8	89.3
Non-Users	7	14	13.2	10.7
Total	53	131	100	100

Table 4. Use of the tablet by age groups.

	Quantity				Percentage			
Users/Non-Users	55–60 years old	61–70 years old	71–80 years old	Total	55–60 years old	61–70 years old	71–80 years old	Total
Users	7	72	84	163	87.5	92.3	85.7	88.6
Non-Users	1	6	14	21	12.5	7.7	14.3	11.4
Total	8	78	98	184	100	100	100	100

and 56% did not. There are no appreciable differences in frequency of use discriminated by sex. According to age cohorts, 55.6% of the older adults between 61–70 years old use the tablet every day, when just 40.5% between 71–80 years old use it daily.

Living alone is a variable of great interest for the interpretation of information behaviors and information practices and there was a high percentage without company at home:

among the users, 40.5% live alone and of the non-users, 62% live alone. A lower daily usage frequency was detected in those who live alone: 36.4%, very distant from the 55.7% of those who use it daily and did not live alone and 48.5% of those who needed help live alone.

The relationship between educational level and frequency of usage is also confirmed. Those who only have elementary education level use the tablet less frequently than those who reached secondary and tertiary education.

The users show a low level of attendance to places where respondents can meet and socialize: only 46% of the respondents acknowledge to attend to one or two types of socialization places. When asked about the activities of daily life, the most mentioned are (regardless of the frequency): using the tablet (100%), doing domestic chores (97,5%), go shopping (95%), taking care of plants (85%), visiting family or neighbors (68%), going for a walk for pleasure (49%) and going out with friends (44%). Other options included in the list are done by less than 40% of the users consulted. 59% perform between 6 to 8 activities and the rest less than that.

The question about Internet Search using the tablet, included as a critical incident, revels that 55% performed a search. Of those, 54% have 70 or less years old and 45% 71+ years old and 33% live alone. 12% needed help when searching, 72% of them live alone and are women, and 68% are +71 years old. The ones that never searched the Internet are 31%, 51% of them live alone, 72% are women and 28% men; 37% are 70 or younger and 63% are 71 or older. Regarding the educational level, low education level corresponds to those which did not search on the Internet (63% attended only elementary education), represent 37% of the total. In summary, the critical incident confirms the profile of those who do not seek information on the Internet and those who need help in their searches.

The results collected coincide with the statements of the referents from the area of aging and use of ICT in the lower use of ICT with related variables with increased age, a lower degree of education, and lower income [42].

As described through previous tables, women users were 117 (89.3%) and non-users 14 (10.7%). Table 5 present the frequency of the use of tablet according to age-groups.

Table 5. Percentages. Total users (frequency of use) by age group

Frequency of use of the tablet	55 to 60 years old	61 to 70 years old	71 to 80 years old	Total
Every day	66.7	57.4	36.8	47.9
Sometime per week	3.3	31.5	45.6	38.5
In the month	0	9.3	1.5	12.8
No data*	0	1.9	0	0
Total	100%	100%	100%	100%

The frequency of use of the tablet decreases with the older groups, especially thoseaged 70+, in daily and monthly use. The important incidence of the educational level in all the frequencies of use is also confirmed; users who have not completed secondary-education level use it less than those who completed secondary education and have complete or incomplete tertiary studies (Table 6).

Table 6. Percentages. Total users (frequency of use), by educational level

Frequency of use of the tablet	Incomplete primary education	Complete primary education	Incomplete secondary education	Complete secondary education	Incomplete university/ tertiary education	Complete university/ tertiary education	Total
Every day	34.8	45.7	53.8	60	0	66.7	47.9
Sometime per week	56.5	40	25.6	40	100	16.7	38.5
In the month	4.3	14.3	20.5	0	0	16.7	12.8
No data*	4.3	0	0	0	0	0	0.9
Total	100 %	100 %	100 %	100 %	100 %	100 %	100 %

The percentage of low daily use of the tablet is relevant if we compare whether they live alone or not, which we had already observed in the data between users and non-users, men and women, although it rises in the use sometime per week and in the month (Table 7).

Table 7. Percentages. Total users (frequency of use), by way of life.

Frequency of use of the tablet	Lives alone	Does not live alone	Total
Every day	35.4	56.5	47.9
Sometime per week	47.9	31.9	38.5
In the month	14.6	11.6	12.8
No data*	2.1	0	0.9
Total	100%	100%	100%

Another interesting fact is the low percentage in the social activities significant for a social integration of these older women, such as associations, clubs, neighborhood commissions or choirs. It is also important to check their low percentage of attendance to libraries and digital inclusion centers where they can be supported in their use of tablets (Table 8).

Table 8. Attendance to each type/place of meeting.

Type/place of meeting for elderly people	Number of respondents who attend*	Percentage over the total respondents (117)
Excursions	61	52.1
Gym	51	43.6
Church	43	36.7
Others (parties, dances, etc.)	41	35
Retirees associations	39	33.3
Neighborhood or city square	37	31.6
Clubs	18	15.4
Library	18	15.4
Neighborhood commissions or other social organizations	14	12
Choirs	12	10.3
Digital inclusion center	11	9.4

*Each type/place of meeting is analyzed and it is taken into account if they attend, regardless of the frequency (weekly, monthly or annual). Each percentage is calculated over the total respondents. That is why the column does not add 100%.

40.2% of the respondents (47) attend only 2 or less places or types of meetings on which they are asked. 59.8% attend more than two places (up to 8 places/types of meeting).

Finally, but relevant to the research, are the answers to the question about Internet Search using the tablet revels that 55% performed a search, 72% of them live alone and are women, and 68% are +71 years old. The ones that never searched the Internet are 31%, 51% of them live alone, 72% are women.

Therefore, as Vorrink et al. [42] say for the development and implementation of technologies for this user group, these variables should be taken into account as influencing factors. Likewise, the data show the need to deepen through observation and focus groups other factors that determine information behavior.

Observations in Trainers of the Courses Dictated by the Plan and Interviewed.
Observations of 15 training courses taught by the plan's trainers when distributing tablets were done by the FIC team in Paysandú and Rocha. Between 8 to 10 women attended each one. All of them meet predetermined guidelines, create a friendly climate and generally have empathy with the users. But, for the participants, it is difficult to keep up with the explanations. The different parts and functionalities are explained. With regard to the core of our research, the tablet as a *bridge* of searching for information, right after finishing the workshop, they start to mention Internet searches (tablet browser). They explain what the browser is, and they recommend: "*They have to be specific with what they are searching. If what they want is the recipe for a chocolate cake they put 'chocolate cake recipe' and not 'cooking recipes'. If they want to see goals from Suárez*

they put'goals from Luis Suarez." The tablet asks me 'what are you looking for? 'and I put my finger on that question and write. Before the question: *Any questions about the browser".* They answer 'no' ". In total they spend less than ten minutes searching on the Internet and in some cases, they do not refer to it.

These limitations coincide with the answers of the questionnaire and what they expressed in the focus groups and the need to design and incorporate a technological proposal to the tablets that motivate them to search inclusive information.

Focus Groups. The focus groups formed by older women of the Ibirapitá plan was a data collection technique used in large part of the projects developed by the research line on informative behavior and inclusive information. The organization was supported by civil society organizations with which we had a link from the beginning, association of retirees (CAJUPAY, Paysandú; AJUPENRO, Rocha; APUPENQUE, Quebracho) and the Municipal Public Library of Rocha. They totaled 7 focus groups with an average of 12 members. The moderation was in charge of a team member with predetermined guidelines focused on obtaining data on their behavior with the tablet, especially in the process of searching for information and their local information needs.In general, there was a very enthusiastic participation, contributing to the warm reception of the associations of retirees and pensioners, where their leaders' ability to convene and empathize was highlighted. The FIC team also invited them to lunch or has tea, helping to create a relaxed and friendly environment.

The participants of the focus groups focused their concerns on the following topics: health, safety, procedures, tourism, work, services and local information, and the difficulties arising from the use of the tablet. They described the topics and subtopics of greatest interest, which were collected by the team observers, who prepared an exhaustive report that allowed identifying the contents to provide to the INCO team.

"Local information and access to services" are configured as the most interesting topics. It is proposed that the tablet could be a fast and reliable way to access information that would facilitate their daily life: transport, cultural activities, courses and even commercial or work information, and there are elements that prove the interest and social value that older people have for local information. The demand for information emerges with affection and is also based on the exercise of freedom and the strong sense of belonging to their communities. It is interesting to stress that information is experienced as a product that acquires meaning within the framework of the social relationships that each context produced/produces in people's daily experience. The *"social utility of information"* attribute is clearly expressed as people understand that having or not having information is directly related to the decision making about their life (what to do, when, where to do it, by what means, budget of the decisions). The use of the tablet and the difficulties that it entails is a repeated topic. They demand that the support service be more personalized and immediate. In that sense, they would accept that the advice be online but still prefer personalized and face-to-face treatment. The connectivity restricted to 1 Giga and the subsequent expense that implies wanting to remain connected is a determining factor in how they relate to the tablet, even causing its abandonment or disinterest.

A collective mention was also made of technological tools such as social networks, which very few of the participants make use of without having any inconvenience when it comes to safely navigating them. The reasons why they join these networks (Facebook mainly) respond to the desire to keep in touch with family members living in Montevideo or abroad. The latter remained present in all the focus groups carried out: the desire for belonging and group connection, and the collective experience of dialogue and peer exchange. The use of tacit information from this perspective had a lot of value for the participants, since among them they took knowledge of data relevant to their informative needs. From the emotional and cognitive vision, the participation of the beneficiaries became more present in moments where the stimulus of the conversation appealed to the memorial and retrospective. Emphasis was placed on the interest in revisiting places and moments that represented an important occasion on the participants' lives, and from these moments, a transversal consensus was maintained in their stories regarding the "times" lived by the generations to which they belong. Undoubtedly, the concepts of Savolainen's ELIS were very present in this technique. On the technologies and the changes that the use of a tablet supposes in their lives, they made reference to the fears that this "new world" of the tablet awakens to them at the same time that it is received with great curiosity and opening. The role of the trainers is mentioned as decisive for the beneficiaries when crossing that bridge. Patience is an essential virtue that participants emphasize in their trainers.

Interviews with Trainers as Social Mediators of Information. Within the framework of the research, in-depth interviews were conducted in Paysandú and Rocha with 5 trainers of the Ibirapitá plan and 5 library clerks, *Digital Inclusion Spaces and Production Training Centers* (Cecap-MEC) that conducted training courses for the elderly who received tablets. The training offered by the Ibirapitá plan to the elderly to whom the tablet is delivered consists of an introductory, basic, mandatory class of three hours during which the devices are delivered to a group of approximately 30 people. In Paysandú, the trainers do not perceive large differences between the number of men and women attending these workshops; in Rocha, the audience has a marked feminine bias (70 to 80%). There is consensus in the trainers' narratives to consider *"women make more use of the devices and are more interested in understanding them"*. Taking pictures, listening to the radio, reading the newspaper and surfing the Internet are other functions of the tablet that trainers say they do in their workshops. Internet browsing is always the last mentioned, which is in line with the results of the questionnaires and observations.

The interviews with trainers will be analyzed specifically in other dissemination works (papers, articles in journals and books in 2020–2021), as well as the workshops observations, focusing on the mediation role of the trainers, especially the volunteers. But, at least, let's quote one comment very shared in the texts, about the behavior of the families of the users: *"When they ask the grandchildren, they don't teach them. If they ask for help to watch a video, they search for it but they don't show them how to search, and they want to learn"."In the family there are many people who understand the devices but don't pay attention to them […] They come here and tell us: 'I have grandchildren, I have children, I have everything, but they don't know how to explain to me"*.

3.5 Conclusions

Some emerging trends of the questionnaires, interviews, observations and focus groups, with a prior triangulation, allow us some conclusions from the FIC team: the information acquires meaning within the framework of the social relations that each context produced/produces in people's daily experience; close relationship between the social utility of information and decision making about their life; information practices are linked to the isolation or family and/or social relationship of the elderly woman and her tablet; the data show a high percentage of tablet users and non-user users living alone and in an encapsulation at home, with few links in the environment. Their life is focused on the tasks inside the home and half of them go for a walk, and less of them go out with friends; the family nucleus does not appear as a support pillar for the access and use of the tablet (children and grandchildren); personal characteristics: being active, optimistic, friendly, with self-esteem, they clearly appear as fundamental dimensions in the search and use of information on the tablet; the interest and social value that older people have for local information and the role to motivate the search for information on tablets is evidenced.

4 The Design of the Technological Solution for Tablets of Older Women Within the Framework of Interdisciplinary and Participatory Research

4.1 The Research Team and Its Undergraduate Project in Computer Engineering

The INCO team built a content system consisting of an Android application for Ibirapitá Plan tablets, a React web application and a web server, in a collaborative manner with its recipients, in order to facilitate access to relevant information requested by FIC team. The objectives and stages are described in the School of Engineering of University of the Republic's Computer Engineering undergraduate project entitled *Portal de accebilidad del Plan Ibirapitá* [Portal of accessibility of the Ibirapitá Plan] of Alejandro Miguel, Luciano Montero and Inés Saint Martin, guided by the teacher tutors Cecilia Apa, Ewelina Bakala and Laura González [45].

The following specific objectives are defined: i) investigate the state of the art of applications for older adults and investigate existing applications for similar purposes, analyze their characteristics, types of information they provide and design aspects; ii) build a solution that is compatible and can be included in the tablets delivered by the Ibirapitá Plan, taking the technological requirements they present into account; and iii) design and implement the product in a participatory manner with end users, using the focus groups with which the FIC team works in Rocha and Paysandú. To achieve this objective, it was necessary to take into account the usual needs and behaviors of potential users in order to make an application that could adapt to them [45].

4.2 Ibirapitá Tablets and the Product Design Process

The Ibirapitá Plan tablets have an Android operating system, but provide a launcher specially designed for the Ibirapitá Plan audience. On the home screen you can distinguish buttons with large icons that group applications under the same theme and a lower bar from where you can access the main applications: camera, radios, newspapers, books and browser. It was evaluated that icons with size and iconography adapted for older adults favored accessibility, so they deserved to be taken into account in the design to be proposed. At the same time, some opportunities for improvements were visualized, such as the language used and the shortcuts to specific pages in the web browser, similar to web bookmarks, which hindered their manipulation expressed in the FIC Report. This report was received by the InCo team at the beginning of 2018, with the results of the FIC team's research on information behavior and information practices in the departments of Paysandú and Rocha, and in the towns of Quebracho and La Paloma, presented in this communication.

In the *Analysis* (Sect. 2) the *User Profile,* the *State of the Art of Similar Solutions* (applications for older adults existing in the market or provided by the Ibirapitá Plan) and the *Concepts of Usability and Accessibility* are analyzed. The requirements survey and its different phases are presented: discovery, analysis and validation, and definition of scope. It is highlighted how the analysis and survey were carried out concurrently, using an iterative, incremental, creative and collaborative process. Together with the FIC team, ideas were generated to shape the solution. In Sect. 3, they describe the *Solution*: system architecture, web server, content manager: implementation, functionality, Android application; technical decisions: Internet use optimization, content and user administration, authentication, location of the Android application user; problems found: integration with external sources. In Sect. 4, they include the *Development Process*. Basically, in mid 2018, they created an initial application proposal using the Justinmind tool, which allows interactive design prototypes. This took into account the needs of accessibility, utilities, information/themes, leisure and interest. This stage allowed us to review the viability of some requirements and to verify if it complied with what was requested by the FIC team.

4.3 Product Design

The final solution proposed building a system consisting of three subsystems: an Android application, to allow viewing of content by end users; a content manager, to allow content generation; and a web server, to store and provide the contents. The different subsystems communicate with each other, each of them deployed independently and communicate among them using the HTTP protocol. The contents represent the information shown in the Android application to the users. These can be of the type *article, event, point of interest, or reference content.* The *articles* generally model broad texts of any subject, analogous to an article in a newspaper, magazine or book. The *events* model happenings to be developed on a certain date and place; they also explain the cost, the name of the organizer and contact information. The contents of the *point of interest* type model iconic, emblematic, cultural or recreational places that can be visited. The *reference contents* model those contents that are consumed from sources external to the system such as those obtained by the RSS mechanism [45, p. 25–26]. Each content has a title and an image that can be displayed as a cover and/or an image gallery, and that belong to a *category* and a *location* identified by the administrator. For the administration, roles were created: collaborator, creator or administrator.

4.4 Validations and Versions of the Technological Solution with the Users in Participatory Workshops

The technological solution was validated in three stages that took place in the chosen departments, Paysandú and Rocha, using the technique of integrated workshops with the users accessing and using the tablets with the solution incorporated into them.

The aspects observed in the first stage focused on usability with respect to navigation within the application and the use of the different functionalities. The incorporation of filters with buttons was simple, allowing overcoming the difficulty of operating the keyboard. Also the adaptation of the font size and colors was welcomed by the users.

The main proposal of the *InfoCoMayores* Project, allowing access to local information, aroused great interest. The participants read carefully and gave great value to the contents about the events held in the place where they live. *Events* was one of the points of greatest attraction and commented on the possibility of filtering by free events, adding notifications, recommending events to other users and the importance of the event information including contact information, price, time and place.

The second version of the application, validated in the second stage, not only sought to improve the initial prototype, but also to be a tool to validate new features and ideas that emerged after the workshops of the previous stage. The new features were: calendar events list, event visualization, "Like" action within *Events*, article display, increase font size by pinch gesture, font size selection button and bar. Visualization of contents of *Reference* type and content filter in general. Due to the main problems presented by users in the use of the application, it was decided to perform a general redesign of the application in the third stage. Redesign was finally validated in October 2018, where a more fluid access to the detail of the contents, a good understanding of the filters functionality, and a good reception of the new disposition of the events and all the features were noted.

5 Conclusions and Perspectives of the Research for Access to Inclusive Digital Information on Older Women's Tablets

In spite of the difficulties to identify the elderly with tablets, due to the anonymity that protects Ibirapitá plan's data, we had the support of several institutions and referents of the free social housing complexes for retirees in Paysandú and Rocha.

There was also such support and commitment to conduct focus groups and observations of the courses in the distribution of tablets. Undoubtedly, the professionalism of the team members, their excellent team spirit, and rigor in the work helped to successfully fulfill the stages. The participation of experienced researchers, young researchers, and students who joined the project with great enthusiasm is remarkable.

Finally, but most important to achieve integration with the elderly, it is also remarkable the role played by the regional coordinators of the Ibirapitá plan and the interviewed referents of each institution visited, some of which became indispensable mediators for the social insertion of the project. Also, the design, creation, implementation and evaluation of new quality information content for tablets (digital products) in a participative approach, involving the recipients of the Ibirapitá plan will seek to overcome the challenges and has meant an advance in exploratory studies to deepen on ageing, genre and

ICT for a line of research to be continued on the Ibirapitá plan and its innovative impacts for a desirable informative inclusion.

References

1. United Nations: Political declaration and Madrid international plan of action on ageing. Second World Assembly of Aging (2002)
2. United Nations, Department Of Economic and Social Affairs, Population Division. World Population Prospects 2019: Highlights. ST/ESA/SER.A/423 (2019)
3. United Nations, Department Of Economic and Social Affairs, Population Division. World Population Prospects 2019: Volume I: Comprehensive Tables (2019)
4. Slaght, E., Stampley, C.: Promoting intergenerational practice. J. Intergenerational Relat. **4**(3), 73–86 (2006)
5. Cummings, S., Williams, M., Ellis, R.: Impact of an intergenerational program on 4th graders attitudes towards elders and school behaviors. J. Hum. Behav. Soc. Environ. **6**, 91–107 (2002)
6. Fletcher, S.K.: Intergenerational dialogue to reduce prejudice. J. Intergenerational Relat. **5**(1), 6–19 (2007)
7. International Telecommunication Union: Measuring the Information Society Report 2018. EB/O L (2018)
8. International Telecommunication Union: Measuring the Information Society Report 2016 (2016)
9. Grupo Radar: El perfil del internauta uruguayo: resumen ejecutivo. Radar, Montevideo 2018
10. Thevenet, N.: Cuidados en personas adultas mayores: análisis descriptivo de los datos del censo 2011. MIDES, Montevideo (2013)
11. Batthyány, K.: Las políticas y el cuidado en América Latina: una mirada a las experiencias regionales. CEPAL, Santiago de Chile. Serie Asuntos de Género **124** (2015)
12. Batthyány, K.: Estudio sobre trabajo doméstico en Uruguay (No. 470799). International Labour Organization (2012)
13. Aguirre, R.: La política de cuidados en Uruguay: ¿ un avance para la igualdad de género? Estudos Feministas **22**(3), 798–813 (2015)
14. Aguirre, R., Solari, S.S.: Cuidar y ser cuidado Identity Research. Int. J. Collective Identity Res. **1**, 7 (2016)
15. Ezquerra, S., Pérez Salanova, M., Pla, M., Subirats, J. (eds.): Edades en transición. Envejecer en el siglo XXI. Planeta, Barcelona (2016)
16. Aguirre, R., Scavino, S.: Vejeces de las mujeres: desafíos para la igualdad de género y la justicia social en Uruguay. Doble clik, Montevideo (2019)
17. Chatman, E.A.: Opinion leadership, poverty and information sharing. R.Q. **26**(3), 341–353 (1988)
18. Chatman, E.A.: The impoverished life-world of outsiders. J. Am. Soc. Inf. Sci. **47**(3), 193–206 (1996)
19. Chatman, E.A.: A theory of life in the round. J. Am. Soc. Inf. Sci. **50**(3), 207–217 (1999)
20. Savolainen, R.: The role of the Internet in information seeking in context. Inf. Process. Manag. **35**(6), 765–782 (1999)
21. Savolainen, R.: Network competence and information seeking on the Internet: from definitions towards a social cognitive model. J. Documentation **58**, 211–226 (2002)
22. Savolainen, R.: Enthusiastic, realistic and critical: discourses of Internet use in the context of everyday life information seeking. Inf. Res. **10**(1), n1 (2004). paper 198
23. Savolainen, R.: Everyday life information seeking. In: Fisher, K.E., Erdelez, S., McKechnie, S.L. (eds.) Theories of Information Behaviour, pp. 143–148. Information Today, Inc., Medford (2005)

24. Savolainen, R.: Source preferences in the context of seeking problem-specific information. Inf. Process. Manag. **44**(1), 274–293 (2008)
25. Fisher, K.E., Erdelez, S., Mckechnie, L. (eds.) Theories of Information Behavior. Information Today Medford, New Jersey (2005)
26. Fisher, K.E., Landry, C.F., Naumer, C.: Social spaces, casual interactions, meaningful exchanges: "information grounds" characteristics based on the college student experience. Inf. Res. **12**(2), 12 (2007). paper 291
27. Fisher, K.E., Naumer, C.M.: Information grounds: theoretical basis and empirical findings on information flow in social settings. In: Spink, A., Cole, C. (eds.) New directions in human information behavior, pp. 93–111. Kluwer Academic Publishers, Amsterdam (2006)
28. Fisher, K.E., Naumer, C., Durrance, J., Stromski, L., Christiansen, T.: Something old, something new preliminary findings from an exploratory study about people's information habits and information grounds. Inf. Res. **10**(2), n2 (2005). paper 223
29. Williamson, K: The information needs and information-seeking behaviour of older adults: an Australian study. In: Vakkari, P., Savolainen, R., Dervin (eds.) Information Seeking in Context: Proceedings of an International Conference on Research in Information Needs, Seeking, and Use in Different Contexts, Tampere, Finland, 1996, pp. 337–350. Taylor Graham, Los Angeles (1997)
30. Williamson, K., Asla, T.: Information behaviour of people in the fourth age: implications for the conceptualizacion of information literacy. Libr. Inf. Sci. Res. **31**(2), 76–83 (2009)
31. Williamson, K., Bow, A., Wale, K.: Older people, new technology and public libraries. In: Reading the future: Proceedings of the Australian Library and Information Association Biennial Conference, pp. 161–170. ALIA, Canberra, Australia (1996)
32. Williamson, K., Bow, A., Wale, K.: Older people and the Internet. Link-up, 9–12 March (1997)
33. Williamson, K., Stayner, R.: Information and library needs of the aged. Austr. Libr. J. **29**(4), 188–195 (1980)
34. Vroman, K.G., Arthanat, S., Lysack, C.: "Who over 65 is online?" Older adults' dispositions toward information communication technology. Comput. Hum. Behav. **43**, 156–166 (2015)
35. Barnard, Y., Bradley, M.D., Hodgson, F., Lloyd, A.D.: Learning to use new technologies by older adults: perceived difficulties, experimentation behaviour and usability. Comput. Hum. Behav. **29**(4), 1715–1724 (2013)
36. Wright, P.: Digital tablet issues for older adults. Gerontechnology **13**(2), 306 (2014)
37. Magsamen-Conrad, K., Dowd, J., Abuljadail, M., Alsulaiman, S., Shareefi, A.: Life-span differences in the uses and gratifications of tablets: implications for older adults. Comput. Hum. Behav. **52**, 96–106 (2015)
38. Alvseike, H., Brønnick, K.: Feasibility of the iPad as a hub for smart house technology in the elderly; effects of cognition, self-efficacy, and technology experience. J. Multidiscip. Healthc. **5**, 299–306 (2011)
39. Talja, S., Nyce, J.M.: The problem with problematic situations: differences between practices, tasks, and situations as units of analysis. Libr. Inf. Sci. Res. **37**, 61–67 (2015)
40. Talja, S., Hartel, J.: Revisiting the user-centred turn in information science research: an intellectual history perspective. Inf. Res. **12**(4), 4 (2007)
41. Talja, S., Tuominen, K., Savolainen, R.: "Isms" in information science: constructivism, collectivism and constructionism. J. Documentation **61**(1), 79–101 (2005)
42. Vorrink, S.N.W., Antonietti, A.M., Kort, H.S.M., et al.: Technology use by older adults in the Netherlands and its associations with demographics and health outcomes. Assistive Technol. **29**(4), 188–196 (2017)
43. Peral-Peral, B., Arenas-Gaitán, J., Villarejo-Ramos, Á.F.: From digital divide to psycho-digital divide: elders and online social networks. Comunicar **23**(45), 57–64 (2015)

44. Hong, S.J., et al.: How old are you really? Cognitive age in technology acceptance. Decis. Support Syst. **56**, 122–130 (2013)
45. Miguel, A., Montero, L., Saint Martin, I.: Portal de accebilidad del Plan Ibirapitá [Portal of accessibility of the Ibirapitá Plan]. Undergraduate project, teacher tutors Cecilia Apa, EwelinaBakala and Laura González. Universidad de la República, Uruguay. Facultad de Ingeniería. Instituto de Computación, Montevideo, Uruguay. https://www.fing.edu.uy/inco/grupos/lins/informes/pg-portal-accesibilidad-ibirapita.pdf. Accessed 10 Dec 2019

Smartwatch Use Among Older Adults: Findings from Two Large Surveys

Alexander Seifert[(✉)]

Institute of Sociology, University of Zurich, 8050 Zurich, Switzerland
alexander.seifert@uzh.ch

Abstract. Access to modern mobile information and communication technologies (ICT) such as smartphones, tablets, smartwatches, and other wearables in later life remains poorly understood, as does the use of such technologies. Even though modern ICT devices permeate daily life, little is known about the distribution of modern handheld assistances such as smartwatches among older adults. This paper presents data on the distribution of smartwatches among older adults (and the predictors of this usage) by utilizing two representative data sets from Switzerland. Secondary analyses were based on two cross-sectional surveys of 1,824 participants (study 1: n = 811, age ≥ 56 years; study 2: n = 1,013, age ≥ 50 years). Both univariate and multivariate analyses were conducted. The results indicate that 4.4% (study 1) and 6.6% (study 2) of participants owned a smartwatch, and most used the technology daily. Univariate analysis showed that education, age, technological affinity, and the use of mobile ICT devices (smartphones, tablets, and fitness trackers) in particular distinguished smartwatch users from nonusers, whereas gender, income, quality of life, subjective health, participation in education offers and sports, and the use of classical ICT devices (such as radio, TV, and computers) were not significant predictors of group differences between user and non-user of smartwatch. Multivariate analyses confirmed the univariate findings by showing that education, interest in technology, and the use of mobile ICT devices predicted smartwatch usage. While the results must be viewed with caution because of the generally low number of smartwatch users, this initial evaluation of smartwatch use among older adults should nevertheless enrich discussions of the acceptance of wearables among them.

Keywords: Wearables · Information and communication technologies · Seniors · Smartwatches · Smart devices

1 Introduction

New information and communication technologies (ICT) tend to become embedded in the daily lives of older adults in digitalized societies. In response, the field of gerontology has recently placed technology usage on the research agenda [1]. Since the mid-1990s, the population in general has often viewed wearables as an opportunity to access information on the go and to communicate independently of location. Such technologies thus act as a "visual-memory prosthetic" and a "perception enhancer" [2]. Meaning that

Q. Gao and J. Zhou (Eds.): HCII 2020, LNCS 12207, pp. 372–385, 2020.
https://doi.org/10.1007/978-3-030-50252-2_28

wearables can serve as body-near personal information repositories and human capability enhancer. The smartwatch in particular has been the focus of increased attention in recent years, notably since the release of the Apple Watch and the Samsung Galaxy Watch. A smartwatch is a wearable computer worn on the wrist that primarily acts as an extension of a mobile phone. Smartwatches can show notifications and track physical activities, heart rate, and other related metrics, among other uses [3, 4]. The newest smartwatches often include a touch screen and can support advanced features and display high-resolution information; they usually include mobile apps and have their own mobile operating systems.

Smartwatch ownership rates among the general population are lower than for smartphones or tablets, although current statistics show an increased number of uses [5]. One in six US adults owned a smartwatch in 2018, when the top three manufacturers (Apple, Samsung, and Fitbit) accounted for 88% of smartwatch sales [6]. Marketing reports predict that older adults will likely make up the fastest-growing segment of the population to adopt wearable devices such as smartwatches because of the growth of new health-related features (such as health monitoring and reminders of health-related behavior) that are appealing to older people [7].

Although increasing numbers of older people have started to use mobile digital devices such as smartphones, tablets, and fitness trackers [8–11], a divide [12, 13] still exists between younger and older people in both access and usage rates [9, 14]. For this reason, older adults must still be considered a special target group when discussing the use of handheld technologies and wearables. Studies have also shown that older adults have specific requirements when they handle mobile devices (and the applications on those devices) and that lack of familiarity or lack of need for such technologies are important reasons for nonuse [10, 15–17].

Due to the recent diffusion of smartwatches within the global market, older people increasingly use smartwatches to assist in everyday life, such as by managing emergencies, helping with reminders to take medication, controlling health indicators, encouraging physical activity, and helping them navigate new locations [18–24]. Current research shows that older adults use smartwatches in different ways and for various purposes, for example, a recent Spain-based qualitative study showed that the most common uses were to manage notifications and to keep track of sports activities [18].

Research on smartwatches among older adults remains scarce regarding the general distribution of smartwatch users among the older population. Almost nothing is known about the use of smartwatches within the general older population and the integration of these watches within older adults' everyday lives. Data about the distribution of smartwatches to some extent exists only for the general population (typically based on marketing reports), but the same is not true for the older population. Research on which factors influence the acceptance of smartwatch use among older adults remains scarce or is often based on convenience samples or small sample sizes [18]. For this reason, generalization to the general older population is almost impossible. Considering the potential benefits of smartwatches for users, reaching an understanding of older adults' intentions to use this type of technology and examining actual usage behaviors are becoming increasingly important research activities.

2   Research Questions

Given this current research background and the fact that current research on smartwatch usages among older adults remains scare regarding the general share of users and non-users of smartwatches, the present study has investigated the distribution of smartwatches among older adults by using two representative samples from Switzerland. From an empirical perspective, older people often exhibit lower usage rates of modern ICT devices such as computers, smartphones, tablets, or wearables than the younger population [9]. Older adults are generally not the first to adopt new technologies, which has led to a situation known as the "digital divide" [12, 13, 17]. The field of critical gerontology, however, reminds us to view technologies not only as helping seniors to improve their quality of life and to cope with everyday life tasks but also as daily expressions of individuality and leisure behavior [25]. The first question to be asked in this paper is thus not only why older adults often do not use smartwatches but also how many older adults *do* use smartwatches and include those technologies in their everyday lives for different purposes.

The second goal of this paper is to evaluate, using a more explorative approach, the significant predictors of smartwatch ownership. Bearing in mind previous geron-technology research and technology-acceptance models on wearables usage among older adults [1, 16, 17, 26], the assumption in the present study is that socio-demographic variables such as age, gender, education, income, and health situation can help predict whether people are smartwatch users. Research has shown that beyond socio-demographic variables, having information about people's affinity for technology and current technology use in general is also important for examining people's intentional motivation to use smartwatches [27]. The assumption in this study is thus that those with an interest in new technologies and broader ICT experience in general will more often own smartwatches than those who lack such interest and experience.

Third, beyond examining general usage rates, individual reasons for using smart-watches should also be studied, which leads to another research question: What are the most common reasons for smartwatch usage? Based on previous work [18, 28], the study's assumption is that sports activities and the continuous monitoring of health-related information are important reasons for smartwatch usage.

3   Method

3.1   Samples

An important characteristic of this study's secondary data analysis is that the data was drawn from two large surveys performed in Switzerland. For this reason, replicating what emerged in one study in an independent second sample should add to the robustness of the findings.

The first study is based on data drawn from a representative survey [29] of 811 participants enrolled in the University of the Third Age at the University of Zurich and ETH Zurich, the Swiss Federal Institute of Technology, Switzerland (UZH3). The study was a self-guided survey administered in August 2018 that was given via paper and pencil or online. All participants of UZH3 were invited via mailed invitations to be involved in the study; no financial incentives were offered to participate. The response rate of this survey was 28%. UZH3 offers periodic open lectures from different departments on various scientific topics for an annual participation fee. The survey participants had attended a talk an average of 12 times during the previous 12 months (standard deviation [SD]: 10.89). The participants included in this study (N = 811) were at least 56 years old, with an average age of 72.49 years (SD = 5.97); 48% were female. Table 1 provides a description of the study 1 sample.

Table 1. Study 1: Sample description and smartwatch user group description.

Parameter	Range	*M* or %	Smartwatch nonusers (n = 741)	Smart-watch users (n = 34)	T-test T (p) or Cramér's V (p)
Gender					
Female		50.2%	51.0%	35.3%	.065 (.073)
Male		49.8%	49.0%	64.7%	
Age					
Age mean	56–94	71.95	71.96	70.09	2.006 (.052)
Age group: < 60		0.4%	0.4%	–	.072 (.406)
Age group: 60–69		41.4%	41.0%	52.9%	
Age group: 70–79		44.9%	45.2%	44.1%	
Age group: 80–89		12.8%	12.8%	2.9%	
Age group: ≥ 90		0.5%	0.5%	–	
Education					
Primary		0.3%	0.3%	–	
Secondary		48.7%	49.4%	24.2%	**.104 (.017)**
Tertiary		51.1%	50.3%	75.8%	
Household income[1]	1–6	4.07	4.07	4.50	-1.974 (.056)
Quality of life[2]	1–6	5.49	5.50	5.41	.612 (.544)
Subjective health[3]	1–6	4.98	4.98	5.00	-.179 (.859)
Interest in technology[4]	1–5	3.79	3.77	4.15	**-2.040 (.049)**
Technology use difficulty[5]	1–5	2.65	2.68	1.97	**3.594 (.001)**
Classical ICT device count[6]	0–3	2.88	2.88	2.91	-.460 (.648)
Mobile ICT device count[7]	0–3	1.51	1.45	2.44	**-7.161 (<.001)**
Lecture visitation[8]	0–50	12.10	12.08	14.16	-.939 (.355)

Notes: 1: *Household income* (in Swiss francs [CHF]), from 1 (< 2,001) to 6 (> 10,000). 2: *Perceived quality of life*: scale from 1 (very bad) to 6 (very good). 3: *Subjective health*: scale from 1 (very bad) to 6 (very good). 4: *Interest in technology* ("I'm very interested in new technical things"): scale from 1 (does not apply at all) to 5 (applies fully). 5: *Technology use difficulty* ("I find it difficult to operate modern technical equipment"): scale from 1 (does not apply at all) to 5 (applies fully). 6: *Classical ICT device count* (count of three ICT devices: radio, TV, and computers). 7: *Mobile ICT device count* (count of three ICT devices: smartphones, tablets, and fitness trackers). 8: *Lecture visitation* (active lecture visits at the Senior University of the Third Age within the last 12 months).

The second study was conducted in November 2016 under the project title "Mobile Health Tracking in Old Age (mHealth50+)" [8]. A total of 1,013 adults aged 50 years and older from the German- and French-speaking regions of Switzerland were interviewed using a computer-assisted telephone interview (CATI) format. The response rate of the survey was 19%. All participants approved of the telephone interviews. A standardized questionnaire was administered with 24 questions about personal details (age, sex, education, sports, subjective health, and subjective quality of life) and mobile device usage for health tracking. A random sample of the permanent-resident population of Switzerland aged 50 years and older was selected from the AZ-Direct database (based on the public phonebook). The age of the respondents in the sample ranged from 50 to 95 years, with a mean age of 65.3 years; 53% were female. Table 2 provides a description of the study 2 sample.

Table 2. Study 2: Sample description and smartwatch user group description.

Parameter	Range	M or %	Smartwatch nonusers (n = 934)	Smartwatch users (n = 66)	T-test T (p) or Cramér's V (p)
Gender					
Female		53.1%	53.5%	48.5%	.025 (.427)
Male		46.9%	46.5%	51.5%	
Age					
Age mean	50–95	65.28	65.35	62.62	**2.282 (.025)**
Age group: < 60		38.0%	37.8%	45.5%	.070 (.301)
Age group: 60–69		28.8%	29.0%	28.8%	
Age group: 70–79		20.0%	19.8%	21.2%	
Age group: 80–89		12.0%	12.3%	4.5%	
Age group: ≥ 90		1.1%	1.1%	−	
Education					
Primary		19.1%	18.6%	19.4%	.070 (.086)
Secondary		56.6%	57.7%	45.2%	
Tertiary		24.4%	23.7%	35.5%	
Household income[1]	1–5		2.56	2.91	-1.802 (.077)
Quality of life[2]	1–5	4.37	4.36	4.38	-.153 (.879)
Subjective health[3]	1–5	4.07	4.07	4.08	-.036 (.971)
Interest in technology[4]	1–5	3.18	3.14	3.79	**-3.820 (<.001)**
Technology use difficulty[5]	1–5	2.73	2.75	2.55	.922 (.325)
Mobile ICT device count[6]	0–3	1.18	1.12	1.97	**-8.401 (<.001)**
Sports[7]	0–5	3.49	3.49	3.61	-.670 (.505)

Notes: 1: *Household income* (in CHF), from 1 (< 4,001) to 5 (> 12,000). 2: *Perceived quality of life*: scale from 1 (very bad) to 5 (very good). 3: *Subjective health*: scale from 1 (very bad) to 5 (very good). 4: *Interest in technology* ("I'm very interested in new technical things"): scale from 1 (does not apply at all) to 5 (applies fully). 5: *Technology use difficulties* ("I find it difficult to operate modern technical equipment"): scale from 1 (does not apply at all) to 5 (applies fully). 6: *Mobile ICT device count* (count of three ICT devices: smartphones, tablets, and fitness trackers). 7: *Sports*: sports activity in general, rated from 0 (never) to 5 (daily).

3.2 Measures of Study Variables

The dependent variable "smartwatch use" was defined as smartwatch usage and was rated on a five-point scale (1 = daily, 2 = once a week, 3 = once a month, 4 = seldom, and 4 = never or I do not own). Smartphone users were defined as those who had used a smartwatch, regardless of frequency, whereas smartwatch nonusers were defined as those who did not own a smartwatch.

To examine whether standard demographic variables were significant predictors for smartwatch use, a set of variables was included in the univariate and multivariate models: age (in years), gender (female/male), education (primary/secondary/tertiary), and household income (gross household income in Swiss francs [CHF], from low to high).

Tables 1 and 2 include specific details of the scales used within the two surveys. In addition to those basic variables, information on life situation was also used, including perceived quality of life and subjective health (both measured with a five- or six-point Likert scale, from low to high). Tables 1 and 2 provide details.

As described in the introduction, the acceptance of new mobile technologies such as smartwatches is often influenced by people's "technological affinity" and the use of other technologies. The secondary analyses thus included information about people's attitudes toward technologies: more precisely their interest in technology (based on the statement "I'm very interested in new technical things") and their technology usage difficulty (based on the statement "I find it difficult to operate modern technical equipment"), rated on a Likert scale from 1 ("does not apply at all") to 5 ("applies fully"). Information about other ICT device use was also included, including "classical ICT device count," which is a count of the three ICT devices of radio, TV, and computers (used only in study 1), and "mobile ICT device count," which is a count of three modern mobile ICT devices (smartphones, tablets, and fitness trackers).

For the bivariate analyses, study-specific variables for the two survey studies were also included. For study 1, information about the frequency of lecture visits at the Senior University of the Third Age within the last 12 months (ranging from 0 to 50 visits) was included to examine whether active participation in educational settings influenced smartwatch usage, such as by using smartwatches as a tool for "situated reflection" within educational contexts [30]. For study 2, information about sports activities (sports activity in general, rated from 0 [never] to 5 [daily]) was used to examine whether participation in sports influenced smartwatch usage, such as using the devices to track one's physical activity [3, 8].

3.3 Analytic Strategies

SPSS (version 25) was used for the statistical analyses. Univariate analyses were used to describe the differences in the characteristics of the smartwatch user and nonuser groups by applying the Student's t-test and chi-square testing. In addition, two binary logistic regressions based on the two groups were calculated to analyze the statistical predictors of smartwatch use.

4   Results

4.1 Descriptive Data on Smartwatch Use

In study 1, which involved participants from the Senior University of the Third Age, 4.4% (n = 34) of participants were smartwatch users. Of these smartwatch users, 55.9% used their smartwatches daily, 5.9% used them once a week, 8.8% used them once a month, and the rest (29.4%) used them more infrequently than once a month. All smartwatch users were also smartphone users, and 90.9% of all smartwatch users also used a tablet; 61.8% of all smartwatch users also owned a fitness tracker in addition to their smartwatch.

In terms of standard demographics, the bivariate analyses (see Table 1) showed that only education was a significant distinguisher between smartwatch users and nonusers.

The regular descriptive frequency differences, however, showed that males, younger people, and those with higher incomes were more likely to be smartwatch users, although these findings were not significant. Quality of life and subjective health also showed no significant effects, whereas technological affinity showed significant explanatory power. Smartwatch users were more often interested in new technology in general and had less difficulty in the use of these technologies. Whereas the use of classical ICT devices (radio, TV, and computers) did not distinguish between users and nonusers, the use of modern mobile ICT devices (smartphones, tablets, and fitness trackers) did. People who used other mobile devices in addition to smartwatches were more often smartwatch owners. For the survey-specific variable "lecture visitation," which showed information about participation in educational settings, no significant relation was found within the bivariate analysis. If the findings are viewed descriptively, however, then smartwatch users visited these lectures more often on average.

In study 2, which was conducted among the 50+ population in Switzerland, 6.6% (n = 66) of participants were smartwatch users. Among these smartwatch users, 71.2% used smartwatches daily, 16.7% used them once a week, and the rest (12.1%) used them more infrequently than once a week. Among all smartwatch users, 92.3% also owned a smartphone, 76.9% also used a tablet, and 30.3% also owned a fitness tracker in addition to their smartwatch.

Regarding standard demographics, the bivariate analyses (see Table 2) showed that only mean age was a significant distinguisher between smartwatch users and nonusers: smartwatch users were younger on average than nonusers. The regular descriptive frequency differences, however, showed that males, and those with higher education levels and incomes, were more likely to be smartwatch users, although these findings were not significant. Again, quality of life and subjective health also showed no significant effects, whereas interest in technology showed significant explanatory power. Smartwatch users were more often interested in new technology in general. The use of modern mobile ICT devices was a significant distinguisher between users and nonusers. Smartwatch users often owned more than one additional mobile device. For the survey-specific variable "sports," which covered information about participation in sports activities in general, no significant relation was found within the bivariate analysis. If viewed descriptively, however, then smartwatch users were found to participate in sports more than nonusers on average.

Different standard demographic variables were found to be significant in the bivariate analyses of both studies: study 1's significant variable was education, while study 2's was age. In neither study were quality of life and subjective health significant distinguishers between users and nonusers. The same trend of group differences was noted in both studies; interest in technology and the use of mobile ICT devices were significant distinguishers between smartwatch users and nonusers in both studies.

To control for the different age ranges of the two studies, the frequency of smartwatch users was examined only between the ages of 65 (the retirement age in Switzerland) and 90: 4.1% owned a smartwatch in study 1, compared to 5.7% in study 2 within the same age range. These findings show that differences did exist, but they were not significant between the two studies (χ^2 [1, n = 1178] = 1.557, p = .212).

4.2 Multivariate Test of Group Differences

Additional analyses were conducted to check the bivariate results using a multivariate approach. Table 3 shows the results of two binary logistic regressions to address studies 1 and 2. In both models, smartwatch groups (1 = user, 0 = nonuser) were considered as the dependent variable, while age, gender, education, household income, quality of life, subjective health, interest in technology, technology use difficulty, and ICT device count were included as dependent variables. The tests of both full models showed statistical significance, which indicates that the predictors, as a set, reliably distinguished between users and nonusers (study 1: $\chi^2 = 57.563$ [10], $p \le .001$, Nagelkerke's $R^2 = .263$, n = 714; study 2: $\chi^2 = 39.426$ [9], $p \le .001$, Nagelkerke's $R^2 = .126$, n = 827).

Table 3. Multivariate binary logistic regression analysis for the predictors of smartwatch use.

Parameter	Study 1[A]			Study 2[B]		
	OR	p-value	95 % CI	OR	p-value	95 % CI
Female (ref. male)	.719	.493	.280, 1.847	.959	.893	.520, 1.768
Age	.969	.452	.892, 1.052	.992	.623	.959, 1.026
Tertiary education (ref. primary and secondary)	3.395	.014	1.276, 9.032	1.241	.528	.635, 2.425
Household income	1.122	.522	.789, 15.97	.996	.978	.763, 1.300
Quality of life	.468	.056	.223, .985	1.019	.935	.652, 1.592
Subjective health	1.176	.585	.657, 2.103	.958	.807	.676, 1.356
Interest in technology	.673	.129	.403, 1.123	1.346	.033	1.024, 1.768
Technology use difficulty	.557	.018	.343, .905	1.238	.064	.988, 1.552
ICT device count	.659	.530	.180, 2.419	–	–	–
Mobile ICT device count	4.242	<.001	2.289, 7.860	2.403	<.001	1.630, 3.543

Notes: The dependent variable is smartwatch use: 0 (no use) or 1 (use). A: study 1 model fit ($\chi^2 = 57.563$ [10], $p = <.001$, Nagelkerke's $R^2 = .263$, n = 714). B: study 2 model fit ($\chi^2 = 39.426$ [9], $p = <.001$, Nagelkerke's $R^2 = .126$, n = 827).

Study 1's model 1 showed that education, technology use difficulty, and mobile ICT device usage were significant prediction factors, whereas gender, age, income, quality of life, health, interest in technology, and classical ICT device usage were not found to be predictors in the multivariate analysis. People who had a tertiary education, those with few technology use difficulties, and those who used mobile ICT devices other than smartwatches were more often smartwatch users than those with lower education levels and more technology use difficulties, as well as those who used few or no mobile ICT devices.

Study 2's model 2 showed that interest in technology and mobile ICT device usage were significant predictors, whereas gender, age, education, income, quality of life, health, and technology use difficulty were not found to be predictors in the multivariate analysis. Participants who were particularly interested in technologies, and those who used mobile ICT devices, were more often smartwatch users than those with less interest in technology and those who used few or no mobile ICT devices.

4.3 Additional Findings on the Purpose of Smartwatch Use

Additional information about the purpose of wearables usage was available in study 2. Those participants who used a smartphone, smartwatch, or fitness tracker were asked why they used these technologies; they could choose among five different health-related purposes, and multiple answers were possible. Using only the subsample of smartwatch users (n = 66), the ranked answers were as follows (ordered by frequency): "to motivate myself to remain healthy" (53.3%), "to track daily physical activity" (42.6%), "to exchange health-related data with my physician" (21.3%), "to exchange health-related data with my friends" (18.6%), and "to track my sleep quality" (14.8%).

5 Discussion

Based on data drawn from Switzerland, this paper has presented the dispersion of smartwatches among older Swiss adults. Following the first research question of who among the older population uses smartwatches, the analysis of two large surveys revealed that roughly five people among 100 older adults aged 65 years and older owned a smartwatch.

As a comparison, data from a Swiss marketing study [31] of people aged 18 years and older found that 10% of participants used a smartwatch; in the present study, 4.4% (study 1) and 6.6% (study 2) used a smartwatch. Although older age groups have yet to match the usage rates of younger age groups, a growing number of older people are now incorporating mobile ICT devices into their daily routines. Researchers have discussed whether the digital divide between younger and older people could diminish or even vanish in the near future [32].

Even though few older adults use smartwatches, their usage rates are not markedly different from those of the general population. But the existing data on today's older smartwatch users indicates that these users are early purchasers of smartwatches. Such users are known as Roger's "early adopters" [33], meaning that, regardless of age, they belong to the first wave of users of a technical innovation. As a result, smartwatches cannot yet be thought of as a mass product within the ICT field. This situation also means that researchers who want to develop smartwatch-based interventions (for example, to monitor health-related information) should be aware of the scarcity of these devices among the older population as well as possible barriers to the use of these wearables [34]. Design requirements for developing wearables or applications for smartwatches for older adults should be developed accordingly [35, 36].

This paper's second research question addresses differences between smartwatch users and nonusers. The univariate analysis showed that education, age, technological affinity (having interest in and experiencing few difficulties with new technologies), and the use of mobile ICT devices (smartphones, tablets, and fitness trackers) were significant distinguishing factors between smartwatch users and nonusers, whereas gender, income, quality of life, subjective health, participation in education offers and sports, and the use of classical ICT devices (radio, TV, and computers) were not significant predictors of group differences. The multivariate analyses confirmed the univariate findings by showing that education, technological affinity, and the use of mobile ICT devices all predicted smartwatch usage. Even though the findings differed to some extent between the two studies, we may summarize by saying that typical parameters such as gender, income, and subjective health did not distinguish significantly between smartwatch users and nonuser. In addition, age was only a significant distinguisher in study 2 and was not significant within the multivariate analyses. Interest in technology and one's current use of mobile ICT devices were found to be far more important factors.

Given that today's bestselling smartwatches interact with smartphones (and indeed require a smartphone to operate fully), this study's finding that nearly all smartwatch users were also smartphone users is not surprising. The analyses also showed, however, that large numbers of smartwatch users also used tablets and fitness trackers, neither of which are necessary to operate a smartwatch. Smartwatch users thus are familiar with modern mobile technologies in general and are also users of these technical innovations, which speaks to a lifestyle of technical affinity.

The findings show that, regardless of age, people who use smartwatches are often pioneers or early adopters, as Rogers [33] defines the term, meaning that age or other personal characteristics are not as important as factors such as technology affinity and having a lifestyle where people often use modern technologies and technical innovations. Smartwatches thus present a good example for the study of daily ICT use among older adults beyond mere functionality and perceived ease of use and usefulness. In addition to health-related functionality, fashionability, or the aesthetic appeal of smartwatches [27, 37–39], is often associated with older adults' usage of wearables. For example, Chuah et al. [4] suggest that smartwatches represent a type of "fashnology" (a portmanteau of "fashion" and "technology"). These attributes are influenced by people's perception of smartwatches as a technology and/or as a fashion accessory.

This study's third research question addresses the purpose of smartwatch use. The study participants' responses indicated that they used these devices to remain healthy and physically active more than they used them for social reasons, such as exchanging personal data with friends or documenting data for their physicians. Previous studies [28] have identified self-control and incentives to be active as reasons for using wearables. These findings also fit well with the fact that the most commonly used behavior-change techniques in current wearables interventions for older adults are to provide feedback, self-monitoring, and goal-setting [40]. Nevertheless, to return to the fashion aspect of smartwatches, neither study in the present research involved information about other reasons for buying smartwatches. Future studies thus should investigate people's different reasons for using smartwatches in more detail and within a large population sample, as recommended by Chuah et al. [4]. Longitudinal studies are also needed to investigate the long-term use of wearables among older adults: research shows, for example, that wearables such as fitness trackers are often used within certain timeframes but not on a permanent basis [41]. Finally, developing a quantitative analysis of smartwatch logs [42] would be helpful to better understand their usage patterns, particularly regarding usage and the "sense-giving" processes of smartwatch use within older adults' daily lives.

Smartwatches could be an interesting field for researchers in the future because of the opportunity they provide to use smartwatches as a data-collection tool for older adults' daily lives. This approach belongs to the family of ambulatory assessment and experience sampling, both of which allow for assessing and tracking older people's ongoing thoughts, feelings, behaviors, and physiological processes in daily life while using a mobile device [43]. The primary goal of mobile data collection via smartwatches is to collect in-the-moment active data (e.g., subjective self-reports) and/or passive data (e.g., data collected from smartphone sensors). This method has become increasingly popular because of its many advantages [44]. First, the findings are ecologically valid, because they are collected during people's day-to-day lives in their real environments; second, the reports are collected in the moment and are therefore less prone to memory bias than retrospective assessments; third, intensive, repeated measurements of one participant can be used to capture within-person information; and fourth, real-life data is rich in contextual information, as the data allows for the combination of self-reports and objective activity assessments by using sensors that are already built into smartwatches.

5.1 Limitations

Several limitations must be noted. First, the present study has a specific regional focus (Switzerland), so the findings have limited generalizability. Second, while one could argue that the sample of active participants at the University of the Third Age is selectively biased, the group that was selected is believed to represent a heterogenic group of high educated and sometimes technology-friendly older adults in Switzerland. Third, the data has provided only a cross-sectional view of the various interplays examined in the study. Future researchers should investigate the dynamics of these interplays within the background of today's persistent digital transformation. Fourth, because of the limited width of the study variables that could be used, other important background factors could not be controlled for, such as technophobia [45], personality, technical skills, or attitudes toward wearables in general. Further studies using longitudinal designs and with a wider range of variables will therefore be required to examine this topic in more detail.

5.2 Conclusion

This study has presented representative data for Switzerland on the actual use of smartwatches in a population where new mobile devices are not in everyday use. The results indicate that 4.4% (study 1) and 6.6% (study 2) of participants aged 50 years or older owned a smartwatch, and most used the technology daily. Multivariate analyses showed that education, interest in technology, and the use of mobile ICT devices predicted smartwatch usage. The study showed, that, today, it is mainly those seniors with a marked interest in technology and a technology-friendly lifestyle in general who own smartwatches. The current study has provided evidence of the potential of smartwatch use by older people. Although very few older adults use these mobile devices today, such people make for interesting study subjects [46], since researchers can examine their daily use of new, commercially available technologies. Such people also offer the opportunity to investigate technologies that are especially designed for the aged population.

References

1. Schulz, R., Wahl, H.-W., Matthews, J.T., De Vito Dabbs, A., Beach, S.R., Czaja, S.J.: Advancing the aging and technology agenda in gerontology. Gerontologist **55**, 724–734 (2015). https://doi.org/10.1093/geront/gnu071

2. Mann, S.: Wearable computing: a first step toward personal imaging. Computer **30**, 25–32 (1997). https://doi.org/10.1109/2.566147

3. Henriksen, A., et al.: Using fitness trackers and smartwatches to measure physical activity in research: analysis of consumer wrist-worn wearables. J. Med. Internet Res. **20**, e110 (2018). https://doi.org/10.2196/jmir.9157

4. Chuah, S.H.-W., Rauschnabel, P.A., Krey, N., Nguyen, B., Ramayah, T., Lade, S.: Wearable technologies: the role of usefulness and visibility in smartwatch adoption. Comput. Hum. Behav. **65**, 276–284 (2016). https://doi.org/10.1016/j.chb.2016.07.047

5. Liu, S.: Smartwatches - Statistics & Facts. https://www.statista.com/topics/4762/smartwatc hes/. Accessed 04 Nov 2019

6. Whitwam, R.: 1 in 6 US Adults Now Own a Smartwatch. https://www.extremetech.com/mob ile/285724-1-in-6-us-adults-now-own-a-smartwatch. Accessed 04 Nov 2019

7. Musli, S.: One in 10 American adults expected to have a smartwatch next year. https:// www.cnet.com/news/one-in-10-american-adults-expected-to-have-a-smartwatch-next-year/. Accessed 04 Nov 2019

8. Seifert, A., Schlomann, A., Rietz, C., Schelling, H.R.: The use of mobile devices for physical activity tracking in older adults' everyday life. Digit. Health **3**, 1–12 (2017). https://doi.org/ 10.1177/2055207617740088

9. Pew Research Center: Tech Adoption Climbs Among Older Adults (2017). http://www.pew internet.org/wp-content/uploads/sites/9/2017/05/PI_2017.05.17_Older-Americans-Tech_F INAL.pdf

10. Rosales, A., Fernández-Ardèvol, M.: Smartphone usage diversity among older people. In: Sayago, S. (ed.) Perspectives on Human-Computer Interaction Research with Older People. HIS, pp. 51–66. Springer, Cham (2019). https://doi.org/10.1007/978-3-030-06076-3_4

11. Katz, S., Marshall, B.L.: Tracked and fit: FitBits, brain games, and the quantified aging body. J. Aging Stud. **45**, 63–68 (2018). https://doi.org/10.1016/j.jaging.2018.01.009

12. Korupp, S.E., Szydlik, M.: Causes and trends of the digital divide. Eur. Sociol. Rev. **21**, 409–422 (2005). https://doi.org/10.1093/esr/jci030

13. Compaine, B.M. (ed.): The Digital Divide: Facing a Crisis or Creating a Myth?. MIT Press, Cambridge (2001)

14. Seifert, A., Schelling, H.R.: Mobile use of the Internet using smartphones or tablets by Swiss people over 65 years. Gerontechnology **14** (2015). https://doi.org/10.4017/gt.2015. 14.1.006.00

15. Hunsaker, A., Hargittai, E.: A review of Internet use among older adults. New Media Soc. **20**, 3937–3954 (2018). https://doi.org/10.1177/1461444818787348

16. Berkowsky, R.W., Sharit, J., Czaja, S.J.: Factors predicting decisions about technology adoption among older adults. Innov. Aging **1** (2017). https://doi.org/10.1093/geroni/igy002

17. Francis, J., Ball, C., Kadylak, T., Cotten, S.R.: Aging in the digital age: conceptualizing technology adoption and digital inequalities. In: Neves, B.B., Vetere, F. (eds.) Ageing and Digital Technology, pp. 35–49. Springer, Singapore (2019). https://doi.org/10.1007/978-981-13-3693-5_3

18. Rosales, A., Fernández-Ardèvol, M., Comunello, F., Mulargia, S., Ferran-Ferrer, N.: Older people and smartwatches, initial experiences. El Prof. Inf. **26**, 457 (2017). https://doi.org/10. 3145/epi.2017.may.12

19. Manini, T.M., et al.: Perception of older adults toward smartwatch technology for assessing pain and related patient-reported outcomes: pilot study. JMIR MHealth UHealth **7**, e10044 (2019). https://doi.org/10.2196/10044

20. Ehrler, F., Lovis, C.: Supporting elderly homecare with smartwatches: advantages and drawbacks. Stud. Health Technol. Inform. 667–671 (2014). https://doi.org/10.3233/978-1-61499-432-9-667

21. Lee, H., Joseph, B., Enriquez, A., Najafi, B.: Toward using a smartwatch to monitor frailty in a hospital setting: using a single wrist-wearable sensor to assess frailty in bedbound inpatients. Gerontology **64**, 389–400 (2018). https://doi.org/10.1159/000484241

22. Antos, S.A., Danilovich, M.K., Eisenstein, A.R., Gordon, K.E., Kording, K.P.: Smartwatches can detect walker and cane use in older adults. Innov. Aging **3** (2019). https://doi.org/10.1093/geroni/igz008

23. Rosales, A., Fernández-Ardèvol, M., Ferran-Ferrer, N.: Long-term appropriation of smartwatches among a group of older people. In: Zhou, J., Salvendy, G. (eds.) ITAP 2018. LNCS, vol. 10926, pp. 135–148. Springer, Cham (2018). https://doi.org/10.1007/978-3-319-92034-4_11

24. Fernández-Ardèvol, M., Rosales, A.: My interests, my activities: learning from an intergenerational comparison of smartwatch use. In: Zhou, J., Salvendy, G. (eds.) ITAP 2017. LNCS, vol. 10298, pp. 114–129. Springer, Cham (2017). https://doi.org/10.1007/978-3-319-58536-9_10

25. Peine, A., Neven, L.: From intervention to co-constitution: new directions in theorizing about aging and technology. Gerontologist **59**, 15–21 (2019). https://doi.org/10.1093/geront/gny050

26. Czaja, S.J.: Factors predicting the use of technology: findings from the center for research and education on aging and technology enhancement (create). Psychol. Aging **21**, 333–352 (2006). https://doi.org/10.1037/0882-7974.21.2.333

27. Dehghani, M.: Exploring the motivational factors on continuous usage intention of smartwatches among actual users. Behav. Inf. Technol. **37**, 145–158 (2018). https://doi.org/10.1080/0144929X.2018.1424246

28. Schlomann, A.: A case study on older adults' long-term use of an activity tracker. Gerontechnology **16**, 115–124 (2017). https://doi.org/10.4017/gt.2017.16.2.007.00

29. Seifert, A.: Senioren-Universität Zürich: Befragung der Teilnehmenden. PsyArXiv (2019). https://doi.org/10.31234/osf.io/z5v8p

30. Garcia, B., Chu, S.L., Nam, B., Banigan, C.: Wearables for learning: examining the smartwatch as a tool for situated science reflection. In: Proceedings of the 2018 CHI Conference on Human Factors in Computing Systems, CHI 2018, pp. 1–13. ACM Press, Montreal (2018). https://doi.org/10.1145/3173574.3173830

31. Mändli-Lerch, K.: Jeder Fünfte besitzt eine Smartwatch oder ein Smartband. https://gfs-zh.ch/wp-content/uploads/2016/04/Medienmitteilung_Smartwatch.pdf. Accessed 13 June 2017

32. Gilleard, C., Jones, I., Higgs, P.: Connectivity in later life: the declining age divide in mobile cell phone ownership. Sociol. Res. Online. **20**, 1–13 (2015). https://doi.org/10.5153/sro.3552

33. Rogers, E.M.: Diffusion of Innovations. Free Press, New York (2010)

34. Seifert, A., Reinwand, D.A., Schlomann, A.: Designing and using digital mental health interventions for older adults: being aware of digital inequality. Front. Psychiatry **10**, 568 (2019). https://doi.org/10.3389/fpsyt.2019.00568

35. Klebbe, R., Steinert, A., Müller-Werdan, U.: Wearables for older adults: requirements, design, and user experience. In: Buchem, I., Klamma, R., Wild, F. (eds.) Perspectives on Wearable Enhanced Learning (WELL), pp. 313–332. Springer, Cham (2019). https://doi.org/10.1007/978-3-319-64301-4_15

36. Czaja, S.J., Boot, W.R., Charness, N., Rogers, W.A.: Designing for Older Adults: Principles and Creative Human Factors Approaches. CRC Press, Boca Raton (2019)

37. Choi, J., Kim, S.: Is the smartwatch an IT product or a fashion product? A study on factors affecting the intention to use smartwatches. Comput. Hum. Behav. **63**, 777–786 (2016). https://doi.org/10.1016/j.chb.2016.06.007

38. Kim, K.J., Shin, D.-H.: An acceptance model for smart watches: Implications for the adoption of future wearable technology. Internet Res. **25**, 527–541 (2015). https://doi.org/10.1108/IntR-05-2014-0126

39. Nimrod, G., Ivan, L.: The dual roles technology plays in leisure: insights from a study of grandmothers. Leis. Sci. 1–18 (2019). https://doi.org/10.1080/01490400.2019.1656123

40. Middelweerd, A., Mollee, J.S., van der Wal, C.N., Brug, J., te Velde, S.J.: Apps to promote physical activity among adults: a review and content analysis. Int. J. Behav. Nutr. Phys. Act. **11**, 97 (2014). https://doi.org/10.1186/s12966-014-0097-9

41. Li, L., Peng, W., Kononova, A., Bowen, M., Cotten, S.R.: Factors associated with older adults' long-term use of wearable activity trackers. Telemed. E-Health. tmj.2019.0052 (2019). https://doi.org/10.1089/tmj.2019.0052

42. Ørmen, J., Thorhauge, A.M.: Smartphone log data in a qualitative perspective. Mob. Media Commun. **3**, 335–350 (2015). https://doi.org/10.1177/2050157914565845

43. Seifert, A., Harari, G.M.: Mobile data collection with smartphones. In: Gu, D., Dupre, M.E. (eds.) Encyclopedia of Gerontology and Population Aging. Springer, Cham (2019). https://doi.org/10.1007/978-3-319-69892-2_562-1

44. Seifert, A., Hofer, M., Allemand, M.: Mobile data collection: smart, but not (yet) smart enough. Front. Neurosci. **12**, 971 (2018). https://doi.org/10.3389/fnins.2018.00971

45. Nimrod, G.: Technophobia among older Internet users. Educ. Gerontol. **44**, 148–162 (2018). https://doi.org/10.1080/03601277.2018.1428145

46. Loos, E., Haddon, L., Mante-Meijer, E.A.: Generational Use of New Media. Ashgate, Burlington (2012)

Author Index

Printed in the United States
By Bookmasters